Practice in a Second Language

THE CAMBRIDGE APPLIED LINGUISTICS SERIES

Series editors: Michael H. Long and Jack C. Richards

This series presents the findings of work in applied linguistics that are of direct relevance to language teaching and learning and of particular interest to applied linguists, researchers, language teachers, and teacher trainers.

Recent publications in this series:

Practice in a Second Language

Perspectives from Applied Linguistics and Cognitive Psychology

Edited by

Robert M. DeKeyser
University of Maryland at College Park

CAMBRIDGE
UNIVERSITY PRESS

CAMBRIDGE UNIVERSITY PRESS
Cambridge, New York, Melbourne, Madrid, Cape Town, Singapore, São Paulo

Cambridge University Press
32 Avenue of the Americas, New York, NY 10013-2473, USA

www.cambridge.org
Information on this title: www.cambridge.org/9780521865296

First published 2007

Printed in the United States of America

A catalog record for this publication is available from the British Library.

Library of Congress Cataloging in Publication Data

Practice in a second language : perspectives from applied linguistics and cognitive
psychology / edited by Robert M. DeKeyser.
   p.   cm. – (The Cambridge applied linguistics series)
Includes bibliographical references and index.
ISBN-13: 978-0-521-86529-6 (hardback)
ISBN-10: 0-521-86529-8 (hardback)
ISBN-13: 978-0-521-68404-0 (pbk.)
ISBN-10: 0-521-68404-8 (pbk.)
1. Language and languages – Study and teaching.   2. Second language acquisition.
I. DeKeyser, Robert.   II. Title.   III. Series.
P51.P68   2007
418.0071–dc22   2006049272

ISBN   978-0-521-86529-6 hardback
ISBN   978-0-521-68404-0 paperback

Contents

III INDIVIDUAL DIFFERENCES   227

Contributors

Robert M. DeKeyser, *University of Maryland, USA*
Jennifer Leeman, *George Mason University, USA*
Ronald P. Leow, *Georgetown University, USA*
Roy Lyster, *McGill University, Canada*
Alison Mackey, *Georgetown University, USA*
Carmen Muñoz, *University of Barcelona, Spain*
Hitoshi Muranoi, *Tohoku Gakuin University, Japan*
Lourdes Ortega, *University of Hawai'i at Mānoa, USA*
Leila Ranta, *University of Alberta, Canada*
Peter Robinson, *Aoyama Gakuin University, Japan*
Kris Van den Branden, *Katholieke Universiteit Leuven, Belgium*

Series editors' preface

Sometimes maligned for its allegedly behaviorist connotations but critical for success in many fields from music and sport to mathematics and language learning, *practice* is undergoing something of a revival in the applied linguistics literature, and this latest volume in the *Cambridge Applied Linguistics Series* will undoubtedly heighten interest. To the extent that language is a skill, it behooves us to determine optimal ways of providing opportunities for skill development as well as the optimal timing of those opportunities.

Robert M. DeKeyser's introduction to *Practice in a Second Language* reminds us, among other things, of progress in this area in cognitive psychology and that the notion of practice lies at the intersection of a number of other issues of fundamental importance in second language learning and teaching. They include relationships between declarative and procedural knowledge/skill, automatization, rule-based and item-based learning, implicit and explicit knowledge, the value and timing of feedback, and the transferability, or not, of potentially skill-specific and task-specific abilities. In other words, the practice issue and theory and research findings on practice are important for a wide variety of theoretical and practical issues in second and foreign language acquisition and teaching.

The book you have before you consists entirely of original contributions authored by some of the leading researchers in the field, assembled and edited by Professor DeKeyser of the University of Maryland. Professor DeKeyser has himself published groundbreaking empirical studies on practice, broadly construed. *Practice in a Second Language* is a major contribution to scholarship in SLA and applied linguistics, of value to researchers and classroom practitioners alike, and a worthy addition to the *Cambridge Applied Linguistics Series*.

Michael H. Long
Jack C. Richards

Introduction: Situating the concept of practice

Robert M. DeKeyser

Practice gets a raw deal in the field of applied linguistics. Most lay-people simply assume that practice is a necessary condition for language learning without giving the concept much further thought, but many applied linguists eschew the term *practice*. For some, the word conjures up images of mind-numbing drills in the sweatshops of foreign language learning, while for others it means fun and games to appease students on Friday afternoons. *Practice* is by no means a dirty word in other domains of human endeavor, however. Parents dutifully take their kids to soccer practice, and professional athletes dutifully show up for team practice, sometimes even with recent injuries. Parents make their kids practice their piano skills at home, and the world's most famous performers of classical music often practice for many hours a day, even if it makes their fingers hurt. If even idolized, spoiled, and highly paid celebrities are willing to put up with practice, why not language learners, teachers, or researchers? The concept of second language practice remains remarkably unexamined from a theoretical point of view. Misgivings and misunderstandings about practice abound and are often rooted in even deeper misunderstandings about what it is that language learners are supposed to learn. In this introductory chapter, I will try to provide some conceptual and terminological clarification in preparation for the rest of the book. In the concluding chapter, I will then formulate tentative recommendations for "the praxis of practice," as they follow from these conceptual distinctions and from the other chapters.

It should be clear from the outset, of course, that the word *practice* in the title is not meant as the opposite of theory, as in "foreign language teaching policy vs. actual practice in secondary schools," "practicing professionals," or "the praxis of second language teaching." The contributors to this book all understand practice in a much more focused way, as specific activities in the second language, engaged in systematically, deliberately, with the goal of developing knowledge of and skills in the second language. But within this broad definition there are still many different ways one can understand the concept of practice. Before we zero in on the meanings of practice in applied linguistics, however, let us have a brief look at how cognitive and educational psychologists have used the term.

The notion of practice in cognitive psychology

The study of skill acquisition is an important area within cognitive psychology (for a good, concise overview see Carlson, 2003). Researchers in that area have documented the acquisition of skills in a wide variety of domains, from algebra, geometry, and computer programming to learning how to drive a car or how to roll cigars. Increasingly, they also employ neuroimaging and other neurological data to document how different skills and different stages in the acquisition of the same skill are represented in the brain (e.g., Anderson, Bothell, Byrne, Douglass, Lebiere, & Qin, 2004; Posner, DiGirolamo, & Fernandez-Duque, 1997). Researchers who study skill acquisition processes all agree that reaction time and error rate decline gradually as a function of practice with a given task. But how is practice defined in this literature?

Carlson, a well-known contemporary theorist of skill acquisition, defines practice simply as "repeated performance of the same (or closely similar) routines" (1997, p. 56). This definition could easily be misinterpreted and may seem a throwback to the heydays of behaviorism; it does not define practice in terms of cognitive processes at all. Clearly, this cannot be what Carlson has in mind, however, because he defines skill as "the ability to routinely, reliably and fluently perform goal-directed activities as a result of practice with those activities" (1997, p. 45). The definition in Newell and Rosenbloom is more precise: "Practice is the subclass of learning that deals only with improving performance on a task that can already be successfully performed" (1981, p. 229). Not only does this definition make the learning/improving component of practice explicit, it also states clearly that practice in the narrow sense applies only to a task that can already be successfully performed. But the definition still remains vague because it does not say what constitutes a task. Is speaking French a task, or requesting a glass of water in French, or does using a conditional verb form to do this constitute a task? Any task outside the laboratory, whether in school or in "the real world," consists of many components. Could practice be defined as referring to repeated engaging/improving in task components that can already be successfully performed? If so, how narrowly could a task component be defined? And would practice of task components separately be better or worse than practice of the whole task? There is no general answer to the latter question (VanLehn, 1989), but Lee and Anderson (2001), for instance, show how the learning of at least one complex task reflects the learning of much smaller parts.

This brings us to the related question of the specificity of practice effects in skill learning. If tasks can be defined at such a low level, then how different can they be before they are different altogether? In other words, how much does practice on a task that shares certain characteristics with another, but also differs from it in a crucial way, contribute to improving performance on this other task? What determines transfer of the effect of practice? A number of studies have shown that the practice effect is quite specific in the sense that there is only minimal transfer between tasks that superficially appear to be each other's mirror image, such as writing versus reading a computer program (see esp. Singley & Anderson, 1989; cf. also Anderson, 1993, chap. 9; Müller, 1999).

This specificity of the practice effect is explained by the well-known distinction between declarative and procedural knowledge. In most forms of skill acquisition, people are first presented with *information*, e.g., rules about how to write a computer program or put a French sentence together in explicit form ("declarative knowledge"). Through initial practice they incorporate this information into *behavioral routines* ("production rules," "procedural knowledge"). This procedural knowledge consists of very specific rules and can be used fast and with a low error rate, but the disadvantage is its lack of generalizability.

Once established, procedural knowledge can become automatized. *Automatization* is a rather difficult concept because the term is used at three levels of generality, at least. In the broadest sense, it refers to the whole process of knowledge change from initial presentation of the rule in declarative format to the final stage of fully spontaneous, effortless, fast, and errorless use of that rule, often without being aware of it anymore. In a narrower sense, it refers to the slow process of reducing error rate, reaction time, and interference with/from other tasks that takes place after proceduralization. In the most specific sense, it designates a merely quantitative change in the subcomponents of procedural knowledge to the exclusion of any qualitative change or restructuring (i.e., excluding changes in which small subcomponents make up procedural knowledge at a given stage of skill development or how they work together).

Automatization in the last two meanings of the word is characterized by the "power law of practice": regardless of the domain of learning, both reaction time and error rate decline over time according to a very specific function that is mathematically defined as a power function; hence the term (see esp. Anderson, 2000; Newell & Rosenbloom, 1981). While the exact nature of the processes underlying the shape of this function (e.g., quantitative vs. qualitative change) is still a matter of debate, and while some question the universality of the power law (see esp. Anderson, 2000; Delaney, Reder, Staszewski, & Ritter, 1998; Haider & Frensch, 2002; Logan, 1988, 1992, 2002; Palmeri, 1997, 1999; Rickard, 1997,

1999, 2004), all agree that reaction time and error rate (some studies also document decreased interference with/from simultaneous tasks) decline gradually as a function of practice with a given task.

The more automatized procedural knowledge becomes the clearer these effects. The transfer found between program reading/writing or, in the case of L2 learning, between production/comprehension skills, then, is explained by the fact that practice in each skill reinforces to some extent the declarative knowledge that is applicable to both. The procedural knowledge, however, is too specific to be transferred from one skill to another; therefore, the practice effect is highly skill-specific.

It should be pointed out here that automatized knowledge is not exactly the same as implicit knowledge. While implicit knowledge or implicit memory is always defined with reference to lack of consciousness or awareness (see, e.g., Reingold & Ray, 2003), absence of awareness is *not* a requirement for automaticity. Hence, one can have knowledge that is implicit but not automatic (because error rate is too high and speed is too low) in cases of incomplete implicit learning (the pattern may be merely probabilistic, so the learner feels unsure, hesitates, and often gets it wrong). On the other hand, one can have knowledge that is automatic but not implicit (because the learner has attained high speed and low error rate but is still conscious of rules, for instance, because he or she is a language teacher, whether of L1 or L2, or a linguist).

A further question concerns the nature of the practice effect for relatively complex tasks: Does it reflect speeding up small components (automatization in the narrowest sense), changing the nature of small components (restructuring), speeding up the way they work together, or changing the nature of how they work together (strategic change)? Increasingly, researchers find that automatization in the narrowest sense is probably much more limited than often assumed and that "attention is subject to a far greater degree of top-down control" (Pashler, Johnston, & Ruthruff, 2001, p. 648).

In the same way that it is hard to decide whether and how to break up a task into components to be practiced separately, it is hard to decide how often to provide feedback on performance in complex tasks. Wulf, Schmidt, and Deubel (1993) found that constant feedback was better for learning fine parameters of a task, whereas intermittent feedback (63 percent of the time) was better for learning the task as a whole. As this study involved a perceptual-motor task, it is unclear to what extent its findings would generalize to a cognitive skill such as language learning, however. Moreover, decisions need to be made about when to provide feedback. On the one hand, immediate feedback may disrupt the execution of higher-order routines that are also being learned (cf. Schooler & Anderson 1990, quoted in Anderson, 2000), but on the other hand, feedback should not be delayed too much because it may be most efficient when it is provided while the procedural "knowledge" that led to the error is still active in memory. Most importantly, perhaps, a substantial amount of evidence suggests that what is best for improving performance in the short run can be worst in the long run, especially for transfer. Less frequent feedback leads to less immediate improvement but to better performance in the long run, at least for a variety of perceptual and motor tasks (Schmidt & Bjork, 1992). Needless to say, eventual performance and transfer are more important in real life and even to some extent in school contexts than short-term performance.

The notion of practice in educational psychology

Educators and educational psychologists do not doubt the importance of practice. Even during the heydays of the cognitive revolution, Ausubel, Novak, and Hanesian wrote:

> Although much significant meaningful learning obviously occurs during initial presentation of the instructional material, both overlearning and most long-term retention presuppose multiple presentations of trials (practice). Both learning process and outcome customarily encompass various qualitative and quantitative changes that take place during these several trials. Learning and retention, therefore, ordinarily imply practice. Such practice, furthermore, is typically specific (restricted to the learning task) and deliberate (intentional). (1978, p. 311)

Much more recently, Bransford, Brown, and Cocking, for instance, stated that "in deliberate practice, a student works under a tutor (human or computer based) to rehearse appropriate practices that enhance performance" (1999, p. 166) and pointed out that deliberate practice can lead to an enormous reduction in the time it takes individuals to reach real-world performance criteria. Ericsson and associates (Ericsson, Krampe, & Tesch-Römer, 1993; Ericsson & Charness, 1994; Starkes & Ericsson, 2003; see also Ericsson, 1996; Ericsson & Lehmann, 1996) have documented in astounding detail the enormous amount of deliberate practice it takes to become a truly expert performer such as a world-class musician, chess player, or athlete. Others (e.g., Maguire, Valentine, Wilding, & Kapur, 2003; Wilding & Valentine, 1997; cf. also Ericsson, 2003) have documented large effects of deliberate practice in performance of highly specific memory tasks.

As is often the case, however, terminology varies from author to author. Legge, for instance, makes a distinction between practice, which may "simply involve using the skills that have been acquired, sometimes imperfectly" (1986, p. 228), and training, which involves "a deliberate scheme to assist learning." On the other hand, Haskell (2001) gives training a more narrow, negative meaning of drilling or teaching recipes, which leads to the well-known lack of transfer. It should be clear that we will use the term *practice* in a sense that is both narrower than Legge's (for we are dealing with activities planned to assist initial learning of new elements of a language) and much broader than mere drilling (for we include a variety of loosely structured communicative activities).

A large part of the educational literature on practice concerns the issue of transfer, whether it be from one classroom task to another or from the classroom to performance on the job. A central concept here is that of transfer-appropriate processing: transfer is likely to occur to the extent that the cognitive operations involved in the new context, task, or test recapitulate or overlap with those engaged in during initial learning (see, e.g., Whittlesea & Dorken, 1993). "Knowledge that is overly contextualized can reduce transfer; abstract representations of knowledge can help promote transfer" (Bransford et al., 1999, p. 41). One particular form that this problem can take is that of trying to teach procedural knowledge without an adequate declarative base. Singley and Anderson (1989) point out not only that transfer between related skills such as reading and writing computer programs is limited but that where it does happen it appears to occur via declarative knowledge of the underlying rules. If a student only grasps a problem through a limited number of examples, learning may be quick but transfer is doubtful. If the principle or rule underlying the examples is thoroughly understood, transfer will be much easier, but examples are still necessary for establishing usable knowledge (see esp. Anderson, Fincham, & Douglass, 1997). "Without an adequate level of initial learning, transfer cannot be expected. The point seems obvious, but it is often overlooked" (Bransford et al., 1999, p. 41).

On the other hand, narrow procedural knowledge, while it is less generalizable, is not only the most efficient in those contexts where it is applicable but it is also more durable (Healy, King, Clawson, Sinclair, Rickard, Crutcher et al., 1995; Healy, Barshi, Crutcher, Tao, Rickard, Marmie et al., 1998).

The concept of practice in applied linguistics

Few applied linguists have attempted to define what exactly constitutes practice. Ellis has been among the most explicit. He states that "practice...involves an attempt to supply the learner with plentiful opportunities for producing targeted structures in controlled and free language use in order to develop fully proceduralized implicit knowledge" (1993, p. 109). This may seem uncontroversial, but what Ellis says in the next few sentences makes it clear that the concept is far from obvious. Because of the emphasis he puts on procedural knowledge, he takes the point of view that (production) practice is important for teaching pronunciation and formulaic knowledge but not for the teaching of grammar rules: "What is being challenged here is the traditional role it has played in the teaching of grammatical items" (p. 109). This point of view, of course, reflects the Chomskyan distinction between competence and performance: practice is to improve performance, not to teach competence, the most prototypical form of which is our intuitive knowledge of grammar rules. This competence has always been seen as either acquired or not, but not something gradual; furthermore, once something has been acquired, Chomskyan theory sees it as available for use in performance, except for certain constraints on the latter which are considered to be beyond the scope of linguistics proper (see e.g., Chomsky, 1965, p. 3; 1980; 1986, chaps. 1 and 2).

The Chomsky/Ellis point of view, however, is at odds with both the cognitive psychology of skill acquisition and much current theorizing in applied linguistics, most notably with VanPatten's theory of input processing. Cognitive psychologists stress the role of practice in transforming declarative/explicit knowledge into procedural/implicit knowledge. Clearly, it is implicit knowledge that corresponds to the Chomskyan notion of linguistic competence, not explicit, and clearly practice is needed to achieve it, unless one believes it is also *acquired* completely implicitly – and Ellis does not seem to believe *that*: "Perhaps we do not have to bother with trying to teach implicit knowledge directly" (2002, p. 234).

VanPatten's theory of input processing (e.g., 1996, 2003), on the other hand, clearly aims at building the procedural knowledge needed for the use of grammar rules in comprehension *after* the declarative knowledge of these rules has been taught explicitly. (VanPatten's thinking is clearly in line with skill acquisition theory on this point; whether this procedural knowledge transfers easily to production skills is a different matter, as will be discussed.) Ellis himself appears to have shifted recently toward a less radical competence/performance, rule/item, declarative/procedural, implicit/explicit view: "Production, then, may constitute the mechanism that connects the learner's dual systems, enabling movement to occur from the memory-based to the rule-based system and vice versa. If this interpretation is correct, learners may not be so reliant on input as has been generally assumed in SLA. They may be able to utilize their own internal resources, via using them in production, to both construct and complexify their interlanguages" (2003, p. 115). This also seems to be the position of Diane Larsen-Freeman: "Output practice, then, does not simply serve to increase access to previously acquired knowledge. Doing and learning are synchronous" (2003, p. 114).

As previously stated, in this book we define practice as specific activities in the second language engaged in systematically, deliberately, with the goal of developing knowledge of and skills in the second language. Contributors to this volume put different emphases on the importance of practicing what one already knows in principle (see Legge's definition above, and the chapters by Muranoi and DeKeyser in this volume) versus deliberately engaging in tasks that are supposed to draw attention to new phenomena or engender new insights (see esp. the chapters by Leow and Mackey in this volume). As Robinson (this volume) points out, the two processes typically go together anyhow. While accessing existing knowledge, the learner becomes aware of gaps or inconsistencies in it, which may lead to restructuring or expansion of this knowledge, potentially by incorporation of input from a native-speaking interlocutor.

Issues surrounding practice in applied linguistics

While much of the literature quoted in the first two sections of this chapter is couched in language that may be unfamiliar to second language acquisition researchers, parallels abound between the questions asked in cognitive and educational psychology and those that bedevil our own field. How skill-specific and how task-specific is the effect of practice; in other words, how much transfer can be expected? How much feedback should be given, how, and at what time to maximize the effect of practice? Can explicit knowledge be automatized through practice to the point of becoming equivalent to implicit acquired knowledge? How does automaticity develop in the course of practice? These issues will be outlined here and discussed in more depth in the final chapter of this book.

Complete answers to these questions are not available in large part because empirical research on practice has been quite limited in recent decades. Between the bad memories of audiolingual mechanical drills and the subsequent emphases in the 1970s, 1980s, and 1990s on authentic communication, focus on meaning, and task-based learning, few researchers in the post-audiolingual period have addressed the issue of practice head-on (cf. also Larsen-Freeman, 2003, pp. 102 and 106).

The skill-specificity issue is probably the one that has drawn the most attention in applied linguistics lately (see esp. DeKeyser, Salaberry, Robinson, & Harrington, 2002; Izumi, 2002, 2003; Muranoi, this volume; VanPatten, 2002a, 2002b, 2003, 2004). Cognitive psychology has much to say about the specificity of skills (see esp. Anderson, 1993; Anderson & Fincham, 1994; Anderson, Fincham, & Douglass, 1997; Müller, 1999; Singley & Anderson, 1989), but of course its findings cannot be transferred blindly to issues of second language acquisition. Both

Ellis (1992, 1993, but see the 2003 quote on page 7) and VanPatten (see esp. VanPatten & Cadierno, 1993; VanPatten & Oikkenon, 1996) take the view that while input practice leads to acquisition, output practice merely serves to improve fluency. On the other hand, studies such as those by DeKeyser (1997), DeKeyser and Sokalski (1996), and Izumi (2002) clearly show a lack of transfer between receptive and productive skills at the level of both proceduralized and automatized knowledge.

The problem of transfer, discussed so often in cognitive psychology and even more in educational psychology, applies also at the broader level of transfer from declarative knowledge to procedural skill and of knowledge and skill from one context to another, in particular from the classroom to the native-speaking environment. Transfer from declarative knowledge to procedural skill has been discussed very widely (see e.g., Carroll, 2001; DeKeyser, 1997, 2003; Doughty, 2003; Ellis, 1992, 1993, 2003; Hulstijn, 2002; Krashen, 1982, 1999; McLaughlin, 1987; Skehan, 1998), and is often referred to as the interface issue. A typical case of the other kind of transfer, from the classroom context to the real world, is, of course, the semester abroad context. Research on the latter topic illustrates both that this transfer is far from obvious and that study abroad is not as obviously ideal for practicing foreign language skills as is often assumed (see esp. Brecht & Robinson, 1993; Brecht, Davidson, & Ginsberg, 1995; DeKeyser, this volume). DeKeyser argues that these two transfer issues, from one kind of knowledge and skill to another and from one context to another, are intertwined in study abroad programs.

Another prominent issue already mentioned is the separation of a complex skill into separate components in terms of teaching, practicing, and providing feedback. Most L2 teaching methodologies of the last 30 years, such as communicative language teaching, the natural approach, and task-based learning, are much less inclined to take language apart into small components than was the case for older methods such as grammar-translation, audiolingualism, or cognitive code. But what exactly the ideal point is on the analytic/synthetic dimension of curriculum design, and what this implies for practice activities, is still far from resolved, especially in the foreign language context (see esp. Ortega, this volume).

The usefulness of feedback in general, and of specific techniques such as explicit error correction, negotiation of meaning, or recasts has been the subject of much debate in applied linguistics but has only recently become the subject of a considerable number of empirical studies (see esp. Iwashita, 2003; Leeman, 2003; Nicholas, Lightbown, & Spada, 2001; Pica & Washburn, 2002). It appears from this literature that feedback tends to have a substantial positive effect (see esp. Leeman, this volume, and the meta-analysis in Russell & Spada, 2006), but the amount of empirical evidence gathered so far is insufficient to answer more specific questions about when and how to give feedback with any degree of certainty. Clearly, we need to know more about these questions, and about others, which have hardly been addressed at all. How useful is feedback for different elements of language, not just for pronunciation versus grammar versus vocabulary, but even, say, for rules versus items versus prototypes, simple rules versus complex rules, frequent items versus infrequent items? And, perhaps most important, how should the frequency and the nature of feedback be adapted to the stage of learning or skill acquisition? Much work remains to be done in this area.

Automatization, on the other hand, is an issue that has not drawn much focused attention yet, let alone provided the accumulation of evidence that is needed to guide practice. As argued on page 3, automatization in the broad sense has many faces. In applied linguistics these are illustrated, for instance, in the work of Healy et al. (1998), who show that strategy shifts from rules to items as well as from items to rules can both occur as a result of ample practice with linguistic structures, and in that of DeKeyser (1997), who shows that automatization in a more narrow sense can take place for second language grammar rules following the same power-function learning curve documented in the acquisition of skills in other domains. Many questions remain, however, especially about the integration of such findings from a skill acquisition perspective with findings from the second language acquisition literature.

While the acquisition of complex skills, skill specificity, skill transfer, feedback on performance, and automatization of skills are issues for which applied linguists can certainly find much inspiration in the cognitive and educational literature, we also face a number of difficult choices that are characteristic of second language teaching, such as the relationship between form and meaning and the difference between teaching form and teaching forms. Clearly, form-meaning connections are the essence of language, and taking them apart more than necessary for practice activities would be unwise, but there are areas of language such as phonetics, phonology, and morphological paradigms where narrowly focused, repeated practice activities with forms can be useful (DeKeyser, 1998). Such practice activities have traditionally been called drills. They have been alternately advocated, demonized, derided, and resuscitated, often even without making the distinction between different kinds of drills.

As (talking about) drilling has been so out of fashion for a number of years, it may be good to remind some younger readers of this volume of the three-way distinction made by several authors after the concern for communicative language teaching became well established but before it evolved, at least at the level of academic debate, into an almost exclusive focus on meaning. Paulston (1970, 1972; cf. also Paulston & Bruder, 1976) made a three-way distinction between mechanical, meaningful, and communicative drills (MMC). Mechanical drills were defined as drills "where there is complete control of the response and only one correct way of responding" (1976, p. 3). Such drills can be carried out without any knowledge of the L2 or even any understanding of the rule being practiced by mere superficial analogy; replacing all lexemes with nonsense words would leave the drill intact. Meaningful drills are very different in the sense that "the student cannot complete these drills without fully understanding structurally and semantically what is being said" (p. 7). In other words, they require that the student access the form-meaning links characteristic of the L2 in order to understand what is asked and to respond with an answer that is correct not only in terms of form but also in terms of intended meaning. In communicative drills there is still control over the structures used by the student, but the immediate goal from the student's point of view becomes actual exchange of information: the student is telling the teacher or other students something they did not know. "The main difference between a meaningful drill and a communicative drill is that in the latter the speaker adds new information about the real world" (p. 9).

Byrne (1986) also made a three-way distinction between presentation, practice, and production (PPP). It is clear from Byrne's discussion (esp. p. 5), however, that the practice stage roughly corresponds to Anderson's proceduralization stage, and the production stage to automatization. In other words, PPP is completely different from MMC: presentation precedes MMC, practice combines the mechanical and meaningful, and production includes but goes beyond the communicative in MMC (because it goes beyond drills).

As I have argued previously (DeKeyser, 1998), mechanical drills can only serve a very limited purpose, because they do not make the learner engage in what is the essence of language processing, i.e., establishing form-meaning connections. Far too often, however, all drills are equated with mechanical drills. The debate between Wong and VanPatten (2003, 2004) and Leaver, Rifkin, and Shekhtman (2004) clearly illustrates this point: where Wong and VanPatten saved their sharpest criticisms for mechanical drills, other kinds of drills appeared to be guilty by association, which led to the reaction by Leaver, Rifkin, and Shekhtman.

While we did not include the idea of multiple repetition as implied by drills as a necessary component of our definition of practice (see above) any more than the idea of mechanical practice, we definitely do not exclude it either. It is an element of the definition used by cognitive psychologists such as Carlson (see above), it continues to be an important element of the praxis of practice all over the world, and it is gradually gaining respectability again in empirical research on second language learning (e.g., Bygate, 2001; Gass, Mackey, Alvarez-Torres, & Fernández-García, 1999; Lynch & Maclean, 2000, 2001; Van den Branden, 1997; see also Van den Branden, this volume).

The real question is not so much whether repeated performance of a narrowly construed task has a role to play in second language learning, but how strongly form-focused activities such as drills should be integrated into the curriculum without reverting to a structural syllabus that merely teaches "the structure of the day" or becoming obsessed with a mere focus on forms instead of focus on form (see esp. Doughty & Williams, 1998; Long 1988; Long & Robinson, 1998). Discussions of task-based learning (Ellis, 2003; Long & Crookes, 1992; Long & Norris, 2000; Skehan, 1996; Wesche & Skehan, 2002), in particular, continue to deal with this issue.

Finally, as the table of contents for this book suggests, the need for and usefulness of different kinds of practice varies considerably depending on the institutional context and the characteristics of the individual learner. Second language teaching, foreign language teaching, bilingual immersion programs, and study abroad are all characterized by their own opportunities for and constraints on practice, and students of different ages, with quantitative and qualitative differences in aptitude, can benefit differentially from different forms of practice.

Far from being an outdated concept, then, practice stands at the crossroads where many different questions intersect: questions about the relationship between competence and performance, implicit and explicit learning, production and comprehension, analytic versus synthetic syllabi, accuracy versus fluency, and about individualization of instruction.

The structure of this volume

The first section in the book discusses the basic forms of practice and feedback that are applicable to most circumstances, whether they emphasize input or output. The second section deals with variations in institutional context and what impact they have on conditions for different kinds of practice. The third section discusses how practice activities could be adapted to differences in age and aptitude between learners. Short introductions to the issues dealt with in the individual chapters can be found at the beginning of each of these sections. The final chapter of this book draws together the findings from the previous sections against the background of the conceptual distinctions made in the introductory chapter and provides a differentiated view of what constitutes good L2 skill practice. The book ends with a glossary, which provides definitions of terms used in more than one chapter in this book along with some core concepts from individual chapters.

While the concept of practice certainly applies to the four skills of listening, speaking, reading, and writing, many chapters in this book focus on oral skills, largely because that is where the issue of practice has been perceived as most problematic and has generated the most empirical research and theoretical debate. Even there, however, much remains to be done. While much SLA research has dealt with oral input, there is little empirical research on systematic listening practice – learning to listen and listening to learn have been seen as very different issues (cf. Vandergrift, 2004). "At present a [second language] course based primarily on psychological principles has not been realized" (Healy et al., 1998). It is the aim of this book to contribute to such a goal.

References

Anderson, J. R. (1993). *Rules of the mind.* Hillsdale, NJ: Lawrence Erlbaum.

Anderson, J. R. (2000). *Learning and memory. An integrated approach* (2nd ed.). New York: John Wiley.

Anderson, J. R., Bothell, D., Byrne, M. D., Douglass, S., Lebiere, C., & Qin, Y. (2004). An integrated theory of the mind. *Psychological Review, 111*(4), 1036–60.

Anderson, J. R., & Fincham, J. M. (1994). Acquisition of procedural skills from examples. *Journal of Experimental Psychology: Learning, Memory and Cognition, 20*(6), 1322–40.

Anderson, J. R., Fincham, J. M., & Douglass, S. (1997). The role of examples and rules in the acquisition of a cognitive skill. *Journal of Experimental Psychology: Learning, Memory and Cognition, 23*(4), 932–45.

Ausubel, D. P., Novak, J. D., & Hanesian, H. (1978). *Educational psychology: A cognitive view.* New York: Holt, Rinehart, and Winston.

Bransford, J. D., Brown, A. L., & Cocking, R. R. (1999). *How people learn: Brain, mind, experience, and school.* Washington, DC: National Academy Press.

Brecht, R. D., Davidson, D. E., & Ginsberg, R. B. (1995). Predictors of foreign language gain during study abroad. In B. Freed (Ed.), *Second language acquisition in a study abroad context* (pp. 37–66). Amsterdam/ Philadelphia: Benjamins.

Brecht, R. D., & Robinson, J. L. (1993). *Qualitative analysis of second language acquisition in study abroad: The ACTR/NFLC project.* Washington, DC: National Foreign Language Center.

Bygate, M. (2001). Effects of task repetition on the structure and control of oral language. In M. Bygate, P. Skehan, & M. Swain (Eds.), *Researching pedagogic tasks: Second language learning, teaching, and testing* (pp. 23–48). New York: Longman.

Byrne, D. (Ed.). (1986). *Teaching oral English* (2nd ed.). Harlow, UK: Longman.

Carlson, R. A. (1997). *Experienced cognition.* Mahwah, NJ: Lawrence Erlbaum.

Carlson, R. A. (2003). Skill learning. In L. Nadel (Ed.), *Encyclopedia of cognitive science* (Vol. 4, pp. 36–42). London: Macmillan.

Carroll, S. E. (2001). *Input and evidence.* Amsterdam: John Benjamins.

Chomsky, N. (1965). *Aspects of the theory of syntax.* Cambridge, MA: MIT Press.

Chomsky, N. (1980). *Rules and representations.* New York: Columbia University Press.

Chomsky, N. (1986). *Knowledge of language: Its nature, origin, and use.* New York: Praeger.

DeKeyser, R. M. (1997). Beyond explicit rule learning: Automatizing second language morphosyntax. *Studies in Second Language Acquisition, 19*(2), 195–221.

DeKeyser, R. M. (1998). Beyond focus on form: Cognitive perspectives on learning and practicing second language grammar. In C. Doughty & J. Williams (Eds.), *Focus on form in classroom second language acquisition* (pp. 42–63). New York: Cambridge University Press.

DeKeyser, R. M. (2003). Implicit and explicit learning. In C. Doughty & M. Long (Eds.), *Handbook of second language acquisition* (pp. 313–48). Oxford: Blackwell.

DeKeyser, R. M., Salaberry, R., Robinson, P., & Harrington, M. (2002). What gets processed in processing instruction? A commentary on Bill VanPatten's "Processing instruction: An update." *Language Learning, 52*(4), 805–23.

DeKeyser, R. M., & Sokalski, K. J. (1996). The differential role of comprehension and production practice. *Language Learning, 46*(4), 613–42.

Delaney, P. F., Reder, L. M., Staszewski, J. J., & Ritter, F. E. (1998). The strategy-specific nature of improvement: The power law applies by strategy within task. *Psychological Science, 9*(1), 1–7.

Doughty, C. (2003). Instructed SLA: Constraints, compensation, and enhancement. In C. Doughty & M. H. Long (Eds.), *Handbook of second language acquisition* (pp. 256–310). Oxford: Blackwell.

Doughty, C., & Williams, J. (1998). Pedagogical choices in focus on form. In C. Doughty & J. Williams (Eds.), *Focus on form in classroom second language acquisition* (pp. 197–261). New York: Cambridge University Press.

Ellis, R. (1992). *Second language acquisition and language pedagogy.* Clevedon, UK: Multilingual Matters.

Ellis, R. (1993). The structural syllabus and second language acquisition. *TESOL Quarterly, 27* (1), 91–113.

Ellis, R. (1994). *The study of second language acquisition.* Oxford: Oxford University Press.

Ellis, R. (2002). Does form-focused instruction affect the acquisition of implicit knowledge? *Studies in Second Language Acquisition, 24*(2), 223–36.

Ellis, R. (2003). *Task-based language learning and teaching.* Oxford: Oxford University Press.

Ericsson, K. A. (Ed.). (1996). *The road to excellence: The acquisition of expert performance in the arts and sciences, sports, and games.* Mahwah, NJ: Lawrence Erlbaum.

Ericsson, K. A. (2003). Exceptional memorizers: made, not born. *Trends in Cognitive Sciences, 7*(6), 233–5.

Ericsson, K. A., & Charness, N. (1994). Expert performance. *American Psychologist, 49*(8), 725–47.

Ericsson, K. A., Krampe, R. T., & Tesch-Römer, C. (1993). The role of deliberate practice in the acquisition of expert performance. *Psychological Review, 100*(3), 363–406.

Ericsson, K. A., & Lehmann, A. C. (1996). Expert and exceptional performance: Evidence of maximal adaptation to task constraints. *Annual Review of Psychology, 47*, 273–305.

Gass, S., Mackey, A., Alvarez-Torres, M. J., & Fernández-García, M. (1999). The effects of task repetition on linguistic output. *Language Learning, 49*(4), 549–81.

Haider, H., & Frensch, P. A. (2002). Why aggregated learning follows the power law of practice when individual learning does not: Comment on Rickard (1997, 1999), Delaney et al. (1998), and Palmeri (1999). *Journal of Experimental Psychology: Learning, memory and cognition, 28*(2), 392–406.

Haskell, R. E. (2001). *Transfer of Learning: Cognition, instruction, and reasoning*. New York: Academic Press.

Healy, A. F., King, C. L., Clawson, D. M., Sinclair, G. P., Rickard, T. C., Crutcher, R. J. et al. (1995). Optimizing the long-term retention of skills. In A. F. Healy & L. E. Bourne, Jr. (Eds.), *Learning and memory of knowledge and skills. Durability and specificity* (pp. 1–29). Thousand Oaks, CA: Sage.

Healy, A. F., Barshi, I., Crutcher, R. J., Tao, L., Rickard, T. C., Marmie, W. R. et al. (1998). Toward the improvement of training in foreign languages. In A. F. Healy & L. E. J. Bourne (Eds.), *Foreign language learning. Psycholinguistic studies on training and retention* (pp. 3–53). Mahwah, NJ: Lawrence Erlbaum.

Hulstijn, J. (2002). Towards a unified account of the representation, acquisition, and automatization of second-language knowledge. *Second Language Research, 18*(3), 193–223.

Iwashita, N. (2003). Negative feedback and positive evidence in task-based interaction: Differential effects on L2 developments. *Studies in Second Language Acquisition, 25*(1), 1–36.

Izumi, S. (2002). Output, input enhancement, and the noticing hypothesis: An experimental study on ESL relativization. *Studies in Second Language Acquisition, 24*(4), 541–77.

Izumi, S. (2003). Comprehension and production processes in second language learning: In search of the psycholinguistic rationale of the output hypothesis. *Applied Linguistics, 24*(2), 168–96.

Krashen, S. D. (1982). *Principles and practice in second language acquisition*. Englewood Cliffs, NJ: Prentice-Hall.

Krashen, S. D. (1999). Seeking a role for grammar: A review of some recent studies. *Foreign Language Annals, 32*(2), 245–57.

Larsen-Freeman, D. (2003). *Teaching language: From grammar to grammaring*. Boston, MA: Heinle.

Leaver, B. L., Rifkin, B., & Shekhtman, B. (2004). Apples and oranges are both fruit, but they don't taste the same: A response to Wynne Wong and Bill VanPatten. *Foreign Language Annals, 37*(1), 125–32.

Lee, F. J., & Anderson, J. R. (2001). Does learning a complex task have to be complex? A study in learning decomposition. *Cognitive Psychology, 42*, 267–316.

Leeman, J. (2003). Recasts and second language development: Beyond negative evidence. *Studies in Second Language Acquisition, 25*(1), 37–63.

Legge, D. (1986). Skills. In R. Harré & R. Lamb (Eds.), *The dictionary of developmental and educational psychology* (pp. 225–8). Oxford: Blackwell.

Logan, G. D. (1988). Toward an instance theory of automatization. *Psychological Review, 95*(4), 492–527.

Logan, G. D. (1992). Shapes of reaction-time distributions and shapes of learning curves: A test of the instance theory of automaticity. *Journal of Experimental Psychology: Learning, Memory and Cognition, 18*(5), 883–914.

Logan, G. D. (2002). An instance theory of attention and memory. *Psychological Review, 109*(2), 376–400.

Long, M. H. (1988). Instructed interlanguage development. In L. Beebe (Ed.), *Issues in second language acquisition: Multiple perspectives* (pp. 115–41). New York: Harper & Row.

Long, M. H., & Crookes, G. (1992). Three approaches to task-based syllabus design. *TESOL Quarterly, 26*(1), 27–56.

Long, M. H., & Norris, J. (2000). Task-based teaching and assessment. In M. Byram (Ed.), *Encyclopedia of language teaching* (pp. 597–603). London: Routledge.

Long, M. H., & Robinson, P. (1998). Focus on form: Theory, research, and practice. In C. Doughty & J. Williams (Eds.), *Focus on form in classroom second language acquisition* (pp. 15–41). New York: Cambridge University Press.

Lynch, T., & Maclean, J. (2000). Exploring the benefits of task repetition and recycling for classroom language learning. *Language Teaching Research, 4*(3), 221–50.

Lynch, T., & Maclean, J. (2001). "A case of exercising": Effects of immediate task repetition on learners' performance. In M. Bygate, P. Skehan & M. Swain (Eds.), *Researching pedagogic tasks. Second language learning, teaching, and testing* (pp. 141–62). New York: Longman.

Maguire, E. A., Valentine, E. R., Wilding, J. M., & Kapur, N. (2003). Routes to remembering: the brains behind superior memory. *Nature Neuroscience, 6*(1), 90–5.

McLaughlin, B. (1987). *Theories of second-language learning*. London: Edward Arnold.

Müller, B. (1999). Use specificity of cognitive skills: Evidence for production rules? *Journal of Experimental Psychology, 25*(1), 191–207.

Newell, A., & Rosenbloom, P. S. (1981). Mechanisms of skill acquisition and the law of practice. In J. R. Anderson (Ed.), *Cognitive skills and their acquisition* (pp. 1–55). Hillsdale, NJ: Lawrence Erlbaum.

Nicholas, H., Lightbown, P. M., & Spada, N. (2001). Recasts as feedback to language learners. *Language Learning, 51*(4), 719–58.

Palmeri, T. J. (1997). Exemplar similarity and the development of automaticity. *Journal of Experimental Psychology: Learning, Memory and Cognition, 23*(2), 324–54.

Palmeri, T. J. (1999). Theories of automaticity and the power law of practice. *Journal of Experimental Psychology: Learning, Memory, and Cognition, 25*(2), 543–51.

Pashler, H., Johnston, J. C., & Ruthruff, E. (2001). Attention and performance. *Annual Review of Psychology, 52*, 629–51.

Paulston, C. B. (1970). Structural pattern drills: A classification. *Foreign Language Annals, 4*(2), 187–93.

Paulston, C. B. (1972). The sequencing of structural pattern drills. *TESOL Quarterly, 6*, 197–208.

Paulston, C. B., & Bruder, M. N. (1976). *Teaching English as a second language: Techniques and procedures*. Cambridge, MA: Winthrop.

Pica, T., & Washburn, G. (2002). Negative evidence in language classroom activities: A study of its availability and accessibility to language learners. *Working Papers in Educational Linguistics, 18*(1), 1–28.

Posner, M. I., DiGirolamo, G. J., & Fernandez-Duque, D. (1997). Brain mechanisms of cognitive skills. *Consciousness and Cognition, 6,* 267–90.

Reingold, E. M., & Ray, C. A. (2003). Implicit cognition. In L. Nadel (Ed.), *Encyclopedia of cognitive science* (Vol. 2, pp. 481–5). London: Macmillan.

Rickard, T. C. (1997). Bending the power law: A CMPL theory of strategy shifts and the automatization of cognitive skills. *Journal of Experimental Psychology: General, 126*(3), 288–311.

Rickard, T. C. (1999). A CMPL alternative account of practice effects in numerosity judgments. *Journal of Experimental Psychology: Learning, Memory, and Cognition, 25*(2), 532–42.

Rickard, T. C. (2004). Strategy execution in cognitive skill learning: An item-level test of candidate models. *Journal of Experimental Psychology: Learning, Memory, and Cognition, 30*(1), 65–82.

Russell, J., & Spada, N. (2006). The effectiveness of corrective feedback for the acquisition of L2 grammar: A meta-analysis of the research. In J. M. Norris & L. Ortega (Eds.), *Synthesizing research on language learning and teaching* (pp. 133–64). Philadelphia / Amsterdam: John Benjamins.

Schooler, L. J., & Anderson, J. R. (1990). The disruptive potential of immediate feedback. In *Proceedings of the 12th annual conference of the Cognitive Science Society* (pp. 702–8). Cambridge, MA.

Schmidt, R. A., & Bjork, R. A. (1992). New conceptualizations of practice: Common principles in three paradigms suggest new concepts for training. *Psychological Science, 3*(4), 207–17.

Singley, M. K., & Anderson, J. R. (1989). *The transfer of cognitive skill.* Cambridge, MA: Harvard University Press.

Skehan, P. (1996). A framework for the implementation of task-based instruction. *Applied Linguistics, 17,* 38–62.

Skehan, P. (1998). *A cognitive approach to language learning.* Oxford: Oxford University Press.

Starkes, J. L., & Ericsson, K. A. (Eds.). (2003). *Expert performance in sports: Advances in research on sports expertise.* Champaign, IL: Human Kinetics.

Van den Branden, K. (1997). Effects of negotiation on language learners' output. *Language Learning, 47*(4), 589–636.

Vandergrift, L. (2004). Listening to learn or learning to listen? *Annual Review of Applied Linguistics, 24,* 3–25.

VanLehn, K. (1989). Problem solving and cognitive skill acquisition. In M. I. Posner (Ed.), *Foundations of cognitive science* (pp. 527–79). Cambridge, MA: MIT Press.

VanPatten, B. (1996). *Input processing and grammar instruction: Theory and research.* Norwood, NJ: Ablex.

VanPatten, B. (2002a). Processing instruction: An update. *Language Learning, 52*(4), 755–803.

VanPatten, B. (2002b). Processing the content of input-processing and processing instruction research: A response to DeKeyser, Salaberry, Robinson, and Harrington. *Language Learning, 52*(4), 825–31.

VanPatten, B. (2003). *From input to output: A teacher's guide to second language acquisition.* New York: McGraw-Hill.

VanPatten, B. (Ed.). (2004). *Processing instruction: Theory, research, and commentary.* Mahwah, NJ: Lawrence Erlbaum.

VanPatten, B., & Cadierno, T. (1993). Input processing and second language acquisition: a role for instruction. *The Modern Language Journal, 77*(1), 45–57.

VanPatten, B., & Oikkenon, S. (1996). Explanation versus structured input in processing instruction. *Studies in Second Language Acquisition, 18*(4), 495–510.

Wesche, M. B., & Skehan, P. (2002). Communicative, task-based, and content-based language instruction. In R. B. Kaplan (Ed.), *The Oxford Handbook of Applied Linguistics* (pp. 207–28). New York: Oxford University Press.

Whittlesea, B. W. A., & Dorken, M. D. (1993). Incidentally, things in general are particularly determined: An episodic-processing account of implicit learning. *Journal of Experimental Psychology: General, 122*, 227–48.

Wilding, J. M., & Valentine, E. R. (1997). *Superior memory.* Hove, UK: Psychology Press.

Wong, W., & VanPatten, B. (2003). The evidence is IN: Drills are OUT. *Foreign Language Annals, 36*(3), 403–23.

Wong, W., & VanPatten, B. (2004). Beyond experience and belief (or, waiting for the evidence): A reply to Leaver et al.'s "Apples and Oranges." *Foreign Language Annals, 37*(1), 133–42.

Wulf, G., Schmidt, R. A., & Deubel, H. (1993). Reduced feedback frequency enhances generalized motor program learning but no parameterization learning. *Journal of Experimental Psychology: Learning, Memory and Cognition, 19*, 1134–50.

Yule, G. (1997). *Referential communication tasks.* Mahwah, NJ: Lawrence Erlbaum.

PART I:
FOUNDATIONS

The chapters in this section form the foundations of the book in the sense that they deal with aspects of practice that should hold true for all learners in all contexts. Part II will deal with variations due to institutional contexts and Part III with individual differences.

Input and output have been discussed many times in the applied linguistics and second language acquisition literature, but only in recent years has attention been focused on what exactly the role of input and output *practice* is. For centuries, language teaching, whether grammar-translation, audiolingual, cognitive-code, or communicative, had put emphasis on output activities but with very divergent underlying philosophies. Krashen's monitor model and Krashen and Terrell's natural approach were radical breaks with that tradition in the sense that they saw only a minimal role for output practice, seeing output as largely unproblematic, provided the relevant competence had been acquired. Acquisition of competence, in turn, was viewed as a matter of enough meaning-focused processing of the right ("comprehensible") kind of input, not a matter of systematic practice in the sense of this book (i.e., specific activities in the second language, engaged in systematically, deliberately, with the goal of developing knowledge of and skills in the second language; see Chapter 1), even though some of the activities advocated by Krashen and Terrell as a means of providing meaningful and comprehensible input would certainly qualify as practice from our point of view. Since then the profession has seen a return to focus on form, but how much of it is necessary, at what stage of the learning process, in particular whether form should be learned through practice with focus on form, or whether form should be taught and then practiced, how much practice is needed in comprehension and how much in production and for what purposes continue to be debated.

The chapters in this section illustrate the various answers to these questions. Ron Leow describes three different ways of looking at input practice: (1) what he calls the "attention strand," i.e., the point of view that learners should engage in systematic activities that will focus their attention on form to start the acquisition process; (2) what VanPatten has called "processing instruction," i.e., activities aimed at the acquisition of form-meaning links through repeated processing of these links in a format that makes them essential to the task, following explicit instruction; and (3) the skill acquisition approach as represented by cognitive psychologists such as Anderson and Newell, which holds that skills in a variety of domains are acquired by proceduralizing and automatizing declarative knowledge, the latter most often being acquired through explicit instruction of rules accompanied by examples.

Hitoshi Muranoi argues strongly that there is a need for output practice. Drawing on Swain's output hypothesis, Levelt's speech production model, and Anderson's model of skill acquisition, he describes a variety of functions of output practice: noticing, hypothesis testing, conscious reflection, and automatization. He advocates output practice through various forms of text reconstruction.

Ideally, of course, input and output practice are integrated in the form of interaction between native and non-native speakers. Not only do learners need to practice skills like holding the floor or getting the floor, which can only be learned in an interactional context; but as Alison Mackey's chapter shows, learners can also benefit from the specific kinds of comprehensible input and pushed output that are brought about through the negotiation of meaning in NS-NNS interaction.

An especially problematic aspect of practice, in particular of interactive practice, is the role of feedback. With its renewed focus on form, the profession is less suspicious of feedback than a generation ago, but exactly how and when to provide what kind of feedback continues to be a question of great concern. Jennifer Leeman guides us through the maze of terminology on this point and argues that, while feedback is clearly beneficial, it can be hard to determine whether it is enhanced salience, metalinguistic information, or pushed output that plays the biggest role, in particular as this may depend on the elements of language in question.

1 Input in the L2 classroom: An attentional perspective on receptive practice

Ronald P. Leow

Introduction

The role of input is undoubtedly crucial in the process of second/foreign language (L2) learning. Input may be defined as the L2 data (form-based and/or meaning-based) that learners receive either in the formal classroom or in a naturalistic setting. Indeed, how L2 input is presented to L2 learners in the classroom and its effects on the processes learners employ to interact with the input (input processing) have been the focus of several strands of second language acquisition (SLA) studies conducted within a psycholinguistic framework. The theoretical underpinnings of most of these psycholinguistic studies appear to include some role for attention (and possibly awareness) in the processing of L2 grammatical or linguistic data in adult learners' L2 development (e.g., Robinson, 1995; Schmidt, 1990, 1993, 1995, 2001; Tomlin & Villa, 1994; VanPatten, 2004).

The term *practice* has several connotations (see DeKeyser, this volume for an elaborated discussion of this term in several fields of inquiry) in both the applied linguistics and cognitive psychology literatures. In applied linguistics, the notion of pedagogical practice in the typical classroom assumes some form of performance by learners in response to L2 grammatical input they receive in this setting, which may be provided prior to or during practice. In addition, the L2 input is usually manipulated in some form by the teacher. For example, learners may be exposed to L2 that has been carefully selected and manipulated by the teacher to highlight some linguistic data and may be requested to interact with it in several ways, such as selecting options related to the linguistic data in the input, performing a task, and so forth.

From an attentional perspective, then, receptive practice will be broadly defined in this chapter as follows: any exposure[1] to manipulated L2 input that provides not only various exemplars of targeted L2 forms or structures upon which learners' attention to (and/or awareness of) is directly or indirectly premised but also some form of opportunity to perform a limited productive or nonproductive task or activity (e.g., selecting one out of two options, completing a problem-solving task, translating) during the exposure. The general assumption is that, via receptive practice, learners pay attention to the targeted linguistic data in the input while processing the grammatical information substantially enough to be capable of recognizing, interpreting, and/or producing such forms or structures after exposure. By definition, studies in which learners were required to simply process the L2 input (e.g., textual or input enhancement, input flooding, some skill acquisition studies) or to produce the targeted forms or structures during exposure (see, for example, Muranoi for output, Leeman for oral feedback, and Mackey for oral interaction in this volume) have been excluded in this chapter. The ultimate goal of receptive practice is to promote robust input processing leading to subsequent internalization of the linguistic data.

It is important to note that this chapter does not presume that receptive practice is the only pedagogical avenue for successful L2 development in the classroom setting given that this type of practice addresses only one aspect of the acquisitional process, usually referred to as an early stage of processing the incoming L2 data. A wealth of studies have addressed, for example, the role of output in L2 development (e.g., de la Fuente, 2002; Izumi & Bigelow, 2000; Izumi, Bigelow, Fujiwara, & Fearnow, 1999; Izumi, 2002; Muranoi, this volume; Swain, 1995; Swain & Lapkin, 1995), that appears to provide abundant empirical support for such a role in SLA.

Theoretical underpinnings

Cognitive psychology and cognitive science have provided an explanation of or theoretical account for the role cognitive processes play in SLA (e.g., Anderson, 1983, 1990; Bialystok, 1978, 1990, 1994; Carr & Curran, 1994; Ellis, 1993; Gass, 1988; Hulstijn, 1989; Hulstijn & Schmidt, 1994; Robinson, 1995; Schmidt 1990 and elsewhere; Sharwood Smith, 1981, 1986, 1991; Tomlin & Villa, 1994; VanPatten, 1996). One premise shared by the fields of cognitive psychology, cognitive science, and SLA is that learning does not take place without attention. The role of attention is deemed crucial for further long-term memory storage of L2 information to take place (for comprehensive reviews of studies that explicate such a role of attention in language learning, see Carr & Curran, 1994; Schmidt, 1990 and elsewhere; Robinson, 1995; Tomlin & Villa, 1994).

Given this role for attention in L2 development, the next section will report on current SLA research that has employed receptive practice in an effort to promote L2 development in the L2 classroom and situate these studies with respect to their theoretical underpinnings and the role of attention in receptive practice.

Receptive practice in SLA classroom-based research

The 1990s witnessed several strands of research (attentional/attention-focusing tasks, processing instruction [PI], and skill acquisition) that shared the same purpose of providing receptive practice to learners to promote their intake and subsequent processing of targeted linguistic data contained in the L2 input. However, the studies seem to differ somewhat with respect to the role attention plays in receptive practice. In the attentional strand, attention appears to be assigned a primary role (e.g., Rosa & Leow, 2004a, 2004b; Rosa & O'Neill, 1999); in the processing instruction (PI) strand, it has a secondary role (e.g., VanPatten, 2004, Wong, 2004a), and in the skill acquisition strand, it is subsumed within the theoretical framework (e.g., de Graaff, 1997; DeKeyser, 1997; DeKeyser & Sokalski, 1996). There are also methodological differences in the timing of the provision or lack thereof of grammatical information on the L2 linguistic data embedded in the input. For example, some studies, as part of their research designs, provided explicit grammatical information prior to practice (e.g., Benati, 2004; Cadierno 1995; Cheng, 2002; DeKeyser & Sokalski, 1996; Farley, 2001a, 2001b, 2004; Morgan-Short & Bowden, 2006; Rosa & Leow, 2004a, 2004b; VanPatten & Cadierno, 1993; VanPatten & Oikkenon, 1996; VanPatten & Sanz, 1995; VanPatten & Wong, 2004), during practice in the form of feedback (e.g., de Graff, 1997; DeKeyser, 1997; Morgan-Short & Bowden, 2006; Rosa & Leow, 2004a, 2004b; Sanz, 2004; Sanz & Morgan-Short, 2004), or none at all (e.g., Benati, 2004; Farley, 2004; Rosa & O'Neill, 1999; Sanz, 2004; Sanz & Morgan-Short, 2004; VanPatten & Wong, 2004b). In addition, whether any research methodology was employed to operationalize and measure the construct of attention, that is, whether learners did indeed pay attention to the targeted forms or structures during practice, can be viewed from an offline (e.g., Benati, 2004; Farley, 2004; de Graaff, 1997; DeKeyser, 1997; Sanz, 2004; Sanz & Morgan-Short, 2004; VanPatten & Cadierno, 1993; VanPatten & Oikkenon, 1996; VanPatten & Sanz, 1995; VanPatten & Wong, 2004) versus an online (Rosa & Leow, 2004a, 2004b; Rosa & O'Neill, 1999) data elicitation perspective. Online data elicitation measures (for example, think-aloud protocols) are employed to gather information on learners' internal processes *during* exposure to and/or interaction with the L2 data. Offline measures are conducted *after* exposure and, consequently, can only make inferences as to whether learners either paid attention to or became aware of targeted forms or structures in the input.[2]

Studies conducted within the attentional strand

The theoretical underpinning of studies conducted within the attentional strand that provided receptive practice to adult L2 learners (e.g., Rosa & Leow, 2004a, 2004b; Rosa & O'Neill, 1999) is derived from Schmidt's (1990 and elsewhere) noticing hypothesis.[3] According to this hypothesis, learners need to consciously notice or demonstrate a conscious apprehension and awareness of some particular form in the input before that form can be processed further. In Schmidt's view, since focal attention is isomorphic with awareness, there cannot be any dissociation between awareness and learning. Schmidt also distinguishes two levels of awareness to account for the distinction between intake/item learning and restructuring/system learning, namely, awareness at the level of noticing and at the level of understanding. At the level of understanding, learners are able to analyze, compare, test hypotheses, and verbalize the underlying rules of the language.[4]

Studies conducted within an attentional framework have employed concurrent data elicitation procedures (e.g., think-aloud protocols) to establish that attention was indeed paid to the targeted forms or structures before its effects were statistically analyzed. In addition, the design of the experimental tasks that provided receptive practice was premised on Loschky and Bley-Vroman's (1993) notion of "task-essentialness" that required learners to pay attention to the targeted grammatical forms in the input in order to successfully complete the task. According to Loschky and Bley-Vroman, "the grammatical point itself is the 'essence' of what is to be attended to" (p. 139). Due to the nature of the experimental tasks, implicit feedback was inherently provided during performance (Rosa & O'Neill, 1999), while type of feedback (whether explicit or implicit) was also addressed in Rosa and Leow (2004a, 2004b).

Rosa and O'Neill (1999) investigated how intake of Spanish contrary-to-fact conditional sentences was affected both by awareness and by the condition under which a problem-solving task was performed. Participants were 67 adult L2 learners of Spanish, with no prior knowledge of the targeted structure, who were randomly divided into four conditions with different degrees of explicitness and one control group. Two factors were varied to create the four experimental conditions: explicit formal instruction (FI) on Spanish contrary-to-fact conditional sentences (provided in a handout prior to practice) and directions to search for rules (RS) while solving each sentence of the puzzle, yielding the following groups: [+FI, +RS], [+FI, −RS], [−FI, +RS], [−FI, −RS]. Participants in the [−RS] conditions were requested to memorize the content information as they solved each sentence of the puzzle. The control group was not provided with any instruction prior to completing the puzzle.

Concurrent data on learners' awareness were gathered through the use of think-aloud protocols performed while participants were completing the problem-solving tasks. Intake was measured through a multiple-choice recognition test administered immediately after practice.

Receptive practice was provided via a problem-solving task (a multiple-choice jigsaw puzzle) divided into two pasted sections on a page: (1) a piece of the puzzle depicting an event, a person, or the result of an event and (2) another piece of the puzzle with the main clause of a conditional sentence of either one of two experimental targeted structures. Each page also had three other pieces of the puzzle each with a subordinate clause written on it. Participants were required to select one of the three unpasted pieces that would correctly fit between the picture and the main subordinate clause. Implicit feedback was inherent in the practice, given that a correct match indicated accuracy. Rosa and O'Neill found that all the experimental groups, including the control, increased significantly their intake from the pre-test to the post-test. In other words, the absence of explicit grammatical presentation of L2 linguistic data did not impede learners' ability to recognize the targeted structure immediately after exposure.

Rosa and O'Neill, like Leow (1997, 2001a), reported that awareness at the level of noticing and at the level of understanding translated into a significant improvement in intake scores from the pre-test to the post-test. Likewise, results indicated that learners who demonstrated understanding of the targeted structure performed significantly better on intake posttests than learners who evidenced noticing only. Finally, Rosa and O'Neill reported significant relationships between learners in the [+FI] and the [+RS] conditions and awareness at the level of understanding. They suggested that "providing learners with formal instruction could be an effective way of directing their attention to form, thus promoting the emergence of high levels of awareness" (p. 544) and "orienting the learners to the formal aspects of the input by simply reminding them to search for rules was almost as powerful as presenting them with the actual rules" (p. 545).

Rosa and Leow (2004a, 2004b) examined (1) whether exposure to L2 input under different computerized task conditions premised on degree of explicitness had a differential impact on learners' ability to recognize and produce both old and new exemplars of the Spanish past conditional immediately after exposure to the input and over time; (2) whether exposure to L2 input under different conditions had a differential impact on learners' awareness; and (3) whether different levels of awareness influenced learners' ability to recognize and produce the targeted structure immediately after exposure to the input and over time. Degree of explicitness was manipulated by combining three features: (a) a pretask providing explicit grammatical information, (b) feedback concurrent to input processing, and (c) in those cases in which feedback was provided, its nature (i.e., implicit or explicit). In the explicit feedback (EFE) condition, if the answer was correct, the participants received a prompt reinforcing the reason their choice was the right one. If the answer was wrong, the participants received a prompt saying that the choice was incorrect together with an explanation of the reason. In this case, the participants were instructed to try again so that they made the correct selection of time frame for each particular sentence before going on to the next card. For the implicit condition, the participants received only feedback that indicated whether the answer was right or wrong.

Exposure to the L2 input took place in a computer-based setting by means of a series of problem-solving tasks involving manipulation of the input. The participants in the control condition were exposed to similar input (a sentence-reading activity) in a computer setting, although not in the form of a problem-solving task.

One hundred adult learners of Spanish with no prior knowledge of the targeted structure were randomly exposed to past conditional sentences under one of six conditions premised on different degrees of explicitness: EPEFE (explicit pretask + explicit feedback), EPIFE (explicit pretask + implicit feedback), EFE (explicit feedback), EP (explicit pretask), IFE (implicit feedback), and control. Receptive practice was provided via a jigsaw puzzle, comprising a series of 28 interactive Libra cards[5] and relatively similar in design to Rosa and O'Neill's puzzle. Duration of practice was 28 minutes with an additional 8 minutes allotted for the pretask phase. L2 development was assessed through recognition and controlled-production tests containing old and new exemplars of the targeted structure.

Results indicated that explicit grammatical explanation prior to practice significantly contributed to learners' superior ability to recognize and produce in writing old and new exemplars of the targeted structure when compared to the control group, an ability that was maintained for a period of three weeks. Among their findings, Rosa and Leow found that, regarding type of task condition, (1) higher degrees of explicitness had a more drastic impact; (2) processing L2 input through a problem-solving task proved to be an efficient way of helping learners internalize the targeted structure; (3) the advantages of processing input under explicit conditions were more evident in production of old and new items and in recognition of new items; (4) in the case of recognition and production of new items, higher levels of accuracy were reached by learners who processed input through a problem-solving task containing (a) two sources of information on the targeted structure (e.g., a pretask and explicit or implicit feedback) or (b) only one source of information, in the form of concurrent explicit feedback; and (5) explicit feedback provided during input processing had stronger effects on accuracy than a pretask alone.

Regarding the role of awareness, Rosa and Leow (2004b) also found that (1) higher levels of awareness (i.e., understanding) were associated with learning conditions providing an explicit pretask as well as implicit or explicit feedback; (2) higher levels of awareness (i.e., understanding) were substantially more effective than lower levels (i.e., noticing) in helping learners recognize and produce novel exemplars of the targeted structure; and (3) higher levels of awareness were associated with sophisticated input-processing strategies such as hypothesis formation and testing, as well as with verbal formulation of rules accounting for the form and function of the targeted structure, corroborating the findings of previous studies on the role of awareness in L2 behavior and learning (e.g., Leow, 1997; Rosa & O'Neill, 1999).

Studies conducted within the processing instruction (PI) strand

The theoretical foundation of processing instruction is based on VanPatten's (1996) model of input processing (IP)[6] (see VanPatten, 2004 for an updated version of his model), which, in turn, appears to draw from the metaphor of a limited capacity channel or processor (e.g., Broadbent, 1958; Kahneman, 1973; Norman, 1968; Treisman, 1964). Capacity theories postulate that there is competition for attentional resources to be paid to incoming information and that what is paid attention to may depend on the amount of mental effort required to process the incoming information. For example, Kahneman's (1973) capacity model of attention, dependent on the participant's state of arousal, postulated the allocation of attentional resources from a pool of cognitive resources to incoming information. Whereas earlier filter theories (e.g., Broadbent, 1958; Treisman, 1964; Norman, 1968) viewed an inevitable competition for the allocation of attentional resources for incoming information, Kahneman's (1973) capacity model allows the possibility of dividing the allocation of resources to different aspects of incoming information. According to Kahneman, performance may not be negatively affected once the state of arousal is adequate and if the task demands are not overwhelming.

In line with the notion that learners have a limited capacity to process L2 information, PI advocates in its guidelines to "present one thing at a time." Providing only one rule at a time can avoid overtaxing learners' processing resources and maximize the potential to pay more focused attention to the targeted form or structure needed for intake (Lee & VanPatten, 1995). According to VanPatten (2004, p. 7), "processing implies that perception and noticing have occurred, but the latter two do not necessarily imply that a form has been processed (linked with meaning and/or form)." As implied in the previous statement, the role of attention (noticing) in PI appears to be secondary to the primary goal of PI, which is to "help L2 learners derive richer intake from input by having them engage in structured input activities that push them away from the strategies they normally use to make form-meaning connections" (Wong, 2004a: 33). Indeed, Wong (2004) appears to view the role of attention during structured input activities as "an incidental byproduct" in that learners' attention is drawn to the relevant form-meaning connection only because the learners are engaging in the structured input activities. This view, however, appears to contradict Sanz' (2004) direct reference to the important role of attention (noticing) in processing instruction when she writes that "[i]ts input-focused practice is crucially structured so that learners need to attend to the target grammatical form/structure to understand the meaning and complete the activity" (p. 241). Sanz relates this practice to the notion of Loschky and Bley-Vroman's (1993) "task-essentialness," which in itself is premised on the role of attention crucial for successful completion of a task.

The three main characteristics of PI are (a) grammatical explanation about the targeted form or structure prior to practice, (b) explicit information about processing strategies (in which learners' attention is explicitly oriented to what to pay attention to and why), and (c) participation in structured input activities to promote further processing of the input data. *Structured input* activities are so called because the input has been manipulated to make the targeted forms or structures more salient (e.g., sentence-initial) and discourage learners' previous incorrect use of a particular processing strategy (e.g., a subject-verb-object [SVO] word order arguably employed by English-speaking students learning Spanish). Two types of structured input activities are used in PI: referential and affective. Referential activities require learners to pay attention to form in order to get meaning. Learners have a correct or an incorrect answer that provides feedback to the teacher concerning the learners' ability to make the correct form-meaning connection. During these activities, learners are provided with implicit feedback about whether their answer was correct. Affective activities require learners to provide an affective response while processing information about the real world. There is no correct or incorrect response. One key feature of structured input activities, then, is to have learners respond to the input in some form or fashion to promote active processing of the targeted form or structure while keeping the focus on meaningful activities. Given the focus on the creation of intake from the input, no production of the targeted structure is promoted during the exposure. Instead, learners are "pushed to make form-meaning connections by requiring them to rely on form or sentence structure to interpret meaning" (Wong, 2004a, p. 37).

The effects of this instructional treatment have been typically compared with traditional instruction, defined as grammatical explanation and output practice of a grammatical point, and meaning-based instruction.[7] Participants were generally from second semester and above with some prior knowledge of the targeted forms or structures (Spanish preverbal direct object pronouns, *ser* and *estar*, preterit, present subjunctive, conditional; Italian future tense). Two exceptions were the French causative (VanPatten & Wong, 2004b) and Spanish preverbal direct object pronouns (Morgan-Short & Bowden, 2006). Assessment tasks were an interpretation task (typically a choice of A or B) and a written fill-in-the-blank or change-the-verb production task (e.g., Cheng, 2002; Farley, 2001a, 2001b, 2004; Morgan-Short & Bowden, 2006; VanPatten & Cadierno, 1993; VanPatten & Oikkenon, 1996) while VanPatten and Sanz (1995) also employed a written video-retelling. The duration of instructional exposure was typically two to four days for approximately two hours.

Overall results indicated significant improvement in PI learners' performances on both the interpretation and written production tasks when compared to a control group without exposure to the linguistic data. When compared to the traditional output group, the results revealed that while the PI group typically outperformed the traditional group on the interpretation assessment task, there was usually no significant difference in performance on the production assessment task.

Subsequent PI studies sought to isolate the variable of explicit grammatical explanation before practice to address its potential effect during practice (Benati, 2004; Farley, 2004; VanPatten & Oikkenon, 1996; Wong, 2004a, 2004b). VanPatten and Oikkenon replicated VanPatten and Cadierno (1993) at a high school level with the groups exposed to one of three conditions: (a) explicit grammatical explanation only (about 10–15 minutes per session followed by activities not related to the targeted structure), (b) structured input activities only (SI), or (c) grammatical explanation and structured input activities (PI). The authors reported that the groups exposed to SI and PI performed significantly better on both the interpretation and production tasks when compared with the explicit grammatical explanation-only group. Indeed, explicit grammatical explanation appeared to play no role in subsequent processing of the targeted structure.

Participants in the more recent studies were from the first quarter to the fourth semester (with some participants possessing some prior knowledge of the targeted forms or structures) that included the use of the *de* with *avoir* in French (Wong), the Italian future tense (Benati), and the Spanish subjunctive (Farley). Wong's and Benati's results were relatively similar to VanPatten and Oikkenon's findings, although Wong found a significant increase in performance between the pre-test and post-test for the EI group on the production task (Benati did not report pre-test-post-test comparisons on the groups' performances on either assessment task). Wong postulated that the type of linguistic structure might be responsible for such a potential improvement. Farley found the PI group to be significantly better than the SI group on both tasks (both groups improved significantly from the pre-test to the post-test; there was no explicit grammatical explanation only group). To explain the discrepancy between this finding and other PI studies, Farley postulated that explicit grammatical information may be "beneficial" in PI for language features that possess "opaque or semantically non-transparent form-meaning connections" (p. 238). Overall, though, when compared to other conditions not receiving grammatical information prior to practice, the findings replicated those found in VanPatten and Oikkenon (1996).

Four studies to date (Benati, 2005; Farley, 2001a, 2001b; Morgan-Short & Bowden, 2006) specifically addressed whether output-based instruction was as effective as PI when all the variables except for practice mode were controlled. In addition, Morgan-Short and Bowden attempted to address methodological limitations found in previous research designs by controlling for prior knowledge of the targeted form, providing a control group that was exposed to the targeted forms approximately matched for time spent on experimental task, providing customized computerized feedback, and delivering the instruction via the computer to eliminate potential teacher bias. Overall, the results were quite inconclusive. For the interpretation task, while Farley (2001a) and Benati (2004) reported PI's superior performance when compared to output-based instruction, both Farley (2001b) and Morgan-Short and Bowden (2006) reported no significant difference in performance between the two groups. For the production task, while all four studies reported no significant difference in performance between PI and output-based instruction on the immediate posttest, Morgan-Short and Bowden also reported that only the output-based instruction group outperformed the control group, indicating that both PI and the control group performed statistically similar on this task. All significant differences in performance between groups on both interpretation and productions tests had disappeared by the delayed posttest, one week later. To account for the control group's differential performance when compared with previous PI studies, Morgan-Short and Bowden suggested that their use of control participants who were exposed to meaningful contexts in a reading passage, differed from the typical nonexposure control group employed in many PI studies.

Sanz and Morgan-Short (2004) went a step further and addressed, within the PI framework, the effects of explicit grammatical explanation [E] not only prior to but also during receptive practice via explicit negative feedback [F] on the acquisition of Spanish word order (preverbal direct-object pronoun) by 69 adult first- or second-year college students of Spanish with some prior knowledge of the targeted structure (see Sanz, 2004 for a report of the feedback component only). Feedback was immediate, personalized (i.e., only provided when an error was made), and focused consistently on the critical form and the source of the error, which was the learners' incorrect use of the strategy of assigning agent status to the preverbal pronoun. Participants were randomly assigned to one of four practice conditions: [+E, +F], [−E, −F], [+E, −F], and [−E, +F]. Assessment tasks were an interpretation, sentence completion, and a written video-retelling. Results indicated that while participants in all practice conditions significantly improved their ability to assign semantic functions correctly to noun phrases in the sentence from the pretest to posttest on all assessment tasks, no significant differences were found among the four practice groups. Sanz and Morgan-Short concluded that (a) explicit grammatical information about the Spanish preverbal direct-object pronoun, whether provided to learners prior to practice or during practice (via feedback), or at both times, might not play an important role in facilitating second language acquisition and (b) exposing learners to practice with structured input premised on the notion of task-essentialness was sufficient to promote acquisition.

Studies conducted within the skill acquisition strand

The theoretical debate on the potential interface between implicit and explicit learning/knowledge (e.g., DeKeyser, 1998; N. Ellis, 1993; R. Ellis, 1994a, 1994b, 1995; Hulstijn & de Graaff, 1994; Krashen, 1982) centers on the extent to which awareness is necessary for L2 development, although the roles of attention and awareness in receptive practice in this strand are not fully explicated or methodologically operationalized and measured. Proponents of a noninterface position (e.g., Krashen, 1982, 1985, 1994) argue that learning under explicit conditions, that is, with awareness, cannot convert into acquisition. In other words, explicit grammatical knowledge (Krashen, 1982) or learned linguistic knowledge (Schwartz, 1993) and implicit knowledge (or competence) are completely separate. Proponents of the strong or weak form of the interface position (e.g., Bialystok 1981; DeKeyser, 1998; N. Ellis, 1993; R. Ellis, 1994a, 1994b; Hulstijn & de Graaff, 1994; McLaughlin, 1987) argue that there is either a direct link (strong interface position) or a potential link (weak interface position) between the two, that is, by practicing new grammatical rules until the rules become automatized, learners can convert explicit knowledge into implicit knowledge.

The strong or weak interface position finds its roots in cognitive psychology models of skill acquisition that include theories of controlled and automatic processing (e.g., McLaughlin, 1987; Shiffrin & Schneider, 1977) and is aptly exemplified by Anderson's Adaptive Control of Thought (ACT) model[8] (Anderson, 1982, 1983, 1990), based on the distinction between declarative and procedural knowledge.

To address empirically the debate on the potential interface between implicit and explicit learning and knowledge, studies have designed so-called experimental implicit and explicit learning conditions to address the effects of different types of instructional exposures or conditions on L2 development (e.g., Alanen, 1995; de Graaff, 1997; DeKeyser, 1995, 1997; N. Ellis, 1993; Robinson, 1996, 1997a, 1997b). In most of these studies (Alanen, 1995; DeKeyser, 1995; N. Ellis, 1993; Robinson, 1996, 1997a, 1997b), explicit grammatical information was provided prior to simple exposure (without any provision of receptive practice) to the L2 that contained the targeted form or structure. In other words, learners were simply requested to read sentences in order to, for example, search for rules, memorize, or comprehend the L2.

Studies that did provide receptive practice within this strand of research (e.g., de Graaff, 1997; DeKeyser, 1997) typically created experimental learning conditions in which the effects of explicit grammatical explanation were investigated. De Graaff (1997) investigated the effects of explicit instruction and the complexity of morphological and syntactic structures on language acquisition of an artificial language called eXperanto, which was presented in a computerized self-study course. The four targeted structures were a simple morphological rule (plural noun form), a complex morphological rule (the inflection of the imperative mode), a simple syntactic rule (the position of the negation forms), and a complex syntactic rule (the position of the object). De Graaff hypothesized that explicit instruction would be more effective in the case of the acquisition of syntactic structures (dependent more exclusively on rule application) than on morphological structures (dependent on both rule application and analogy application).

Fifty-four monolingual native speakers of Dutch were randomly assigned to an explicit or implicit learning condition. The duration of both conditions was 15 hours and included a series of dialogues, vocabulary activities, and grammatical exercises (fill-in-the-blanks and sentence-level activities based on a functional clue in Dutch). The major difference between the two conditions was that the explicit condition received explicit rule presentation and explicit grammatical explanations on the targeted grammatical structures during feedback. The implicit learning group only rehearsed example sentences. Assessment tasks were a time-constrained grammaticality judgment task, a gap-filling task, and a sentence judgment and correction task not constrained by time. These tasks were administered three times: one halfway through the experiment, one immediately after the treatment (which lasted 10 weeks), and one 5 weeks later.

De Graaff found that participants exposed to grammatical explanations scored higher on all assessment tasks on both immediate and delayed post-tests than participants in the implicit condition. No differential effect of explicit instruction on the learning of simple versus complex rules was found nor were the effects of explicit versus implicit instruction significantly different in the case of morphological as opposed to syntactic structures.

DeKeyser (1997) went a step further by addressing the issue of how explicit knowledge of morphosyntactic rules is automatized under different conditions of practice. To address this issue, a miniature computerized linguistic system (an agglutinative language with flexible word order), Autopractan, was designed. All 61 participants were explicitly taught four grammatical rules and 32 vocabulary items twice, tested on their explicit knowledge of vocabulary and grammar, and given detailed explicit feedback on their errors. They were tested once again to ensure complete vocabulary and grammar knowledge and then assigned to one of three practice conditions (A, B, and C). Learners in condition A practiced comprehension of two targeted rules and production of the other two targeted rules. Condition B was the opposite of condition A; that is, learners practiced comprehension of the two targeted rules practiced by A in production and vice versa. Learners under condition C practiced all four targeted rules in both comprehension and production. Thus, all participants received explicit grammatical explanations of the targeted rules, the same amount of practice and exposure for each rule, the same amount of practice in both skills, and the same amount of experience with both practice and testing formats. However, the amount of practice of specific rules in specific skills and formats differentiated the three groups. The practice sessions also incorporated feedback that included an explicit grammatical explanation of the errors.

Exposure lasted 22 sessions (comprising the learning and practice phases) of one hour or less over a period of 11 weeks. In the first 6 sessions, participants received a formal presentation of the grammar, then practiced, based on condition assignment, in the remaining 16. Performance was measured by both comprehension and production assessment tasks, and they included single-task as well as dual-task conditions in order to test for automatization and interference of simultaneous task performance.

DeKeyser reported the following results: practice led to automatization measured as reaction times and error rates. Automatization was evident both in comprehension and production and under single- and dual-task conditions. Practice also appeared to be skill-specific, as learners who had received comprehension practice improved more in comprehension, and learners who had received production practice improved more in production.

According to DeKeyser (1997), these results lend support to a model of skill acquisition that predicts that declarative knowledge changes into qualitatively different procedural knowledge during initial practice. Subsequently, proceduralized knowledge is slowly automatized, a process that requires little or no change in task components; instead, only a quantitative change within the same components is observed.

The DeKeyser and Sokalski (1996) study was designed to address the effects of receptive versus productive practice in a context in which grammatical explanation was provided. They sought to replicate VanPatten and Cadierno's (1993) processing instruction study in relation to the predictions of skill acquisition theory: that is, the issue of specific contribution of production and comprehension practice in SLA and the degree to which relative complexity of structure could affect the usefulness of input and output practice. According to DeKeyser and Sokalski, a "morphological complex structure may be easier to notice but harder to produce correctly than a simpler structure; a simpler structure may be inconspicuous and therefore harder to notice, but easier to produce by virtue of its simplicity" (p. 620). Eighty-two first year English-speaking students of Spanish with some prior knowledge of the targeted Spanish direct-object clitic and the conditional form were assigned to one of three conditions at two levels (Spanish I and Spanish II): input practice, output practice, and control. The experimental groups received a grammatical handout for each targeted item, to which they could have referred during the exposure. The practice exercises were designed to maintain, as far as possible, a similar format, length of sentences, grammatical complexity, vocabulary, and a need to attend to meaning for the experimental groups. The sequence of exercises began with a few mechanical exercises and progressed to meaningful and communicative ones. Comprehension tasks required a choice of one out of two, while the production tasks required participants to fill in the blanks, translate sentences, and answer questions. Practice lasted over six class periods for a total of 85 minutes (10 minutes to read the grammatical handout and 75 minutes for practice). Feedback was provided via teacher-based discussions and corrections. The control group read the grammatical handout for only 10 minutes and for the rest of the treatment period followed the regular class schedule. Assessment tasks were a comprehension test, a fill-in-the-blank test, and a translation test.

For the direct object clitic, results indicated that the input practice group significantly outperformed the control group on the comprehension test, while the output group significantly outperformed the control group on the production test. These significant differences disappeared by the time of the delayed test one week later. For the conditional form, the results revealed that the output practice group significantly outperformed the control group on both the comprehension and production tests while the input practice significantly outperformed the control group on the comprehension test. Like the comprehension test, these significant differences disappeared by the delayed test. DeKeyser and Sokalski concluded that the predictions of skill acquisition theory are largely supported by the findings, in that input practice is better for comprehension skills while output practice is better for production skills, but that "these patterns are obscured when both testing time and the morphosyntactic nature in question favor one skill or the other" (p. 615).

Table 1.1 summarizes the research strands, theoretical frameworks, and receptive practice features reported in SLA research.

Discussion of SLA research on receptive practice

An overall review of the findings reveals several interesting patterns and a relative amount of overlap between the strands for both theoretical and methodological issues. The following section provides responses to important questions regarding the effectiveness of providing explicit grammatical information prior to and during receptive practice, the roles of attention and awareness during the performance of receptive practice, and the issues of the complexity of linguistic items, comprehension and production based on type of practice, and amount of practice and exemplars.

Does providing explicit grammatical information prior to receptive practice have an effect on L2 development?

To address this question, only studies (Benati, 2004; Rosa & O'Neill, 1999; Rosa & Leow, 2004a, 2004b; VanPatten & Oikkenon, 1996; Wong, 2004b) that have isolated the variable of ± grammatical information will be considered, given that in other studies the experimental groups included confounding variables that were not teased out methodologically to make relevant statistical comparisons. All the studies, with the exception of those by Benati and VanPatten and Oikkenon, reported that explicit grammatical information provided prior to receptive practice significantly contributed to learners' intake and their written production of old and new exemplars of the Spanish past conditional (Rosa & Leow, 2004a), learners' intake of Spanish contrary-to-fact conditional sentences (Rosa & O'Neill), and the interpretation and written production of *avoir de* in French (Wong) after practice. However, they also reported that the grammatical information provided in the form of a

TABLE 1.1. STRANDS, THEORETICAL FRAMEWORKS, AND FEATURES OF RECEPTIVE PRACTICE REPORTED IN SLA RESEARCH

Strand of research	Theoretical framework	Receptive practice features reported in SLA research
Attentional/attention-focusing tasks	Schmidt's noticing hypothesis	• problem-solving tasks designed to draw learners' attention to (and awareness of) targeted linguistic items in the input • targeted linguistic items: both morphological and syntactic structures • concurrent feedback (explicit/implicit) • task-essentialness • up to $\frac{1}{2}$ hour of practice • exposure of up to 18 exemplars of targeted forms or structures in the input
Processing instruction	VanPatten's model of input processing	• structured input activities designed to draw learners' attention to targeted linguistic items in the input • targeted linguistic items: both morphological and syntactic structures • explicit rule presentation prior to practice (to raise learners' awareness of targeted linguistic items) • explicit information about processing strategies (in which learners' attention is explicitly oriented to what to pay attention to and why) • concurrent feedback (implicit) • task-essentialness • up to 2 hours of practice • exposure of up to 56 exemplars of targeted forms or structures in the input
Skill acquisition	Cognitive psychology models of skill acquisition (e.g., Anderson's Adaptive Control of Thought [ACT] Model)	• various grammar-based tasks • targeted linguistic items: both morphological and syntactic structures • concurrent feedback (explicit grammatical information plus explicit rule presentation to raise learners' awareness of targeted linguistic items) • up to 16 hours of practice

pretask (Rosa & Leow, 2004a), handout (Rosa & O'Neill), and explanation (Wong), was not essential in the context of their experiments, given that learners not receiving such grammatical information also benefited from their practice. The comparative ineffectiveness of grammatical information prior to practice was also found in Benati and VanPatten & Oikkenon.

Given that receptive practice in both the attentional and PI strands arguably shares the same feature of task-essentialness, premised on both attention and feedback, it may be concluded that the intrinsic characteristics of the experimental exposure (essentialness and provision of feedback) could have been sufficient for grammatical structures to be taken in, regardless of the presence or absence of explicit information or directions to search for rules.

Does providing explicit grammatical information during receptive practice have an effect on L2 development?

To address this question, once again only studies (Rosa & Leow, 2004a; Sanz & Morgan-Short, 2004) that controlled the variable ± feedback during receptive practice are considered. Sanz and Morgan-Short reported that both their [−E, −F] and [−E, +F] groups significantly increased their ability to interpret and produce the targeted O-cliticV sentences after exposure to receptive practice in the PI strand. Rosa and Leow also reported that their EFE and IFE groups significantly improved their ability to recognize new exemplars of the targeted structure as well as to produce in writing both old and new exemplars. These results indicate that providing grammatical information via feedback, whether implicit or explicit, contributes to L2 development.

However, when the issue of explicitness is considered, there is a clear disparity between the findings of the two sets of studies. While Sanz and Morgan-Short found no difference between the performances of their [−E, −F] and [−E, +F] groups, the EFE group in Rosa and Leow demonstrated superior ability to produce old exemplars and recognize new exemplars when compared to the IFE group. Sanz and Morgan-Short suggested that the disparity in results may result from, among other reasons, their interpretation of the notion of "task-essentialness," which views not only the need to pay attention to the targeted structure in the input but also the need to provide some form of explicit grammatical feedback during performance of the task. Consequently, Sanz and Morgan-Short suggested that Rosa and Leow's IFE group's practice without the provision of any explicit grammatical information "may not have been task-essential, as was the practice for the other groups" and without the appropriate feedback, "they might not have noticed the corresponding aspectual difference inherent in the form" (p. 70). Rosa and Leow did employ concurrent data elicitation procedures that revealed that some participants in this IFE group did indeed notice the aspectual difference (a discussion of the representative nature of experimental cells follows).

At issue here may not be between-group differences as a function of the task-essential aspect of receptive practice but as a function of the degree of explicitness between the various learning conditions in relation to the assessment tasks. This perspective is exemplified in both Rosa and O'Neill (1999) and Rosa and Leow, whose research designs included (a) participants with no prior knowledge of the targeted structures, thereby controlling for potential interaction between prior knowledge and practice, (b) control of the amount of provision of feedback during practice (Rosa & Leow), and (c) operationalization of attention and awareness to methodologically account for their effects on learners' performances.

For example, as reported by Rosa and Leow on the recognition assessment task, all experimental groups, including the control group, significantly improved from the pretest to the posttest after practice. The control group's performance largely supports Robinson's (1997a) view that behavior in tests containing old exemplars of a structure is determined by memory rather than by ability to generalize knowledge. However, the control group was the only one that showed no significant growth in ability to produce old and new exemplars from the pretest to the posttest and to the delayed posttest. These results seem to be consistent with the hypothesis that the more explicit the conditions of exposure to L2 input, the higher the likelihood that learners will learn a given targeted structure (e.g., Berry, 1994; Ellis, 1993).

Given the short duration of the practice phase in both Rosa and O'Neill and Rosa and Leow (just under half an hour), those conditions that favored the development of explicit knowledge (i.e., those containing some form of explicit linguistic information) were more effective than less explicit conditions in helping learners improve their ability to recognize old (Rosa & Leow; Rosa & O'Neill) and new exemplars (Rosa & Leow), and produce old and new items and recognize new exemplars (Rosa & Leow).

While the explicitness of a given learning condition may have an influence on how much previous and generalizable information learners extract from a set of input data, other variables that may impact the provision of grammatical information during receptive practice include amount of practice and amount of exemplars (see below) and the role of prior knowledge of the targeted structure.

What role does attention play in receptive practice?

It is not surprising that only the attentional strand of the three discussed employed research designs that operationalized and measured the construct of attention (and awareness), given that the primary role attention played was theoretically driven by Schmidt's noticing hypothesis. However, if it is accepted that attention plays some role in receptive practice, then methodologically establishing that attention was indeed paid to the targeted structures before statistically analyzing the effects of receptive practice on learners' L2 development should improve a study's internal validity (see below). Many studies have designed experimental conditions with specific features that differentiate them from other conditions with the expectation that participants assigned to one condition will perform according to the specified features of that condition. The use of a pretest-posttest design without any data collection of learners' concurrent processes while exposed to receptive practice assumes that participants perform differentially based on the instructions provided for each experimental group.

The use of concurrent data elicitation procedures (e.g., think alouds)[9] directly addresses the representative nature of participants' performances in experimental groups in studies premised on some role for attention in L2 development (see Leow, 2000, for a discussion of the advantages and disadvantages of online/concurrent versus offline data elicitation procedures), which in turn addresses the internal validity of the study (see Leow, 1999, for validity issues regarding the role of attention in SLA research methodology). Recent studies (e.g., Alanen, 1995; Leow, 1997, 1998a, 2000; Rosa & Leow, 2004a, 2004b; Rosa & O'Neill, 1999) that have employed online data collection procedures have revealed that not all participants in one experimental group followed the specific instructions assigned to that group.[10] In other words, what they did during the exposure period did not truly reflect the expected nature of the task that differentiated one group from another in the study. Consequently, statistically contrasting the mean scores of experimental conditions to address the effects of practice may not be an accurate indication of such effects. In addition, concurrent data also provide the answer to several assumptions made by researchers in regard to learners' attention to and/or awareness of particular linguistic items in the input during practice.

What role does awareness play in receptive practice?

It is of interest to note that the construct awareness appears to arguably permeate the three strands (attentional, PI, and skill acquisition) (cf. Table 1.1). Given that the attentional strand is grounded in Schmidt's noticing hypothesis, not surprisingly the issue of awareness has been empirically and methodologically addressed in this strand. In the PI strand, providing explicit grammatical information on the targeted linguistic data may be viewed as an obvious methodological attempt to raise participants' awareness of the so-called mismatch between their prior strategy (presumably incorrect) and the targeted and correct one in the L2, following a strict interpretation of processing instruction (VanPatten, 1996, p. 60). Sanz (2004) wrote that "[g]rammar explanation is based on both linguistic and psycholinguistic principles and is geared to make learners aware of the need to change specific processing strategies" (pp. 241–2). The provision of implicit feedback in regard to whether the answer is correct or incorrect during structured input activities may also be viewed as an effort to raise minimally a low level of awareness regarding the targeted structure. Indeed, VanPatten and Oikkenon (1996, pp. 507–8) speculated on the potential role of awareness during learners' performance while exposed to structured input: "However, another possibility exists, namely, that learners developed their own conscious rules for the formation and use of object pronouns in Spanish as a result of being exposed to structured input." Interestingly, this explanation falls in line with the recent labeling of structured input activities as being "task-essential" (Sanz, 2004; Sanz & Morgan-Short, 2004) which, according to Loschky and Bley-Vroman (1993) "causes attention to be paid to the relevant structures, and this attention facilitates initial hypothesis formation or restructuring. . . ." (p. 142). Hypothesis formation has been associated with awareness at the level of understanding in current research (e.g., Leow, 1997; Rosa & Leow, 2004b; Rosa & O'Neill, 1999) and thus leaves open whether awareness does play a role in structured input activities.

Similarly, skill acquisition theory is premised on the role of awareness in explicit learning conditions as opposed to implicit learning conditions. Following the field of cognitive psychology, the distinction between implicit and explicit learning in SLA studies has typically been operationalized by creating (a) a so-called *explicit learning condition* in which learners are either provided with explicit grammatical information or instructed to look for rules underlying the input, and (b) a so-called *implicit learning condition* whereby individuals are instructed to memorize the input without any awareness of the grammatical information embedded in the input. The premise underlying these studies is that explicit learning, that is, learning with awareness, occurs when individuals are provided with explicit grammatical information or instructed to search for rules, whereas implicit learning, that is, learning without awareness, occurs when learners are told to memorize content information.

Studies that have employed concurrent data elicitation procedures appear to explicate the effects of different types of receptive practice on learners' L2 development through the interaction between different levels of awareness and type of learning conditions. For example, the main findings indicate that (1) awareness at the level of noticing and understanding contributed substantially to a significant increase in learners' ability to take in the targeted form or structure (Rosa & Leow, 2004b; Rosa & O'Neill, 1999; cf. also Leow, 1997, 2000, 2001a) and produce in writing the targeted form or structure (Rosa & Leow, 2004b; see also Leow, 1997, 2001a), including novel exemplars (Rosa & Leow, 2004b); (2) awareness at the level of understanding led to significantly more intake when compared to awareness at the level of noticing (Rosa & Leow, 2004b; Rosa & O'Neill, 1999; see also Leow, 1997, 2001a); (3) there is a correlation between awareness at the level of understanding and usage of hypothesis testing/rule formation (Rosa & Leow, 2004b; Rosa & O'Neill, 1999; see also Leow, 1997, 2000; 2001a); (4) there is a correlation between level of awareness and formal instruction and directions to search for rules (Rosa & O'Neill, 1999); and (5) there is a correlation between awareness at the level of understanding and learning conditions providing an explicit pretask (with grammatical explanation) as well as implicit or explicit concurrent feedback (Rosa & Leow, 2004b). Overall, these studies appear to provide empirical support for the facilitative effects of awareness on foreign language behavior and learning.

Does complexity of linguistic items play a role in receptive practice?

The issue of complexity of linguistic items in receptive practice has been addressed by two studies discussed previously, namely de Graaff (1997) and DeKeyser and Sokalski (1996) within the skill acquisition strand. De Graaff investigated the effects of complexity of morphological and syntactic structures on language acquisition of an artificial language (eXperanto) and did not find any evidence for a differential effect of explicit instruction depending on the variables' complexity and morphology/syntax. However, MacWhinney (1997), in a response to de Graaff's study, suggested that the linguistic items selected for the study might not have been dissimilar in complexity, accounting for the insignificant results found in the study.

DeKeyser and Sokalski investigated the degree to which relative complexity of structure could affect the usefulness of input and output practice. They concluded that the findings generally follow the prediction of skill acquisition theory in that input practice is better for comprehension and output practice is better for production, findings that support those reported in DeKeyser (1997).

These predictions, however, appear to be contradicted by the findings reported in the PI (e.g., VanPatten & Cadierno, 1993) and attentional (Rosa & Leow, 2004a) strands. For example, in Rosa and Leow, processing and comprehension of the targeted structure through problem-solving tasks resulted in a significant improvement in controlled written production of both old and new exemplars. Recall that the participants in this study did not possess any prior knowledge of the targeted structure prior to the input-based practice. Rosa and Leow concluded that their results were more in line with the position that well-designed comprehension practice alone might be robust enough to bring about significant improvement both in comprehension and in production. They pointed out, however, that whereas the results of DeKeyser's (1997) investigation referred to the long-term effects of systematic practice (after automatization has taken place), the results of their study together with those of the PI strand referred to short-term effects before automatization. Further research into the skill acquisition strand is warranted.

How much receptive practice is needed?

The receptive practice phases (excluding the provision of any prior explicit grammatical information) of the studies reported above range from just under half an hour (Rosa & Leow, 2004a, 2004b) to approximately 16 hours (DeKeyser, 1997). Processing instruction studies typically provided approximately 2 hours of practice (DeKeyser and Sokalski, 1996, provided $1\frac{1}{4}$ hour) while de Graaff's (1997) participants practiced for 15 hours. However, whether amount of practice plays a role in L2 development remains to be investigated, given that this variable has not been empirically explored.

An issue related to the amount of practice is that of amount of exemplars embedded in the input during practice. While it is quite difficult to glean this information from several of the studies, two sets of studies (Rosa & Leow, 2004a, 2004b versus Sanz & Morgan-Short, 2004) that shared several methodological features in their research designs reveal a difference of 200 percent in the number of exemplars (18 in the former set an 56 in the latter set) provided to participants during practice. Frequency of occurrence has been well documented in the psycholinguistic literature (see Goldschneider & DeKeyser, 2001 and Larsen-Freeman & Long, 1991 for frequency on morpheme acquisition; Lee, 2002 and Rott, 1999 for incidental vocabulary gain in reading; Leow, 1998b for double exposure to targeted forms). The overall conclusions of these studies indicate that frequency of occurrence appears to play a role in learners' subsequent L2 development. This is an area of research that clearly warrants future investigation within the receptive practice strand.

Conclusion

Empirical findings suggest that providing learners with explicit grammatical information prior to and/or during practice may be positive for

SLA in that the levels of accuracy appear to be higher than those found for conditions not exposed to such information. At the same time, receptive practice that incorporates task-essentialness and feedback appears to reduce the need for such explicit grammatical information prior to or during practice, most likely due to the importance of attending to the targeted structure and feedback on the potential accuracy of the structure. The degree of explicitness in relation to receptive practice based on task-essentialness and feedback may account for the superior performances of learners exposed to several sources of explicit grammatical information both prior to and during practice. In other words, "increasing the sources of explicit grammatical information and placing them at strategic points during input processing may enhance learners' capacity to acquire generalizable knowledge from a limited set of input data" (Rosa & Leow, 2004a, p. 211). However, there is one caveat that needs to be noted: current research on receptive practice has typically employed controlled or nonspontaneous assessment tasks (e.g., translation, controlled production, fill-in-the-blank) to measure learners' L2 development. It may then be argued that explicit grammatical explanation favors superior postexposure performance on such tasks. Whether similar performance can be extrapolated to more spontaneous postexposure tasks needs to be empirically addressed.

The roles of attention and awareness appear to be of relative importance in receptive practice, irrespective of the theoretical underpinnings of the different strands. The strands appear to differ in their methodological approach to these roles in their respective research designs. It is noted that, methodologically, there appears to be a trend toward the provision of experimental exposure administered through computerized tasks. This direction suggests that it may be advantageous to incorporate technology, in both research designs and instructional exposure, by means of carefully designed activities founded on theoretical SLA underpinnings to help learners process L2 structures and establish form-function relationships. There may also be the need for further research on learners' cognitive processes during practice in order to determine whether the external conditions created by each given task or activity prompted the types of processes that had been initially predicted by the researchers.

There is clearly a need to increase our understanding of the input processes involved in language learning and become more aware of the variables that contribute to language learning and development in the classroom setting. With this better understanding and awareness, we can then pay even closer attention to the way we provide receptive practice with the L2 input in the formal classroom to promote our learners' L2 development from an informed, psycholinguistic perspective.

Notes

1. Following Leow (1998b, p. 63), the term *exposure* refers to both formal grammatical explanation/presentation (which, in this chapter, will be subsumed under the generic term *information*) and formal exposure, given that learners may be *exposed* to, and not necessarily *instructed* on, grammatical information with the expectation that they will somehow pay attention to targeted L2 forms or structures during exposure.

2. Online process measures are inherently higher in internal validity by providing relatively more substantial evidence of what is being measured than offline measures. Online process measures also lend themselves to qualitative analyses that provide a richer source of information on learners' attention and awareness than quantitative analyses can.

3. See Truscott (1998) for a critique of the noticing hypothesis.

4. Several studies (e.g., Leow, 1997, 2000, 2001a, 2001b; Leow, Egi, Nuevo, & Tsai, 2003; Rosa & Leow, 2004a, 2004b; Rosa & O'Neill, 1999) have addressed the constructs of attention and/or awareness in L2 development by employing concurrent data elicitation procedures (e.g., think-aloud protocols). The findings appear to provide empirical support for the facilitative effects of attention and awareness on foreign language behavior and learning and, consequently, of Schmidt's noticing hypothesis. In addition, the online data gathered in Leow (1997) revealed at least three different levels of awareness: [+cognitive change, −meta-awareness, −morphological rule], where learners made no report of their subjective experience nor did they verbalize any rules; [+cognitive change, +meta-awareness, −morphological rule], where learners did verbalize their subjective experience but without any rule formulation; and [+cognitive change, +meta-awareness, +morphological rule], where both a report of a subjective experience together with a rule statement were present.

5. Each Libra card contained a Spanish contrary-to-fact conditional sentence presented in the form of a jigsaw puzzle. The participants' task was to solve all 28 puzzles, each containing the following structure: There were two puzzle pieces on the computer screen, a main clause piece and, to the right of it, an empty piece. Located under the two puzzle pieces were four moveable subordinate clauses, the only difference between them being the tense of the verbs. The participants were informed in boldface font that only one of the fragments was appropriate to complete the puzzle. This feature contributed to the essentialness of the task in that the participants were primed to focus their attention on the targeted structure (both on the morphology of the four candidate verbal forms and on the function of the correct form, that is, on the reason why some tenses worked in certain contexts but not in others). The participants solved each puzzle by filling the empty piece with the appropriate moveable subordinate clauses and finding out which of these four clauses corresponded to the given main clause piece. After participants solved a puzzle, they completed the missing information on the answer sheet provided to them.

6. See DeKeyser, Salaberry, Robinson, and Harrington (2002) for a critique of VanPatten's model and VanPatten (2002) for a response to their critique.

7. Several studies (e.g., Allen, 2000; Collentine, 1998; DeKeyser & Sokalski, 1996; Nagata, 1993; Salaberry, 1997) have attempted to replicate this line

of investigation but may not have methodologically followed the appropriate designing of the SI activities, thereby failing to contribute to any potential alteration of learners' previous incorrect processing of targeted forms or structures. Consequently, these studies have not been included in the reporting of this strand.

8. See DeKeyser's introductory chapter for more information on these concepts. DeKeyser (1998), in an attempt to apply skill theory to focus on form instruction, draws some implications that affect how L2 activities should be sequenced.

9. See Leow and Morgan-Short (2004) and Bowles and Leow (2005) for empirical support for the use of think-aloud protocols as one kind of concurrent data elicitation procedure. In these studies, the issue of reactivity, that is, the potential detrimental impact of thinking aloud during performance of a task, was found not to play a significant role between a think-aloud and a nonthink-aloud group.

10. Similar findings are found in studies that have employed offline data collection questionnaires (e.g., Robinson, 1997b).

References

Alanen, R. (1995). Input enhancement and rule presentation in second language acquisition. In R. Schmidt (Ed.) *Attention & awareness in foreign language learning* (pp. 259–302). Honolulu, HI: University of Hawaii Press.

Anderson, J. (1982). Acquisition of cognitive skill. *Psychological review*, 89, 369–406.

Anderson, J. (1983). *The architecture of cognition*. Cambridge, MA: Harvard University Press.

Anderson, J. (1990). *Cognitive psychology and its implications*. New York: Freeman.

Allen, L. Q. (2000). Form-meaning connections and the French causative: An experiment in processing instruction. *Studies in Second Language Acquisition*, 22, 69–84.

Benati, A. (2004). The effects of structured input activities and explicit information on the acquisition of the Italian future tense. In B. VanPatten (Ed.), *Processing instruction: Theory, research, and commentary* (pp. 207–25). Mahwah, NJ: Lawrence Erlbaum.

Berry, D. (1994). Implicit and explicit learning of complex tasks. In N. Ellis (Ed.), *Implicit and explicit learning of languages* (pp. 147–64). London: Academic Press.

Bialystok, E. (1978). A theoretical model of second language acquisition. *Language Learning*, 28, 69–84.

Bialystok, E. (1981). The role of linguistic knowledge in second language use. *Studies in Second Language Acquisition*, 4, 31–45.

Bialystok, E. (1990). The competence of processing: Classifying theories of second language acquisition. *TESOL Quarterly*, 24, 635–48.

Bialystok, E. (1994). Analysis and control in the development of second language proficiency. *Studies in Second Language Acquisition*, 16, 157–68.

Bowles, M. A., & Leow, R. P. (2005). Reactivity and type of verbal report in SLA research methodology: Expanding the scope of investigation. *Studies in Second Language Acquisition, 27,* 415–40.

Broadbent, D. E. (1958). *Perception and communication.* New York: Pergamon.

Cadierno, T. (1995). Formal instruction from a processing perspective: An investigation into the Spanish past tense. *Modern Language Journal, 79,* 179–93.

Carr, T. H., & Curran, T. (1994). Cognitive factors in learning about structured sequences: Applications to syntax. *Studies in Second Language Acquisition, 16,* 205–30.

Cheng, A. (2002). The effects of processing instruction on the acquisition of *ser* and *estar. Hispania, 85,* 308–23.

Collentine, J. (1998). Processing instruction and the subjunctive. *Hispania, 81,* 576–87.

de Graaff, R. (1997). The eXperanto experiment: Effects of explicit instruction on second language acquisition. *Studies in Second Language Acquisition, 19,* 249–97.

de la Fuente, M. J. (2002). Negotiation and oral acquisition of L2 vocabulary: The roles of input and output in the receptive and productive acquisition of words. *Studies in Second Language Acquisition, 24,* 81–112.

DeKeyser, R. M. (1995). Learning second language grammar rules: An experiment with a miniature linguistic system. *Studies in Second Language Acquisition, 17,* 379–410.

DeKeyser, R. M. (1997). Beyond explicit rule learning: Automatizing second language morphosyntax. *Studies in Second Language Acquisition, 19,* 195–221.

DeKeyser, R. (1998). Beyond focus on form: Cognitive perspectives on learning and practicing second language grammar. In C. Doughty & J. Williams (Eds.), *Focus on form in classroom SLA* (pp. 42–63). Cambridge, UK: Cambridge University Press.

DeKeyser, R. M., & Sokalski, K. J. (1996). The differential role of comprehension and production. *Language Learning, 46,* 613–42.

DeKeyser, R., Salaberry, M., Robinson, P., & Harrrington, M. (2002). What gets processed in processing instruction? A commentary on Bill VanPatten's "Processing instruction: An update." *Language Learning, 52,* 805–23.

Ellis, N. (1993). Rules and instances in foreign language learning: Interactions of implicit and explicit knowledge. *European Journal of Cognitive Psychology, 5,* 289–319.

Ellis, R. (1993). The structural syllabus and second language acquisition. *TESOL Quarterly, 27,* 91–113.

Ellis, R. (1994a). A theory of instructed second language acquisition. In N. Ellis (Ed.), *Implicit and explicit learning of languages* (pp. 79–114). London: Academic Press.

Ellis, R. (1994b). *The study of second language acquisition* (2nd ed.). Oxford: Oxford University Press.

Ellis, R. (1995). Interpretation tasks for grammar teaching. *TESOL Quarterly, 29,* 87–106

Farley, A. P. (2001a). Authentic processing instruction and the Spanish subjunctive. *Hispania, 84,* 289–99.

Farley, A. P. (2001b). Processing instruction and meaning-based output instruction: A comparative study. *Studies in Applied Linguistics, 5,* 57–93.

Farley, A. P. (2004). Processing instruction and the Spanish subjunctive: Is explicit information needed? In B. VanPatten (Ed.), *Processing instruction: Theory, research, and commentary* (pp. 227–39). Mahwah, NJ: Lawrence Erlbaum.

Gass, S. (1988). Integrating research areas: A framework for second language studies. *Applied Linguistics, 9*, 198–217.

Goldschneider, J. M., & DeKeyser, R. M. (2001). Explaining the "natural order of L2 morpheme acquisition" in English: A meta-analysis of multiple determinants. *Language Learning, 51*(1), 1–50.

Hulstijn, J. H. (1989). Implicit and incidental second language learning: Experiments in the processing of natural and partially artificial input. In H. W. Dechert & M. Raupach (Eds.), *Interlingual processes* (pp. 49–73). Tübingen: Narr.

Hulstijn, J., & de Graaff, R. (1994). Under what conditions does explicit knowledge of a second language facilitate the acquisition of implicit knowledge? A research proposal. *AILA Review, 11*, 97–112.

Hulstijn, J. H. & Schmidt, R. W. (1994). Guest editors' introduction. In J. H. Hulstijn & R. W. Schmidt (Eds.), *AILA Review: Consciousness and second language learning: Conceptual, methodological and practical issues in language learning and teaching, 11*, 5–10.

Izumi, S., (2002). Output, input enhancement, and the noticing hypothesis: An experimental study on ESL relativization. *Studies in Second Language Acquisition, 24*, 541–77.

Izumi, S. and Bigelow, M. (2000). Does output promote noticing and second language acquisition? *TESOL Quarterly, 34*, 239–78.

Izumi, S., Bigelow, M., Fujiwara, M., & Fearnow, S. (1999). Testing the output hypothesis. *Studies in Second Language Acquisition, 21*, 421–52.

Kahneman, D. (1973). *Attention and effort*. Englewood Cliffs, NJ: Prentice-Hall.

Krashen, S. (1982). *Principles and practice in second language acquisition*. Oxford: Pergamon.

Krashen, S. (1985). *The Input Hypothesis: Issues and implications*. London: Longman.

Krashen, S. (1994). The input hypothesis and its rivals. In N. Ellis (Ed.), *Implicit and explicit learning of languages* (pp. 45–77). London: Academic Press.

Larsen-Freeman, D., & Long, M. (1991). *An introduction to second language research*. London: Longman.

Lee, J. F. (2002). The incidental acquisition of Spanish: Future tense morphology through reading in a second language. *Studies in Second Language Acquisition, 24*, 55–80.

Lee, J. F. & VanPatten, B. (1995). *Making communicative language teaching happen*. New York: McGraw-Hill.

Leow, R. P. (1997). Attention, awareness, and foreign language behavior. *Language Learning, 47*, 467–506.

Leow, R. P. (1998a). Toward operationalizing the process of attention: Evidence for Tomlin and Villa's (1994) fine-grained analysis of attention. *Applied Psycholinguistics, 19*, 133–59.

Leow, R. P. (1998b). The effects of amount and type of exposure on adult learners' L2 development in SLA. *Modern Language Journal, 82*, 49–68.

Leow, R. P. (1999). The role of attention in second/foreign language classroom research: Methodological issues. In F. Martínez-Gil & J. Gutiérrez-Rexach

(Eds.), *Advances in Hispanic linguistics: Papers from the 2nd. Hispanic Linguistics Symposium* (pp. 60–71). Somerville, MA: Cascadilla Press.

Leow, R. P. (2000). A study of the role of awareness in foreign language behavior: Aware vs. unaware learners. *Studies in Second Language Acquisition, 22,* 557–84.

Leow, R. P. (2001a). Attention, awareness, and foreign language behavior. *Language Learning, 51,* 113–55.

Leow, R. P. (2001b). Do learners notice enhanced forms while interacting with the L2?: An online and offline study of the role of written input enhancement in L2 reading. *Hispania, 84,* 496–509.

Leow, R. P., Egi, T., Nuevo, A-M., & Tsai, Y. (2003). The roles of textual enhancement and type of linguistic item in adult L2 learners' comprehension and intake. *Applied Language Learning, 13,* 93–108.

Leow, R. P., & Morgan-Short, K. (2004). To think aloud or not to think aloud: The issue of reactivity in SLA research methodology. *Studies in Second Language Acquisition, 26,* 35–57.

Loschky, L., & Bley-Vroman, R. (1993). Grammar and task-based methodology. In G. Crookes & S. M. Gass (Eds.), *Tasks and language learning: Integrating theory and practice* (pp. 123–67). Clevedon, UK: Multilingual Matters.

MacWhinney, B. (1997). Implicit and explicit processes. *Studies in Second Language Acquisition, 19,* 277–81.

McLaughlin, B. (1987). *Theories of second language learning.* London: Edward Arnold.

Morgan-Short, K., & Bowden, H. W. (2006). Processing instruction and meaningful output-based instruction: Effects on second language development. *Studies in Second Language Acquisition, 28,* 31–65.

Nagata, N. (1993). Intelligent computer feedback for second language instruction. *Modern Language Journal, 77,* 330–9.

Norman, D. A. (1968). Toward a theory of memory and attention. *Psychological Review, 84,* 522–36.

Robinson, P. (1995). Attention, memory, and the "noticing" hypothesis. *Language Learning, 45,* 283–331.

Robinson, P. (1996). Learning simple and complex second language rules under implicit, incidental, rule-search and instructed conditions. *Studies in Second Language Acquisition, 18,* 27–68.

Robinson, P. (1997a). Generalizability and automaticity of second language learning under implicit, incidental, enhanced, and instructed conditions. *Studies in Second Language Acquisition, 19,* 223–47.

Robinson, P. (1997b). Individual differences and the fundamental similarity of implicit and explicit adult second language learning. *Language Learning, 47,* 45–99.

Rosa, E. & Leow, R. P. (2004a). Computerized task-based instruction in the L2 classroom: The effects of explicitness and type of feedback on L2 development. *Modern Language Journal, 88,* 192–216.

Rosa, E. & Leow, R. P. (2004b). Awareness, different learning conditions, and second language development. *Applied Psycholinguistics, 25,* 269–92.

Rosa, E. & O'Neill, M. (1999). Explicitness, intake, and the issue of awareness: Another piece to the puzzle. *Studies in Second Language Acquisition, 21,* 511–56.

Rott, S. (1999). Relationships between the process of reading, word inferencing, and incidental vocabulary acquisition. In J. Lee & A. Valdman (Eds.), *Form and meaning: Multiple perspectives* (pp. 255–82). Boston, MA: Heinle & Heinle.

Salaberry, M. R. (1997). The role of input and output practice in second language practice. *The Canadian Modern Language Review, 53*, 422–51.

Sanz, C. (2004). Computer delivered implicit vs.explicit feedback in processing instruction. In B. VanPatten (Ed.), *Processing instruction: Theory, research, and commentary* (pp. 241–55). Mahwah, NJ: Lawrence Erlbaum.

Sanz, C. & Morgan-Short, K. (2004). Positive evidence versus explicit rule presentation and explicit negative feedback: A computer-assisted study. *Language Learning, 54*, 35–78.

Schmidt, R. W. (1990). The role of consciousness in second language learning. *Applied Linguistics, 11*, 129–58.

Schmidt, R. W. (1993). Awareness and second language acquisition. *Annual Review of Applied Linguistics, 13*, 206–26.

Schmidt, R. W. (1995). Consciousness and foreign language learning: A tutorial on the role of attention and awareness in learning. In R. W. Schmidt (Ed.), *Attention and awareness in foreign language learning* (Technical Report #9), (pp. 1–63). Honolulu, HI: University of Hawaii.

Schmidt, R. (2001). Attention. In P. Robinson (ed.), *Cognition and second language instruction* (pp. 3–32). New York: Cambridge University Press.

Schwartz, B. (1993). On explicit and negative data effecting and affecting competence and linguistic behavior. *Studies in Second Language Acquisition, 15*, 147–63.

Sharwood Smith, M. (1981). Consciousness-raising and the second language learner. *Applied Linguistics, 2*, 159–69.

Sharwood Smith, M. (1986). Comprehension vs. acquisition: Two ways of processing input. *Applied Linguistics, 7*, 239–56.

Sharwood Smith, M. (1991). Speaking to many minds: On the relevance of different types of language information for the L2 learner. *Second Language Research, 17*, 118–36.

Sharwood Smith, M. (1993). Input enhancement in instructed SLA: Theoretical bases. *Studies in Second Language Acquisition, 15*, 165–80.

Shiffrin, R., & Schneider, W. (1977). Controlled and automatic human information processing: Perceptual learning, automatic attending, and a general theory. *Psychological Review, 84*, 127–190.

Swain, M. (1995). Three functions of output in second language learning. In G. Cook and B. Seildlhofer (Eds.), *Principles and practice in applied linguistics: Studies in honor of H. Widdowson* (pp. 125–44). Oxford: Oxford University Press.

Swain, M., & Lapkin, S. (1995). Problems in output and the cognitive processes they generate: A step towards second language learning: *Applied Linguistics, 16*, 371–91.

Tomlin, R. S., & Villa, V. (1994). Attention in cognitive science and second language acquisition. *Studies in Second Language Acquisition, 16*, 183–203.

Treisman, A. M. (1964). Verbal cues, language, and meaning in selective attention. *American Journal of Psychology, 77*, 533–46.

Truscott, J. (1998). Noticing in second language acquisition: A critical review. *Second Language Research, 14,* 103–35.

VanPatten, B. (1996). *Input processing and grammar instruction in second language acquisition.* Norwood, NJ: Ablex.

VanPatten, B. (2002). Processing the content of input processing and processing instruction research: A response to DeKeyser, Salaberry, Robinson, & Harrington. *Language Learning, 52,* 825–31.

VanPatten, B. (2004). Input processing in SLA. In B. VanPatten (Ed.), *Processing instruction: Theory, research, and commentary* (pp. 5–31). Mahwah, NJ: Lawrence Erlbaum.

VanPatten, B., & Cadierno, T. (1993). Input processing and second language acquisition: A role for instruction. *Modern Language Journal, 77,* 45–57.

VanPatten, B., & Oikkenon, S. (1996). Explanation versus structured input in processing instruction. *Studies in Second Language Acquisition, 18,* 495–510.

VanPatten, B., & Sanz, C. (1995). From input to output: Processing instruction and communicative tasks. In F. Eckman, D. Highland, P. Lee, J. Mileham, & R. Rutkowski Weber (Eds.), *Second language acquisition: Theory and pedagogy* (pp. 169–85). Mahwah, NJ: Lawrence Erlbaum.

VanPatten, B., & Wong, W. (2004). Processing instruction and the French causative: Another replication. In B. VanPatten (Ed.), *Processing instruction: Theory, research, and commentary* (pp. 87–118). Mahwah, NJ: Lawrence Erlbaum.

Wong, W. (2004a). The nature of processing instruction. In B. VanPatten (Ed.), *Processing instruction: Theory, research, and commentary* (pp. 33–63). Mahwah, NJ: Lawrence Erlbaum.

Wong, W. (2004b). Processing instruction in French: The roles of explicit information and structured input. In B. VanPatten (Ed.), *Processing instruction: Theory, research, and commentary* (pp. 187–205). Mahwah, NJ: Lawrence Erlbaum.

2 Output practice in the L2 classroom

Hitoshi Muranoi

Introduction[1]

Most second language (L2) teachers and learners likely believe that practice in production (i.e., speaking and writing), or output practice, is crucial for developing L2 proficiency. This belief in the usefulness of output practice is reflected in conventional foreign language teaching methodologies, which typically employ teaching procedures consisting of three major stages: presentation, practice, and *production* (i.e., the PPP model; see Byrne, 1976; Harmer, 2001). The role of output practice, however, remains a contentious issue in second language acquisition (SLA) research as characterized by a number of ongoing debates.

Advocates of the Input Hypothesis, for instance, argue that producing output serves only for generating comprehensible input from the interlocutor (Krashen, 1982, 1985, 1998). Krashen (1998) further argues that output does not make a real contribution to the development of linguistic competence because (1) output, especially comprehensible output, is too scarce, (2) it is possible to attain high levels of linguistic competence without output,[2] and (3) there is no direct evidence that output leads to language acquisition. In the Natural Approach, which is based upon Krashen's Input Hypothesis, teachers are guided not to force their students to produce the target language but rather to expect that "speech (and writing) production emerges as the acquisition process progresses" (Krashen & Terrell, 1983, p. 58). VanPatten (1996) also advocates abandoning mechanical output practice. He argues that output practice of a form or structure without processing input that is necessary for the construction of the mental representation of the form itself is "analogous to attempting to manipulate the exhaust fumes (output) of a car to make run it better" (p. 6). Similarly, Ellis (1991, 1994, 1997) assumes that production practice plays only a limited role in L2 acquisition. Reviewing previous studies of the effects of production-based activities (e.g., the garden-path technique, text-manipulation, and text-creation activities), Ellis (1997) concludes that there is no strong evidence that output-practice is beneficial for L2 acquisition, though it might at least work to raise learners' consciousness of certain linguistic forms.

He also points out that it is not clear whether production practice can result in the acquisition of *new* linguistic features (Ellis, 1994).

In contrast to these dismissive views, a number of scholars have argued that output plays crucial roles in L2 acquisition. Swain (1985, 1995, 1998, 2000, 2005), for example, has claimed that output is crucial to L2 acquisition not only as a way of practicing already-existing linguistic knowledge but also as a way of creating new linguistic knowledge. She argues that L2 learners notice new linguistic features, formulate hypotheses about new grammatical forms, and test the hypotheses when they are provided proper opportunities to produce L2 output. Others have emphasized the role of output in enhancing fluency and the automaticity of processing particular linguistic knowledge (e.g., de Bot, 1996). Gass (1997), for example, claims that consistent practice, in which learners are required to map grammar to output, results in automatic processing of the grammar.

Notwithstanding this controversy over the role of output practice, a great number of L2 teachers probably know well from their experience that opportunities to produce the target language are critical for developing learners' abilities to communicate in an L2, especially the abilities to speak and write. They are also aware that neither mere decontextualized output practice such as mechanical pattern practice nor mere opportunities for free conversation lead L2 learners to develop well-balanced communicative competence.[3] What is not clearly known yet is what kind of output practice is required to develop productive skills with which L2 learners can communicate with other speakers appropriately in real life. To examine the effectiveness of output practice, we need to understand the psycholinguistic mechanisms of L2 production. Understanding the cognitive processes involved in L2 production will be a foundation both for investigating the possible roles of output practice and for determining how best to construct output practice.

This chapter aims to demystify the possible roles of output practice in L2 acquisition by reviewing previous and ongoing studies on L2 output. In the first half of the discussion, cognitive processes of L2 production are examined based on psycholinguistic models, including Levelt's language production model, Swain's Output Hypothesis, and Anderson's skill acquisition theory. In the second half of this chapter, empirical studies of the effects of output practice are reviewed. These studies include those on the effects of text reconstruction, essay writing, output-oriented interaction, and communication tasks. Such a review of theory and empirical studies enables us to make psycholinguistically based predictions for the effects of output practice.

In this chapter, the term *output practice* is used to refer to any activity designed to provide L2 learners with opportunities to produce output. The term *practice*, therefore, is used in a wider meaning than that used in the traditional Presentation-Practice-Production sequence, in which practice refers to a mechanical drill-like activity such as repetition and manipulation. Here, practice broadly means any "activity with the goal of becoming better at it" (DeKeyser, 1998, p. 50).

Models of L2 production

Levelt's language production model

Several models of language production, which are useful for framing the discussion on the role of output production in SLA, have been proposed in psycholinguistics (see Harley, 2001; Wheeldon, 2000, for reviews of production models). Among them, Levelt's (1989, 1993) speech production model, originally developed for first language production has been widely used to describe and explain processes involved in L2 production (e.g., Bygate, 2001; de Bot, 1992, 1996; de Bot, Paribakht, & Wesche, 1997; Dörnyei & Kormos, 1998; Doughty, 2001; Izumi, 2000, 2003; Pienemann, 1998; Towell, Hawkins, & Bazergui, 1996, and others).

According to Levelt (1989, 1993), speech production consists of three major components: the Conceptualizer, the Formulator, and the Articulator (see Figure 2.1 for a schematic representation of the model). The conceptualizing component, the Conceptualizer, includes conceiving of an intention, selecting the relevant information, ordering this information for expression, keeping track of what was said before, and so on. At this level, the speaker attends to his or her own production, monitoring what he or she is saying and how. The product of these mental activities is a preverbal message. The formulating component, the Formulator, converts the preverbal message into a speech plan. The Formulator involves two major processes that translate a conceptual structure into a linguistic one. The first step is the grammatical encoding of the message, a process consisting of procedures for accessing lemmas (the syntactic and morphological information of lexical items) and of the syntactic building procedures. Levelt claims that the speaker's lemma information is declarative knowledge stored in his or her mental lexicon. A lexical item's lemma information contains the lexical item's semantic information, or meaning of the word. For example, *give* (verb) has semantic information of "some actor X causing some possession Y to go from actor X to recipient Z" (Levelt, 1989, p. 11). Also, the lemma information of *give* contains syntactic information that "the verb *give* is categorized as a verb which can take a subject expressing the actor X, a direct object expressing the possession Y, and an indirect object expressing the recipient Z (as in John gave Mary the book)" (Levelt, 1989, p. 11). Levelt argues that a lemma is activated when its meaning matches part of the

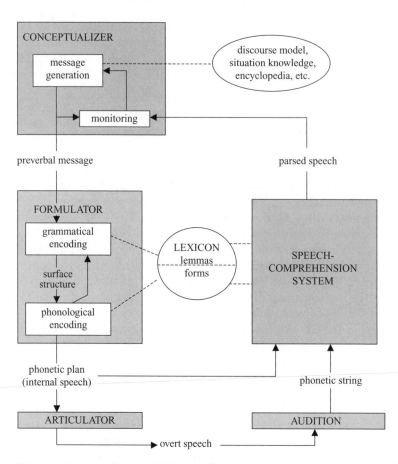

Figure 2.1 Levelt's (1989) production model (A blueprint for the speaker). From Speaking: From intention to articulation *(p. 9), by W. J. M. Levelt, 1989, Cambridge, MA: The MIT Press. Copyright 1989 by the MIT Press. Reprinted with permission.*

preverbal message and that this activation leads to certain syntactic building procedures. For example, the conceptual structure of a message to be conveyed activates the lemma of *give*, and its syntactic information activates the verb-phrase-building procedure. Levelt regards this syntactic building process as procedural knowledge, which has the format IF X THEN Y, following Anderson's ACT Model (Anderson, 1983, 1993, 2000). Such syntactic building procedures, along with the relevant lemmas, produce a surface structure – "an ordered string of lemmas grouped in phrases and subphrases of various kinds" (Levelt, 1989, p. 11). The interim results of grammatical encoding are temporarily deposited in a buffer called the syntactic buffer, which stores results of grammatical encoding.

The second step of formulating is phonological encoding. This includes retrieving or building detailed phonetic and articulatory planning for lemmas and for the whole utterance. The phonetic and articulatory plan is executed in the third major processing component, the Articulator. Articulating is the execution of the phonetic plan through retrieving chunks of internal speech from a temporary storage called the articulatory buffer (which stores results of the phonetic plans) and through motor execution. This is a component in which speakers' internal linguistic knowledge turns into audible sounds.

Levelt (1989) discusses these processing components from the perspective of automaticity. Working on the distinction between controlled processing that demands intention and attention and automatic processing that is executed without intention or awareness, Levelt addresses to what degree the major processing components are automatic. He argues that conceptualizing involves highly controlled processing that demands attentional resources. Other processing components such as formulating and articulating are claimed to be largely automatic, demanding very little executive control. This is the point at which L1 production differs from L2 production. For L2 learners who have not yet had full command of the target language, formulating and articulating are likely to be controlled. Regarding this issue, Towell et al. (1996) report an interesting finding from their study on advanced learners of French, who spent at least six months in a French-speaking country. From the results of quantitative and qualitative analyses of the learners' performance data, they conclude that increases in fluency are attributable to increases in the degree of proceduralization of linguistic knowledge. They claim that L2 learners who spent a period of residence abroad increased fluency because proceduralization took place in the Formulator, in which messages are grammatically and phonetically encoded. This finding suggests that it is the formulating component, especially grammatical and phonological encoding, that classroom teachers should seek to facilitate through instruction in order to develop learners' spontaneous productive skills. Task-based/supported instruction which emphasizes planning and repetition of tasks can be beneficial to promoting proceduralization in the Formulator component (see the sections on task repetition and task planning in this chapter).

Levelt's production model, which is intended to account for speech production by adult native speakers, does not provide any direct explanation for the process of language learning by L2 learners. Also, this model does not specify how grammatical encoding is derived for complex structures such as relative clauses and WH questions. Similarly, Dörnyei and Kormos (1998) point out that it is not clear where some grammar rules that are not tied to specific lexical items are stored in Levelt's model (see Izumi, 2000, 2003; Dörnyei & Kormos, 1998 for other problems of Levelt's model). It can be said, however, that Levelt's model provides L2 teachers with a model of language production mechanisms on which they can rely to evaluate the psycholinguistic validity of a particular pedagogical treatment. Levelt's model helps us hypothesize that output practice that gives learners ample opportunities for conceptualizing, formulating, and articulating in contexts where learners are encouraged to convey messages relying on their existing lexical, grammatical, and phonological knowledge, should activate cognitive processes crucial for interlanguage production such as hypothesis testing. It can be predicted, for instance, that the following output-based L2 activities affect these cognitive processes: text reconstruction, essay writing, guided summarizing, dictogloss, interaction, communication tasks, planned tasks, repeated tasks, automatization tasks, simple and complex tasks (see the section on empirical studies of the effects of output practice). In particular, Levelt's model, which is heavily lexically driven, leads us to recognize the importance of lexical items in promoting grammatical encoding in L2 (see Muranoi, 2000a, reported in the section below on studies of output practice through text reconstruction and writing for an example of lexically driven L2 instruction).

Swain's Output Hypothesis

Another important requisite for the discussion of the role of output practice is to understand in what way L2 output affects various cognitive processes involved in SLA (Swain, 1985, 1995, 1998, 2005). Swain (1985) first documented the potential roles of output in L2 learning based on a large-scale research project on Canadian French immersion programs. From an analysis of the observation data from immersion classes, she points out that the immersion students are not pushed enough in their output. There is little social or cognitive pressure to produce more target-like language because the students can be understood by their interlocutors by means of their strategic competence. Swain concludes that comprehensible output, defined as "output that extends the linguistic repertoire of the learner as he or she attempts to create precisely and appropriately the meaning desired" (Swain, 1985, p. 252), is a necessary mechanism of L2 acquisition.

Swain (1985, 1995, 1998, 2005) identified the following specific roles of output in L2 learning: noticing, hypothesis formulation and testing, and metalinguistic function and syntactic processing.

NOTICING

Output is assumed to trigger at least two types of noticing (i.e., noticing a gap and noticing a hole) under certain circumstances. Learners may notice a form in L2 input that is different from their own interlanguage (Schmidt, 1990, 1992, 2001; Swain, 1998). Swain (1998), citing Doughty and Williams (1998), hypothesizes that this type of noticing (i.e., noticing the gap between the target language and the interlanguage) may be stimulated by noticing a hole in one's interlanguage. Producing output helps learners notice that there is something that they cannot say precisely (in her terms, a "hole") though they want to say it in the target language (Swain, 1995). In this way, learners consciously recognize some of their linguistic problems and, more importantly, the learners' attention may be selectively led to relevant input (Swain, 1998; Swain & Lapkin, 1995). Learners may "notice the difference between what they themselves can or have said (or even what they know they cannot say) and what more competent speakers of the TL [target language] say instead to convey the same intention under the same social condition" (Doughty, 2001, p. 225). This process is called cognitive comparison and has been seen as one of the crucial processes in language acquisition (Doughty, 2001; Ellis, 1997; Nelson, 1987; Slobin, 1985). It can be assumed, therefore, that producing output promotes both noticing a hole in the interlanguage system and noticing the gap between the interlanguage and the target language, both of which trigger important cognitive processes such as selective attention and cognitive comparison.

HYPOTHESIS FORMULATION AND TESTING

It is also hypothesized that noticing, which is stimulated by producing output, can trigger other cognitive processes that might generate new linguistic knowledge for the learners or that consolidates the learners' existing knowledge (Swain, 1998; Swain & Lapkin, 1995). These processes include formulating, testing, confirming, modifying, and rejecting hypotheses about the target language systems (collectively termed hypothesis formulation and testing). Hypothesis formulation and testing are processes in which L2 learners use their output as a way of trying out new language forms (hypotheses) to convey their intended messages (Swain, 1998). A language learner's hypothesis is defined by Schachter (1984) as "a prediction that a certain aspect of the language is organized in a certain way" (p. 169). Schachter (1993) assumes that this prediction largely depends on inductive inferencing, in which the learner scans the input data, discerns regularities in the data, and generalizes (i.e., formulation of a hypothesis; see also Tomlin & Villa, 1994, for the discussion of how a learner formulates a hypothesis). This newly formulated hypothesis may be tried out in another type of inferencing – deductive inferencing – to see if the data are consistent with the hypothesis (testing a hypothesis). Schachter (1986) also claims that a hypothesis is contingent upon feedback and that L2 production is a way for L2 learners to gain two types of feedback from interlocutors, i.e., both direct and indirect metalinguistic information. Direct metalinguistic information includes overt corrections, and indirect metalinguistic information includes such responses as clarification requests, confirmation checks, overt failures to respond, misunderstandings, delays, laughters, and so on (Schachter, 1986). By producing output, therefore, learners can test hypotheses against feedback from external resources. When feedback from an external source is not available, learners might rely on their internal knowledge to test their hypotheses (Bley-Vroman, 1986; Cook, 1985; Swain, 1998). That external feedback exerts a positive effect on learner production has been reported in a number of empirical studies on interaction (e.g., Carroll & Swain, 1993; Doughty & Varela, 1998; Leeman, this volume; Long, Inagaki, & Ortega, 1998; Mackey, this volume; Muranoi, 2000b). These studies lend support to the claim that non-native speakers (NNSs) modify their output when native speakers (NSs) signal an explicit need for clarification in interactions (see Gass, 1997; Long, 1996; Pica, 1994, for reviews of interaction studies).

The modified, or reprocessed, output is considered to represent the leading edge of a learner's interlanguage (Swain, 1998). Hypothesis testing is seen as a process through which L2 learners push the limits of their interlanguage systems when they are required to produce output that their current interlanguage system cannot deal with (see also Tarone & Liu, 1995).

METALINGUISTIC FUNCTION AND SYNTACTIC PROCESSING

The third function of output identified by Swain is the metalinguistic. Swain claims that learners use language to reflect on language (Swain, 1995, 1998). The language produced by learners to reflect on language use is termed metatalk and demonstrates how learners are consciously thinking about their target language (Swain, 1998). This metatalk, Swain argues, may serve the function of deepening learners' awareness of forms and linguistic rules and helping them understand the relationship between meaning, forms, and function in a highly context-sensitive situation (Swain, 1998).

Closely related to the metalinguistic function is that which promotes syntactic processing. In Swain's Output Hypothesis, it is assumed that producing output in L2, as opposed to simply comprehending the language, may force the learner to move from semantic processing to syntactic processing (Kowal & Swain, 1997; Swain, 1985). As Krashen points out, we do not always utilize syntax in understanding language because "in many cases we get the message with a combination of verb, or lexical information plus extra-linguistic information" (1982, p. 66). Swain (1985) argues that producing the target language pushes learners to process the language syntactically by leading them to pay attention to the means of expression necessary for conveying their intended meaning successfully. In a similar vein, Long (1996) points out the usefulness of spoken production, claiming that "it elicits negative input and encourages analysis and grammaticization" (p. 440). In Levelt's (1989) terms, it is grammatical encoding that opportunities for output particularly facilitate. Grammatical encoding, in which a conceptual structure is translated into a linguistic structure, operates through accessing lemmas stored in the learners' mental lexicon. It can be assumed, therefore, that messages to be conveyed and relevant lexical items activate grammatical encoding, or syntactic processing.

Swain's Output Hypothesis implies that output practice eliciting opportunities for L2 production can facilitate L2 acquisition if the practice successfully affects cognitive processes such as noticing, hypothesis testing, metalinguistic reflection, and syntactic processing. In other words, output practice that leads learners to notice gaps in their interlanguage systems, test their existing knowledge, reflect consciously on their own language, and process language syntactically is expected to be the most beneficial for L2 development.

While there can be no doubt that the Output Hypothesis provides us with useful pedagogical implications, it must be noted that the hypothesis has not been extensively verified yet. Only a few studies have empirically investigated the effects of output on L2 development. Although several empirical studies have examined the role of output in noticing (e.g., Izumi, 2000) and output modification (Pica, Holliday, Lewis, & Morgenthaler, 1989; Takashima & Ellis, 1999), the impact on other internal processes such as hypothesis formulation and testing, cognitive comparison, and syntactic processing has not been directly examined. Swain and her colleagues present insightful evidence in support of the Output Hypothesis (e.g., Swain & Lapkin, 1995; Kowal & Swain, 1994). However, as most studies have investigated relatively simple grammatical rules, more evidence is needed (see Izumi, 2000, and Koyanagi, 1998, for exceptions). L2 researchers must examine the roles of output in acquiring various linguistic rules, especially complex syntactic rules. Whether output plays a significant role in L2 learning of completely *new* linguistic items is another issue to be worked out. We need to examine how output-based instruction can assist learners in formulating a new interlanguage hypothesis (de Bot, 1996; Ellis, 1994, 1999). Longitudinal studies are also important to investigate whether output treatment actually contributes to interlanguage development (e.g., whether the effects of output treatment last for a certain period of time). We also need research with valid tests that measure L2 production in both oral and written modes. Future research should be conducted employing more rigorous research methodology and using quantitative and qualitative analyses complementarily.

Taking into account these methodological limitations of the Output Hypothesis, we should be careful not to assume that output practice can be useful for any learner with any linguistic form under any condition. Whether output practice leads to L2 development heavily depends on various factors, including learners' psycholinguistic readiness and linguistic features of the target form.

Fluency and Anderson's skill acquisition theory

In a review article of the Output Hypothesis, de Bot (1996) proposes a fourth function of output: enhancing fluency through practice. Enhancing fluency is important for L2 learning not only because it enhances the speed of delivery but because fluency on one level allows learners' attentional resources to be used on higher-level processes (de Bot, 1996, p. 552). Following the information processing approach to skill acquisition proposed by Anderson (1982, 1983, 1993), de Bot argues that output practice plays an important role in enhancing fluency by turning declarative knowledge into procedural knowledge.

Anderson's ACT (Adaptive Control Theory) model of cognitive development is greatly relevant to our discussion of the role of output practice in that it puts emphasis on the role of practice in the transitional change of knowledge. Anderson assumes that conversion of declarative knowledge into procedural knowledge is crucial for learning complex skills including speech production (see DeKeyser, this volume, for a detailed description of the ACT model; see also DeKeyser, 1997, 1998, 2001; Johnson, 1996; O'Malley & Chamot, 1990, Schmidt, 1992; Towell & Hawkins, 1994, for the application of the ACT model to SLA research).

Anderson's theory, which has been widely applied to SLA studies, is informative for L2 teachers in constructing and evaluating L2 practice. His theory helps us explain why it is highly difficult for the majority of L2 learners to use the target language in spontaneous online communication; the transition from declarative to automatized knowledge takes a very long time and requires a lot of good practice. One of the requirements for good practice is that the practice match the three stages of skill acquisition (see Johnson, 1996, for teaching procedures; O'Malley & Chamot, 1990, for learning strategies, both of which correspond to the three stages).

Although Anderson's skill acquisition theory can account for some aspects of language learning, especially the transition from controlled to automatic processing of linguistic knowledge, it should be noted that the theory has limitations in explaining other aspects of L2 acquisition. For example, as Anderson makes no distinctions between language and other cognitive systems, his models provide little explanation for the acquisition of properties unique to language (Cook, 1993; Johnson & Johnson, 1998). Cook (1993) points out that Anderson's ACT models and other information processing models ignore the notion of grammatical structure, which makes up the core of language knowledge. Consequently, it is difficult to see how production systems operate in the acquisition of complex grammatical structures. It can be concluded that ACT models are useful for explaining how knowledge is proceduralized, not for explaining how new linguistic knowledge, especially complex knowledge, develops in learners' minds (i.e., hypothesis formulation). There has been an attempt to integrate a linguistic model (i.e., a universal grammar-based SLA model) into Anderson's skill acquisition model (e.g., Towell & Hawkins, 1994). Such integration should be further developed in order to obtain a comprehensive model of L2 learning and acquisition.

In summary, the three psycholinguistic theories of language production (Levelt's language production model, Swain's Output Hypothesis, and Anderson's skill acquisition theory) are very useful for L2 teachers in that these theories help teachers understand why giving L2 learners opportunities for producing output through practice facilitates the acquisition of certain linguistic features. Output triggers cognitive processes crucial for SLA such as noticing, hypothesis testing, conscious reflection, and automatization, all of which operate within the three major components of language production: conceptualizing, formulating, and articulating.

The three psycholinguistic models discussed in this section represent the mechanisms of output from somewhat different perspectives. However, it can be assumed that the three models strongly interface with each other. The interconnected relations are schematically represented in Figure 2.2. The figure shows that proceduralization of linguistic knowledge must be promoted in the formulator component, especially in grammatical and phonological encoding to enhance fluency in L2 production. Swain's Output Hypothesis also depicts what happens in an L2 learner's mind when a message flows from the Conceptualizer to the Formulator and when his or her speech is overtly articulated. The following section discusses what kinds of L2 instruction can affect these interconnected cognitive processes.

Empirical studies of the effects of output practice

This section reviews empirical studies, most of which take cognitive approaches to SLA, which were conducted to examine the roles and functions of output in L2 learning. Though the number of such studies is still rather limited, several important findings on the roles of output practice in L2 learning have been reported. This section introduces four bodies of recent research investigating whether output-oriented activities are effective for the development of proficiency in L2: studies comparing comprehension and production practice, of output practice through text reconstruction, of interaction, and of communication tasks.

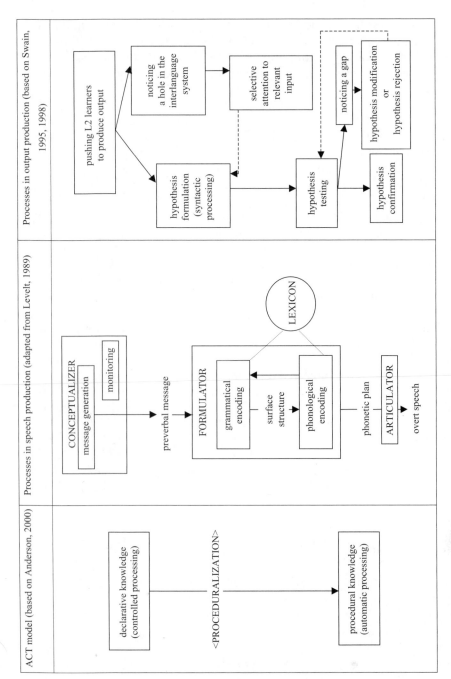

Figure 2.2 Summary of three models of language production

Studies comparing comprehension and production practice

The effects of output practice in L2 acquisition compared with comprehension practice have been investigated in several studies motivated by VanPatten and his associates' claims that practice in production does not make a significant contribution to L2 acquisition and that comprehension practice alone is enough to bring about significant development, not only in comprehension but also in production (Cadierno, 1992; VanPatten, 1996; VanPatten & Cadierno, 1993; VanPatten & Sanz, 1995). These claims are based upon the findings from empirical studies of input processing instruction (see VanPatten, 1996 for a review of input processing studies), which involves explanation and promoting form-meaning connections during processing input data (see Leow, this volume, for details of input processing). Summarizing the findings of these studies, VanPatten (1996) reports that traditional instruction involving explanation and output practice developed only L2 learners' production abilities, while input processing instruction helped learners develop both production and comprehension abilities. He argues that grammar translation and output-based traditional instruction foster L2 learners' explicit knowledge that can be used on fairly simple and time-controlled language tasks, while input processing instruction facilitates the formation and growth of the L2 developing system involving the accommodation of the intake and the restructuring of the system itself (VanPatten, 1996).

Responding to VanPatten's argument, DeKeyser and Sokalski (1996) conducted an experimental study to examine whether what was found in the input processing studies (e.g., VanPatten & Cadierno, 1993) on a particular structure (the direct object clitics) was applicable to the acquisition of other structures (the conditionals) by students from a different population. DeKeyser and Sokalski reported that the effect of input and output practice was basically skill-specific; input practice was significantly better for comprehension skills and output practice significantly better for production skills. DeKeyser and Sokalski, however, expressed reservations about making strong generalizations from the results because the patterns found in their study were obscured when both testing time (immediate versus delayed) and the morphosyntactic nature of the structure (simple versus complex) favored one skill or the other.

As pointed out in DeKeyser, Salaberry, Robinson, and Harrington (2002), it is noteworthy that recent empirical studies on processing have reported that both processing and output-based instruction have equally beneficial effects on the acquisition of semantically complex target forms (e.g., the subjunctive in Spanish) (see Cheng, 2002; Collentine, 2002; Farley, 2001). In these studies, the output-based treatments are much more meaning-based, containing no mechanical output drills. In the earlier processing instruction studies, traditional output-based instruction was composed of mechanical drills (e.g., VanPatten & Cadierno, 1993).[4] Therefore, whether output-based instruction has positive effects equal to those of processing instruction seems to depend on the operationalization of the treatments. DeKeyser et al. (2002) argue that key constructs including output-based instruction are not properly operationalized in the earlier processing instruction studies.

Also, it should be noted that most input processing studies (e.g., Cadierno, 1992; VanPatten & Cadierno, 1993) rely only on measures of controlled language comprehension and controlled written production; spontaneous oral production was not measured. In VanPatten and Sanz (1995), learners' production was measured with a sentence-level completion task and a storytelling (video narration) task, which requires spontaneous language use. However, the effect of processing instruction on oral production, as measured by the storytelling task, was not statistically significant, though it was observable. It is not clear, therefore, whether input processing is effective for the development of oral production ability in less-controlled tasks. Findings of the input processing studies should be interpreted with caution due to this methodological limitation.

In an experimental study on the automatization of explicitly learned rules of morphosyntax in L2, DeKeyser (1997) provides further evidence of the differential effects of computer-controlled comprehension practice and production practice on the learning of morphosyntactic rules and vocabulary items in an artificial language. Results indicated that the learning of morphosyntactic rules was highly skill-specific; large amounts of practice in comprehension and production of L2 grammatical rules led to significant improvements in the skill practiced but had far less impact on the reverse skill. Results of this study also suggest that L2 skills develop very gradually over time, in the same way as learning in other cognitive domains such as geometry and computer programming. DeKeyser (1997) reports that the learning curves observed in the study followed the same power law as the acquisition of other cognitive skills.[5] He argues, "This evidence supports the model of skill acquisition that posits that during initial practice declarative knowledge is turned into qualitatively different procedural knowledge and that subsequently a much slower process of gradual automatization takes place, which requires little or no change in task components, only a quantitative change within the same components" (p. 214).

Findings reported in DeKeyser and Sokalski (1996) and DeKeyser (1997) have the important pedagogical implication that specific practice is necessary for different skills in L2: input practice for reception skills and output practice for production skills. DeKeyser's (1997) finding that the acquisition of grammar follows the power law of learning (i.e., the performance with L2 grammar gradually improves through practice) is also highly significant because it indicates that practice plays an essential role in the development of performance with interlanguage grammar.

In interpreting the results of these studies that rely heavily on skill acquisition theory, we should keep in mind the already discussed limitations of the theory itself; there may be a number of linguistic rules that are acquired by L2 learners following other paths than the transition from declarative to procedural processing (e.g., rules underlying complex systems such as the English article system). Also, it should be noted that whether production practice has positive impact on the acquisition (i.e., automatization) of particular grammatical forms heavily depends on the linguistic features of the target form and various learner factors (DeKeyser, 1998). Also, as DeKeyser (1997, 1998) points out, findings of such laboratory studies as DeKeyser (1995, 1997) should not be overgeneralized or directly applied to actual language teaching in classrooms because these experimental studies employed a research methodology that emphasized testing specific hypotheses in highly controlled conditions, which were different from natural conditions in classrooms. Lack of testing measures for spontaneous oral production in these studies also limits the generalizability of the findings. More empirical studies should be accumulated under various conditions, especially in classroom settings, to obtain more direct recommendations for classroom language teaching.

Studies of output practice through text reconstruction and writing

Having learners reconstruct a text (story) that they have comprehended is one of the most effective instructional techniques that elicit learner output and eventually promote L2 learning. Kowal and Swain (1994) used a text reconstruction procedure called dictogloss to provide learners with opportunities for production in L2. In this procedure, a short but dense text is read to the learners, who jot down words and phrases they recognize and then work together in small groups to reconstruct the text from their shared information (Wajnryb, 1990). Kowal and Swain analyzed the dictogloss data taken from L2 learners in a French immersion class in Toronto. Based on the results of quantitative and qualitative analyses, Kowal and Swain maintain that the students became aware of gaps in their existing knowledge and points of uncertainty as they worked on the dictogloss task. Kowal and Swain's data suggest the learners were pushed to reflect on the sentence and seek a solution by hypothesizing about language and applying prior knowledge when the students were faced with an apparent discrepancy. Kowal and Swain emphasize that the subsequent discussion on the reconstructed text helped the learners deepen their understanding of form-function relationships (see LaPierre, 1994, reported in Swain, 1998; Swain, 2000, for further data of positive effects of dictogloss; see Swain & Lapkin, 1995, for analyses of essay writing data). Kowal and Swain conclude the data obtained in these dictogloss studies strongly support the output hypothesis. In particular, the data suggest that the noticing, hypothesis formulation and testing, and metalinguistic functions are actually at work during the dictogloss task.

In a study utilizing computer-assisted reconstruction/reading tasks, Izumi (2002) investigated whether and how output (i.e., text reconstruction), visual input enhancement, or the combination of both promoted noticing and the acquisition of relativization in English by adult ESL learners in the United States. Izumi reports that (1) those engaged in output-input activities outperformed those exposed to the same input for the sole purpose of comprehension in learning English relativization; (2) those who received visual input enhancement failed to show any measurable effect on learning. From these findings, Izumi concludes that pushed output, when provided along with relevant input, has three advantages in learning complex L2 grammatical forms: (1) detection of formal elements in the input, (2) integrative processing of the target form, and (3) noticing of the mismatches between one's interlanguage form and the target language input. Izumi also asserts that the lack of any significant impact of visual input enhancement suggests that the superficial external manipulation of the target form in the input can affect only detection, but not necessarily such processes as integration of the form and noticing gaps between the TL and IL forms (see also Izumi, Bigelow, Fujiwara & Fearnow, 1999; Izumi & Bigelow, 2000, for the effects of text reconstruction).

Findings of Izumi (2002) clearly indicate that output practice coupled with relevant input leads L2 learners to notice their linguistic problems under certain circumstances. These studies lend support for Swain's Output Hypothesis. They also point out the importance of extended opportunities for producing output; improvement in output is caused cumulatively.

One limitation of Izumi (2002) is that learner performance with the target form in the oral mode was not examined; learner performance was measured by controlled (nonspontaneous) written tests such as a sentence completion test, a picture-cued production test, and a grammaticality judgment test.

The effect of output practice through text reconstruction on L2 production in both written and oral modes was examined by Muranoi (2000a) within the research framework of focus on form (Doughty, 2001, 2003; Doughty & Williams, 1998; Long, 1991; Long & Robinson, 1998).[6] Muranoi proposes a focus-on-form treatment that emphasizes the role of pushed output in L2 learning through guided summarizing. The instructional treatment is termed *focus on form through guided summarizing* (FFGS), in which L2 learners are directed to reproduce the story of a text they have comprehended through reading. Guided summarizing is an instructional procedure that is usually used as a postreading or postlistening activity predominantly focusing on meaning. In this study, however, a focus-on-form treatment is integrated into guided summarizing by means of a concept map (i.e., a schematic representation of key words and phrases) that directly leads learners to use specific lexical items and indirectly guides them to use relevant grammatical forms. Learners are directed to reconstruct the story they have comprehended in the written mode and then in the oral mode without looking at the original text, relying on the lexical items assigned by the concept map. The lexical items in the concept map are arranged to indirectly lead learners to use certain grammatical forms (i.e., eliciting hypothesis formulation). The learners are then given an opportunity to revise their reproduced text by comparing it with the original texts (i.e., eliciting hypothesis testing against positive evidence). Muranoi investigated whether this output-oriented, focus-on-form treatment would bring about positive effects on the learning of a relatively complex grammatical form (the English perfect passive) by Japanese university students learning English as a foreign language (EFL). Results indicated that (1) FFGS enhanced EFL learners' accuracy in the use of the perfect passive as measured by oral and written sentence completion tests; (2) FFGS performed in both oral and written modes had better effects than that performed in the written mode only; and (3) FFGS was effective only for those who were psycholinguistically ready to learn the target form (i.e., the acquisition of the simple passive and the perfect active was a developmental requisite for the learning of the perfect passive). Based on the Output Hypothesis, Muranoi (2000a) argues that FFGS was effective because it promoted cognitive processes including noticing, comparing, and formulating and testing hypotheses. Also he claims, following Levelt's (1989) production model, that FFGS seems to be particularly helpful in leading learners to formulate a hypothesis about their IL grammar because the treatment was designed to facilitate learners' grammatical encoding by providing learners with messages to be conveyed (i.e., a news story) and lexical items whose lemma information stimulates syntactic building procedures. Further research is in order to see whether similar findings can be obtained with tests that elicit more spontaneous online use of the target form in less-controlled communicative tasks.

Studies of output practice through interaction

A number of studies have investigated whether and how interaction and negotiation of meaning elicit learner output (i.e., pushed output) and consequently promote L2 acquisition. Based on the findings of these studies it is now assumed that negotiated interaction provides opportunities to produce and modify output, which are crucial to L2 learning (for reviews of interaction studies, see Gass, 1997; Leeman, this volume; Long, 1996; Mackey, this volume; Pica, 1992, 1994).

Findings of interaction studies lend support to the claim that L2 learners respond linguistically when asked by their interlocutors to clarify or confirm what they have said during interaction and thereby attempt to make their output comprehensible for mutual understanding (see also Doughty & Varela, 1998; Ellis & He, 1999; Koyanagi, 1998; McDonough, 2005; Pica, 1992, 1994; Pica, Lincoln-Porter, Paninos, & Linnell, 1996; Shehadeh, 1999; Takashima & Ellis, 1999). Muranoi (2000b), for instance, reports the positive effects of a treatment that aims at guiding learners to modify and restructure their output by providing interactional modifications (requests for repetition and recasts) during a problem-solving task (i.e., strategic interaction, Di Pietro, 1987). The treatment is termed interaction enhancement (IE) because both input and output are enhanced in the treatment. The request for repetition has a dual function: as a flag to an incorrect form (input enhancement) and as a facilitator that guides the learner to produce modified output (output enhancement). After having the learner produce modified output, the teacher repeats the learner's correctly modified form (input enhancement), or he or she provides a corrective recast if the learner does not modify the output correctly. In the quasi-experimental study investigating the effects of IE on the oral and written performance of English articles by Japanese university students, two types of IE were employed: IE plus formal debriefing (IEF), which provided learners with explicit presentations of the target rule after the performance of the task; and IE plus meaning-focused debriefing (IEM), which provided a debriefing on how successfully the intended communication was carried out. Results indicate that IE had positive effects, which lasted for at least five weeks, on L2 learning of English articles and that IEF had a greater effect than IEM. In particular it seemed the explicit grammar explanation the IEF group received helped prevent the learners from overgeneralization of the target form. These findings suggest that an instructional treatment that systematically combines such techniques as output enhancement, input enhancement, a problem-solving task, and explicit presentation of target rules can be beneficial for guiding L2 learners to develop their IL grammar. Further research with more rigorous research methods is necessary to test if IE is effective under other conditions.

In his quasi-experimental study, Van den Branden (1997) examined the effects of various types of negotiation (negotiation of meaning, negotiation of forms) on L2 learners' output. The participants, child learners of Dutch at a Flemish primary school, were asked to solve a murder case by orally describing a series of drawings to an NS partner or a teacher partner who was not allowed to see the drawings. Results showed that (1) children negotiated each other's output at the levels of meaning and context but not (deliberately) at the level of form while performing the task; (2) children were able to modify their output interactionally when confronted with negative feedback; (3) the type of interactional modification children produced was more strongly influenced by the type of feedback they received than by the person who gave it; and (4) the feedback the learners received and the interactional modifications they made during negotiations had delayed effects on their output production in subsequent interactions. Performing the same task with another partner, the learners who had been pushed in preceding negotiations provided more important information and used a wider range of vocabulary than the contrast students. Van den Branden reports, however, that the negotiations exerted no significant effects on the syntactic complexity nor on the grammatical correctness of the learner output produced in the post-test. These findings suggest that negotiations push children to modify their output semantically and, in particular, lexically. However, Van den Branden claims that further research is necessary to examine the possible effects of negotiation on the grammatical accuracy of learner output.

Regarding this finding on accuracy, L2 researchers and teachers should keep in mind that variables such as syntactic complexity and grammatical correctness are less easily affected by external interventions than semantic and lexical complexity (Bygate, 2001). Also, as this study had no specific grammatical target items, it should be noted that previous studies that examined the effects of interactional modifications without any particular grammatical target (e.g., Lyster, 1998; Lyster & Ranta, 1994) have reported weaker impact of instructional treatments than studies that targeted specific grammatical items such as past tense forms and question formation (e.g., Doughty & Varela, 1998; Mackey, 1999).

These studies on the effects of interactional modifications on learner output indicate that negotiated interactions push L2 learners to generate and modify output with the help of external or internal feedback, especially within the framework of focus on form, though it is not clear whether negotiated interactions affect syntactic development. These findings encourage L2 teachers to use various types of meaningful practice that require negotiation of meaning, taking into account such factors as task type, age, and linguistic features of the target items.

Studies of output practice through communication tasks

L2 researchers and teachers have recognized the potential of task-based instruction to create more opportunities to negotiate meaning than traditional instruction (Long, 1985, 1991; Long & Crookes, 1992; Loschky & Bley-Vroman, 1993; Pica, Kanagy, & Falodun, 1993; Robinson, 2001a, 2001b). DeKeyser (2001) points out that task-based language teaching is particularly profitable for fostering the development of accuracy in production. He predicts that communication tasks can be used to provide learners with systematic, meaningful and context-embedded practice, which ensures automatization of linguistic forms.

The potential of task-based instruction has been documented empirically, and L2 researchers have found that communication tasks such as an information-gap task bring about conditions for comprehension, feedback, and modified production (Pica, 1992, 1994). In this section, studies investigating how task activities affect interlanguage – in particular, L2 production in terms of accuracy, fluency, and complexity – will be reviewed from four different but closely related variables: planning, repetition, automatization, and cognitive complexity.

TASK PLANNING

It has been reported that pretask planning influences learner output while performing communication tasks. Foster and Skehan (1996), for instance, examined the effects of planning time on learner performance on three different types of communication tasks (a personal information exchange task, a narration, and a decision-making task). These tasks were performed by three groups of ESL learners in the United Kingdom. Group 1 had no planning time. Group 2 had 10 minutes of unguided planning time. Group 3 had 10 minutes of detailed planning time with detailed guidance as to how to use the planning time and how to develop ideas for the completion of the tasks. Performance on the communication tasks was measured in terms of fluency (the number of repetitions, reformulations, replacements, false starts, pauses, and silence), complexity (the number of clauses per c-unit/syntactic variety) and accuracy (the proportion of error-free to total clauses). Results indicate that there were strong effects of planning on fluency and clear effects on complexity, with a linear relationship between degree of planning (no planning, undetailed planning, and detailed planning) and degree of complexity. However, the relationship between planning and accuracy was rather complex; the most accurate performance was produced by less detailed planning. Foster and Skehan also reported complex relationships between task type and planning conditions. The effects of planning were greater with the narrative and decision-making tasks than with the personal information exchange task. These findings imply that task planning is one of the crucial conditions that L2 teachers can control in order to help learners develop their performance in tasks. Foster and Skehan's study, however, suggests that further research is necessary to understand what kind of planning is particularly beneficial for enhancing accuracy of task performance.

Ortega (1999) also investigated the effect of planning on L2 oral performance by native speakers of American English who were learning Spanish. Ortega reports that planning opportunities before story-retelling tasks increased the syntactic complexity (words per utterance) and fluency (pruned speech rate) of planned output, but that no effects were found for lexical range (type-token ratio) and that mixed results were found concerning the effect of planning on grammatical accuracy (target-like use of noun-modifier agreement and the Spanish article system). Ortega also analyzed the learners' retrospective interview protocols to examine the cognitive and attentional processes during planning. Results showed that task planning helped adult learners of Spanish produce more fluent and complex language but that there were no effects on lexical range. Findings regarding accuracy were inconclusive. Results from the retrospective analyses suggest that opportunity to plan before performing a task in L2 can enhance learners' attention to form during pretask planning. Ortega reports that learners given opportunities for planning employed a wide variety of cognitive and metacognitive strategies and that they were engaged in morphosyntactic and utterance-level processing, as well as lexical and semantic processing. Ortega (1999) concludes that pretask planning has two facilitative effects on L2 acquisition: (1) "Planning removes some of the cognitive load and communicative pressure of a given task, thus freeing up attentional resources for the learners to reach the upper limits of his or her interlanguage and to ease on-line performance" (p. 138) and (2) "creates a space for the learner to assess task demands and available linguistic resources and to prioritize strategic allocation of effort and attention accordingly" (p. 138). These effects, Ortega argues, promote such cognitive processes as making form-function connections, noticing the gap, hypothesis testing, restructuring, and development.

Similarly, Mehnert (1998) investigated the effect of different amounts of planning time (1, 5, 10 minutes) on the speech performance of L2 learners of German. Results indicate that fluency and lexical density of speech increased as a function of planning time. Accuracy of speech improved with only one minute of planning but did not increase with more planning time. Complexity of speech was higher for the 10-minute planning condition only.

Findings of the effects of task planning have indicated that teachers should provide learners with a proper amount of planning time with proper guidance as to how to prepare for a task. It is also important to note that planning should be systematically incorporated into the whole process of task performance. On this point, it may be relevant to refer to Di Pietro (1987)'s three-phase task performance, which proposes that each interactive task session should consist of a rehearsal phase, a performance phase, and a debriefing phase (see Di Pietro, 1987 for examples).

TASK REPETITION

Repetition is another factor that influences the impact of task on L2 production. Bygate (2001) investigated whether the repeated use of the same and similar communication tasks promoted development of an L2. Following Levelt's (1989, 1993) production model, Bygate assumes that repetition is facilitative for L2 development because "part of the work of conceptualization, formulation and articulation carried out on the first occasion is kept in the learners' memory store and can be reused on the second occasion, thereby freeing up some of the learners' capacity to pay attention to other aspects of the task, particularly in the processes of formulation and articulation" (2001, p. 29). Using overseas NNS students in the United Kingdom, Bygate investigated the effects of task-type practice (10 weeks' exposure to either narrative or interview tasks), repetition (of a version of each task type 10 weeks earlier), and task type (narrative or interview). Bygate investigated learner performances on one repeated and one new version of each of the task types by three groups – one participating in narrative tasks, one in interview tasks, and one receiving no treatment – in terms of fluency (the number of unfilled pauses per t-unit), accuracy (the incidence of errors per t-unit), and complexity (number of words per t-unit). Results indicated that there was a strong effect of task repetition. Bygate reports that a brief encounter with a task 10 weeks earlier affected subsequent performance of the same task. He also reports that the results of his study partially confirmed the hypothesis that different versions of the same type of task had positive effects on learner performance. He also found that the effects of task type and task repetition varied depending on the aspect of learner performance; accuracy was "less open to influence from task-type practice or task repetition than fluency or complexity" (p. 43).

Bygate's findings imply that repetition of task is effective to help learners perform the task in more fluent and complex manners. This is because task repetition can change learners' allocation of attention; learners can pay more attention to linguistic aspects, including syntactic and phonological processing, during the second and later performances of a task because most parts of semantic processing do not require as much of the learners' attentional resources as in the first performance of the task.

Contrary to Bygate's findings, Gass, Alvarez-Torres, Fernández-García, and Mackey (1999) found that task repetition had limited effects on overall proficiency, morphosyntax, and lexical sophistication by English-speaking learners of Spanish. Results indicate that a group that saw the same video four times had some improvement, but there was no carryover effect when the content of the video changed. Gass et al. (1999) comment that this is not surprising because overall fluency is likely to be partially context dependent.

AUTOMATIZATION

Another strand of research concerns the relation between learners' attentional resources and task repetition. It is possible for L2 teachers to guide their learners to spend their cognitive (attentional) resources for higher processing by automatizing lower processing. Johnson (1996), for example, maintains that L2 teachers should help learners automatize their linguistic knowledge (declarative knowledge) by controlling the amount of attention a learner can give to a language form. Johnson quotes Huey (1968) to summarize the role of automatization: "Repetition progressively frees the mind from attention to details . . . and reduces the extent to which consciousness must concern itself with the process" (Huey, 1968, cited in Johnson, 1996, p. 138).

Johnson claims that to facilitate automatization (*automization* in Johnson's terminology) teachers should manipulate tasks in various ways to progressively decrease the amount of attention required for a learner to perform a subskill such as complex grammatical encoding. He proposes several ways this can be achieved in practice. One of them is to introduce "artificial attention distracters" into communication tasks, which aim at consuming learners' conscious attention. Noting that message-focused communicative activities often involve mere language reproduction, Johnson stresses the importance of tasks that contain something that deflects learners' attention from form (form defocus) for facilitating automatization of linguistic knowledge (see Johnson, 1996, for examples of form defocus tasks).

Arevart and Nation (1991) report the positive effects of a technique that facilitates automatization of existing linguistic knowledge by having learners tell the same story three times to different listeners, decreasing the time for each retelling (4 / 3 / 2 minutes). They examined the effects of this 4 / 3 / 2 technique with intermediate to low-advanced level English learners in New Zealand. Learners automatized use of the existing linguistic knowledge, or fluency was measured by calculating the speaking speed in words per minute and the frequency of hesitations per 100 words following Lennon (1990). Results indicate that the participants significantly improved their fluency over the three deliveries of their talks. Arevart and Nation argue that spoken fluency activities that provide the opportunity for repetition with a focus on the message can assist learners who have difficulty in accessing lexical and grammatical items when their attention is focused on conveying a message. Such a technique is expected to lead learners to "gradual automatization by making the learner go through the same production routines under conditions of increased time pressure and increased integration with other cognitive demands" (DeKeyser, 2001, p. 150).

COGNITIVE COMPLEXITY

Another factor highly related to learner attentional resources while performing communication tasks is the cognitive complexity of the task. It has been reported that the degree of cognitive complexity greatly affects learner performance in tasks (see Robinson, 2001a; Skehan, 1998). Robinson (2001b), for example, examined the effects of the cognitive complexity of tasks on language production and learner perceptions of task difficulty for Japanese university students of English. The participants engaged in a direction-giving task. Two versions of the map task were used: a simpler version (the use of a map covering a familiar and small area) and a more complex one (a larger and unfamiliar area). The effects of the sequence of the tasks (from simple to complex, from complex to simple) were also examined. The information givers' production was assessed for accuracy (error free C-units), fluency (the number of words per C-unit), and complexity (clauses per C-unit and lexical complexity or variety of words per C-unit).[7] The information receivers' production was assessed by calculating the number of clarification requests and confirmation checks. Robinson also employed a questionnaire to examine learner perception of task difficulty. Results indicate that increasing the cognitive complexity of the task significantly affected information givers' production (e.g., more lexical variety on the complex version of the task and greater fluency on the simpler version). Robinson reported that information-receivers' production was also affected (e.g., more confirmation checks on the complex version). Moreover, learners perceived the complex version to be more stressful than the simpler one. Results also show that sequencing from simple to complex did not affect the learners' ratings of task difficulty, but that task sequencing increased the accuracy of speaker production in the simple-complex sequence and fluency in the complex-simple sequence. Based on these findings, Robinson concludes that "cognitive complexity is a robust, and manipulable influence on learner production, and is therefore a feasible basis for design and sequencing decisions which operationalize a task-based syllabus" (2001b, p. 52).

Results of Robinson's study tell us that one responsibility of L2 teachers is to control the cognitive complexity of communication tasks carefully. What is most important is to choose and sequence tasks of different degrees of complexity, depending on learner readiness and linguistic characteristics of the target form.

The studies discussed in this section clearly indicate that authentic communicative tasks are valuable for teachers who want to push learners to produce output in the classroom. These studies also suggest that teachers can make the best use of tasks to develop learners' production abilities if they consider factors such as task planning, task repetition, task type, task complexity, and task selection and sequencing.

The inconclusive findings regarding the effects of task variables on learners' linguistic accuracy are noteworthy because they indicate that accuracy is an aspect of L2 proficiency that is not easily affected through performing a communication task alone. In addition to planning, repetition, and complexity manipulation, L2 teachers must further supplement task-based instruction in order to enhance learners' accuracy (e.g., explicit formal instruction of the target forms). The positive effect of presenting explicit grammatical rules immediately following the performance of a communicative task has been identified in Muranoi's (2000b) quasi-experimental study, in which explicit grammar instruction was provided as a part of focus on form (see the previous section). Pedagogically, such a treatment aiming at enhancing learner accuracy during task-based instruction should be given importance because communication tasks have serious pitfalls that stem from an almost complete emphasis on meaning (Long, 1985). As Skehan (1996) claims, it is likely that a task-based approach will "teach learners simply how to do tasks better, to proceduralize strategic solutions to problems, and to engage in lexicalized communication" (p. 42). Loschky and Bley-Vroman (1993) similarly argue that information-gap tasks may do more to develop strategic than linguistic competency because "in most common information-gap tasks learners seem to be able to exchange information solely through use of semantic- and pragmatic-based strategies combined with their background knowledge" (p. 125). These statements underscore the fact that mere participation in communication tasks may be insufficient for leading learners to develop their linguistic competence and particularly to accurate and appropriate production. Skehan (1996) argues that it is necessary "to devise methods of focusing on form without losing the values of tasks as realistic communicative motivators, and as opportunities to trigger acquisitional processes" (p. 42). More research on focus on form in light of task-based instruction will provide us with insights on how to realize Skehan's proposal.

Future research on the relationship between task-based instruction and L2 production should include more detailed examination of the influence of learner factors such as needs, motivation, attitudes, cognitive styles, working memory capacity, cognitive abilities, personality, and so on. Research in this line is of importance because L2 production is greatly influenced by these individual differences (Ellis, 1999). Also, the validity of measurements of task performance (accuracy, fluency, and complexity) must be confirmed in future research. As shown in this review of task studies, there has been no consensus on how to quantify learner performance in tasks. The validity of specific measures has been questioned, too. For example, the use of temporal variables (e.g., the number of pauses as an index of fluency) has been criticized because these often accidental features of speech production reveal only limited aspects of language use rather than language acquisition (Cook, 1993; Griffiths, 1991). Researchers also must verify the validity of measures of accuracy (e.g., the number of error-free T-units) and complexity (e.g., the number of words per T-unit). As these indexes are developed to measure over-all proficiency levels (e.g., Larsen-Freeman, 1983), it is possible that the positive effects of instruction on specific linguistic items are being over-looked. To examine L2 production in a more valid manner, it is necessary for L2 researchers to complementarily employ both data collection tasks that focus on specific structures and more extensive elicitation tasks that characterize overall language abilities (see Doughty & Long, 2000, for comprehensive descriptions and evaluations of various L2 production data collection methods). The use of introspective methodology (e.g., stimulated recall method, Gass & Mackey, 2000) is also beneficial, espe-cially when used alongside quantitative measures of L2 production (e.g., Ortega, 1999).

Summary and conclusions

The studies reviewed in this chapter indicate that output practice (i.e., any activity designed to provide L2 learners with opportunities to produce output) is effective for developing L2 learners' well-balanced commu-nicative competence. Based upon the findings of empirical studies, it can be concluded that instructional treatments eliciting learner output in con-textualized practice can develop L2 learners' productive proficiency. This is presumably because output promotes major cognitive processes in SLA, including noticing, hypothesis formulation and testing, conscious reflec-tion, and automatization. Psycholinguistic models of language produc-tion help us understand that L2 production is executed through a series of highly complex interrelated processes such as conceptualizing, formu-lating, and articulating. It can be inferred that formulating is the pro-cess that needs to be proceduralized through output practice to enhance fluency in L2. Skill acquisition theory also claims that linguistic knowl-edge, including lexical, grammatical, and phonological knowledge, must be processed automatically as procedural knowledge for spontaneous communication. These theories provide a foundation for L2 teachers to construct psycholinguistically valid opportunities for practice which aim at facilitating cognitive processes crucial for L2 development.

Results of empirical studies on the effects of output-based instruc-tion, especially those conducted in classroom situations, generally indi-cate that providing learners with opportunities for producing output in language-use contexts is facilitative in developing learners' interlanguage, especially productive skills. Instructional techniques aiming at eliciting learner output through text reconstruction, interaction, and other tasks have been empirically proven to be effective for L2 acquisition, though the strength of the effects heavily depends on various factors, including learner individual differences and the complexity of the target linguistic items. These studies on output have shed light on the theoretically and practically significant issue of how output practice contributes to L2 acquisition. However, as the number of empirical studies is still limited and the methodological limitations remain, further research is needed on the impact of output. In particular, we need to examine in what way and in what order the interrelated cognitive processes are affected through different types of output practice. Also, we know little about how much practice L2 learners need to acquire a particular linguistic form. Future integration of more advanced theories and research on the psycholinguistic mechanisms of language production and dynamic instructional techniques for L2 teaching devised by well-informed teachers will help L2 researchers understand what factors affect production and at the same time provide practitioners with insightful pedagogical implications that help them evaluate whether their instruction is psycholinguistically valid.

Notes

1. I thank Robert DeKeyser, Catherine J. Doughty, and anonymous reviewers for insightful comments on earlier drafts of this chapter. All errors are, of course, my own.
2. Long (1996) cautions that cases of individuals who allegedly learned languages with minimal or no opportunity to speak, as reported in Krashen (1985), should be interpreted as highly exceptional and that these cases are "somewhat poorly documented" (p. 447).
3. See DeKeyser (1998) for drawbacks of mechanical drills used in the Audiolingual Method, which was popular in the 1950s through the 1970s. See Schmidt (1983) for evidence of the inadequacy of mere output opportunities.
4. It should be noted that in his recent book VanPatten (2003) claims that output plays a facilitative role in acquisition and that making output pushes learners "to be better processors of input" (VanPatten, 2003, p. 69). He maintains, however, that decontextualized output practice such as mechanical pattern practice plays a limited role in L2 acquisition.
5. The power law of learning is defined by Anderson (2000) as "the phenomenon that memory performance improves as a power function of practice" (p. 469). That is, a memory can be rapidly retrieved when it is strengthened with practice following a curve defined by a power function (see DeKeyser, 2001; Newell & Rosenbloom, 1981).
6. Focus on form is defined as a meaning-oriented instructional treatment that "consists of an occasional shift of attention to linguistic code features – by

the teacher and for one or more students – triggered by perceived problems with comprehension or production" (Long & Robinson, 1998, p. 23).
7. A C-unit (communication unit) is an independent grammatical predication, which is similar to a T-unit (minimal terminable unit: any syntactic main clause and its associated subordinate clauses). In the C-unit analysis elliptical answers to questions are considered complete predications (Chaudron, 1988). Robinson (2001b), therefore, assumes that C-units are more suitable for analyzing interactive discourse than T-units.

References

Anderson, J. (1982). Acquisition of cognitive skill. *Psychological Review, 89*, 4, 369–406.
Anderson, J. (1983). *The architecture of cognition.* Cambridge, MA: Harvard University Press.
Anderson, J. (1993). *Rules of the mind.* Hillsdale, NJ: Lawrence Erlbaum.
Anderson, J. (2000). *Cognitive psychology and its implications* (5th ed). New York: Worth.
Arevart, S., & Nation, P. (1991). Fluency improvement in a second language. *RELC Journal, 22*, 1, 84–94.
Bley-Vroman, R. (1986). Hypothesis testing in second-language acquisition theory. *Language Learning, 36*, 3, 353–76.
Bygate, M. (2001). Effects of task repetition on the structure and control of oral language. In M. Bygate, P. Skehan, & M. Swain (Eds.), *Researching pedagogic tasks: Second language learning, teaching and testing* (pp. 23–48). London: Longman.
Byrne, D. (1976). *Teaching oral English.* Harlow, UK: Longman.
Cadierno, T. (1992). *Explicit instruction in grammar: A comparison of input based and output based instruction in second language acquisition.* Unpublished doctoral dissertation, University of Illinois at Urbana-Champaign.
Carroll, S., & Swain, M. (1993). Explicit and implicit negative feedback: An empirical study of the learning of linguistic generalizations. *Studies in Second Language Acquisition, 15*, 3, 357–86.
Chaudron, C. (1988). *Second language classrooms: Research on teaching and learning.* Cambridge, UK: Cambridge University Press.
Cheng, A. (2002). The effects of processing instruction on the acquisition of *ser* and *estar. Hispania, 85*, 2, 308–23.
Collentine, J. (2002). On the acquisition of the subjunctive and authentic processing instruction: A response to Farley. *Hispania, 84*, 4, 900–9.
Cook, V. (1985). Chomsky's universal grammar and second language learning. *Applied Linguistics, 6*, 2, 2–18.
Cook, V. (1993). *Linguistics and second language acquisition.* Basingstoke, UK: Macmillan.
de Bot, K. (1992). A bilingual production model: Levelt's "Speaking" model adapted. *Applied Linguistics, 13*, 1, 1–24.
de Bot, K. (1996). The psycholinguistics of the output hypothesis. *Language Learning, 46*, 3, 529–55.
de Bot, K., Paribakht, T. S., & Weshe, M. B. (1997). Toward a lexical processing model for the study of second language vocabulary acquisition:

Evidence from ESL reading. *Studies in Second Language Acquisition, 19*, 249–75.

DeKeyser, R. (1995). Learning second language grammar rules. An experiment with a miniature linguistic system. *Studies is Second Language Acquisition, 17*, 379–410.

DeKeyser, R. (1997). Beyond explicit rule learning: Automatizing second language morphosyntax. *Studies in Second Language Acquisition, 19*, 2, 195–221.

DeKeyser, R. (1998). Beyond focus on form: Cognitive perspectives on learning and practicing second language grammar. In C. Doughty & J. Williams (Eds.), *Focus on form in classroom second language acquisition* (pp. 42–63). Cambridge, UK: Cambridge University Press.

DeKeyser, R. (2001). Automaticity and automatization. In P. Robinson (Ed.), *Cognition and second language instruction* (pp. 125–51). Cambridge, UK: Cambridge University Press.

DeKeyser, R., Salaberry, R., Robinson, P., & Harrington, M. (2002). What gets processed in processing instruction? A commentary on Bill VanPatten's "Processing instruction: An update." *Language Learning, 52*, 4, 805–23.

DeKeyser, R., & Sokalski, K. (1996). The differential role of comprehension and production practice. *Language Learning, 46*, 4, 613–42.

Di Pietro, R. (1987). *Strategic interaction: Learning languages through scenarios.* Cambridge, UK: Cambridge University Press.

Dörnyei, Z., & Kormos, J. (1998). Problem-solving mechanisms in L2 communication: A psycholinguistic perspective. *Studies in Second Language Acquisition, 20*, 349–85.

Doughty, C. (2001). Cognitive underpinnings of focus on form. In P. Robinson (Ed.), *Cognition and second language instruction* (pp. 206–57). New York: Cambridge University Press.

Doughty, C. (2003). Instructed SLA: Constraints, compensation, and enhancement. In C. Doughty & M. H. Long (Eds.), *The handbook of second language acquisition* (pp. 256–310). Oxford: Blackwell.

Doughty, C., & Long, M. (2000). Eliciting second language speech data. In L. Menn & N. Bernstein Ratner (Eds.), *Methods for studying language production* (pp. 149–77). Mahwah, NJ: Lawrence Eralbaum.

Doughty, C., & Varela, E. (1998). Communicative focus on form. In C. Doughty & J. Williams (Eds.), *Focus on form in classroom second language acquisition* (pp. 114–38). New York: Cambridge University Press.

Doughty, C., & Williams, J. (1998). Pedagogical choices in focus on form. In C. Doughty & J. Williams (Eds.), *Focus on form in classroom second language acquisition* (pp. 197–261). New York: Cambridge University Press.

Ellis, R. (1991). The role of practice in classroom learning. In R. Ellis (Ed.), *Second language acquisition and language pedagogy* (pp. 101–20). Clevedon, UK: Multilingual Matters.

Ellis, R. (1994). *The study of second language acquisition.* Oxford: Oxford University Press.

Ellis, R. (1997). *SLA research and language teaching.* Oxford: Oxford University Press.

Ellis, R. (Ed.). (1999). Theoretical perspectives on interaction and language learning. In R. Ellis (Ed.), *Learning a second language through interaction* (pp. 3–31). Amsterdam/Philadelphia: John Benjamins.

Ellis, R., & He, X. (1999). The role of modified input and output in the incidental acquisition of word meanings. *Studies in Second Language Acquisition, 21,* 285–301.

Farley, A. P. (2001). Authentic processing instruction and the Spanish subjunctive. *Hispania, 84,* 289–99.

Foster, P., & Skehan, P. (1996). The influence of planning and task type on second language performance. *Studies in Second Language Acquisition, 18,* 3, 299–323.

Gass, S. (1997). *Input, interaction, and the second language learner.* Mahwah, NJ: Lawrence Erlbaum.

Gass, S., & Mackey, A. (2000). *Stimulated recall methodology in second language research.* Mahwah, NJ: Lawrence Erlbaum.

Gass, S., Mackey, A., Alvarez-Torres, M., & Fernández-García, M. (1999). The effects of task repetition on linguistic output. *Language Learning, 49,* 4, 549–81.

Griffiths, R. (1991). Pausological research in an L2 context: A rationale and review of selected studies. *Applied Linguistics, 12,* 4, 345–64.

Harley, T. (2001). *The psychology of language: From data to theory*(2nd ed.). East Sussex, UK: Psychology Press.

Harmer, J. (2001). *The practice of English language teaching*(3rd ed.). London: Longman.

Huey, E. (1968). *The psychology and pedagogy of reading.* Cambridge, MA: MIT Press.

Izumi, S. (2000). *Promoting noticing and SLA: An empirical study of the effects of output and input enhancement on ESL relativization.* Unpublished doctoral dissertation, Georgetown University, Washington, DC.

Izumi, S. (2002). Output, input enhancement, and the noticing hypothesis. *Studies in Second Language Acquisition, 24,* 541–77.

Izumi, S. (2003). Comprehension and production processes in second language learning: In search of the psycholinguistic rationale of the output hypothesis. *Applied Linguistics, 24,* 2, 168–96.

Izumi, S., & Bigelow, M. (2000). Does output promote noticing and second language acquisition? *TESOL Quarterly, 34,* 2, 239–78.

Izumi, S., Bigelow, M., Fujiwara, M., & Fearnow, S. (1999). Testing the Output Hypothesis: Effects of output on noticing and second language acquisition. *Studies in Second Language Acquisition, 21,* 3, 421–52.

Johnson, K. (1996). *Language teaching & skill learning.* Oxford: Blackwell.

Johnson, K., & Johnson, H. (Eds.) (1998). *Encyclopedic dictionary of applied linguistics.* Oxford: Blackwell.

Kowal, M., & Swain, M. (1994). Using collaborative language production tasks to promote students' language awareness. *Language Awareness, 3,* 73–93.

Kowal, M., & Swain, M. (1997). From semantic to syntactic processing: How can we promote it in the immersion classroom? In R. K. Johnson & M. Swain (Eds.), *Immersion education: International perspectives* (pp. 284–309). Cambridge, UK: Cambridge University Press.

Koyanagi, K. (1998). *The effect of focus-on-form tasks on the acquisition of a Japanese conditional "to": Input, output, and "task-essentialness."* Unpublished doctoral dissertation, Georgetown University, Washington, DC.

Krashen, S. (1982). *Principles and practice in second language acquisition.* Oxford: Pergamon.

Krashen, S. (1985). *The input hypothesis: Issues and implications.* London: Longman.

Krashen, S. (1998). Comprehensible input? *System, 26,* 175–82.

Krashen, S., & Terrell, T. (1983). *The Natural Approach: Language acquisition in the classroom.* Oxford: Pergamon/Alemany.

LaPierre, D. (1994). *Language output in a cooperative learning setting: Determining its effects on second language learning.* Unpublished master's thesis, University of Toronto, Canada.

Larsen-Freeman, D. (1983). Assessing global second language proficiency. In H. Seliger & M. Long (Eds.), *Classroom-oriented research in second language acquisition* (pp. 287–305). Cambridge, MA: Newbury House.

Lennon, P. (1990). Investigating fluency in EFL: A quantitative approach. *Language Learning, 40,* 387–417.

Levelt, W. J. M. (1989). *Speaking: From intention to articulation.* Cambridge, MA: MIT Press.

Levelt, W. J. M. (1993). Language use in normal speakers and its disorders. In G. Blanken, J. Dittman, H. Grimm, J. C. Marshall, & C. W. Wallesch (Eds.), *Linguistic disorders and pathologies* (pp. 1–15). Berlin: de Gruyter.

Long, M. (1985). A role for instruction in second language acquisition: Task-based language teaching. In K. Hyltenstam & M. Pienemann (Eds.), *Modeling and assessing second language development* (pp. 77–99). Clevedon, UK: Multilingual Matters.

Long, M. (1991). Focus on form: A design feature in language teaching methodology. In K. de Bot, R. Ginsberg, & C. Kramsch (Eds.), *Foreign language research in cross-cultural perspective* (pp. 39–52). Amsterdam: John Benjamins.

Long, M. (1996). The role of the linguistic environment in second language acquisition. In W. Ritchie & T. Bhatia (Eds.), *Handbook of research on second language acquisition* (pp. 413–68). New York: Academic Press.

Long, M., & Crookes, G. (1992). Three approaches to task-based syllabus design. *TESOL Quarterly, 26,* 1, 27–56.

Long, M., Inagaki, S., & Ortega, L. (1998). The role of implicit negative feedback in SLA: Models and recasts in Japanese and Spanish. *The Modern Language Journal, 82,* 357–71.

Long, M., & Robinson, P. (1998). Focus on form: Theory, research, and practice. In C. Doughty & J. Williams (Eds.), *Focus on form in classroom second language acquisition* (pp. 15–41). New York: Cambridge University Press.

Loschky, L., & Bley-Vroman, R. (1993). Grammar and task-based methodology. In G. Crookes and S. Gass (Eds.), *Tasks and language learning: Integrating theory and practice* (pp. 123–67). Clevedon, UK: Multilingual Matters.

Lyster, R. (1998). Recasts, repetition and ambiguity in L2 classroom discourse. *Studies in Second Language Acquisition, 20,* 50–81.

Lyster, R., & Ranta, L. (1994). Corrective feedback and learner uptake: Negotiation of form in communicative classrooms. *Studies in Second Language Acquisition, 19,* 37–66.

Mackey, A. (1999). Input, interaction, and second language development: An empirical study of question formation in ESL. *Studies in Second Language Acquisition, 21,* 557–87.

McDonough, K. (2005). Identifying the impact of negative feedback and learners' responses on ESL question development. *Studies in Second Language Acquisition, 27,* 1, 79–103.

Mehnert, U. (1998). The effects of different lengths of time for planning on second language performance. *Studies in Second Language Acquisition, 20,* 1, 83–108.

Muranoi, H. (2000a, November). *Focus on form through guided summarizing and EFL learners' interlanguage development.* Paper presented at the 39th annual conference of Japan Association of College English Teachers (JACET), Okinawa, Japan.

Muranoi, H. (2000b). Focus on form through interaction enhancement: Integrating formal instruction into a communicative task in EFL classrooms. *Language Learning, 50,* 4, 617–73.

Nelson, K. (1987). Some observations from the perspective of the rare event cognitive comparison theory of language acquisition. In K. Nelson & A. van Kleeck (Eds.), *Children's language, Vol. 6.* Norwood, NJ: Lawrence Erlbaum.

Newell, A., & Rosenbloom, P. S. (1981). Mechanisms of skill acquisition and the law of practice. In J. R. Anderson (Ed.), *Cognitive skills and their acquisition* (pp. 1–55). Hillsdale, NJ: Lawrence Erlbaum.

O'Malley, M., & Chamot, A. (1990). *Learning strategies in second language acquisition.* New York: Cambridge University Press.

Ortega, L. (1999). Planning and focus on form in L2 oral performance. *Studies in Second Language Acquisition, 21,* 1, 109–48.

Pica, T. (1992). The textual outcomes of native speaker-non-native speaker negotiation: What do they reveal about second language learning? In C. Kramsch & S. McConnell-Ginet (Eds.), *Text and context* (pp. 198–237). Cambridge, MA: Heath.

Pica, T. (1994). Research on negotiation: What does it reveal about second language learning conditions, processes, and outcomes? *Language Learning, 44,* 493–527.

Pica, T., Holliday, L. Lewis, N., & Morgenthaler, M. (1989). Comprehensible output as an outcome of linguistic demands on the learner. *Studies in Second Language Acquisition, 11,* 63–90.

Pica, T., Kanagy, R., & Faldun, J. (1993). Choosing and using communication tasks for second language research and instruction. In G. Crookes and S. Gass (Eds.), *Tasks and language learning: Integrating theory and practice* (pp. 9–34). Clevedon, UK: Multilingual Matters.

Pica, T., Lincoln-Porter, F., Paninos, D., & Linnell, J. (1996). Language learners' interaction: How does it address the input, output, and feedback needs of L2 learners? *TESOL Quarterly, 30,* 59–84.

Pienemann, M. (1998). *Language processing and second language development: Processability theory.* Amsterdam/Philadelphia: John Benjamins.

Robinson, P. (2001a). Task complexity, cognitive resources, and syllabus design: a triadic framework for examining task influences on SLA. In P. Robinson (Ed.), *Cognition and second language instruction* (pp. 287–318). Cambridge, UK: Cambridge University Press.

Robinson, P. (2001b). Task complexity, task difficulty, and task production: Exploring interactions in a componential framework. *Applied Linguistics, 22,* 1, 27–57.

Schachter, J. (1984). Universal input condition. In W. Rutherford (Ed.), *Language universals and second language acquisition* (pp. 167–83). Amsterdam/Philadelphia: John Benjamins.

Schachter, J. (1986). Three approaches to the study of input. *Language Learning, 36*, 2, 211–25.

Schachter, J. (1993). A new account of language transfer. In S. Gass & L. Selinker (Eds.), *Language transfer in language learning (Rev. ed.)* (pp. 32–46). Amsterdam/Philadelphia: John Benjamins.

Schmidt, R. (1983). Input, acculturation and the acquisition of communicative competence. In N. Wolfson & E. Judd (Eds.), *Sociolinguistics and second language acquisition* (pp. 137–74). Rowley, MA: Newbury House.

Schmidt, R. (1990). The role of consciousness in second language learning. *Applied Linguistics, 11*, 129–58.

Schmidt, R. (1992). Psychological mechanisms underlying second language fluency. *Studies in Second Language Acquisition, 14*, 357–85.

Schmidt, R. (2001). Attention. In P. Robinson (Ed.), *Cognition and second language instruction* (pp. 3–32). Cambridge, UK: Cambridge University Press.

Shehadeh, A. (1999). Non-Native speakers' production of modified comprehensible output and second language learning. *Language Learning, 49*, 4. 627–75.

Skehan, P. (1996). A framework for the implementation of task-based instruction. *Applied Linguistics, 17*, 1, 38–62.

Skehan, P. (1998). *A cognitive approach to language learning.* Oxford: Oxford University Press.

Slobin, D. I. (1985). Crosslinguistic evidence for the language-making capacity. In D. I. Slobin (Ed.), *The crosslinguistic study of language acquisition*, Vol. 2: *Theoretical issues* (pp. 1157–1259). Hillsdale, NJ: Lawrence Erlbaum.

Swain, M. (1985). Communicative competence: Some roles of comprehensible input and comprehensible output in its development. In S. Gass & C. Madden (Eds.), *Input in second language acquisition* (pp. 235–53). Cambridge, MA: Newbury House.

Swain, M. (1995). Thee functions of output in second language learning. In G. Cook, & B. Seidlhoffer (Eds.), *Principles & practice in applied linguistics: Studies in honor of H. G. Widdowson* (pp. 125–44). Oxford: Oxford University Press.

Swain, M. (1998). Focus on form through conscious reflection. In C. Doughty & J. Williams (Eds.), *Focus on form in classroom second language acquisition* (pp.64–81). New York: Cambridge University Press.

Swain, M. (2000). The output hypothesis and beyond: Mediating acquisition through collaborative dialogue. In J. Lantolf (Ed.), *Sociocultural theory and second language learning* (pp. 97–114). Oxford: Oxford University Press.

Swain, M. (2005). The output hypothesis: Theory and research. In E. Hinkel (Ed.), *Handbook of research in second language teaching and learning* (pp. 471–81). Mahwah, NJ: Lawrence Erlbaum.

Swain, M., & Lapkin, S. (1995). Problems in output and the cognitive processes they generate: A step towards second language learning. *Applied Linguistics, 16*, 371–91.

Takashima, H., & Ellis, R. (1999). Output enhancement and the acquisition of the past tense. In R. Ellis (Ed.), *Learning a second language through interaction* (pp. 173–88). Amsterdam/Philadelphia: John Benjamins.

Tarone, T., & Liu, G. Q. (1995). Situational context, variation, and second language acquisition theory. In G. Cook & B. Seidlhoffer (Eds.), *Principles & practice in applied linguistics: Studies in honor of H. G. Widdowson* (pp. 107–24). Oxford: Oxford University Press.

Tomlin, R., & Villa, V. (1994). Attention in cognitive science and second language acquisition. *Studies in Second Language Acquisition, 16*, 2, 183–204.

Towell, R., & Hawkins, R. (1994). *Approaches to second language acquisition.* Clevedon, UK: Multilingual Matters.

Towell, R., Hawkins, R., & Bazergui, N. (1996). The development of fluency in advanced learners of French. *Applied Linguistics, 17*, 1, 84–119.

Van den Branden, K. (1997). Effects of negotiation on language learners' output. *Language Learning, 47*, 589–636.

VanPatten, B. (1996). *Input processing and grammar instruction: Theory and research.* Norwood, NJ: Ablex.

VanPatten, B. (2003). *From input to output: A teacher's guide to second language acquisition.* Boston: McGraw-Hill.

VanPatten, B., & Cadierno, T. (1993). Explicit instruction and input processing. *Studies in Second Language Acquisition, 15*, 2, 225–43.

VanPatten, B., & Sanz, C. (1995). From input to output: Processing instruction and communicative tasks. In F. Eckman, D. Highland, P. W. Lee, J. Mileham, & R. R. Weber (Eds.), *Second language acquisition theory and pedagogy* (pp. 169–85). Mahwah, NJ: Lawrence Erlbaum.

Wajnryb, R. (1990). *Grammar dictation.* Oxford: Oxford University Press.

Wheeldon, L. (Ed.). (2000). *Aspects of language production.* East Sussex, UK: Psychology Press.

3 Interaction as practice

Alison Mackey

Introduction

Research on interaction in second language acquisition points to the importance of a range of interactional processes in the second language learning process. These processes include negotiation for meaning, the provision of feedback, and the production of modified output, as well as cognitive (learner-internal) factors such as attention, noticing, and memory for language. Research on interaction is often applied in second language classrooms through corrective feedback practices and the use of communicative tasks, and it brings together a number of related processes. Accordingly, this chapter integrates several of the constructs and processes discussed independently in other chapters in this volume, most notably input (Leow), feedback (Leeman), and output (Muranoi).

The development of the Interaction Hypothesis

One of the innovations in second language (L2) work over the last 25 years has been the development of research into the cognitive mechanisms that underlie second language acquisition. Research into L2 interaction can be traced to several lines originating in the 1970s. For example, Krashen's (1978) formulation of the input hypothesis suggested that adult second language learning was driven primarily by exposure to sufficient amounts of comprehensible input – that is, input that learners can understand. These ideas represented a shift in thinking from earlier claims about language learning, such as those made by Lado (1957) whose contrastive analysis hypothesis emphasized descriptions of what learners might find more or less difficult to learn. Krashen's hypothesis centered around the notion that comprehension was the primary site for language learning, while production was viewed as a reflection of what had been learned. The promotion of comprehensible input is currently one of the primary goals of many immersion programs, comprehension-based programs, and communicative language teaching. However, research into second language learning in settings where learners had access to large quantities of comprehensible input has indicated that comprehensible input alone might not be sufficient for second language learning. For example, in Swain's (1985) influential study of the L2 comprehension and production of Anglophone learners in French immersion schools, learners who demonstrated near-nativelike comprehension on direct language measures and in performance on the content of their coursework nonetheless evidenced significantly non-nativelike production. Findings such as these led Swain to focus on the importance of output in the L2 learning process and to suggest that output was more than a reflection of learning, representing, in fact, a crucial part of the L2 learning process (Swain, 1985, 1995, 1998, 2005). Another important line of research associated with the Interaction Hypothesis was developed by Hatch (1978) and Wagner-Gough and Hatch (1975), who were among the first L2 researchers to consider the role of conversation in the development of a second language, suggesting that "language learning evolves out of learning how to carry on conversations, out of learning how to communicate" (Hatch, 1978, p. 63). Hatch and her colleagues' work took both input and output into consideration, suggesting that conversational interaction was an important means for learners to gain access to comprehensible input as well as for opportunities to produce linguistic output.

These early arguments about comprehensible input, modified output, and the role of conversation were synthesized in a set of specific claims initially proposed by Long (1981) and known in the second language acquisition (SLA) field as the Interaction Hypothesis. Simply put, the hypothesis suggests that participating in conversational interaction facilitates L2 learning. Long's (1996) influential update of the Interaction Hypothesis brings claims about input, interaction, and output together with suggestions that learners' internal capacities are part of the L2 learning process. This reformulated hypothesis describes helpful types of interaction as including the opportunity to receive comprehensible input, the provision of feedback on L2 form, and the opportunity to produce modified output (Gass, 1997; Long, 1996; Pica, 1994). Work by Gass (1997) and Pica (1994) has further specified the nature of the claims made in the Interaction Hypothesis, suggesting that interaction may provide learners with opportunities to make connections between L2 form and meaning. Gass (1997) also comments on learner-internal processes during interaction, arguing that "learners gain additional information about the language and focus their attention on particular parts of the language. This attention primes language for insertion into a developing interlanguage system" (p. 87). More recently, the interaction hypothesis has been further specified, with Gass & Mackey's (in press) overview in Williams & VanPatten's (in press) collection on theories in SLA, and Mackey's (in press) further specification of the mechanisms involved in interaction driven learning.

Interactional Processes

Claims have been made individually and collectively about the importance of interactional processes in L2 learning, including comprehensible input, feedback, and modified output. Long (1996) proposes that feedback obtained during conversational interaction promotes interlanguage development because interaction "connects input, internal learner capacities, particularly selective attention, and output in productive ways" (pp. 451–2). Swain has claimed that modified output benefits L2 development because "learners need to be pushed to make use of their resources; they need to have their linguistic abilities stretched to their fullest; they need to reflect on their output and consider ways of modifying it to enhance comprehensibility, appropriateness and accuracy" (1993, p. 160–1). Pica has claimed that language learning should be seen as the "interaction among the cognitive, psycholinguistic and social processes of language learning as well as the interaction of various processes within them" (1998, p. 10).

Input, interaction and SLA theory construction

SLA researchers suggest that interaction provides learners with learning opportunities through input and output processes involving critical linguistic information during exchanges of communicative importance and that the cognitive mechanisms that drive learning are optimally engaged in processing form/meaning relationships in linguistic data. Interaction is claimed to be necessary but not sufficient for L2 learning. Current work suggests that there is more than one route to L2 development through interaction, with learners perceiving feedback differently depending on the type, the relevant area of language (e.g., morphosyntax, lexis, phonology), and possibly the specific target of the feedback (Mackey, Gass, & McDonough, 2000). To date, there is no claim that one or more of the interactional processes, including comprehensible input, feedback, and modified output, work better than any of the others, although it is possible that these processes may be differentially effective for various aspects of language, learner characteristics, contexts, and task demands. Indeed, interactional processes may work in concert or in unique ways.

The applicability of research on interaction to theory construction in SLA can be seen in a range of different paradigms. One of the most important recent claims about L2 learning, and one which seems destined to drive the field of SLA forward, is Ellis's (2002) frequency-based account of SLA. In concluding his account, Ellis claims that "the role of frequency has largely been ignored in theoretical and applied linguistics for the last 40 years or so.... There is now ample evidence for its reinstatement as an all-pervasive causal factor. In the final analysis of successful language acquisition and processing, it is the language learner who counts" (p. 179). In building his argument, Ellis gives some credit to the processes involved in interaction for making form-meaning connections salient to the learner, maintaining that these processes provide input, time on task and the opportunity to relate form and function, all of which he claims are necessary for developing the associations required for language learning. Gass and Mackey (2002) have argued that one of the functions of interaction may be to provide learners with multiple exemplars of targetlike input in a way that allows learners, as active participants in interaction, to connect form and meaning at exactly the right time; in other words, interaction may repeatedly provide and strengthen more targetlike schemata at precisely the moments when problems arise. It also provides opportunities to produce output, which may act to sensitize learners to associations in future input. The relationship between input frequency and SLA is clearly an important one that requires more research.

In an alternative perspective on SLA, Carroll (2000) points to a restricted role for interactional feedback in her autonomous induction theory, which is based on her interpretation of Universal Grammar. Carroll claims that learners can learn exceptions to generalizations, inducing the generalizations themselves on the basis of both direct and indirect forms of feedback. She also notes that in her model there is no causal relationship between feedback and correction in learning distinctions "too far removed" from the conceptual system (pp. 340–1).

The importance and relevance of research findings on input and interaction to SLA theory construction is clear. Claims about the relationship of interactional processes in the linguistic environment to language acquisition have also been advanced in relation to the first language context. For example, Tomasello (2003) has made arguments similar to those of Ellis (2002) about frequency-based accounts in first language acquisition, explicitly rejecting any role for Universal Grammar. Sokolov and Snow (1994) have argued for the importance of findings on input and interaction in first language acquisition in relation to first language acquisition theory, claiming that children need not be viewed as passive learners, driven either by innate constraints or by contingencies in the environment and that every learning pattern is the product of a learner-environment interaction.

In summary then, several processes that take place during interaction have been claimed to benefit L2 learning, often in different ways. While not intended to be a comprehensive, causal theory of L2 learning, interaction can be seen as a window through which to view important aspects of the L2 learning process and as a facilitator of many of the processes. In order to explore the interaction-learning relationship, researchers have examined the developmental benefits of a range of processes that often overlap. These include negotiation for meaning, feedback, recasts, and output. Each of these will be discussed in turn in the following sections. As noted earlier, other chapters in this volume also discuss some of these processes, including output (Muranoi) and feedback (Leeman). However, the focus in the next section is the role these processes play in interaction, not an in-depth exploration of the processes themselves.

Negotiation for meaning

During negotiation for meaning, learners work to achieve comprehensibility of what is being said. Negotiation involves feedback and modifications to input or output. When negotiating for meaning, interlocutors shift the flow of conversation to clarify misunderstandings caused by insufficient or faulty linguistic knowledge (Gass & Varonis, 1985, 1989; Long, 1996; Pica, 1994). Long (1996) defines negotiation as "the process in which, in an effort to communicate, learners and competent speakers provide and interpret signals of their own and their interlocutor's perceived comprehension, thus provoking adjustments to linguistic form, conversational structure, message content, or all three, until an acceptable level of understanding is achieved" (p. 418). In interactions between native speakers and learners, learner-initiated negotiation often leads to the provision of modified input by the interlocutor, while native speaker-initiated negotiation often leads to the production of modified output by the learner. Negotiation may also provide learners with additional time to focus on how meaning is encoded (Gass & Varonis, 1985). Pica (1994, 1996) describes how negotiation contributes to the language learning process by addressing a number of L2 learners' needs. She argues that negotiation facilitates comprehension of second language input, and that through the processes of repetition, segmentation, and rewording, negotiation serves to draw learners' attention to second language form-meaning relationships.

An example of how negotiated interaction may be operating to facilitate L2 development can be seen in Example 1. The learner does not understand the word *glasses*. The word is repeated, the original phrase is extended and rephrased, a synonym is provided, and the learner eventually seems to understand the word.

Example 1: Negotiation for meaning

NS:	there's there's a a pair of reading glasses above the plant
NNS:	a what?
NS:	glasses reading glasses to see the newspaper?
NNS:	glassi?
NS:	you wear them to see with, if you can't see reading glasses

NNS: ahh ahh glasses glasses to read you say reading glasses
NS: yeah

(Mackey, 1999, p. 559)

Gass (1997) also describes how negotiation facilitates second language learning by triggering clarification and elaboration of the input. She claims that negotiation can provide learners with enhanced and salient input as well as feedback on their production. She further argues that negotiation can draw learners' attention to linguistic problems, proposing that an initial step in grammar change is the learners' noticing of a mismatch between the input and their own organization of the target language.

Much of the early work on interaction described interactional processes in terms of negotiation for meaning and focused on the role of negotiation in promoting comprehensible input, providing many descriptions and models of negotiation (see Gass, Mackey, & Pica, 1998; Long, 1996, for summaries). In the 1990s, researchers moved on from describing the ways in which interactional modifications led to improved comprehension; they began to focus on more direct testing of how interaction impacted L2 production (Gass & Varonis, 1994; Polio & Gass, 1998; Silver, 2000) and in a few cases how interaction impacted L2 learning (Mackey, 1999). Simply put, a significant body of empirical work has provided support for claims that interaction benefits learning. Studies have been carried out with both children and adults, and in both classroom (e.g., Doughty & Varela, 1998; Ellis, Tanaka, & Yamazaki, 1994; Mackey, 2000, 2006; Oliver, 2000; Storch, 2002) and laboratory settings (e.g., Ayoun, 2001; Braidi, 2002; Gass & Varonis, 1994; Han, 2002; Iwashita, 2003; Leeman, 2003; Long, Inagaki, & Ortega, 1998; Mackey, 1999; Mackey & Oliver, 2002; Mackey, Oliver, & Leeman, 2003; Mackey & Philp, 1998; Oliver, 1998; Philp, 2003). The operationalization of L2 learning has varied across the studies; some studies measured development using pre- and post-tests (e.g., Ayoun, 2001; Doughty & Varela, 1998; Ellis et al., 1994; Han, 2002; Iwashita, 2003; Leeman, 2003; Long et al., 1998; Mackey, 1999; Mackey & Oliver, 2002; Mackey & Philp, 1998), while others regarded learners' uptake as evidence of learning (e.g., Braidi, 2002; Mackey et al., 2003; Oliver, 1998, 2000).

Current work on interaction also focuses on directly examining the interaction-L2 learning relationship. However, in addition to exploring interactional processes such as negotiation as monolithic constructs or collectively beneficial processes, recent studies have sought to characterize and explain the interaction-learning relationship by utilizing a more finely grained analysis of the components of interaction. This approach has led to a deconstruction of many of the general constructs of interactional processes and a trend toward the operationalization and experimental isolation of more specific aspects of each of them in order to examine their impact on learning individually as well as collectively. The next sections describe current interaction research in terms of how it has isolated and tested the L2 learning outcomes of feedback, recasts, and output.

Feedback during interaction

Following a long line of work in the field of first language acquisition (see the interesting review by Nicholas, Lightbown, & Spada, 2001, for more details), current theoretical work in SLA has suggested that an important source of interactional benefits is the feedback learners receive on their utterances (Gass, 1997; Long, 1996; Swain, 1995). As Leeman (this volume) explains in more detail, feedback provides learners with information about the success of their utterances. Feedback can be positive or negative, and it can be more or less explicit. Negative feedback refers to information that informs learners that their utterances were problematic. Through negative feedback, learners receive information about the accuracy, communicative success, or content of their production. Such feedback may also provide learners with additional opportunities to focus on their production or comprehension. In Example 2, an excerpt of interaction between a native speaker (NS) and a non-native speaker (NNS) shows feedback being provided on L2 grammar in the form of a simple repetition and clarification request ("floors?"). This example is taken from a study that utilized a retrospective interview procedure known as stimulated recall protocol and, as explained in depth in Gass and Mackey (2000) investigated learners' insights into negative feedback after it had been provided (the study is reported in Mackey et al., 2000). The NNS's retrospective comment about the interaction implies she recognized that the feedback suggested a problem with her phonology.

Example 2: Feedback

NNS:	There are /flurs/?
NS:	Floors? ← **Feedback**
NNS:	/fluw'rs/ uh flowers.
NNS retrospective comments:	I was thinking my pronounce, pronunciation is very horrible.

(Mackey et al., 2000, p. 486)

A number of interaction studies have shown that interactional feedback is associated with L2 learning (e.g., Ayoun, 2001; Braidi, 2002; Doughty & Varela, 1998; Han, 2002; Leeman, 2003; Long et al., 1998; Mackey et al., 2003; Mackey & Philp, 1998; Oliver, 1998, 2000). Much of the current research focuses on understanding the specific contributions of negative feedback provided during interaction. One form of feedback, recasts, is proving to be a particularly fertile area of investigation with the aim of increasing our understanding of interactional processes in SLA.

RECASTS AS INTERACTIONAL FEEDBACK

Long (1996) has argued that recasts and negotiation for meaning both function to direct learners' attention toward linguistic form in the context of interaction. Nicholas et al. (2001) have defined recasts as "utterances that repeat a learner's incorrect utterance, making only the changes necessary to produce a correct utterance, without changing the meaning" (p. 733). Recasts are more linguistically targetlike reformulations of what a learner has just said.

Negotiation for meaning inevitably requires learner involvement, as shown in Examples 1 and 2. Recasts themselves, on the other hand, do not always make participatory demands on the learner. As some researchers (e.g., Lyster, 1998a, 1998b) have pointed out, while recasts provide the learner with more targetlike forms, they may be perceived by the learner as an optional and alternative way to say the same thing. Thus, learners may not repeat or rephrase their original utterances following recasts, and they may not even perceive recasts as feedback at all (Mackey et al., 2000). Of course, the fact that learners sometimes fail to identify feedback as such does not necessarily imply that the feedback is not beneficial for learners. Regardless of responses, recasts provided during interaction have been implicated in L2 learning in a number of studies (Ayoun, 2001; Braidi, 2002; Han, 2002; Leeman, 2003; Mackey & Philp, 1998; Morris, 2002; Philp, 2003; Storch, 2002). Whereas some researchers such as Lyster (1998a, 1998b) and Panova and Lyster (2002) have suggested that recasts do not lead to responses, or uptake, other researchers such as Mackey and Philp (1998) have pointed out that it may be a mistake to equate responses and L2 learning because an immediate response may or may not be indicative of a more permanent restructuring. Oliver has also pointed out that examination of the discourse context is important because responses may occur more in some settings and contexts than others and may in fact be problematic because of the discourse constraints in certain contexts (Oliver, 1995, 1998, 2000; Oliver & Mackey, 2003).

Output during interaction

Current claims about the L2 learning process emphasize the role of modified output (Ellis & He, 1999; Muranoi, this volume; Shehadeh, 2002; Swain, 1985, 1995, 1998, 2005). Learners may modify their utterances after receiving feedback. In Example 3, two learners are collaborating on a task that involves finding routes on a map. After producing an initially problematic utterance ("turn another side") and receiving feedback about its lack of comprehensibility, Learner 1 appears to realize that her utterance was not understood. She then reformulates her initial utterance, modifying her output from "turn another side" to the (more grammatical) "turn to the left side." Learner 2 comprehends, and the conversation (and task-completion process) proceeds.

Example 3: Modified output

Learner 1:   In front of library, turn another side from grocery store
Learner 2:   Which side from the grocery?
Learner 1:   Ah, er turn to the left side ← **Modified Output**
Learner 2:   Ok turn left, I did it, now which way to turn?

(Mackey, 2000)

Researchers have argued that when learners modify their output, positive developmental effects occur (Gass, 1997; Swain, 1995). Swain has claimed that learners may be "pushed" to produce more accurate, appropriate, complex, and comprehensible forms following feedback from an interlocutor (Swain, 1993; Swain & Lapkin, 1995; see also Gass, 1988, 1997; Long, 1996; Pica, 1994). When interlocutors signal that an utterance has been incomprehensible or ill-formed, learners may reflect on their language and modify the linguistic and pragmatic features of their output. Claims for the benefits of modified output apply whether the modified production is more, less, or equally as grammatical as the learner's first (problematic) utterance. It has been argued that modified production is useful in part because it may promote cognitive processing of morphosyntax, or grammar, as well as of semantics, or meaning, thereby promoting automaticity (Anderson, 1993; de Bot, 1996; DeKeyser, 1997, 2001; Doughty, 2001; Logan, 1992). As DeKeyser (1997, see also DeKeyser, 2001) has shown, automatic comprehension can be achieved through comprehension practice, but only production practice leads to lower reaction times and higher accuracy in the production of linguistic targets. Such findings indicate that output is essential for integrating new linguistic representations into the existing schema. There has also been speculation that modified output may be developmentally useful because of the role it plays in promoting learner awareness of form, encouraging learners to pay attention to L2 grammar (Schmidt, 1995, 2001; Schmidt & Frota, 1986). Proponents of modified output claim that it operates by drawing learners' attention to grammatical structures, making the structures salient and thereby creating a context for L2 learning (McDonough, 2001, 2005; Swain, 1995). A number of empirical studies have been carried out to identify the amount and type of modified output that learners produce in response to different types of negative feedback (Iwashita, 2001; Pica, 1988; Pica, Holliday,

Lewis, & Morgenthaler, 1989; Shehadeh, 1999, 2001; Van den Branden, 1997). Although the majority of this research has been descriptive (Shehadeh, 2002), some experimental studies have found positive relationships between modified output and L2 learning (Ellis & He, 1999; Izumi, 1999, 2002; Izumi, Bigelow, Fujiwara, & Fearnow, 1999; Mackey, 1997; McDonough, 2001, 2005; Nobuyoshi & Ellis, 1993; Silver, 2000) and between output and noticing of L2 form (Qi & Lapkin, 2001; Swain & Lapkin, 1998).

UNMODIFIED OUTPUT DURING INTERACTION

Of course, despite interactional contexts that provide negative feedback with opportunities to modify output, learners do not always reformulate their ungrammatical forms correctly. Instead, they may repeat their original utterances, modify grammatical features in the direction of the target or not, or not respond to the feedback at all. In Example 4 (from a small-scale study by Nobuyoshi & Ellis, 1993), the learner was telling a story requiring past tense forms. After her interlocutor requested clarification ("sorry?"), the learner repeated the initial utterance ("but he sleep") without any more targetlike modifications.

Example 4: Output without TL modification

Learner: But he sleep. He becomes asleep.
Teacher: Sorry?
Learner: But he sleep. He become asleep.
                                        (Nobuyoshi & Ellis, 1993, p. 208)

Learners may not perceive interlocutors' feedback as providing information about the acceptability of their utterances (Birdsong, 1989; Carroll, 1995); they may not perceive the targets of the feedback or may not be at the correct developmental level to modify their utterances (Mackey et al., 2000). Nonetheless, it is possible that the feedback might be associated with some sort of change in their underlying interlanguage systems even when there is no immediate surface manifestation of that change in the learners' production. Evidence for this might come in the form of studies that demonstrate a relationship between feedback and short- or long-term learning, but without a change in immediate production (Gass, 1988; Mackey & Philp, 1998).

MODIFIED OUTPUT (UPTAKE) DURING INTERACTION

Learners' immediate incorporation of interactional feedback is referred to as uptake in much of the research on classroom interaction. (Ellis, Basturkmen, & Loewen, 2001a, 2001b; Lyster, 1998a, 1998b; Lyster & Ranta, 1997; Panova & Lyster, 2002). Uptake is related to the construct of modified output and has been defined as "a student's utterance that immediately follows the teacher's feedback and that constitutes a reaction in some way to the teacher's intention to draw attention to some aspect of the student's initial utterance" – in other words, an acknowledgement of feedback (Lyster & Ranta, 1997, p. 49). Whereas modified output generally implies a modification of an original linguistic form, the term *uptake* extends the meaning of modified output since uptake encompasses simple acknowledgements of feedback, such as "OK." In examining the utility of feedback, Oliver (1995) investigated whether non-native speakers correctly incorporated native speaker feedback into subsequent turns. Oliver calculated the percentage of incorporation of feedback based on the number of cases where learners had a discoursally appropriate *opportunity* to incorporate feedback, rather than on the total number of times learners actually received feedback. In more recent work, Ellis et al. (2001a, 2001b) have extended the meaning of uptake to include any incorporation by the learner of previously provided explicit or implicit information about a linguistic feature. As discussed above, some interaction researchers have argued that in addition to serving as evidence of "noticing" or "attending" to feedback, constructs such as uptake and modified output also function as helpful opportunities for production practice. These are interesting ideas, but such claims clearly require careful empirical attention. McDonough's (2005) study, which demonstrates that modified output in response to negative feedback facilitated L2 learning, provides a helpful model for how such questions can be explored.

In summary then, much of the recent interaction research has isolated different aspects of interaction and has found them to be associated with various sorts of learning or interlanguage change. One of the questions being asked in current interaction studies is *how* interaction-driven learning comes about.

How does interaction work to impact L2 learning?

Learners' internal capacities: Attention and noticing in interaction

As shown in the earlier descriptions of interactional processes, claims about attention, awareness, and noticing have been made in the context of feedback, recasts, output, and negotiation for meaning in general. Leow (this volume) also discusses these issues, providing his attentional perspective on input. The influential concept of noticing in SLA can be traced to research by Schmidt and Frota (1986), which centered on a diary study of L2 learning in an immersion environment supplemented by periodic language tests. The trend apparent in their data is that the learner acquires forms soon after evidence of noticing the forms in the input or during classroom experiences. This study led to the development of two major theoretical perspectives on the role of attention in the field of SLA: the work of Schmidt (1990, 1993, 1995, 2001) and Robinson (1995, 2001, 2002) on the one hand and that of Tomlin and Villa (1994) on the other.

According to Schmidt (1990, 1993, 1995), learning cannot take place without awareness because the learner must be consciously aware of linguistic input for it to become internalized; thus, awareness and learning cannot be dissociated. Schmidt differentiates between two levels of awareness: at the level of noticing linguistic input and at the level of understanding linguistic input. Schmidt claims that awareness at the level of noticing is necessary for language learning, while awareness at the level of understanding is facilitative but not necessary for SLA. Robinson's (1995, 2001, 2002) perspective is similar, concurring with Schmidt about the crucial role of awareness in SLA. In Robinson's model, detection of linguistic input involves awareness and rehearsal processes. Robinson also claims that attention to input is a consequence of encoding in working memory, and only input encoded in working memory may be subsequently transferred to long-term memory. Thus, in Robinson's model, as in Schmidt's, attention is crucial for learning, and no learning can take place without attention and some level of awareness.

An alternative and distinct perspective, emerging from work in cognitive psychology (Posner, 1988, 1992; Posner & Peterson, 1990), is presented by Tomlin and Villa (1994) and advocates a disassociation between learning and awareness. They divide attention into three components: *alertness* (a general readiness to deal with incoming stimuli); *orientation* (the directing of attentional resources to specific stimuli); and *detection* (the cognitive registration of the stimuli). They claim that SLA and awareness can be dissociated, contending that it is the attentional function of detection of linguistic input that is crucial for L2 learning to take place. Claims about attention have also been debated. Truscott's (1998) critical review of claims about attention, awareness, and noticing points out how difficult it is to falsify such claims; Leow (1998) points to problems in operationalizing noticing empirically, and Simard and Wong (2001) have discussed problems with modeling attention.

Interaction research has typically made little reference to specific models of noticing, awareness, and attention, although most researchers place importance on these processes. Rather, these terms have been used in a general (and often seemingly interchangeable) way in claims about the utility of interaction. For example, Long (1996) describes the importance in interaction of "internal learner capacities, particularly selective attention" (pp. 451–2). Ellis (1999) claims that interaction can alert learners to potential gaps in their interlanguage which they can then address by paying attention to input. Swain's (1998) claims about the noticing function of output and Pica's (1994) suggestions about noticing of input are similarly nonspecific. Gass (1997) states that "attention, accomplished in part through negotiation, is one of the crucial mechanisms in this process" (p. 132). Mackey et al. (2000) argue that "it is assumed that, through interaction, some aspects of attention may become focused on the parts of their language that deviate from target language norms . . . a second assumption is that this attention, or noticing of the gap (Schmidt & Frota, 1986) between learner language forms and target language forms, is a step toward change" (p. 473). It would be desirable for future claims about the role of attention in interaction-driven learning to be formulated in more specific and testable ways.

Interaction-driven learning and individual differences

While some researchers have focused on empirically researching the interaction-learning relationship and have looked to general claims about attention to explain their findings, others have sought to make connections between the cognitive capacities of individual learners and engagement in interaction or learning from interaction. Research on individual differences is gaining in importance in the SLA field. As Sawyer and Ranta (2001) explain, the fact that "individuals who attempt to learn a foreign language differ dramatically in their rate of acquisition and in their ultimate attainment" (p. 319) fuels much research. The role of learners' internal capacities in shaping and utilizing learning opportunities during interaction is thus an emerging theme in recent research. If internal capacities constrain interactional processes, for example, in the allocation of attentional resources for noticing input/output mismatches, as suggested by Robinson (2002), learners' engagement in interaction may be impacted, as may their developmental outcomes.

Individual differences in second language learning in general have been attributed to a range of factors including language aptitude, working memory, cognitive styles, social context, learning strategies, and motivation. Within interaction research in particular, specific claims about sources of individual variation have been made in relation to constructs from cognitive psychology such as working memory (Mackey, Philp, Egi, Fujii, & Tatsumi, 2002) and aptitude (Robinson, 1997). Research on aptitude and motivation is discussed by Robinson (this volume), so those topics will not be revisited here. Instead, this section discusses individual differences in working memory in the context of interaction.

WORKING MEMORY AND SLA RESEARCH

There seems to be a consensus in the general SLA literature that the cognitive processes that underlie working memory capacity and attention are related. For example, Engle, Kane, and Tuholski (1999) argue that working memory capacity refers to controlled attention in the face of distraction, and individual differences in working memory capacity reflect individual differences in controlled attention. Miyake and Shah (1999) refer to the "already well-accepted point that working memory, attention and consciousness are related to one another" (p. 461). Interpreting such claims for the SLA community, Sawyer and Ranta (2001) note that if "attention at any moment is limited by working memory capacity, then there must logically be a close relationship between amount of learning and size of WM" (p. 342).

Within the general framework of cognitive and psycholinguistic accounts of SLA (e.g., DeKeyser, 1998; Ellis, 1998, 1999; Healy & Bourne, 1998; Segalowitz & Lightbown, 1999; Skehan, 1998), an important role has been ascribed to working memory capacity in relation to verbal input during L2 learning (Ellis, 1996; Ellis & Schmidt, 1997; Ellis & Sinclair, 1996; Miyake & Friedman, 1998; Robinson, 1995, 2002; Sawyer & Ranta, 2001; Skehan, 1998; Williams & Lovatt, 2003). Studies of working memory and SLA have focused on the relationship between individual differences in working memory and L2 performance, as well as on investigating the role of various components of working memory in L2 learning. For example, a number of SLA researchers have focused on phonological short-term memory, which is one component of what Baddeley (1990) refers to as the "working memory system." Findings generally support an important role for different aspects of working memory in L2 learning. Early experimental studies such as Daneman and Case (1981), Papagno, Valentine, and Baddeley (1991), and Papagno and Vallar (1992) demonstrated that phonological short-term memory played a role in the learning of novel lexical items. A similar relationship was found between working memory and L2 vocabulary acquisition in a longitudinal study of Finnish children by Service (1992) and Service and Kohonen (1995). More recent studies have suggested that phonological short-term memory may be involved not only in lexical acquisition but also in the acquisition of grammatical rules (Ellis & Schmidt, 1997; Ellis & Sinclair, 1996; Williams, 1999; Williams & Lovatt, 2003). Ellis and Sinclair (1996), for example, compared the effects of learners' phonological rehearsal of Welsh utterances on elements such as comprehension, metalinguistic knowledge, and acquisition, concluding that "individual differences in STM and working memory can have profound effects on language *acquisition*" (p. 247, emphasis in the original). These claims find support in a number of studies, most recently in one by Williams and Lovatt (2003), who report that three distinct measures of phonological short-term memory were related to the learning of grammatical rules in artificial microlanguages. Other research (e.g., Ando, Fukunaga, Kurahashu, Suto, Nakano, & Kage, 1992; Harrington & Sawyer, 1992;

Miyake & Friedman, 1998) has addressed a more active, simultaneous storage/processing function of memory, sometimes referred to as verbal working memory. Taken together, the studies in this area provide both indirect and direct empirical support for the involvement of various aspects of working memory in L2 learning.

WORKING MEMORY AND INTERACTION-DRIVEN LEARNING

Empirical studies of second language interaction have pointed to claims about individual differences in working memory in order to explain their findings that learners vary in terms of how and whether they learn following communicative interactional feedback. In research conducted by Ando et al. (1992) and Mackey et al. (2002) addressing this issue, learners with higher working memory capacities tended to demonstrate more lasting benefits from communicative instruction and interaction, whereas those with lower working memory capacities seemed to make more immediate use of the communicative interaction. Explanations suggest that learners with higher working memory capacities may be engaged in cognitive comparisons between target language forms and their own versions of the forms, impacting processing loads and immediate performance. Learners with lower working memory capacities, in contrast, may be better equipped to engage in immediate modifications to output at a potential longer-term cost to comparison, storage, and subsequent retrieval mechanisms. Miyake and Shah (1999) have suggested that "limitations in working memory may facilitate certain types of learning" with lower working memory capacities being "particularly beneficial for detecting subtle yet important probabilistic regularities in the environment, an ability crucially important for language acquisition" (p. 465). As Williams (1999) points out, "individual differences in memory ability that are apparent even in the earliest stages of exposure have consequences for ultimate levels of learning" (p. 22). Such research suggests that learners with different working memory capacities may benefit from different kinds of interactional feedback. Specifically, learners with lower working memory capacities might benefit more from feedback, such as recasting, which provides them with opportunities to make cognitive comparisons without also requiring modifications to their output for longer-term interlanguage change. Robinson (2002) claims that memory for contingent speech may be "particularly relevant to distinguishing between learners who benefit from implicit negative feedback provided by targeted recasts during oral interaction" (p. 118), exemplifying the link between internal learner capacities and effective learning conditions. These notions are clearly speculative. Factors such as learners' working memory capacities may interact with their developmental levels amongst many other things. However, second language researchers are beginning to investigate these issues.

Interactional processes, communicative tasks and pedagogy

Findings from second language learning through interaction research have been linked to the L2 classroom in several ways. One of the most widely known is in the form of empirical support for communicative language teaching. Claims about form-focused instruction (Spada, 1997) and focus on form (Long & Robinson, 1998) are also supported by some of the interaction research results. Findings from interaction research suggest that positive outcomes obtain when language learners have opportunities to negotiate for comprehensible input, receive feedback, and modify their output. Interaction research findings thus provide an empirical basis for communicative instructional approaches that support these processes and provide opportunities for learners to make form-meaning connections while they are engaged in communicating meaning. Interaction research also points to the crucial nature of feedback in the L2 learning process. The provision of feedback is a critical issue for L2 instructors, who often have questions about when, how, and on which forms to provide feedback. These factors are discussed by Leeman (this volume), who also points out that the most effective types of feedback depend, to some extent, on the source of the linguistic problem.

A common bridge between classroom methodology and interaction research is found in communicative tasks, through an approach known as task-based language teaching (Bygate, Skehan, & Swain, 2001; Ellis, 2003). One of the principal motivations behind some, although certainly not all, SLA research is the promotion of second language pedagogy, and second language researchers have come to believe that certain types of activities may be particularly effective in promoting language development because of the interactional processes they involve. The Interaction Hypothesis, with its emphasis on cognitive implications and learning outcomes of interactional processes, is often cited in support of claims about the importance of tasks in L2 learning, or as support for the task-based language teaching approach (Bygate et al., 2001; Ellis, 2003). Ellis (2003) points out that because interaction has been seen as central to SLA, the study of how task design and implementation affect interaction affords important insights for both instructional course design and language teaching methodology. For example, research findings on task repetition lead us to believe that repetitions of tasks (i.e., practice) are associated with improvements in accuracy, complexity, and fluency (Bygate, 1996, 2001; Gass, Mackey, Fernandez, & Alvarez-Torres, 1999; Lynch & Maclean, 2000, 2001). Research on task familiarity suggests that increased familiarity (gained, one assumes, through practice with the type and/or the content of the task by interacting with one's interlocutor) is associated with beneficial interaction (Plough & Gass, 1993). In a recent study, Mackey, Oliver, and Kanaganas (in press) found that while the children in their study negotiated more and provided more feedback on unfamiliar tasks, they *attended* more to the feedback when the task was familiar. Overall, it seems possible that various types of practice with a task might be associated with more positive language learning opportunities.

Conclusion

The research on the processes of interaction, individual differences in cognition, and communicative tasks reviewed in this chapter reveals many areas of intersection and overlap. The majority of interaction research has demonstrated positive outcomes for interactional processes including negotiation for meaning, feedback, and output in the L2 learning process. The interaction-learning relationship is one of much current interest in SLA, and interaction research has been applied to classrooms through communicative tasks. While research findings such as those reviewed here can help us understand which types of tasks and task features might work best to provide contexts for certain interactional features and linguistic forms, the role of the instructor cannot be underestimated in task-based interaction in the classroom. Instructors select and sequence tasks, provide feedback during interaction, assign learners to pairs and small groups while they carry out the tasks, decide on the instructions and implementation of tasks, and provide opportunities or prompts for modified output and uptake. The learners' level of participation in task-based interaction is clearly also of consequence, so it is important that in managing tasks from their initial phases, instructors frame them in ways that motivate their learners. Dörnyei (2002) suggests that framing strategies that result in learners eagerly anticipating their tasks will have helpful outcomes. Instructors may also decide to provide planning time since planning may result in more complex language and focus on form (Ortega, 1999). Samuda (2001) emphasizes the importance of pre-seeding tasks, not only with structures of interest to instructors but also with contexts for useful interactional processes to occur, a system she refers to as "(p)recasting." Instructors can tailor tasks to the interests and goals of their learners, manipulating features such as task complexity and reasoning demands, both to appeal to learners and to stimulate the productive sorts of interaction that may drive learning. Following the tasks, instructors can provide opportunities for reflection on task performance, including encouraging learners to pay attention to forms that were problematic during the interaction.

In summary, interaction research to date suggests that there is more than one route to L2 development. Interactional processes such as negotiation for meaning, feedback, recasts, and modified output have individually and collectively been shown to be developmentally helpful. The effects of individual differences in aptitude and working memory, along with fluctuating levels of attention and awareness, also suggest that there are many factors involved in interaction-driven L2 development, and these factors often come together during interactional processes. Interaction research can inform classroom practice by illustrating how instructors can utilize task-based activities to create contexts where interactional processes promote learning. In promoting such learning opportunities in the classroom, instructors can utilize research suggesting that different kinds of tasks and implementations facilitate different kinds of input as well as output from learners and can lead to a range of short- and longer-term linguistic outcomes. Of course, practitioners should always consider the pedagogical implications of interaction research in terms of their own teaching context and determine the practices and techniques appropriate for their learners.

References

Anderson, J. R. (1993). *Rules of the mind*. Hillsdale, NJ: Lawrence Erlbaum.

Ando, J., Fukunaga, N., Kurahashu, J., Suto, T., Nakano, T., & Kage, M. (1992). A comparative study on two ESL teaching methods: The communicative and the grammatical approach. *Japanese Journal of Educational Psychology, 40*, 247–56.

Ayoun, D. (2001). The role of negative and positive feedback in the second language acquisition of the *passé composé* and *imparfait*. *Modern Language Journal, 85*, 226–43.

Baddeley, A. D. (1990). *Human memory: Theory and practice*. London: Lawrence Erlbaum.

Birdsong, D. (1989). *Metalinguistic performance and interlinguistic competence*. New York: Springer.

Braidi, S. M. (2002). Reexamining the role of recasts in native-speaker/ nonnative-speaker interactions. *Language Learning, 52*, 1–42.

Bygate, M. (1996). Effects of task repetition: Appraising the developing language of learners. In J. Willis & D. Willis (Eds.), *Challenge and change in language teaching* (pp. 134–46). London: Heinemann.

Bygate, M. (2001). Effects of task repetition on the structure and control of oral language. In M. Bygate, P. Skehan, & M. Swain (Eds.), *Researching pedagogic tasks: Second language learning, teaching, and testing* (pp. 23–48). Harlow, UK: Pearson.

Bygate, M., Skehan, P., & Swain, M. (2001). *Researching pedagogic tasks: Second language learning, teaching, and testing*. Harlow, UK: Pearson.

Carroll, S. (1995). The irrelevance of verbal feedback to language learning. In L. Eubank, L. Selinker, & M. Sharwood Smith (Eds.), *The current state of interlanguage: Studies in honor of William E. Rutherford* (pp. 73–88). Amsterdam: John Benjamins.

Carroll, S. (2000). *Input and evidence: The raw material of second language acquisition.* Amsterdam: John Benjamins.

Daneman, M., & Case, R. (1981). Syntactic form, semantic complexity, and short-term memory: Influence on children's acquisition of new linguistic structures. *Developmental Psychology, 17,* 367–78.

de Bot, K. (1996). The psycholinguistics of the output hypothesis. *Language Learning, 46,* 529–55.

DeKeyser, R. (1997). Beyond explicit rule learning: Automatizing second language morphosyntax. *Studies in Second Language Acquisition, 19,* 195–222.

DeKeyser, R. (1998). Beyond focus on form: Cognitive perspectives on learning and practicing second language grammar. In C. Doughty & J. Williams (Eds.), *Focus on form in classroom second language acquisition* (pp. 42–63). Cambridge, UK: Cambridge University Press.

DeKeyser, R. (2001). Automaticity and automatization. In P. Robinson (Ed.), *Cognition and second language instruction* (pp. 125–51). Cambridge, UK: Cambridge University Press.

Dörnyei, Z. (2002). The motivational basis of language learning tasks. In P. Robinson (Ed.), *Individual differences and instructed language learning* (pp. 137–58). Amsterdam: John Benjamins.

Doughty, C. (2001). Cognitive underpinnings of focus on form. In P. Robinson (Ed.), *Cognition and second language instruction* (pp. 206–57). Cambridge, UK: Cambridge University Press.

Doughty, C., & Varela, E. (1998). Communicative focus on form. In C. Doughty & J. Williams (Eds.), *Focus on form in classroom second language acquisition* (pp. 114–38). Cambridge, UK: Cambridge University Press.

Ellis, N. (1996). Sequencing in SLA: Phonological memory, chunking, and points of order. *Studies in Second Language Acquisition, 18,* 91–126.

Ellis, N. (1998). Emergentism, connectionism and language learning. *Language Learning, 48,* 631–64.

Ellis, N. (1999). Cognitive approaches to SLA. *Annual Review of Applied Linguistics, 19,* 22–42.

Ellis, N. (2002). Frequency effects in language processing. *Studies in Second Language Acquisition, 24,* 143–88.

Ellis, N., & Schmidt, R. (1997). Morphology and longer distance dependencies: Laboratory research illuminating the A in SLA. *Studies in Second Language Acquisition, 19,* 145–71.

Ellis, N., & Sinclair, S. (1996). Working memory in the acquisition of syntax: Putting language in good order. *The Quarterly Journal of Experimental Psychology, 49,* 234–50.

Ellis, R. (2003). *Task-based language learning and teaching.* Oxford: Oxford University Press.

Ellis, R., Basturkmen, H., & Loewen, S. (2001a). Learner uptake in communicative ESL lessons. *Language Learning, 51,* 281–318.

Ellis, R., Basturkmen, H., & Loewen, S. (2001b). Preemptive focus on form in the ESL classroom. *TESOL Quarterly, 35,* 407–32.

Ellis, R., & He, X. (1999). The roles of modified input and output in the incidental acquisition of word meanings. *Studies in Second Language Acquisition, 21,* 285–301.

Ellis, R., Tanaka, Y., & Yamazaki, A. (1994). Classroom interaction, comprehension and the acquisition of L2 word meanings. *Language Learning, 44,* 449–91.

Engle, R., Kane, M., & Tuholski, S. (1999). Individual differences in working memory capacity and what they tell us about controlled attention, general fluid intelligence, and functions of the prefrontal cortex. In A. Miyake & P. Shah (Eds.), *Models of working memory: Mechanisms of active maintenance and executive control* (pp. 442–81). Cambridge, UK: Cambridge University Press.

Gass, S. M. (1988). Integrating research areas: A framework for second language studies. *Applied Linguistics, 9,* 198–217.

Gass, S. M. (1997). *Input, interaction, and the second language learner.* Mahwah, NJ: Lawrence Erlbaum.

Gass, S. M., & Mackey, A. (2000). *Stimulated recall methodology in second language research.* Mahwah, NJ: Lawrence Erlbaum.

Gass, S. M., & Mackey, A. (2002). Frequency effects and second language acquisition. *Studies in Second Language Acquisition, 24,* 249–60.

Gass, S. & Mackey, A. (in press). Input interaction and output in SLA. In Williams, J. & VanPatten, B. (Eds.). *Theories in SLA.* Mahwah, NJ: Lawrence Erlbaum.

Gass, S. M., Mackey, A., Fernandez, M., & Alvarez-Torres, M. (1999). The effects of task repetition on linguistic output. *Language Learning, 49,* 549–80.

Gass, S. M., Mackey, A., & Pica, T. (1998). The role of input and interaction in second language acquisition: Introduction to the special issue. *Modern Language Journal, 82,* 299–307.

Gass, S. M., & Varonis, E. (1985). Variation in native speaker speech modification to nonnative speakers. *Studies in Second Language Acquisition, 7,* 37–58.

Gass, S. M., & Varonis, E. (1989). Incorporated repairs in nonnative discourse. In M. Eisenstein (Ed.), *The dynamic interlanguage* (pp. 71–86). New York: Plenum Press.

Gass, S. M., & Varonis, E. (1994). Input, interaction and second language production. *Studies in Second Language Acquisition, 16,* 283–302.

Han, Z. (2002). A study of the impact of recasts on tense consistency in L2 output. *TESOL Quarterly, 36,* 543–572.

Harrington, M., & Sawyer, M. (1992). L2 working memory capacity and L2 reading skill. *Studies in Second Language Acquisition, 14,* 25–38.

Hatch, E. (1978). Acquisition of syntax in a second language. In J. C. Richards (Ed.), *Understanding second and foreign language learning* (pp. 34–70). Rowley, MA: Newbury House.

Healy, A., & Bourne, L. (Eds.). (1998). *Foreign language learning: Psycholinguistic studies on training and retention.* Mahwah, NJ: Lawrence Erlbaum.

Iwashita, N. (2001). The effect of learner proficiency on interactional moves and modified output in nonnative-nonnative interaction in Japanese as a foreign language. *System, 29,* 267–87.

Iwashita, N. (2003). Negative feedback and positive evidence in task-based interaction: Differential effects on L2 development. *Studies in Second Language Acquisition, 25,* 1–36.

Izumi, S. (1999). *Promoting, noticing and SLA: An empirical study of the effects of output and input enhancement on ESL relativization.* Unpublished doctoral dissertation, Georgetown University, Washington, DC.

Izumi, S. (2002). Output, input enhancement, and the noticing hypothesis: An experimental study on ESL relativization. *Studies in Second Language Acquisition, 24,* 541–77.

Izumi, S., Bigelow, M., Fujiwara, M., & Fearnow, S. (1999). Testing the output hypothesis: Effects of output on noticing and second language acquisition. *Studies in Second Language Acquisition, 21,* 421–52.

Krashen, S. (1978). Second language acquisition. In W. Dingwall (Ed.), *A survey of linguistic science* (pp. 317–38). Stamford, CT: Greylock.

Lado, R. (1957). *Linguistics across cultures: Applied linguistics for language teachers.* Ann Arbor, MI: University of Michigan.

Leeman, J. (2003). Recasts and second language development: Beyond negative evidence. *Studies in Second Language Acquisition, 25,* 37–63.

Leow, R. P. (1998). Toward operationalizing the process of attention in SLA: Evidence for Tomlin and Villa's (1994) fine-grained analysis of attention. *Applied Psycholinguistics, 19,* 133–59.

Logan, G. D. (1992). Shapes of reaction-time distributions and shapes of learning curves: A test of the instance theory of automaticity. *Journal of Experimental Psychology: Learning, Memory, and Cognition, 18,* 883–914.

Long, M. H. (1981). Input, interaction and second language acquisition. In H. Winitz (Ed.), *Native language and foreign language acquisition: Annals of the New York Academy of Sciences* (Vol. 379), pp. 259–78.

Long, M. H. (1996). The role of the linguistic environment in second language acquisition. In W. C. Ritchie & T. K. Bhatia (Eds.), *Handbook of second language acquisition,* pp. 413–68). New York: Academic Press.

Long, M. H., Inagaki, S., & Ortega, L. (1998). The role of implicit negative feedback in SLA: Models and recasts in Japanese and Spanish. *Modern Language Journal, 82,* 357–71.

Long, M. H., & Robinson, P. (1998). Focus on form: Theory, research and practice. In C. Doughty & J. Williams (Eds.), *Focus on form in classroom second language acquisition* (pp. 15–41). Cambridge, UK: Cambridge University Press.

Lynch, T., & Maclean, J. (2000). Exploring the benefits of task repetition and recycling for classroom language learning. *Language Teaching Journal, 4,* 221–50.

Lynch, T., & Maclean, J. (2001). "A case of exercising": Effects of immediate task repetition on learners' performance. In M. Bygate, P. Skehan, & M. Swain (Eds.), *Researching pedagogic tasks: Second language learning, teaching, and testing* (pp. 141–62). Harlow, UK: Pearson.

Lyster, R. (1998a). Negotiation of form, recasts, and explicit correction in relation to error types and learner repair in immersion classrooms. *Language Learning, 48,* 183–218.

Lyster, R. (1998b). Recasts, repetition and ambiguity in L2 classroom discourse. *Studies in Second Language Acquisition, 20,* 51–81.

Lyster, R., & Ranta, L. (1997). Corrective feedback and learner uptake: Negotiation of form in communicative classrooms. *Studies in Second Language Acquisition, 19,* 37–66.

Mackey, A. (1997). *Interactional modifications and the development of questions in English as a second language.* Unpublished manuscript, Michigan State University, East Lansing, MI.

Mackey, A. (1999). Input, interaction, and second language development: An empirical study of question formation in ESL. *Studies in Second Language Acquisition, 21,* 557–87.

Mackey, A. (2000, October). *Feedback, noticing and second language development: An empirical study of L2 classroom interaction.* Paper presented at the annual meeting of the British Association for Applied Linguistics, Cambridge, UK.

Mackey, A. (2006). Feedback, noticing and instructed second language learning. *Applied Linguistics, 27,* 1–27.

Mackey, A. (in press). Introduction. In Mackey, A. (Ed.). *Conversational interaction in second language acquisition: A series of empirical studies.* Oxford: Oxford University Press.

Mackey, A., Gass, S. M., & McDonough, K. (2000). How do learners perceive interactional feedback? *Studies in Second Language Acquisition, 22,* 471–97.

Mackey, A., Oliver, R. & Kanaganas, A., (in press). Task familiarity and interactional feedback in child ESL classrooms. *TESOL Quarterly.*

Mackey, A., & Oliver, R. (2002). Interactional feedback and children's L2 development. *System, 30,* 459–77.

Mackey, A., Oliver, R., & Leeman, J. (2003). Interactional input and the incorporation of feedback: An exploration of NS-NNS and NNS-NNS adult and child dyads. *Language Learning, 53,* 35–66.

Mackey, A., & Philp, J. (1998). Conversational interaction and second language development: Recasts, responses, and red herrings? *Modern Language Journal, 82,* 338–56.

Mackey, A., Philp, J., Egi, T., Fujii, A., & Tatsumi, T. (2002). Individual differences in working memory, noticing of interactional feedback and L2 development. In P. Robinson (Ed.), *Individual differences and instructed language learning* (pp. 181–209). Philadelphia: John Benjamins.

McDonough, K. (2001). *Exploring the relationship between modified output and L2 learning.* Unpublished doctoral dissertation, Georgetown University, Washington, DC.

McDonough, K. (2005). Identifying the impact of negative feedback and learners' responses on ESL question development. *Studies in Second Language Acquisition, 27,* 79–103.

Miyake, A., & Friedman, N. P. (1998). Individual differences in second language proficiency: Working memory as language aptitude. In A. Healy & L. Bourne (Eds.), *Foreign language learning.* Mahwah, NJ: Lawrence Erlbaum.

Miyake, A., & Shah, P. (Eds.). (1999). *Models of working memory: Mechanisms of active maintenance and executive control.* New York: Cambridge University Press.

Morris, F. (2002, March). *How foreign language learners of Spanish perceive implicit negative feedback.* Paper presented at the Second Language Research Forum, Toronto, Ontario.

Nicholas, H., Lightbown, P. M., & Spada, N. (2001). Recasts as feedback to language learners. *Language Learning, 51,* 719–58.

Nobuyoshi, J., & Ellis, R. (1993). Focused communication tasks and second language acquisition. *ELT Journal, 47,* 203–10.

Oliver, R. (1995). Negative feedback in child NS-NNS conversation. *Studies in Second Language Acquisition, 17,* 459–81.

Oliver, R. (1998). Negotiation of meaning in child interactions. *Modern Language Journal, 82,* 372–86.

Oliver, R. (2000). Age differences in negotiation and feedback in classroom and pairwork. *Language Learning, 50,* 119–51.

Oliver, R. (2002). The patterns of negotiation for meaning in child interactions. *Modern Language Journal, 86,* 97–111.

Oliver, R., & Mackey, A. (2003). Interactional context and feedback in child ESL classrooms. *Modern Language Journal, 87,* 519–33.

Ortega, L. (1999). Planning and focus on form in L2 oral performance. *Studies in Second Language Acquisition, 21,* 109–48.

Panova, I., & Lyster, R. (2002). Patterns of corrective feedback and uptake in an adult ESL classroom. *TESOL Quarterly, 36,* 573–95.

Papagno, C., Valentine, T., & Baddeley, A. D. (1991). Phonological short-term memory and foreign language vocabulary learning. *Journal of Memory and Language, 30,* 331–47.

Papagno, C., & Vallar, G. (1992). Phonological short-term memory and the learning of novel words: The effect of phonological similarity and item length. *Quarterly Journal of Experimental Psychology, 44A,* 47–67.

Philp, J. (2003). Constraints on "noticing the gap": Nonnative speakers' noticing of recasts in NS-NNS interaction. *Studies in Second Language Acquisition, 25,* 99–126.

Pica, T. (1988). Interlanguage adjustments as an outcome of NS-NNS negotiated interaction. *Language Learning, 38,* 45–73.

Pica, T. (1994). Research on negotiation: What does it reveal about second-language learning conditions, processes, and outcomes? *Language Learning, 44,* 493–527.

Pica, T. (1996). Second language learning through interaction: Multiple perspectives. *University of Pennsylvania Working Papers in Educational Linguistics, 12,* 1–22.

Pica, T. (1998). Second language learning through interaction: Multiple perspectives. In V. Regan (Ed.), *Contemporary approaches to second language acquisition* (pp. 1–31). Dublin: University of Dublin Press.

Pica, T., Holliday, L., Lewis, N., & Morgenthaler, L. (1989). Comprehensible output as an outcome of linguistic demands on the learner. *Studies in Second Language Acquisition, 11,* 63–90.

Plough, I., & Gass, S. M. (1993). Interlocutor and task familiarity: Effects on interactional structure. In G. Crookes & S. M. Gass (Eds.), *Tasks and language learning: Integrating theory and practice* (pp. 35–56). Clevedon, UK: Multilingual Matters.

Polio, C., & Gass, S. M. (1998). The role of interaction in native speaker comprehension of nonnative speaker speech. *Modern Language Journal, 82,* 308–19.

Posner, M. I. (1988). Structures and function of selective attention. In M. Dennis, E. Kaplan, M. I. Posner, D. Stein, & R. Thompson (Eds.), *Clinical neuropsychology and brain function: Research, measurement, and practice* (pp. 169–201). Washington, DC: American Psychological Association.

Posner, M. I. (1992). Attention as a cognitive and neural system. *Current Directions in Psychological Science, 1,* 1–14.

Posner, M. I., & Peterson, S. E. (1990). The attentional systems of the human brain. *Annual Review of Neuroscience, 13,* 25–42.

Qi, D. S., & Lapkin, S. (2001). Exploring the role of noticing in a three-stage second language writing task. *Journal of Second Language Writing, 10,* 277–303.

Robinson, P. (1995). Attention, memory, and the "noticing" hypothesis. *Language Learning, 45,* 283–331.

Robinson, P. (1997). Individual differences and the fundamental similarity of implicit and explicit adult second language learning. *Language Learning, 47,* 45–99.

Robinson, P. (2001). Individual differences, cognitive abilities, aptitude complexes and learning conditions in second language acquisition. *Second Language Research, 17,* 368–92.

Robinson, P. (2002). Learning conditions, aptitude complexes, and SLA. In P. Robinson (Ed.), *Individual differences and instructed language learning* (pp. 113–33). Philadelphia: John Benjamins.

Samuda, V. (2001). Guiding relationships between form and meaning during task performance: The role of the teacher. In M. Bygate, P. Skehan, & M. Swain (Eds.), *Researching pedagogic tasks: Second language learning, teaching and testing* (pp. 119–40). London: Longman.

Sawyer, M., & Ranta, L. (2001). Aptitude, individual differences, and instructional design. In P. Robinson (Ed.), *Cognition and second language instruction* (pp. 319–53). Cambridge, UK: Cambridge University Press.

Schmidt, R. (1990). The role of consciousness in second language learning. *Applied Linguistics, 11,* 129–58.

Schmidt, R. (1993). Awareness and second language acquisition. *Annual Review of Applied Linguistics, 13,* 206–26.

Schmidt, R. (1995). Consciousness and foreign language learning: A tutorial on the role of attention and awareness in learning. In R. Schmidt (Ed.), *Attention and awareness in foreign language learning.* Honolulu: University of Hawaii Press.

Schmidt, R. (2001). Attention. In P. Robinson (Ed.), *Cognition and second language instruction* (pp. 3–32). Cambridge, UK: Cambridge University Press.

Schmidt, R., & Frota, S. (1986). Developing basic conversational ability in a second language: A case study of an adult learner of Portuguese. In R. R. Day (Ed.), *Talking to learn: Conversation in second language acquisition* (pp. 237–326). Rowley, MA: Newbury House.

Segalowitz, N., & Lightbown, P. M. (1999). Psycholinguistic approaches to SLA. *Annual Review of Applied Linguistics, 19,* 43–63.

Service, E. (1992). Phonology, working memory, and foreign language learning. *The Quarterly Journal of Experimental Psychology, 45A,* 21–50.

Service, E., & Kohonen, V. (1995). Is the relation between phonological memory and foreign language learning accounted for by vocabulary acquisition? *Applied Psycholinguistics, 16,* 155–72.

Shehadeh, A. (1999). Nonnative speakers' production of modified comprehensible output and second language learning. *Language Learning, 49,* 627–75.

Shehadeh, A. (2001). Self and other-initiated modified output during task-based interaction. *TESOL Quarterly, 35,* 433–57.

Shehadeh, A. (2002). Comprehensible output, from occurrence to acquisition: An agenda for acquisitional research. *Language Learning, 52,* 597–647.

Silver, R. E. (2000). Input, output, and negotiation: Conditions for second language development. In B. Swierzbin, F. Morris, M. E. Anderson, C. A. Klee, & E. Tarone (Eds.), *Social and cognitive factors in second language acquisition: Selected proceedings of the 1999 Second Language Research Forum* (pp. 345–71). Somerville, MA: Cascadilla Press.

Simard, D., & Wong, W. (2001). Alertness, orientation, and detection. *Studies in Second Language Acquisition, 23,* 103–24.

Skehan, P. (1998). *A cognitive approach to language learning.* Oxford: Oxford University Press.

Sokolov, J. E., & Snow, C. E. (1994). *Handbook of research in language development using CHILDES.* Hillsdale, NJ: Lawrence Erlbaum.

Spada, N. (1997). Form-focussed instruction and second language acquisition: A review of classroom and laboratory research. *Language Teaching, 30,* 73–87.

Storch, N. (2002). Patterns of interaction in ESL pair work. *Language Learning, 52,* 119–58.

Swain, M. (1985). Communicative competence: Some roles of comprehensible input and comprehensible output in its development. In S. Gass & C. Madden (Eds.), *Input in second language acquisition* (pp. 235–53). Rowley, MA: Newbury House.

Swain, M. (1993). The output hypothesis: Just speaking and writing aren't enough. *Canadian Modern Language Review, 50,* 158–64.

Swain, M. (1995). Three functions of output in second language learning. In G. Cook & B. Seidlhofer (Eds.), *Principle and practice in applied linguistics: Studies in honour of H.G. Widdowson* (pp. 125–44). Oxford: Oxford University Press.

Swain, M. (1998). Focus on form through conscious reflection. In C. Doughty & J. Williams (Eds.), *Focus on form in classroom second language acquisition* (pp. 64–81). Cambridge, UK: Cambridge University Press.

Swain, M. (2005). *The output hypothesis: Theory and research.* In E. Hinkel (Ed.), *Handbook of research in second language teaching and learning* (pp. 471–83). Mahwah, NJ: Lawrence Erlbaum.

Swain, M., & Lapkin, S. (1995). Problems in output and the cognitive processes they generate: A step towards second language learning. *Applied Linguistics, 16,* 370–91.

Swain, M., & Lapkin, S. (1998). Interaction and second language learning: Two adolescent French immersion students working together. *Modern Language Journal, 82,* 320–37.

Tomasello, M. (2003). *Constructing a language: A usage-based theory of language acquisition.* Cambridge, MA: Harvard University Press.

Tomlin, R., & Villa, V. (1994). Attention in cognitive science and second language acquisition. *Studies in Second Language Acquisition, 16,* 183–203.

Truscott, J. (1998). Noticing in second language acquisition: A critical review. *Second Language Research, 14,* 103–35.

Van den Branden, K. (1997). Effects of negotiation on language learners' output. *Language Learning, 47,* 589–636.

Wagner-Gough, J., & Hatch, E. (1975). The importance of input data in second language acquisition studies. *Language Learning, 25,* 297–308.

Williams, J. N. (1999). Memory, attention, and inductive learning. *Studies in Second Language Acquisition, 21,* 1–48.

Williams, J. N., & Lovatt, P. (2003). Phonological memory and rule learning. *Language Learning, 53,* 67–121.

Williams, J. & VanPatten. B. (Eds.). (in press). *Theories in SLA.* Mahwah, NJ: Lawrence Erlbaum.

4 Feedback in L2 learning: Responding to errors during practice

Jennifer Leeman

Introduction

It is fitting that a volume on practice in second language learning should include a chapter on feedback, as the notion that practice can promote L2 development seems to imply that learners do not yet produce error-free output. Thus, a comprehensive understanding of practice must involve consideration of the ways in which interlocutors respond to learner error, and the implementation of a practice-based pedagogy requires instructors to make decisions about whether to provide feedback, and if so, what type(s) to provide. Indeed, the issue of feedback is intricately linked to other practice-related constructs such as the effects of input, output, and interaction, and thus it has been briefly touched upon in previous chapters. The present chapter, while mentioning these constructs, aims to give readers a fuller appreciation of feedback per se, as well as its role in L2 practice. Because most L2 feedback research has not been conducted within a practice framework, a thorough understanding of feedback and of the empirical research in this area requires a consideration of the different perspectives from which such research has been carried out. Therefore, after defining the relevant terminology, this chapter will examine the role of feedback within different theoretical perspectives on SLA. This will lead to a fine-grained analysis of the characteristics of feedback and will facilitate the interpretation of empirical feedback studies reviewed in a subsequent section. The chapter will conclude with a discussion of the implications of such research for SLA theory and L2 pedagogy.

Clarifying the terms

Feedback is a central issue in scholarship dealing with theoretical concerns as well as with instructional design, with a great number of different terms having been employed over the years. Although various terms referring to feedback are sometimes used interchangeably in contemporary acquisition literature, many are associated with different theoretical

111

frameworks and do not have identical meanings. Moreover, terms once more common have fallen from favor, while others seem to have undergone semantic shift. For this reason, it is important at the outset to clarify the terminology employed in current treatments of feedback: *positive evidence, negative evidence, feedback,* and *error correction* (see Chaudron, 1977, for an in-depth early treatment of response to error and the associated terminology).

Evidence is the most specific of the terms in current use, and it appears most frequently in theoretical discussions about the type of data that learners can utilize in the acquisition process and about whether speakers' abstract linguistic knowledge can be acquired without being constrained by some innate linguistic ability. This term is normally defined as information about whether certain structures are permissible in the language being acquired. *Positive evidence* consists of information that certain utterances are possible in the target language, although this term is perhaps even more frequently used to refer to exemplars of possible utterances. *Negative evidence*, on the other hand, is information that certain utterances or types of utterances are impossible in the language being learned.[1] Although these terms have been used in reference to the acquisition of various aspects of language, including the lexicon and phonology, they are most common in discussions of the acquisition of morphosyntax. Evidence may be provided either in advance of any learner-produced language or in response to it.

A more general term, one commonly used in information-processing models, is *feedback*, which refers to a mechanism which provides the learner with information regarding the success or failure of a given process. By definition, feedback is responsive and thus can occur only *after* a given process. Positive feedback consists of information that the process was successful, whereas negative feedback informs of failure. In the case of language acquisition, feedback consists of a wide variety of responses to learner output and may contain information regarding the accuracy, communicative success, or content of learner utterances or discourse, regardless of how the learner interprets and responds to such information. Most first language (L1) and L2 acquisition research has focused on *negative* feedback, or response to learner error, and its effects on linguistic development. It is important to note that negative feedback, which by definition is contingent on learner error, may contain either positive or negative evidence, or both. Finally, the term *error correction* now generally refers to the pedagogical activity of providing feedback for learner errors and is normally avoided in current language acquisition research, as it seems to imply that feedback provided in response to learner error ultimately leads to the elimination of such errors – a question to be answered empirically (see Chaudron, 1977, for various earlier conceptions of correction).

As many have noted, feedback is an area in which SLA researchers and instructors historically have not seen eye to eye. In some ways, this discrepancy may be related to the view that second language acquisition (SLA) research does not have, and perhaps need not have, direct relevance to language teaching (R. Ellis, 1997). Further, many researchers have argued that language acquisition, or at least L1 acquisition, is different from the learning of other types of skills and knowledge (e.g., Chomsky, 1981; Gregg, 1996; Schwartz, 1993). This has meant that until recently, the large body of research that found feedback beneficial for nonlinguistic learning was considered peripheral to SLA. Moreover, for many years, the belief that negative evidence was of little value in language acquisition led some SLA researchers to avoid the question of whether feedback could have an effect on L2 development (Schachter, 1991). In contrast, many L2 instructors have long viewed error correction as an important aspect of language pedagogy and have remained firmly convinced that the key issue was not *whether* to provide error correction, but rather, *how* to do so most effectively.

In recent years, however, this disjuncture has begun to diminish. Advances in both theoretical and empirical research, as well as a greater integration of research from cognitive psychology, have led to a greater interest among SLA researchers in various types of feedback. In addition, there seems to be a wider acceptance of the notion that although theory-building is one key objective of SLA research, developing a knowledge base on which to design effective pedagogy is another important goal (e.g., R. Ellis, 1997; Mitchell & Myles, 1998). Of particular importance in our current understanding of feedback are studies that have explored the role of interaction in L2 development (see Mackey, this volume), the importance of output and production practice (see Muranoi, this volume), and the effects of various instructional and classroom techniques, as well as studies that have explored the role of attention, skill acquisition, and the development of automaticity in SLA. In order to understand the implications of the empirical studies of feedback reviewed later in this chapter, it will be useful to first consider the various theoretical perspectives in which such research is contextualized.

Theoretical perspectives

The role of negative evidence and feedback

Early views on the irrelevance of feedback were closely linked to the introduction of the generativist model of language and the general rejection of behaviorist psychology, which had conceived of language as a series of habits acquired principally through classical conditioning, reinforcement, and training. Behaviorists emphasized the value of positive feedback, with target behaviors reinforced by means of rewards and other positive responses from the environment. Nonetheless, behaviorists also accorded some role to negative feedback, or aversive conditioning, which could come in the form of implicit negative feedback, including "simply...remaining silent when the occasion demands speech" (Skinner, 1957, p. 167).

In contrast, generativist linguists viewed language as a set of abstract rules acquired via biologically determined constraints on possible human languages. This position was supported in part by *poverty of the stimulus* arguments: (a) speakers' knowledge goes well beyond the linguistic data to which they are exposed; (b) learners are exposed to degenerate input such as false starts, slips of the tongue, and other types of ungrammatical speech; and (c) children apparently are not provided with negative evidence or information regarding the impossibility of certain structures in the language they are acquiring (Chomsky, 1981). According to generativists, it is the presumed innate constraints, frequently referred to collectively as universal grammar (UG), that allow for successful first language acquisition even in the complete absence of negative evidence. Further, it was argued that negative evidence could not play a significant role in L1 acquisition unless it was shown to be (a) available to all children, (b) usable, (c) used, and (d) necessary (Pinker, 1989).

Bolstering these claims regarding the irrelevance of negative evidence for language acquisition was the widely held belief that parents rarely correct children's linguistic errors or provide them with information about the grammaticality of their utterances, despite the fact that the primary empirical support for this belief came from a single small-scale study (i.e., Brown & Hanlon, 1970) and anecdotal reports. Subsequent research on child-directed speech has found that many caregivers do in fact provide various types of implicit feedback to children, such as clarification requests and recasts, defined as grammatical reformulations of the child's ungrammatical utterance (Demetras, Post, & Snow, 1986; Hirsh-Pasek, Treiman, & Schneiderman, 1984). These types of responses to children's errors may signal that the children's utterances were unacceptable, suggesting that negative evidence might in fact be available in L1 acquisition. Nonetheless, given the implicitness of such feedback (which may be difficult to recognize as negative evidence) and the inconsistency with which it is provided, many researchers have questioned children's ability to make use of negative evidence. Although some empirical research has found that exposure to implicit negative feedback is often associated with children's linguistic growth (e.g., Farrar, 1990; Saxton, 1997), the specific theoretical implications of these findings for the role of negative evidence have been hotly debated (e.g., Bohannon, MacWhinney, & Snow, 1990; Morgan, Bonamo, & Travis, 1995).

Positions on the role of feedback and negative evidence in SLA have largely mirrored those of L1 research, despite important differences between L1 and L2 acquisition (Bley-Vroman, 1988, 1990; N. Ellis, 2002; MacWhinney, 2001). Thus, like the L1 researchers who maintained that children acquire an L1 based solely on positive evidence, some L2 researchers working within the UG paradigm have argued that negative evidence is irrelevant for the acquisition of L2 syntax (e.g., Beck, Schwartz, & Eubank, 1995; Gregg, 1996). A role for negative evidence in the acquisition of other aspects of the L2, however, is not always ruled out (e.g., Schwartz, 1993). In part because various types of negative feedback, including explicit negative evidence, are available to many instructed learners, researchers have focused primarily on exploring whether learners are able to make use of the information provided in feedback. Implicit feedback, such as clarification requests or recasts, may be particularly difficult to make use of because learners may mistakenly assume that their interlocutors are responding to the content rather than the form of their utterances, or that non-comprehension is related to non-linguistic features such as background noise (Carroll, 1995, 2001). Further, learners may interpret recasts as simply an alternative way to express the same meaning, rather than a subtle message that their own utterance was unacceptable (Long, 1996). Moreover, clarification requests and reformulations also occur after grammatical utterances (in addition to ungrammatical ones), in conversations between two native speakers (NSs) as well as in conversations between an NS and a non-native speaker (NNS). This reduces the likelihood that learners will interpret implicit feedback as negative evidence. (Empirical studies which have dealt with these issues are discussed later in this chapter.)

Even if learners do interpret some kind of corrective intent, they may have difficulty identifying the specific source of the problem with their original utterance (Carroll, 1995, 2001; Long, 1996; Pinker, 1989). In the case of explicit feedback, these difficulties are reduced somewhat, as such feedback (particularly when provided by instructors) clearly states that a learner's utterance is ungrammatical. It may also explicitly identify the problematic form and even include metalinguistic information about the reasons for its ungrammaticality. Nonetheless, this does not necessarily mean that learners can make use of this information because they may not have enough metalinguistic knowledge to do so or because negative evidence of any kind simply may not be usable for language acquisition.

Indeed, many researchers who maintain that UG constrains SLA argue that negative evidence cannot play a role in the acquisition of L2 syntax (e.g., Beck, Eubank, & Schwartz, 1995; Schwartz & Gubala-Ryzak, 1992). However, the opposite has also been proposed. In particular, White (1991) suggests that negative evidence may not only have a positive effect but may be *necessary* in specific cases where the L2 being acquired allows only a subset of the structures permissible in the L1. In her view, only exposure to negative evidence would lead learners to retreat from an overly general grammar.

In contrast with UG-based accounts of language acquisition that emphasize the importance of internal linguistic constraints, connectionist models assign great significance to the linguistic environment. While there are many different connectionist models, they share a number of characteristics, the most important being that linguistic knowledge is represented as a series of associations among forms, rather than as a series of formal rules (Plunkett, 1995). These associations are strengthened by repeated exposure. Thus, frequency and statistical properties of the input are major factors in acquisition (N. Ellis, 2002). The most successful computer-based simulations include mechanisms to adjust the strength of associations when existing associations do not produce the correct result, mechanisms which rely on information about the success or failure of processes and outputs – in other words, feedback (Broeder & Plunkett, 1994; Plunkett, 1995).

One connectionist framework of particular interest is MacWhinney's (1987) competition model, which posits that because forms compete in their associations with meanings and other forms, positive evidence for any one form (or meaning) effectively constitutes negative evidence for all competing forms (or meanings). At first glance, it would appear that the competition model allows a role for feedback only to the degree that it also constitutes positive evidence. However, while MacWhinney downplays distinctions between positive and negative evidence, he does state that language acquisition will be driven in part by the detection of errors. As learners encounter conflicts between forms, they will discover which language-internal cues are most likely to prevail in such conflicts, consequently increasing reliance on these cues and decreasing reliance on cues with weaker conflict validity. Thus it would seem that input that promotes the detection of error could prove beneficial. Further, positive feedback might serve to increase reliance on the language-appropriate cues and thus prove beneficial during L2 practice.

Another important line of research that views SLA as roughly equivalent to learning other complex cognitive skills, and thus as governed by general learning mechanisms, is skill acquisition theory. This approach is particularly important here, as it provides the theoretical basis for some recent accounts of the value of L2 practice (see DeKeyser, 2001, and this volume), and it reflects the integration of research from cognitive psychology in SLA theory. According to one of the most widely accepted skill acquisition models, there are three cognitive stages through which learners generally progress: (1) acquisition of declarative knowledge, (2) proceduralization, and (3) automatization (Anderson, 1983, 1993). In the first stage, learners acquire new factual knowledge, whether formal rules or exemplar-based analogies. Although this declarative knowledge can be utilized in skill performance, the cognitive demands, in terms of processing and memory requirements, are relatively high. In the second stage, knowledge is proceduralized, permitting learners to carry out skills or subskills with decreasing reliance on declarative knowledge and, thus, with fewer cognitive resources.

Because proceduralization results in a reduced cognitive load, procedures whose execution previously relied on declarative knowledge can now be combined with other procedures, and they can be compiled into a larger overall procedure, allowing increasingly complex skills to be carried out with decreasing cognitive demand. In the final stage, procedural knowledge is fine-tuned and automatized, allowing for skills to be more efficiently performed, in part by changing the scope of the application of rules. In this view of automatization, feedback can play an important role in the acquisition of skills. During the initial stage, feedback can promote the acquisition of declarative knowledge. In proceduralization, fine-tuning, and automatization, it can indicate the need for greater attention and reliance on declarative knowledge as well as the need to change the scope of a given rule or procedure. Furthermore, feedback may be useful in avoiding the automatization of non-target L2 knowledge. Whereas feedback may prove beneficial throughout the process of skill acquisition, some researchers posit that the most useful type of feedback differs according to the learner's specific stage (see Han, 2002). Of course, if practice promotes the automatization of targetlike knowledge, feedback will play a diminishing role as learners commit fewer and fewer errors.

Another way in which negative feedback might facilitate L2 development is by giving learners the opportunity to subdivide complex tasks into smaller, more manageable ones, or to shift attentional resources to their own linguistic output. Because linguistic production requires multiple cognitive processes related to meaning and form, as well as to the relationship between meaning and form, L2 performance involves competition among accuracy, complexity, and fluency (Skehan, 1998; Skehan & Foster, 2001). Further, when task or communication demands require learners to engage in higher order (non-linguistic) cognitive processes, such as abstract reasoning, performance may be negatively affected due to cognitive overload. Thus, feedback that segments or subdivides the production task may make it possible for learners to perform that portion more accurately. Given that one possible effect of negative feedback is that it may lead learners to shift attention from meaning to form (Carroll, 2001), feedback may benefit learners by providing them the opportunity to focus on the linguistic aspects of their output, having already completed the conceptual components of a task at hand (see Muranoi, this volume). Similarly, it may allow learners to alter their performance priorities by assigning greater importance to accuracy. Indeed, the latter possibility appears to be the case in Example 1, taken from a study that utilized a stimulated recall procedure to investigate learners' perceptions about negative feedback (i.e., Mackey, Gass, & McDonough, 2000).

Example 1

NNS:	Three key.
NS:	Three?
NNS:	Key er keys.
NNS (comment during stimulated recall):	After "key" again, I make a little effort to say "keys" because you have three, I was thinking try a little better English.

(Mackey et al., 2000, p. 486)

Feedback on non-target production might also promote greater learner attention to formal aspects of the L2 in the input to which learners are subsequently exposed (Carroll, 2001; Gass, 1997; Gass & Mackey, 2002; Swain, 1995). However, it must be noted that although increased attention to form during production may result in more accurate L2 performance, the effects on linguistic development, or on future performance, are by no means clear.

Although practice can be comprehension- as well as production-based, discussions of feedback, including this chapter, have focused on responses to non-targetlike production. Nonetheless, feedback that follows non-targetlike *comprehension* of L2 input may benefit learners in some of the same ways that feedback on production can. In her rejection of the sufficiency of exposure to comprehensible input (e.g., Krashen, 1981), White (1987) argues that learners should be exposed to incomprehensible input, as failure to comprehend L2 input might lead them to modify their underlying L2 linguistic system. Similarly, the failure to comprehend input may promote learners' recognition of differences between their own L2 linguistic system and the target system (Gass, 1997). If incomprehension of input promotes L2 development by triggering change in the underlying L2 system (Carroll, 2001), it stands to reason that feedback that informs learners that they have not accurately comprehended the L2 input might also prove valuable.

One line of investigation that has utilized comprehension-based feedback in conjunction with other pedagogical techniques is *processing instruction* research (VanPatten, 1996, 2002; VanPatten & Cadierno, 1993; VanPatten & Sanz, 1995). The underpinnings of this pedagogical approach include the prediction that learners will initially utilize L1 strategies to process L2 input, a tendency that will lead not only to comprehension errors but also to subsequent non-target production, as learners' failure to convert key elements of the input to intake precludes the further processing required for acquisition (see Leow, this volume).

Thus, rather than emphasizing production practice, VanPatten argues for L2 instruction in which learners are first provided with information about a given linguistic structure and then complete structured input activities in which they are pushed to process sentences in a targetlike way. Although VanPatten does not provide an in-depth discussion of feedback, it is clear from the sample activities that instructors are meant to immediately inform learners when they misinterpret the L2 input (e.g., VanPatten, 2002). Although the theoretical and empirical validity of the input processing model and of the related processing instruction studies has been questioned (DeKeyser, Salaberry, Robinson, & Harrington, 2002; Salaberry, 1997), this line of investigation is of particular interest in the present context because it seems to assign an important role to comprehension-based feedback.

Characteristics of negative feedback

As the previous two sections have shown, there are many different types of feedback, and researchers have posited different ways in which feedback may be beneficial for learners engaged in L2 practice. Because determining whether negative evidence can play a role in language acquisition is of great importance for theory-building and, in particular, generativist theory building, much L1 feedback-related research has focused on this crucial, and still unresolved, relationship. However, it is essential to look beyond the question of negative evidence and to carry out a more fine-grained analysis of feedback by considering its specific components and characteristics and the effects they may have on development. Indeed, the picture that this chapter has presented of L2 theoretical research shows that the question is not simply whether negative evidence affects the learner's underlying linguistic competence. It is also important to explore whether negative evidence can affect L2 performance and whether there are other aspects of feedback (distinct from negative evidence) that are beneficial to learners. That is, in addition to determining if negative feedback promotes L2 development by offering information about the unacceptability of ungrammatical learner utterances, there is a need to investigate whether negative feedback promotes L2 development in other ways. For example, together with implicit negative evidence about the learners' non-targetlike form, recasts contain positive evidence of a targetlike alternative form (Pinker, 1989). Whether or not learners can make use of the implicit negative evidence, they may benefit from the positive evidence provided in such feedback. Further, it has been argued that recasts can promote L2 development by enhancing the salience of this positive evidence (Leeman, 2003), a proposal that is consistent with current research regarding the importance of perceptual salience in language acquisition (e.g., Goldschneider & DeKeyser, 2001). If this account of recasts is accurate, it suggests that certain types of negative feedback may be beneficial without attributing the benefits to negative evidence per se.

In addition to providing positive and/or negative evidence, feedback sometimes includes metalinguistic information about the language being acquired, particularly in instructed contexts. Because they argue that positive evidence is the primary agent of linguistic growth, researchers working within the UG framework have generally rejected a role for metalinguistic information, just as they rule out a role for negative evidence. Similarly, researchers who maintain that learning and acquisition are distinct cognitive processes which lead to explicit and implicit knowledge, respectively, argue that metalinguistic rule presentation does not promote the development of nativelike L2 competence and can only be used for monitoring one's linguistic output (e.g., Krashen, 1981). However, several recent studies comparing the effects of implicit and explicit teaching have found advantages for L2 learners provided with metalinguistic rule presentation (e.g., Muranoi, 2000; Norris & Ortega, 2000; Robinson, 1996; but see also R. Ellis, 2002). These results are consistent with the view that L2 learning is much like the acquisition of other complex cognitive abilities, as one tenet of skill acquisition theory is that declarative knowledge can become proceduralized and automatized, as was discussed earlier in this chapter.

Empirical studies of negative evidence and feedback in SLA

Because feedback is a multifaceted construct relevant to a broad range of theoretical perspectives on SLA, researchers have carried out empirical studies within a wide variety of frameworks and have explored issues such as negative evidence, interactional feedback, pushed output, and classroom feedback techniques. This section presents a range of these studies, and the following section discusses their implications regarding the effects of feedback in different frameworks. Regardless of the specific theoretical approach adopted by the researchers, feedback research can be divided into two main categories: (1) descriptive studies that have examined the types of feedback provided, as well as NNS responses to such feedback (e.g., Chaudron, 1977; Lyster, 1998; Lyster & Ranta, 1997; Mackey, Oliver, & Leeman, 2003; Oliver, 1995, 2000; Pica, Holliday, Lewis, & Morgenthaler, 1989), and (2) developmental studies that have used experimental or quasi-experimental methodologies to explore the effects of exposure to various feedback types (e.g., Carroll & Swain, 1993; Doughty & Varela, 1998; Leeman, 2003; Long, Inagaki, & Ortega, 1998; Mackey & Philp, 1998). In addition, a number of researchers have included feedback as one of several pedagogical techniques in studies of instructed SLA (e.g., Day & Shapson, 1991; Leeman, Arteagoitia, Fridman, & Doughty, 1995; Harley, 1998; Spada & Lightbown, 1993; White, Spada, Lightbown, & Ranta 1991; Williams & Evans, 1998). However, these latter studies of *focus on form* (Long, 1991) or *form-focused instruction* (Spada, 1997) did not investigate the effects of feedback in isolation, and space limitations preclude an in-depth discussion in the present chapter.

Descriptive studies

By examining the characteristics of feedback, and of learners' responses to different types of feedback, descriptive studies of interactional feedback can shed light on the role of the linguistic environment, as well as on learners' engagement with the environment. Given the emphasis on exploring the role of negative evidence in language acquisition, and in particular on determining whether such evidence is available and used, many descriptive studies have explored whether NNSs have access to information regarding the ungrammaticality of their non-targetlike utterances, and if so, whether they can make use of such information. Further, researchers have investigated which types of feedback are most likely to lead to modified output on the part of the learner. Like L1 research, L2 studies of dyadic interaction have expanded the definition of negative feedback, which originally emphasized explicit forms of correction, to include various types of implicit feedback that seem to be more frequent in both dyadic interaction and classroom contexts. For example, in their analysis of informal NS-NNS English conversations Brock, Crookes, Day, & Long (1986) found that NSs were more likely to respond to morphosyntactic errors with recasts than with explicit feedback.

Other such descriptive research has found that interlocutors do provide NNSs with feedback containing negative evidence in response to at least some of their non-targetlike utterances (e.g., Oliver, 1995, 2000, 2002; Lyster, 1998; Lyster & Ranta, 1997; Mackey et al., 2000; Mackey et al., 2003). Of course, the more important questions, both for SLA theory as well as for the design of instructional programs, are whether learners can utilize negative evidence and, further, what type of negative feedback is most beneficial. The results of some early descriptive studies in this area suggested that NNSs did not consistently produce modified output in response to negative feedback (Brock et al., 1986; Chaudron, 1977; Pica et al., 1989). Further, certain types of feedback, such as recasts, were particularly unlikely to be incorporated in subsequent turns. However, as Oliver (1995, 2000) points out, comparing feedback types based on whether learners produce modified output may be misleading, as discourse constraints may make incorporation of feedback less likely for recasts than for other types of implicit feedback. When she excluded from analysis those recasts where learners either did not have the opportunity to produce modified output or when it would have been inappropriate to do so, Oliver (1995) found that NNSs incorporated 35 percent of recasts in the following turn. In a descriptive study of feedback that explored the effects of the age of the dyads (adults vs. children) and of whether NNSs interacted with NSs or other NNSs, Mackey et al. (2003) found that NNSs incorporated between 25 percent and 41 percent of all negative feedback that offered the opportunity to do so.

Whether NNSs are provided with negative feedback, and how they react to the feedback they do receive, has also been the focus of classroom research. One of the first of such studies is Chaudron's (1977) analysis of French immersion classes. Chaudron found that recasts that reformulated only the non-target portion of the NNS utterance and recasts that did not add additional information were more likely to lead to NNS incorporation of corrections than were recasts that added new information. Like Chaudron, Lyster and Ranta (1997) recognized that an absence of immediate repetition or incorporation of feedback does not necessarily reflect a lack of intake. For this reason, they analyzed *uptake*, or all types of verbal acknowledgment of feedback on the part of the learner, in their analyses of French immersion classes. Lyster and Ranta found that NNSs were more likely to demonstrate uptake in response to clarification requests or explicit elicitations than after instructor recasts of non-target utterances. In a separate study, Lyster (1998) further analyzed the same database and found that ratios of uptake differed according to the type of recast provided. In contrast, Ohta (2001) found that L2 learners of Japanese demonstrated a high ratio of uptake of recasts, although the overall incidence of recasts was low. Nonetheless, uptake is not a robust measure of learner noticing nor of the utility of feedback for L2 development, as it should not be assumed that learners will verbally acknowledge all feedback that they notice.

Given the unreliability of uptake, studies utilizing methods other than immediate incorporation or uptake to assess noticing are an important complement to this line of research. In one classroom feedback study conducted by Roberts (1995), three student volunteers viewed a videotape of their university Japanese class and reported instances in which they believed an instructor had corrected a student in the class. Participants interpreted as correction only between 24 percent and 46 percent of the 92 negative feedback episodes identified by Roberts. In contrast, participants in Mackey et al.'s (2000) laboratory study perceived negative feedback as correction over 85 percent of the time. Possible reasons for this difference include the research context (laboratory vs. classroom) and the methodology employed: Participants in the Roberts study viewed the video several days after the interaction had occurred, while those in the Mackey et al. study performed a stimulated recall immediately following the interaction, when they presumably had better memory of what they were thinking at the time feedback was provided. Further, learner interpretation of interlocutor responses was operationalized and quantified differently in the two studies: Participants in Roberts's study were asked simply to identify "corrections," whereas those in the Mackey et al. study were asked to report what they were thinking at the time of the exchange, and these reports were then coded by the researchers. Roberts's finding that learners infrequently identified confirmation checks and repetition requests as correction may reflect their understanding of this term, as well as possible learner bias in favor of the most explicit types of correction, particularly given the classroom setting. One finding in which Roberts's and Mackey et al.'s results coincide, however, is that learners were often unable to identify the target of feedback. In both studies, learners noticed and correctly identified the target of feedback when it was about lexis or phonology. One thought-provoking possibility is that feedback type and error type might interact in determining whether feedback is noticed: In the Mackey et al. study, recasts, the feedback type least frequently perceived by learners, were provided most often in response to morphosyntactic errors, while negotiation most commonly followed phonological errors.

Another interesting finding from the Mackey et al. (2000) study is that many NNSs who did not report noticing feedback nonetheless produced modified output in response to such feedback. Similarly, Philp (2003) found no correlation between noticing of feedback (operationalized as the ability to accurately reproduce a recast when cued to do so) and subsequent improved production. In addition to highlighting the methodological difficulties of assessing noticing (see Leow, this volume), these findings also suggest that feedback may have a beneficial effect even when learners do not consciously interpret a corrective intent. This prospect is consistent with the view that negative evidence may not be the most important component of negative feedback. As was discussed in the previous section, there are several other characteristics of negative feedback that may promote development, including positive evidence and enhanced salience.

These descriptive studies of dyadic and classroom interaction – together with investigations of learner perceptions, modified production, and uptake in response to feedback – seem to suggest that learners perceive much negative feedback as negative evidence and that they are able to make at least some use of the feedback to which they are exposed. Still, it is only through the use of developmental measures that we can clearly identify any changes resulting from exposure to feedback. Further, developmental measures are crucial to the identification of any long-term or delayed effects of negative feedback on learners' L2 systems (Gass, 1997; Lightbown, 1998; Long, 1996; Mackey, 1999). Moreover, the use of pre- and post-tests can provide a clearer picture of learners' underlying competence than can the description of learner errors and responses to feedback during interaction, because errors may result from task demands and learner priorities in the allocation of attentional resources, rather than from a lack of L2 knowledge per se.

Developmental studies of feedback and SLA

Because many L2 instructors continued to view error correction as an important aspect of classroom pedagogy, even at a time when many SLA researchers were shying away from feedback research and its associations with behaviorism (Schachter, 1991), early developmental studies tended to have a pedagogical focus and attempted to determine the effects of correction on classroom evaluation measures, rather than on specially designed gauges of L2 development (e.g., Ramirez & Stromquist, 1979). In addition, many developmental studies investigated the effects of feedback on written production, often measuring effectiveness based on a rough evaluation of subsequent written work (e.g., Semke, 1984). Nonetheless, thanks in part to the growing interest in exploring the utility of negative evidence and other types of input, as well as in interaction and form-focused instruction, recent years have seen an increase in more carefully controlled experimental and quasi-experimental feedback studies conducted in both classroom (DeKeyser, 1993; Doughty & Varela, 1998; White, 1991) and laboratory settings (e.g., Carroll & Swain, 1993; Long, Inagaki, & Ortega, 1998; Leeman, 2003; Mackey & Philp, 1998). All of these studies have found at least some benefits for learners exposed to various types of negative feedback.

Given the great theoretical interest in determining the role of negative evidence in SLA, it is not surprising that several studies have investigated feedback from this perspective. One such study conducted in a classroom context investigated the effect of negative evidence on the acquisition of adverb placement in English by L1 speakers of French (White, 1991). Participants who were exposed to negative evidence for a disallowed English word order (SVAO), combined with positive evidence of the target order (SAVO) sentences and explicit instruction, outperformed a second group exposed only to positive evidence of the target order. Similar results were obtained in an experimental study of English passive use by native speakers of Japanese (Izumi & Lakshmanan, 1998). Here too, participants exposed to negative evidence, metalinguistic information, and positive evidence of targetlike alternative forms outperformed the control group. White's original interpretation that negative evidence had affected participants' L2 competence was questioned by Schwartz and Gubala-Ryzak, who argued that the improved L2 linguistic behavior of White's participants was based on another type of learned knowledge (Schwartz, 1993; Schwartz & Gubala-Ryzak, 1992). The implications of these studies regarding the theoretical status of negative *evidence* are unclear, especially given that beneficial treatments also included positive evidence and metalinguistic information, although they do seem to suggest a positive role for negative *feedback*, at least for L2 performance.

Feedback containing negative evidence was also combined with other instructional interventions in a series of experiments conducted by Herron and Tomasello (Herron & Tomasello, 1988; Tomasello & Herron, 1988, 1989), which shared the common goal of comparing the effects of feedback and modeling on subsequent L2 production. In one laboratory study, all participants were exposed to metalinguistic explanation and models of the target structures, but only participants in the feedback group were given production opportunities and negative feedback, sometimes including additional metalinguistic explanation. In two subsequent "garden path" studies conducted in the classroom, Tomasello and Herron found that leading learners to overgeneralize L2 rules and then providing feedback on errors was more effective than informing learners in advance of exceptions to L2 patterns. Nonetheless, various aspects of the research design have been criticized, including the choice of target structures, the evaluation measures utilized, and the lack of meaning focus in all aspects of the experiment (see Beck & Eubank, 1991, for a critique; Tomasello & Herron, 1991, for a response; and Long, 1996, for a discussion).

Several types of implicit negative feedback were combined in Muranoi's (2000) classroom study of *interaction enhancement*, in which he also compared the effects of form-oriented and meaning-oriented post-task debriefing on the development of English articles (see also Muranoi, this volume). Muranoi found significant advantages for learners who were provided with grammatical explanations of the target forms and form-focused analysis of their task performance. Importantly, learners who participated in meaning-oriented debriefing but who were provided with repetition requests and recasts in response to errors outperformed those who did not receive feedback. Thus, Muranoi's results suggest that several aspects of negative feedback, including metalinguistic information, may promote development, while they also demonstrate the benefits of implicit feedback provided without form-focused instruction. Advantages for learners exposed to negative feedback without explicit instruction were also observed in Doughty and Varela's (1998) comparison of two content-based ESL classes, only one of which was provided with feedback. In the feedback class, the instructor responded to oral production errors of the target structures (the simple past and conditional) with what these researchers term *focused recasts*, which consisted of first repeating the error with rising intonation and then providing a recast if neither the learner nor classmates provided the targetlike form. The instructor also provided feedback on learners' written errors.

Benefits for implicit negative feedback have also been found in laboratory settings. In two studies comparing the effects of recasts and models, Long, Inagaki, and Ortega (1998) utilized a carefully designed information exchange activity in order to ensure that participants were exposed to an equal number of target exemplars and had equal opportunities for production, regardless of experimental condition. In the L2 Japanese study, participants in the two experimental treatments demonstrated greater learning of both target structures than the control group, but there were no significant differences between them. For one of the structures in the L2 Spanish study, no change was observed in any group, while for the other (adverbial placement), participants in both experimental groups showed increased use of the targeted forms, with greater increases associated with exposure to recasts.

In their study of the effects of providing recasts during interaction, Mackey and Philp (1998) also found significant advantages for learners exposed to recasts of English question structures. Specifically, results showed that developmentally ready participants who participated in communicative tasks with intensive recasting produced significantly more advanced question forms than did participants who interacted but did not receive recasts, as did participants who had not reached the appropriate developmental stage at the outset. In a study discussed later in this chapter, Leeman (2003) also found significant advantages for participants exposed to recasts during the completion of information-gap tasks in comparison with learners who were exposed to positive evidence without receiving any feedback on their non-targetlike production.

Together, this research suggests that exposure to implicit negative feedback, particularly recasts, can promote L2 development, although as Lyster (1998) points out the implicit negative feedback provided in laboratory studies tends to be much more intensive than what is actually provided either in classrooms or in more naturalistic interaction. In this regard, Iwashita's (2003) study of the development of two grammatical structures in L2 Japanese is of particular interest. Rather than manipulate the provision of one type of feedback as was done in previous research, Iwashita asked participants to work together to solve a communicative task and then carefully coded five different interactional moves. By tabulating the frequency of these interactional moves, she was able to use multiple regression analyses to explore the relationship between different discourse structures and development. Iwashita's results suggested benefits for exposure to several types of implicit interactional feedback, with recasts showing the strongest effect.

Having documented the developmental benefits of exposure to feedback, the next step is to determine how feedback promotes development, an endeavor that necessarily requires a comparison among various feedback types. While the large body of descriptive research described in the last section provides valuable comparisons of the provision and immediate use of many types of feedback, studies comparing the effects on development are less common. One of the rare developmental studies to evaluate different types of feedback was conducted by Carroll and Swain (1993) in a laboratory setting. One noteworthy aspect of this study is that it included four different groups, in addition to a control group, each of which received a different type of feedback on the English dative alternation. When an error was committed, the first group received metalinguistic explanation, the second was explicitly told their utterance was wrong, the third was provided with the target form, and the fourth was asked if they were sure of their response. On subsequent production all feedback groups outperformed the control group, which did not receive any feedback. In addition, the metalinguistic information group showed significantly higher performance than all other groups except the one in which participants were provided with target models in response to errors. These findings suggest not only that various types of negative feedback, even implicit negative evidence, can lead to changes in NNSs' developing grammar but also that when feedback is accompanied by metalinguistic information and salient target models, the benefits are increased. However, it must be noted that all participants in the various feedback groups were informed prior to treatment that "they would be told something when they made a mistake" (Carroll & Swain, 193, p. 365), potentially reducing the degree of difference between groups.

Two different types of implicit negative feedback were also compared in another laboratory study that was designed in part to investigate how recasts can promote L2 development (Leeman, 2003). Because recasts had been hypothesized to enhance positive evidence by making target forms perceptually more salient (in addition to providing implicit negative evidence), a group of participants who received recasts during the completion of information-gap tasks were compared to groups that were exposed to (a) implicit negative evidence and unenhanced positive evidence, (b) enhanced positive evidence without negative evidence, and (c) a control group that was exposed to unenhanced positive evidence (without negative evidence). Both the recast group and the group exposed to enhanced positive evidence outperformed the control group on the target structure (Spanish noun-adjective agreement). There was no statistically significant advantage found for exposure to implicit negative evidence alone, lending support to the suggestion that it is the enhanced salience of positive evidence provided by recasts, rather than the negative evidence, that is the crucial factor in recasts. It should be noted, nonetheless, that there were no significant differences between the two negative feedback types investigated in this study, thus precluding strong claims about their relative utility.

Comparisons of the effects of different feedback types on classroom development are even less frequent than laboratory studies. Nonetheless, although DeKeyser (1993) originally planned to compare one class that received negative feedback with one that did not, the difference between groups in his classroom study turned out to be the type and amount of negative feedback provided, rather than its absence or presence. Specifically, DeKeyser's post-hoc analysis revealed that although only the teacher in the so-called feedback class corrected student errors explicitly, both teachers provided implicit feedback via the negotiation of meaning (including clarification requests and recasts, among other things). In addition to comparing development in the two classes, DeKeyser also explored possible interactions between feedback and variables such as prior achievement, anxiety, and motivation. As he had predicted, DeKeyser did not find a significant effect for a group alone. However, there were significant interactions between feedback and previous achievement (students with high previous achievement benefited most from negative feedback) and between feedback and anxiety on a written grammar test (students with low anxiety benefited most from feedback), as well as a marginally significant interaction between feedback and extrinsic motivation on an oral communication task (students with high extrinsic motivation benefited marginally more). DeKeyser's study highlights the need to take these learner variables into account when considering the effects of feedback on L2 development (see Part III of this volume for discussions of other individual differences among learners).

In sum, there is a growing body of research which has documented advantages for learners exposed to various types of negative feedback in both laboratory and classroom settings. Nonetheless, because of the wide range of feedback types investigated and the relative scarcity of comparisons among them, there is still no conclusive evidence of specifically which types of feedback are most beneficial. And further, there is still no definitive answer to the question of how feedback promotes L2 development nor of what is the specific contribution of the various components of feedback.

Implications for L2 theory and pedagogy

When considering the implications of the research reviewed in this chapter, it will be important to keep in mind the terminological distinctions outlined at the outset, as they are crucial for understanding what might otherwise seem like contradictory claims and findings. In particular, we saw that many researchers working within the UG paradigm maintain that exposure to negative evidence cannot lead to change in L2 syntactic competence. On the other hand, descriptive studies of interactional feedback suggest that negative evidence is indeed available to many L2 learners and that even implicit negative evidence is often perceived as correction and can lead to immediate incorporation or uptake. Further, experimental studies have documented developmental benefits associated with exposure to several types of negative feedback. Nonetheless, neither of these lines of investigation provides much empirical data to dispute the generativist claim that negative evidence does not contribute to language acquisition, either because developmental effects were not investigated or because negative evidence co-occurred with other variables. At the same time, it should not be overlooked that although this research may not shed much light on the question of negative *evidence*, it does suggest that various kinds of negative *feedback* can facilitate L2 development.

It is important to emphasize that acknowledging the value of feedback does not require the adoption of any one theoretical perspective and that the feedback research presented here can be interpreted in several ways. Indeed, the entire gamut of theoretical perspectives discussed in this chapter is consistent with results from empirical feedback research. For example, if recasts enhance the salience of positive evidence, both generativist and connectionist models of language acquisition, as well as skill acquisition theory, can easily accommodate the empirically documented benefits of exposure to this feedback type. By the same token, the finding that clarification requests can promote the immediate production of modified output is consistent with the idea that negative feedback can lead learners to allocate greater attentional resources to the form of their L2 utterances. In that case, more accurate L2 performance following clarification requests might not reflect change in the learner's underlying L2 competence; instead, it might be a consequence of improved access to the underlying system or to a greater control of production processes. However, the finding that clarification requests led to modified output is certainly also consistent with the notion that such implicit negative evidence can lead to changes in L2 competence. Similarly, if one posits that at least some aspects of SLA are driven by skill acquisition mechanisms, the benefits of feedback are not surprising, although existing feedback research does not directly address this issue. Clearly then, before making any definitive claims, there is a need for additional research which isolates negative evidence and other components of feedback, such as enhanced salience, modified output, and metalinguistic instruction. Such research can provide one means by which to evaluate various theories of SLA and can contribute to a better understanding of feedback generally as well as of the individual components of various feedback types.

The risks associated with making sweeping pedagogical recommendations on the basis of evolving theoretical positions and still limited empirical research are widely recognized and need not be enumerated here. Nonetheless, current theory and existing research can inform the design of instructional programs, and they can suggest at least tentative answers for some pedagogy-related questions. Regarding the pressing question of whether L2 instructors should provide feedback to learners, we have seen that the majority of studies have found positive effects for exposure to feedback, and thus, in my view, the answer to this question must be affirmative.

Does this mean that instructors should interrupt learners every time they make a mistake? Of course not. Not only would such behavior likely interrupt the flow of communication, but it could be detrimental to the learning process by producing anxiety, frustration, and perhaps resentment among learners. In comparison, the choice of forms on which to provide feedback is somewhat more difficult. Based on studies showing that readiness can mediate the effectiveness of feedback as well as research suggesting that feedback can promote proceduralization and automatization, instructors ideally would provide feedback for those linguistic features that learners are either in the process of learning or are ready to learn. However, determining just what those features are is no easy task. In the case of instruction where grammar is taught explicitly with the goal of helping students move from declarative to procedural knowledge, or in any class where activities are designed to target specific linguistic features or forms, feedback should be provided for the forms in focus. In classes with no such structural organization, it is potentially more difficult for an instructor to assess learners' current stages of development and to decide which forms are appropriate for feedback. Because feedback may be beneficial in some of the same ways as focus-on-form instruction, the choice of forms for feedback is closely related to the choice of forms to focus on and may be based on a wide range of factors such as frequency, complexity, and developmental readiness (see Biber & Reppen, 2002; de Graaff, 1997; Hulstijn & de Graaff, 1994; Pienemann, 1985; Williams & Evans, 1998).

How best to provide feedback is perhaps the most difficult question facing researchers and instructors alike. Like L2 instruction generally, feedback should respond to learners' needs, and therefore the most effective type of feedback will depend to some extent on the source of the L2 error (e.g., non-target L2 linguistic competence, insufficient attention to form, inaccurate declarative knowledge, overgeneralized application of rules). Of course it isn't realistic to think that instructors can make such assessments spontaneously, in the midst of interaction with students, especially given our current state of knowledge on SLA and L2 performance. However, in addition to whatever benefits feedback can provide for the learner, certain types of feedback also have the potential to give instructors a better sense both of the source of the problem and of the learner's current L2 knowledge. For example, clarification requests not only emphasize the connection between form and meaning for the student, but they can also provide the instructor with insights on the learner's current knowledge. As Han (2001) argues, the efficacy of classroom feedback depends on the instructor diagnosing and targeting the causal factor of the L2 error. For this reason, clarification requests are especially valuable in the classroom, as they can provide the instructor with insights on the learner's current knowledge, insights that can help the instructor tailor subsequent input and feedback to the student.

As emphasized earlier, immediate modified output may not be a clear indication of linguistic change. Still, it does inform the instructor that learners have recognized the feedback at some level and are able to produce the target form, whether as the result of a new L2 hypothesis or a reallocation of attentional resources. Thus, feedback that promotes such modified output may be particularly useful, especially since it can be provided without interrupting the flow of classroom interaction (Ellis, Basturkmen, & Loewen, 2001). Within a practice perspective that emphasizes the proceduralization and automatization of skills and/or the allocation of attention to form, the opportunity to engage in more targetlike L2 production can be considered beneficial, even if it is not the result of new linguistic knowledge.

Moreover, when learners do not produce modified output even when discourse norms encourage or require it, this failure to produce more targetlike structures can inform the instructor that there is a need for additional intervention. Although there may be other explanations, one possible reason for a learner not to produce modified output in response to a clarification request is a lack of the linguistic resources to do so. In these situations, when meaning is clear to learners and they may be especially ready to make form-meaning connections, it is useful for instructors to provide them with the target form. Existing research discussed in this chapter suggests that highlighting the aspects of the L2 yet to be acquired will be beneficial, whether this is accomplished by enhancing salience of target items or via metalinguistic information at an appropriate level. Thus, the best L2 feedback will be much like the best L2 instruction: it will keep meaning in focus and will not only make target forms salient but also highlight the relationship between specific forms and meanings. Of course, instructors and SLA researchers alike should keep in mind that, given learners' range of learning styles, the monotony (for both learners and instructors) of unchanging routines, and the likelihood that there are many ways to promote L2 development, the use of a variety of types of feedback, rather than a single technique, will likely best serve learners.

Note

1. See Carroll, 2001, for other, more detailed definitions of these constructs, as well as of input and intake.

References

Aljaafreh, A., & Lantolf, J. (1994). Negative feedback as regulation and second language learning in the zone of proximal development. *Modern Language Journal, 78*(4), 465–83.

Anderson, J. (1983). *The architecture of cognition.* Cambridge, MA: Harvard University Press.

Anderson, J. (1993). *Rules of the mind.* Hillsdale, NJ: Lawrence Erlbaum.

Anderson, J., & Fincham, J. (1994). Acquisition of procedural skill from examples. *Journal of Experimental Psychology: Learning, Memory and Cognition, 20,* 1322–40.

Beck, M., & Eubank, L. (1991). Acquisition theory and experimental design: A critique of Tomasello and Herron. *Studies in Second Language Acquisition, 13,* 73–6.

Beck, M., Schwartz, B. D., & Eubank, L. (1995). Data, evidence and rules. In L. Eubank, L. Selinker, & M. S. Smith (Eds.), *The current state of interlanguage: Studies in honor of William E. Rutherford* (pp. 177–95). Philadelphia: John Benjamins.

Biber, D., & Reppen, R. (2002). What does frequency have to do with grammar teaching? *Studies in Second Language Acquisition, 24,* 199–208.

Bley-Vroman, R. (1988). The fundamental character of foreign language learning. In W. Rutherford, & M. Sharwood Smith (Ed.), *Grammar and second language teaching.* Rowley, MA: Newbury House.

Bley-Vroman, R. (1990). The logical problem of foreign language learning. *Linguistic Analysis, 20*(3), 3–49.

Bohannon, J. N., MacWhinney, B., & Snow, C. (1990). No negative evidence revisited: Beyond learnability or who has to prove what to whom. *Developmental Psychology, 26,* 221–6.

Brock, C., Crookes, G., Day, R. R., & Long, M. H. (1986). The differential effects of corrective feedback in native speaker-nonnative speaker conversation. In R. R. Day (Ed.), *Talking to learn: Conversation in second language acquisition* (pp. 229–36). Rowley, MA: Newbury House.

Broeder, P., & Plunkett, K. (1994). Connectionism and second language acquisition. In N. Ellis (Ed.), *Implicit and explicit learning of languages* (pp. 421–53). London: Academic Press.

Brown, R., & Hanlon, C. (1970). Derivational complexity and order of acquisition in child speech. In R. Brown (Ed.), *Psycholinguistics* (pp. 155–207). New York: Free Press.

Carroll, S. (1995). The irrelevance of verbal feedback to language learning. In L. Eubank, L. Selinker, & M. S. Smith (Eds.), *The current state of interlanguage: Studies in honor of William E. Rutherford* (pp. 73–88). Philadelphia: John Benjamins.

Carroll, S. (2001). *Input and evidence: The raw material of second language acquisition.* Philadelphia: John Benjamins.

Carroll, S., & Swain, M. (1993). Explicit and implicit negative feedback: an empirical study of the learning of linguistic generalizations. *Studies in Second Language Acquisition, 15*, 357–86.

Chaudron, C. (1977). A descriptive model of discourse in the corrective treatment of learners' errors. *Language Learning, 27*(1), 29–46.

Chomsky, N. (1981). Principles and parameters in syntactic theory. In N. Hornstein & D. Lightfoot (Eds.), *Explanation in linguistics: The logical problem of language acquisition*. London: Longman.

Day, E. M., & Shapson, S. M. (1991). Integrating formal and functional approaches to language teaching in French immersion: An experimental study. *Language Learning, 41*, 25–58.

de Graaff, R. (1997). The *Experanto* experiment: Effects of explicit instruction on second language acquisition. *Studies in Second Language Acquisition, 19*, 249–76.

DeKeyser, R. M. (1993). The effect of error correction on L2 grammar knowledge and oral proficiency. *Modern Language Journal, 77*, 501–14.

DeKeyser, R. M. (1998). Beyond focus on form: Cognitive perspectives on learning and practicing second language. In C. Doughty & J. Williams (Eds.), *Focus on form in classroom second language acquisition* (pp. 42–63). Cambridge, UK: Cambridge University Press.

DeKeyser, R. (2001). Automaticity and automatization. In P. Robinson (Ed.), *Cognition and second language acquisition* (pp. 125–151). Cambridge, UK: Cambridge University Press.

DeKeyser, R., Salaberry, R., Robinson, P., & Harrington, M. (2002). What gets processed in processing instruction? A commentary on Bill VanPatten's "Update." *Language Learning, 52* (4) 805–23.

Demetras, M. J., Post, K. N., & Snow, C. E. (1986). Feedback to first language learners: The role of repetitions and clarification questions. *Journal of Child Language, 13*, 275–92.

Doughty, C., & Varela, E. (1998). Communicative focus on form. In C. Doughty & J. Williams (Eds.), *Focus on form in classroom second language acquisition* (pp. 114–38). Cambridge, UK: Cambridge University Press.

Ellis, N. (2002). Frequency effects in language processing: A review with implications for theories of implicit and explicit language acquisition. *Studies in Second Language Acquisition, 24*, 143–88.

Ellis, R. (1997). *SLA research and language teaching*. Oxford: Oxford University Press.

Ellis, R. (2002). Does form-focused instruction affect the acquisition of implicit knowledge? A review of research. *Studies in Second Language Acquisition, 24*, 223–36.

Ellis, R., Basturkmen H., & Loewen, S. (2001). Learner uptake in communicative ESL lessons. *Language Learning, 51*, 281–318.

Farrar, M. J. (1990). Discourse and the acquisition of grammatical morphemes. *Journal of Child Language, 17*, 607–24.

Gass, S. M. (1997). *Input, interaction and the second language learner*. Mahwah, NJ: Lawrence Erlbaum.

Gass, S. M., & Mackey, A. (2002). Frequency effects in and second language acquisition: A complex picture? *Studies in Second Language Acquisition, 24*, 249–60.

Goldschneider, J. M., & DeKeyser, R. M. (2001). Explaining the "natural order of L2 morpheme acquisition" in English: A meta-analysis of multiple determinants. *Language Learning, 51*(1), 1–50.

Gregg, K. R. (1996). The logical and developmental problems of second language acquisition. In W. C. Ritchie & T. K. Bhatia (Eds.), *Handbook of second language acquisition* (pp. 49–81). San Diego: Academic Press.

Halstijn, J., & de Graaff, R. (1994). Under what conditions does explicit knowledge of a second language facilitate the acquisition of implicit knowledge? A research proposal. *AILA Review, 11*, 97–112.

Han, Z. (2001). Fine-tuning corrective feedback. *Foreign Language Annals, 34* (6), 582–99.

Han, Z. (2002). A study of the impact of recasts on tense consistency in L2 output. *TESOL Quarterly, 36* (4), 543–72.

Harley, B. (1998). The role of focus-on-form tasks in promoting child L2 acquisition. In C. Doughty & J. Williams (Eds.), *Focus on form in classroom second language acquisition* (pp. 156–74). Cambridge, UK: Cambridge University Press.

Herron, C., & Tomasello, M. (1988). Learning grammatical structures in a foreign language: Modeling versus feedback. *The French Review, 61*(6), 910–22.

Hirsh-Pasek, K., Treiman, R., & Schneiderman, M. (1984). Brown & Hanlon revisited: mothers' sensitivity to ungrammatical forms. *Journal of Child Language, 11*, 81–88.

Iwashita, N. (2003). Negative feedback and positive evidence in task-based interaction: Differential effects on L2 development. *Studies in Second Language Acquisition, 25*(1), 1–36.

Izumi, S., & Lakshmanan, U. (1998). Learnability, negative evidence and the L2 acquisition of the English passive. *Second Language Research, 14*(1), 62–101.

Krashen, S. (1981). *Second language acquisition and second language learning.* London: Pergamon.

Lantolf, J. P. (Ed.). (2000). *Sociocultural theory and second language learning.* Oxford, UK: Oxford University Press.

Leeman, J. (2003). Recasts and second language development: Beyond negative evidence. *Studies in Second Language Acquisition, 25*, 37–63.

Leeman, J., Arteagoitia, I., Doughty, C., & Fridman, B. (1995). Integrating attention to form with meaning: Focus on Form in Spanish content-based instruction. In R. W. Schmidt (Ed.), *Attention & awareness in foreign language learning (Technical report #9)* (pp. 217–58). Honolulu: University of Hawaii, Second Language Teaching and Curriculum Center.

Lightbown, P. M. (1998). The importance of timing in focus on form. In C. Doughty & J. Williams (Eds.), *Focus on form in classroom second language acquisition* (pp. 177–96). Cambridge, UK: Cambridge University Press.

Long, M. H. (1991). Focus on form: a design feature in language teaching methodology. In K. de Bot, R. Ginsburg, & C. Kramsch (Eds.), *Foreign language research in a crosscultural perspective* (pp. 39–52). Amsterdam: John Benjamins.

Long, M. H. (1996). The role of the linguistic environment in second language acquisition. In W. C. Ritchie & T. K. Bhatia (Eds.), *Handbook of second language acquisition* (Vol. 26), pp. 413–68). San Diego: Academic Press.

Long, M. H., Inagaki, S., & Ortega, L. (1998). The role of implicit feedback in SLA: Models and recasts in Japanese and Spanish. *Modern Language Journal, 82*(3), 357–71.

Loschky, L. (1994). Comprehensible input and second language acquisition: What is the relationship? *Studies in Second Language Acquisition, 16,* 303–23.

Lyster, R. (1998). Recasts, repetition, and ambiguity in L2 classroom discourse. *Studies in Second Language Acquisition, 20,* 51–81.

Lyster, R., & Ranta, L. (1997). Corrective feedback and learner uptake. *Studies in Second Language Acquisition, 19,* 37–66.

Mackey, A. (1999). Input, interaction and second language development: an empirical study of question formation in ESL. *Studies in Second Language Acquisition, 21,* 557–87.

Mackey, A., & Philp, J. (1998). Conversational interaction and second language development: Recasts, responses, and red herrings? *Modern Language Journal, 82*(3), 338–56.

Mackey, A., Gass, S., & McDonough, K. (2000). How do learners perceive interactional feedback? *Studies in Second Language Acquisition, 22,* 471–97.

Mackey, A., Oliver, R., & Leeman, J. (2003). Interactional input and the incorporation of feedback: An exploration of NS-NNS and NNS-NNS adult and child dyads. *Language Learning, 53*(1) 35–56.

MacWhinney, B. (1987). The competition model. In B. MacWhinney (Ed.), *Mechanisms of language acquisition* (pp. 249–308). Hillsdale, NJ: Lawrence Erlbaum.

MacWhinney, B. (2001). The competition model: The input, the context and the brain. In P. Robinson (Ed.), *Cognition and second language acquisition* (pp. 69–90). Cambridge, UK: Cambridge University Press.

Mitchell, R., & Myles, F. (1998). *Second language learning theories.* London: Arnold.

Morgan, J. L., Bonamo, K. M., & Travis, L. L. (1995). Negative evidence on negative evidence. *Developmental Psychology, 31,* 180–97.

Muranoi, H. (2000). Focus on form through interaction enhancement: Integrating formal instruction into a communicative task in EFL classrooms. *Language Learning, 50,* 617–73.

Nicholas, H., Lightbown, P., & Spada, N. (2001). Recasts as feedback to language learners. *Language Learning, 51,* 719–58.

Norris, J., & Ortega, L. (2000). Effectiveness of L2 instruction: A research synthesis and quantitative meta-analysis. *Language Learning, 50,* 417–528.

Ohta, A. S. (2001). *Second language acquisition processes in the classroom.* Mahwah, NJ: Lawrence Erlbaum.

Oliver, R. (1995). Negative feedback in child NS-NNS conversation. *Studies in Second Language Acquisition, 17,* 459–81.

Oliver, R. (2000). Age differences in negotiation and feedback in classroom and pairwork. *Language Learning, 50,* 119–51.

Oliver, R. (2002). The patterns of negotiation for meaning in child interactions. *Modern Language Journal, 86*(1), 97–111.

Philp, J. (2003). Constraints on "noticing the gap": Non-native speakers' noticing of recasts in NS-NNS interaction. *Studies in Second Language Acquisition, 25*(1), 99–126.

Pica, T., Holliday, L., Lewis, N., & Morgenthaler, L. (1989). Comprehensible output as an outcome of the linguistic demands on the learner. *Studies in Second Language Acquisition, 11*, 63–90.

Pienemann, M. (1985). Learnability and syllabus construction. In K. Hyltenstam & M. Pienemann (Eds.), *Modelling and assessing second language acquisition*. Clevedon, UK: Multilingual Matters.

Pinker, S. (1989). *Learnability and cognition: The acquisition of argument structure*. Cambridge, MA: MIT Press.

Plunkett, K. (1995). Connectionist approaches to language acquisition. In P. Fletcher & B. MacWhinney (Eds.), *The handbook of child language* (pp. 36–72). Oxford: Blackwell.

Ramirez, A. G. & Stromquist, N. P. (1979). ESL methodology and student language learning in bilingual elementary schools. *TESOL Quarterly, 13*(2), 145–58.

Roberts, M. A. (1995). Awareness and the efficacy of error correction. In R. W. Schmidt (Ed.), *Attention & awareness in foreign language learning (Technical Report #9)* (pp. 163–82). Honolulu: University of Hawaii, Second Language Teaching and Curriculum Center.

Robinson, P. (1996). *Consciousness, rules and instructed second language acquisition*. New York: Peter Lang.

Salaberry, M. R. (1997). The role of input and output practice in second language acquisition. *Canadian Modern Language Review, 53*, 422–51.

Saxton, M. (1997). The Contrast Theory of negative input. *Journal of Child Language, 24*, 139–61.

Schachter, J. (1991). Corrective feedback in historical perspective. *Second Language Research, 7*(2), 89–102.

Schwartz, B. D. (1993). On explicit and negative data effecting and affecting *competence* and *linguistic behavior*. *Studies in Second Language Acquisition, 15*, 147–63.

Schwartz, B. D., & Gubala-Ryzak, M. (1992). Learnability and grammar reorganization in L2A: Against negative evidence causing the unlearning of verb movement. *Second Language Research, 8*, 1–38.

Semke, H. D. (1984). Effects of the red pen. *Foreign Language Annals, 17*, 195–202.

Skehan, P. (1998). *A cognitive approach to language learning*. Oxford: Oxford University Press.

Skehan, P., & Foster, P. (2001). Cognition and tasks. In P. Robinson (Ed.), *Cognition and second language acquisition* (pp. 183–205). Cambridge, UK: Cambridge University Press.

Skinner, B. F. (1957). *Verbal behavior*. Englewood Cliffs, NJ: Prentice-Hall.

Spada, N. (1997). Form-focused instruction and second language acquisition: A review of classroom and laboratory research. *Language Teaching, 30*, 73–87.

Spada, N., & Lightbown, P. M. (1993). Instruction and the development of questions in L2 classrooms. *Studies in Second Language Acquisition, 15*, 205–24.

Swain, M. (1995). Three functions of output in second language learning. In G. Cook & B. Seidlhofer (Eds.), *Principle and practice in applied linguistics: Studies in honour of H. G. Widdowson* (pp. 125–44). Oxford, UK: Oxford University Press.

Tomasello, M., & Herron, C. (1988). Down the garden path: Inducing and correcting overgeneralization errors in the foreign language classroom. *Applied Psycholinguistics, 9*, 237–46.

Tomasello, M., & Herron, C. (1989). Feedback for language transfer errors. *Studies in Second Language Acquisition, 11*(4), 385–95.

Tomasello, M., & Herron, C. (1991). Experiments in the real world: A reply to Beck and Eubank. *Studies in Second Language Acquisition, 13*, 513–17.

VanPatten, B. (1996). *Input processing and grammar instruction in second language acquisition.* Norwood, NJ: Ablex.

VanPatten, B. (2002). Processing instruction: An update. *Language Learning, 52*(4), 755–803.

VanPatten, B., & Cadierno, T. (1993). Input processing and second language acquisition: A role for instruction. *Modern Language Journal, 77*, (45–57).

VanPatten, B., & Sanz, C. (1995). From input to output: Processing instruction and communicative tasks. In F. Eckman, D. Highland, P. Lee, J. Mileham, & R. Weber (Eds.), *Second language theory and pedagogy* (pp. 169–86). Philadelphia: Lawrence Erlbaum.

White, L. (1987). Against comprehensible input: The Input Hypothesis and the development of L2 competence. *Applied Linguistics, 8*, 95–110.

White, L. (1991). Adverb placement in second language acquisition: Some effects of positive and negative evidence in the classroom. *Second Language Research, 7*, 133–61.

White, L., Lightbown, P. M., Ranta, L., & Spada, N. (1991). Input enhancement and L2 question formation. *Applied Linguistics, 12*(4), 416–32.

Williams, J., & Evans, J. (1998). What kind of focus and on which forms? In C. Doughty & J. Williams (Eds.), *Focus on form in classroom second language acquisition* (pp. 139–55). Cambridge, UK: Cambridge University Press.

PART II:
INSTITUTIONAL CONTEXTS

The chapters in this section illustrate the variety of specific concerns about the nature of practice that follow from different contexts for teaching a second/foreign language. In the foreign language context, Lourdes Ortega argues, one has to make an effort to make sure that practice is meaningful. She explains how pair or group work and electronic communication can help realize this goal and presents evidence that such activities do not necessarily jeopardize all concern for accuracy, evidence that interaction with other speakers of the same L1 presents advantages when it comes to negotiation of meaning or pushed output for grammar. The different native languages involved in a second language context make this negotiation of grammatical form harder, which helps to explain why students focus so much on lexis and pronunciation in that context. In the second language classroom, as Kris Van den Branden argues, drawing on his experience with child L2 learners in Dutch-speaking Belgium, communicating in the L2 may be more natural, but students do not get sufficient practice if no effort is made to bridge the gap between focused practice of the L2 and use of what was practiced in the "real" second language context, be it in other classes or in the world outside of school. Leila Ranta and Roy Lyster discuss a problem that is typical of immersion contexts: repeated L2 practice in the classroom with native speakers of the same L1 leads to students not realizing how far removed their classroom norms are from those of real native speakers. The authors argue for more systematic practice of form, emphasizing the role of feedback. DeKeyser shows that college students going abroad do not get nearly as much good practice as is often assumed, which is probably the reason their progress, if measured objectively, and especially in the area of accuracy, is often far below expectations. He argues that this limited progress largely stems from a failure to proceduralize grammatical knowledge in the classroom, which leaves learners unprepared to take advantage of the semester abroad for automatizing their knowledge.

In spite of the variety of problems for practice posed by these different contexts, however, there clearly are common themes: that practice should be of sufficient quantity and that practice is problematic in all contexts, even those that are traditionally thought of as the most conducive to good practice. The main difference is in what requires the most emphasis in the various contexts: meaningfulness in the foreign language context (without completely sacrificing task-essentialness of form), establishing bridges with L2 practice beyond the L2 class in the second language context, ensuring enough focus on form and quality feedback in the immersion context, and preparing students for the study abroad context by better systematic practice in the classroom, at least up to the level of proceduralization.

5 A cognitive approach to improving immersion students' oral language abilities: The Awareness-Practice-Feedback sequence

Leila Ranta
Roy Lyster

Consider the experiences of a grade-12 student who has studied French for a total of 13 years in Alberta, the first few years of which were in a total immersion program where all instruction was in French. She travels to Montreal for the first time. To her great shock, she finds that she is unable to use her French very much because the bilingual speakers she comes into contact with switch to English the minute they hear her speak. She comments, "I quickly realized . . . that my French is not the same as Quebecois French" (Haynes, 2001). This experience of communicative failure in the second language (L2) puts a human face on the research findings that characterize the oral production of French immersion students as being "non-nativelike." Immersion researchers have studied the effectiveness of different types of pedagogical interventions designed to overcome the limitations of immersion instruction. These interventions have included enriching the input learners are exposed to (Harley, 1989b), drawing learners' attention to non-salient features of the L2 (Lyster, 1994), increasing the amount of student output (Kowal & Swain, 1997), and providing unambiguous feedback on learners' non-targetlike utterances (Lyster, 2004). This chapter examines the issue of the non-nativelike quality of immersion students' L2 production from the perspective of the language practice that occurs in early immersion classrooms. In this discussion, we highlight the value of using cognitive skill-learning theory (Anderson, 1983) as a framework for sequencing instructional activities aimed at improving the formal accuracy of the otherwise fluent speech of immersion students.

L2 speaking abilities of immersion students

In early total immersion programs, anglophone children begin school in kindergarten where all instruction is in the L2. They are encouraged to use the L2 for communication; grammatical and structural errors are not given undue attention. The teachers seek above all to foster positive attitudes toward learning French. The results from evaluations of early immersion programs are widely known thanks to many syntheses of the research (e.g., Genesee, 1987; Rebuffot, 1993; Swain & Lapkin, 1982). The overwhelming pattern is that immersion students do as well in their academic achievement as their peers in the regular English language program while at the same time attaining superior levels of performance on all measures of French proficiency. They also compare favorably to French native speakers on many measures of reading and listening comprehension. However, the oral and written production skills of French immersion students, while comparable to French speakers of the same age in some respects, remain clearly non-targetlike in many others.

With respect to oral proficiency, both fluency and accuracy were assessed in the large-scale evaluations of immersion programs by McGill University researchers in the 1960s and 1970s. The usual procedure was to elicit speech samples from learners and then have these samples rated by native speakers of French on a number of different dimensions using a 5-point scale (Genesee, 1987). Samples from francophone children of the same age were also included, and the raters were unaware of which samples were from the immersion students and which from the native speakers. For example, in one longitudinal study (Genesee, 1978), students' oral production was rated for overall fluency, grammatical correctness, enunciation, rhythm and intonation, and occurrence of liaisons. In addition, word counts were calculated for the whole sample and different word classes. The ratings of the early immersion students at different grades were significantly different from those of native speakers of the same age for grammatical correctness and different aspects of pronunciation (see Genesee, 1978, Tables 3 and 5). However, some of the fluency-related measures for the immersion groups are comparable to those for native speakers (i.e., overall fluency rating for grades 1 and 2, total number of words, and number of nouns and verbs). In the higher grades, differences between L2 learners and native speakers emerge across the board; the mean ratings for the immersion groups are in the 3.5–5.0 range, whereas the mean for the native speaker groups range from 4.9–5.0. This pattern of results for grades 4–6 is consistent with the findings from a number of studies involving immersion students at the end of secondary school. In a synthesis article, Pawley (1985, p. 874) concluded that "the majority of the students are able to communicate, albeit with some hesitation, errors and some vocabulary limitations especially with more specific topics."

These research findings confirm the impressions of parents and teachers that a content-based approach to L2 learning develops children's ability to communicate effectively in French. On the other hand, as the ratings for grammar in Genesee (1978) reveal, their grammatical accuracy is consistently lower than that of native speakers. Studies of the interlanguage of French immersion students have documented immersion students' non-targetlike use of the following types of features in French: verbs and prepositions (Harley, 1989a; Harley, Cummins, Swain, & Allen, 1990), object pronouns (Harley, 1980), word order (Selinker, Swain, & Dumas, 1975), grammatical gender (Harley, 1979), politeness markers such as singular *vous* and mitigating conditionals (Lyster & Rebuffot, 2002; Swain & Lapkin, 1990), informal variants (Mougeon & Rehner, 2001; Rehner & Mougeon, 1999), and discourse markers (Rehner, 2002). Harley (1994) characterized the oral production of immersion students as containing phonologically salient, high-frequency lexical items, along with syntactic patterns that are generally congruent with the first language (L1) but lacking in the less salient morphosyntactic features which are incongruent with the L1 or not crucial for getting one's meaning across.

The picture that emerges from the many studies of the effects of immersion is of L2 speakers who are relatively fluent and effective communicators but non-targetlike in terms of grammatical structure and non-idiomatic in their lexical choices and pragmatic expression. Not surprisingly, when immersion students have the opportunity to interact with native speakers of French of the same age, for example, on a school exchange, they often encounter real difficulties in making themselves understood (MacFarlane, 2001; Warden, Hart, Lapkin, & Swain, 1995).

A search for explanations in the classroom

The results described in the preceding section regarding immersion students' L2 learning outcomes were confirmed by many program evaluations and other product-oriented research designs. Little was initially known, however, about what actually went on in immersion classrooms, apart from the overriding theoretical assumption that the L2 learning of young children in an immersion context was believed to parallel in many respects their L1 acquisition. Since the late 1980s, the search for an explanation of immersion students' oral production abilities (or lack thereof) has focused on the nature of instruction in immersion classrooms.

Teaching subject matter to learners in a language in which they have limited proficiency clearly requires teaching strategies unlike those used in mother tongue instruction. Testimonials from immersion teachers (e.g., Snow, 1987) have indeed revealed their commitment, in addition to ensuring the psychological development of the children in their charge, to transforming subject matter into comprehensible input by drawing extensively on *negotiation of meaning* strategies. Met (1994) explains that immersion teachers help students get their meaning across by encouraging them initially to use both verbal and non-verbal means of communicating. Immersion teachers are expected to maintain open channels of communication and to make rich interpretations of students' attempts to communicate by responding with various reformulations and expansions that also serve as confirmations and comprehension checks. As students expand their productive repertoires, teachers are expected (1) to increase their students' opportunities to use the L2 through, for example, frequent collaborative learning activities, and (2) to assist students in refining their productive skills by means of feedback responses from the teacher or other students.

The Development of Bilingual Proficiency (DBP) Study undertaken in the 1980s by Harley, Allen, Cummins, and Swain (1990) aimed, in part, to link immersion L2 outcomes to immersion classroom processes. The findings from the observational component of the study revealed that what experienced immersion teachers strove to do (cf. Snow, 1987) and what they were expected to do (cf. Met, 1994) did not necessarily happen in the classroom. For example, they found that opportunities for sustained talk by immersion students were infrequent (Allen, Swain, Harley, & Cummins, 1990). Fewer than 15 percent of student turns in French were more than a clause in length, and this represented a considerably smaller proportion of the sustained speech observed during the English portion of the day. A more recent classroom observation study found that Grade 5 immersion students were engaged in group activities during 16 percent of their instructional time, which is still a fairly low percentage of class time (Fazio & Lyster, 1998).

Allen et al. (1990) also reported that the "speech acts which occur naturally in the classroom context may provide little opportunity for students to produce the full range of target language forms" (p. 74). These observations have been used to explain why immersion students develop high levels of comprehension skills but experience persistent grammatical and sociolinguistic difficulties in their productive abilities. It has also been suggested that subject-matter instruction generates functionally restricted input and, thus, does not on its own provide adequate exposure to the L2 (Swain, 1988). For example, analyses of audio recordings revealed only rare occurrences of conditional and imperfect verb forms in classroom input; this parallels the well-attested finding that students fail to master or even use these forms after several years in French immersion. The concept of functional restriction is not limited to grammatical or pragmatic functions. It can also be seen to apply to the level of macrofunctions (Cook, 1989). Tarone and Swain (1995) describe immersion students' use of French as diglossic, with French associated with academic (or referential) functions and English associated with social interaction functions.

The classroom studies reported in Allen et al. (1990) also revealed that immersion teachers' corrective feedback was infrequent as well as confusing. In the analysis of classroom transcripts by Lyster and Ranta

(1997), teachers preferred to give corrective feedback through recasts, that is, reformulations of students' nontarget output without any overt signal. The teachers' use of such implicit corrective feedback can be seen as well suited to the focus on meaning in immersion classrooms. However, precisely because learners are focused on communicating meaning, the implicitness of recasts makes this kind of feedback difficult to notice in the hurly-burly of classroom discourse (Lyster, 1998a). Furthermore, immersion teachers use many positive feedback moves (e.g., "Yes, that's right!") to respond to the content of learners' messages, irrespective of their well-formedness. Consequently, there appears to be considerable linguistic ambiguity in immersion classrooms from the perspective of young L2 learners whose language production, whether well- or ill-formed, is equally likely to be followed by teacher responses that appear to confirm or approve the form of the message.

The DBP researchers also investigated how grammar was taught in immersion. Teachers were found to provide grammar instruction during language arts lessons but did so in isolated grammar activities that required students to manipulate forms in a decontextualized way (Chaudron, 1986; Swain, 1996). Immersion teachers tended to separate language teaching from content teaching, considering attention to language form in a history or mathematics class to be inappropriate and thus delaying attention to form until the language arts class. Yet even in the language arts class, it is not certain that an explicit focus on grammatical form will take place. Dicks (1992) found that language arts classes tended to be more experiential for early immersion classes and more analytic for middle- and late-immersion classes. For example, in one early-immersion language arts class, the activity was a class debate on euthanasia in which "there was no explicit reference to functional, discoursal, or sociolinguistic language use. The teacher's reference to language form was largely restricted to vocabulary and expressions that were needed for communication. If an incorrect expression was repeated, this was written on the board and the correct expression was given" (p. 59).

A call for pedagogical interventions

In response to this state of affairs, immersion researchers articulated a number of solutions (Allen et al., 1990). They recommended:

> ... *carefully planned and guided communicative practice* that will push students towards the production of comprehensible output. One form of guidance is to engage students in activities contrived by the teacher to focus attention on potential problems, that will naturally elicit particular uses of language. Another form of guidance is to develop activities that make use of functions which would otherwise rarely be encountered in the classroom. (p. 76, emphasis added)

These recommendations provided a research agenda that motivated a whole decade of research (see overviews by Lyster, 2004b; Spada, 1997).

These pedagogical intervention studies demonstrated that form-focused instruction can lead to enhanced learner performance to varying degrees. Consider four frequently cited studies that included carefully planned and guided communicative practice. Harley (1989b) found some immediate but no long-term benefits for immersion students' oral and written production of the *passé composé/imparfait* distinction. Day and Shapson (1991) found long-term benefits in students' use of the conditional, but only on paper-and-pencil tasks. Students in Lyster's (1994) study made gains in their appropriate use of *tu/vous* in both speech and writing and maintained these gains over time. Finally, in her study of the acquisition of grammatical gender by Grade 2 immersion students, Harley (1998) found gains on aural discrimination tasks as well as in oral performance, but only in the case of familiar words; the children were unable to apply what they had learned to new, unfamiliar nouns in oral production.

The more recent work of Swain and Lapkin (1998, 2001) has focused on the metalinguistic function of output, which has been investigated through the use of collaborative writing tasks. The researchers argue that dictogloss and jigsaw tasks serve to focus learners' attention on their own language use, which may provide an opportunity for language learning to take place. It is not certain, however, that collaborative metalinguistic discussion tasks will lead to higher levels of grammatical accuracy in learners' *spoken* French. The theory of transfer-appropriate learning posits that "a learning condition will be transfer appropriate if it activates cognitive operations that are likely to be reinstated later when the individual attempts to put the learning into practice" (Segalowitz, 2000, p. 213). In other words, the kind of cognitive processing that occurs while performing learning tasks must be similar to the kind of processing involved during communicative language use. If immersion students are to speak a more nativelike French, cognitive processing needs to be taken into account in any attempt to improve immersion pedagogy.

A cognitive perspective

The theoretical assumption underlying the first immersion programs was that the L2 "is acquired in much the same manner as children acquire their first language, by interacting with speakers of the language in authentic and meaningful communicative situations" (Swain & Lapkin, 1982, p. 5). SLA researchers who first studied the L2 development of French immersion students were naturally influenced by the SLA theory of the 1970s and 1980s, which emphasized learner-internal processes and considered input to be a trigger for acquisition (Gass & Selinker, 1994). According to this view, learners who are exposed to meaningful input will develop an implicit grammatical system which underlies L2 use in production and comprehension. The L1 model also offers justification for using implicit correction in response to learner errors because parents do not generally correct children's formal errors. Not surprisingly, Krashen (1984), whose Monitor Model has as its foundation the similarity between L1 and L2, has touted the immersion model as the best illustration of his theory. However, the results concerning the non-nativelike grammar of immersion students suggests that they need something more than meaningful input in order to attain high levels of accuracy (Swain, 1985). The idea of a pedagogical intervention to help learners focus on form is incompatible with Krashen's theoretical model in which neither metalinguistic information nor output practice can influence the developing L2 system (Krashen, 1994). In contrast, cognitive theory offers a framework to interpret attested learning outcomes and to guide the development of pedagogical treatments.

Cognitive theory is a fairly recent newcomer to the field of SLA (see McLaughlin, 1987; McLaughlin & Heredia, 1996; Robinson, 2001) and has had limited application in French immersion research (but see Day & Shapson, 1991; Lyster, 1994). This model considers skill development in terms of a broader, information-processing framework in which performance is examined in the light of limitations on the amount of effort humans can allocate to any particular cognitive task (e.g., Shiffrin & Schneider, 1977). Two separate modes of processing have been proposed: automatic and controlled. Initially, new tasks can be handled only using controlled processing. Practice plays an important role in improving performance so that it becomes more rapid and stable. This occurs when components of a skill become automatized, which then liberates attentional resources for use in higher-level processing.

In general terms, the concept of automaticity refers to performance which has become faster, more reliable, and apparently effortless through extensive practice (Segalowitz & Gatbonton, 1995). Despite disagreements among researchers as to the criteria defining automaticity, it is generally accepted that such notions as the power law of practice, specificity of practice, and memory load independence are characteristic of the automatization process (see comprehensive review by DeKeyser, 2001). According to Segalowitz (1997, 2000, 2003; Segalowitz & Lightbown, 1999), L2 fluency in speaking and reading involves the ability to rapidly retrieve from memory appropriate linguistic knowledge and routines, to perform in a smooth manner in the face of distractions, and to perform without disruption when confronted with the unexpected. These abilities reflect high levels of automaticity and of attention-based controlled processing. The development of automaticity requires repetition with consistent associations between stimuli and the learner's cognitive responses. Unlike audiolingual drills, where the words were changed in order to highlight the underlying abstract pattern, automaticity practice requires that the same words and meanings be associated. Segalowitz (2000) argues that attention-based or controlled processing is affected by the transfer appropriateness of the learning situation. In the case of L2 learning, this means using learning tasks that involve processing words and formulae for communicative purposes. Thus, fluent performance is the result of practice that (1) has been extensive and repetitive (thus building automaticity) and (2) has been genuinely communicative in nature (therefore, transfer-appropriate).

The concept of automaticity is important for understanding the oral production abilities of French immersion students who are fluent but non-targetlike. It suggests that learners have automatized interlanguage forms rather than target-language forms. Lyster (1987) and Harley (1989a, 1992) have argued that immersion students' interlanguage is heavily influenced by the L1 (e.g., "*j'étais six*" instead of "*j'avais six ans*"). The connection of interlanguage forms to their corresponding L1 representations in memory is likely to contribute to their greater accessibility in spontaneous communication. As immersion classes consist of learners who share English as either a first or dominant language and, to a large degree, share the same interlanguage, common non-target forms are further reinforced by peer input.

In addition to the effect of what Wong Fillmore (1992) refers to as "learnerese input" provided by peers, teachers' feedback habits may also serve to reinforce interlanguage forms. On the one hand, teachers give priority to teaching content and do not necessarily provide corrective feedback for forms that are ungrammatical but comprehensible. On the other hand, the feedback that teachers do give usually takes the form of recasts and may not be noticed by students (Lyster, 1998a; Lyster & Ranta, 1997). Finally, as Lyster (1998a) has demonstrated, the affective feedback that teachers provide in the form of signs of approval conveys mixed messages to the learner. When a teacher responds to a learner's errorful utterance with "Excellent!" she is thinking of the child's psychological development. Unfortunately, this kind of response may cause errors to fossilize. Feedback that is too implicit or ambiguous to be noticed as negative feedback, along with various signs of approval confirming the veracity of learner utterances irrespective of form, converge to convey to students the message that "more of the same" (Vigil & Oller, 1976, p. 286) is desirable.

Clearly, changing learners' tendency to use highly accessible interlanguage forms is no small undertaking. The challenge is to help learners develop new targetlike representations that can compete with the interlanguage forms, and this necessarily requires incorporating a larger role for automatization practice in pedagogical interventions (de Bot, 2000). This is not a new idea in the literature on form-focused instruction in French immersion; Day and Shapson (1991) and Lyster (1994) emphasized learners' need to automatize new knowledge and suppress old routines. However, there does not appear to be much awareness in immersion pedagogy of the ongoing need for automaticity/fluency-building activities in addition to interesting content-based activities. Following DeKeyser (1998), we propose using the cognitive skill-learning model developed by Anderson (1983, 1993) as the basis for organizing form-focused instruction that can be integrated into content-based L2 instruction.

The three-phase model of skill learning

Anderson's Adaptive Control of Thought (ACT)[1] model views skill learning as the proceduralization of rule-bound declarative knowledge through practice and feedback. Declarative knowledge refers to knowledge about facts and things whereas procedural knowledge refers to knowledge about how to perform various cognitive activities (Anderson, 1983). Anderson, Corbett, Koedinger, and Pelletier (1995) summarize the main tenets of ACT as follows: declarative knowledge is encoded directly from observation and instruction. Skill development depends on transforming this knowledge into production rules that represent procedural knowledge. Production rules can only be acquired through practice. In order to facilitate skill learning, instructional activities should "set up contexts in which these skills can be displayed, monitored, and appropriate feedback given to shape their acquisition" (Anderson et al., 1995, p. 171).

Following Fitts (1964), Anderson (1983) describes skill learning in terms of three phases or stages of learning. The sequence begins with the *cognitive* phase, which is dominated by learning rules and items of factual knowledge. Learners either receive instruction about how to do a task, observe an expert, or attempt to do it themselves. This involves conscious effort on the part of the learner, and the knowledge gained is typically declarative; performance is slow and full of errors. At the next stage, which is called *associative*, declarative knowledge is turned into procedural knowledge through practice, but the declarative representation is not lost. Here performance is still slower and more errorful than expert performance. Given extensive practice and feedback, learners may attain the final or *autonomous* stage, which is characterized by performance which is automatic, error free, and with little demand on working memory or consciousness. Models with four or five stages have also been proposed (see DeKeyser, 1998, p. 127 for discussion), but the advantage of Anderson's framework is that it parallels the well-established instructional sequence of Presentation-Practice-Production

(PPP). Although proponents of task-based L2 instruction like Willis (1996) and Skehan (1998) dismiss the PPP approach on a number of points, little empirical evidence is offered to support the claims. As DeKeyser (1998) has argued, this learning model has not really been adequately tested by SLA researchers, so dismissing it entirely from consideration is premature.

The value of Anderson's three-part structure for the immersion context is that it provides a logical sequence for selecting activities that promote awareness of target-language structures, on the one hand, and activities that build fluency, on the other. Furthermore, as learners progress from fluency-building tasks to those with a greater content focus, the provision of feedback on errors becomes ever more important. Thus, the cognitive skill-building sequence brings together in a coherent framework the concepts of output, noticing the gap, fluency, automaticity, and feedback, which have often been discussed in the SLA literature in isolation. In applying this sequence to immersion, the term *cognitive-associative-autonomous* appears too abstract and the term *presentation-practice-production* too closely tied to audiolingual teaching methods. We have therefore chosen to label the sequence in as transparent a manner as possible (with apologies for adding new terminology): *Awareness-Practice-Feedback*. In the sections that follow, the pedagogical features of each of the three phases are explored.

The awareness phase

The purpose of the awareness phase is to draw learners' attention to the target feature. This could take the form of metalinguistic statements, such as "In French, the conditional verb form is used to express hypothetical relationships." There is, however, no reason to view the awareness stage in a language lesson as limited to deductive, metalinguistic statements of this kind. Indeed, the use of decontextualized grammar rules and metalanguage is unlikely to hold the attention of children who are used to meaningful language activities in the immersion classroom. What is needed are tasks which will help students notice the gap between what they say and the corresponding target-language forms (Schmidt & Frota, 1986; Swain, 1995).

Rather than using deductive tasks to focus on grammatical features, it is likely that learners would find inductive tasks more motivating. For example, Harley (1989b) designed an activity for teaching two tenses in French, the *imparfait* and the *passé composé*. Learners had a text in which the *passé composé* and *imparfait* occurred with clearly differentiated functions. Students were to induce the rules underlying the choice between the *imparfait* and the *passé composé*. Another motivating technique is the consciousness-raising task (Fotos, 1994) in which learners work cooperatively in groups to complete a task that is designed to focus their attention on a particular grammatical feature of the target language. In Lyster (1994), for example, a cooperative jigsaw task was used to teach the differences between formal and informal registers in French. Swain's program of research on the benefits of using collaborative dictogloss and jigsaw tasks is also relevant here (e.g., Kowal & Swain, 1994, 1997; Swain & Lapkin, 1998, 2001). Through the attempt to construct collaboratively a correct written text in French (either through the reconstruction of an aural text or creation of a text based on pictures), learners gain awareness about what aspects of the target language they do not know (Swain & Lapkin, 2001).

The practice phase

According to Anderson (e.g., 1983), once new knowledge is available in declarative form, learners need practice opportunities to make access to this knowledge automatic. Proceduralization is achieved through "communicative drills" where students communicate something while they keep the relevant declarative knowledge in working memory. At first glance, the image of boring drills like those typical of audiolingual materials seems inconsistent with pedagogical practices in French immersion. But the crucial characteristic of a drill is repetition within a narrow context. Indeed, the games and songs of children in the earliest years of immersion can be considered communicative drills. Recent years have seen a greater recognition of the role of repetition in L2 learning (DeKeyser, 1997, 2001; Hulstijn, 2001; Gatbonton & Segalowitz, 1988; Segalowitz & Lightbown, 1999). Gatbonton and Segalowitz (1988, 2005) were among the first to argue for what they called "creative automatization" within communicative language teaching. They argued that tasks should be both inherently repetitive and psychologically authentic. Hulstijn (2001) discusses the value of exposing students to reading and listening texts more than once. Nation (1989) describes the 4/3/2 technique, which provides both repetition and a time constraint. Each learner prepares a talk on a given topic and then is paired up with another student to whom the learner delivers his or her talk uninterrupted for four minutes; the students then change partners and the same speaker gives the same talk to a different listener in three minutes. Finally, the learners change partners again and this time the speaker has two minutes to give the same talk. The language game described by Day and Shapson (1991) is an example of an activity with a grammatical focus and a time constraint. The teacher chooses from a list of hypothetical clauses of the type "If I had a million dollars, I would take a trip to Europe" (i.e., "*Si j'avais 1,000,000$, alors je voyagerais en Europe*") and asks competing teams of students to complete it in as many ways as possible in 30 seconds.

The role-plays in Lyster (1994) and the songs and rhymes used in Harley (1998) also provide opportunities for repetition in an enjoyable way.

An excellent example of content-driven activities which are inherently repetitive and psychologically authentic is described in Doughty and Varela (1998). The study took place in a content-based ESL science class; the form-focused instruction targeted the simple past and the conditional past in the context of science experiments. For example, in one of the experiments, students were asked to first make the following prediction: *Which will go farthest across a desk when blown: a plastic cup with three pennies, one with six pennies, one with nine pennies, or one with twelve pennies?* After completing the experiment, students were asked to write a science report in which they described the steps they followed (using the past tense) and to report their initial predictions (using the conditional past). Thus, the experiments and reports that were designed to address content area curricular objectives also created obligatory contexts for the repeated use of the simple past and the conditional past.

The feedback phase

In a traditional foreign language classroom, controlled practice is gradually replaced by communicative practice. In immersion, content-based lessons take up the greater part of instructional time. These lessons typically include a variety of teacher-led lessons, cooperative learning activities, and group projects. How can teachers ensure that students use in their science and social studies lessons the grammatical forms that they have been made aware of and practiced during the language arts lesson? In this phase, teacher feedback plays a crucial role.

In Lyster and Ranta (1997), teacher feedback was characterized as participant moves in an interaction. In our present view, all corrective feedback moves belong to one of two kinds: either reformulations or prompts. Reformulation includes recasts and explicit correction because both these moves supply learners with target reformulations of their non-target output (see Lyster & Ranta, 1997 for definitions of the feedback categories). Prompts include a variety of signals, other than alternative reformulations, that push learners to self-repair. These include elicitation, metalinguistic clues, clarification requests, and teacher repetition. Although these four prompting moves represent a wide range of feedback types, they have one important feature in common that differentiates them from reformulation moves: They withhold correct forms and instead provide clues to prompt students to retrieve correct forms from what they already know. Previously these moves were referred to as the "negotiation of form" (Lyster, 1998b; Lyster & Ranta, 1997) or "form-focused negotiation" (Lyster, 2002). In the present discussion these moves are referred to as prompts in order to avoid confusion with negotiation strategies comprising the negotiation of meaning, which aim for comprehensibility of message through various input and conversational modifications (e.g., Long, 1996; Pica, 1994).

In Lyster and Ranta (1997), recasts did not provide opportunities to self-repair whereas prompting, by definition, did provide learners with such opportunities. The significance of this finding has been a matter of debate. Doughty (2001) claims that recasts are the optimal form of feedback because acquisition depends on input, and the recast offers the opportunity for learners to notice the input and make cognitive comparisons. De Bot (2000) disputes this claim on psycholinguistic grounds, arguing that the form of an utterance is lost once it has been processed for meaning. From the perspective of the present discussion, we would argue that the modified output which follows prompting during content lessons is in fact practice and therefore contributes to the proceduralization of declarative knowledge gained during language arts lessons.

The aim here is not to downplay the role of input. However, the Canadian early French immersion context is unique in many respects. By the end of elementary school, learners have had years of exposure to L2 input, including the linguistic forms that they consistently have problems acquiring. More input is not going to make a difference; learners need to be pushed when their focus is on academic content to use target forms which are in competition with highly accessible interlanguage forms. One way to ensure that immersion students use the target forms is by offering feedback in the form of prompts.

The Awareness-Practice-Feedback sequence in French immersion research

To varying degrees, the pedagogical sequence of Awareness-Practice-Feedback underlies the instructional materials used in studies of the impact of form-focused instruction on French immersion students' target language accuracy mentioned above (Day & Shapson, 1991; Harley, 1998, 1989b; Lyster, 1994). Instructional treatments in these studies promoted awareness of specific target features and then allowed for oral practice in a variety of meaningful contexts related to the students' subject matter instruction. To do so, a variety of genres were exploited (e.g., short stories, legends, scientific reports, newspaper articles, informal letters, invitations, childhood albums, novels), including texts that were directly linked to the students' regular science or social studies curriculum but enhanced so as to draw attention to form. Cooperative learning activities as well as language games and exercises were also used to encourage both awareness and practice of the target features. The activities used in these studies appeared to provide opportunities for genuine communicative use of the target forms, but the results with respect to oral production were inconsistent across studies. It seems likely that the lack of impact on accuracy in the learners' oral production in some studies may be because insufficient time was allotted to fluency-building practice and feedback was not integrated systematically into the instructional materials.

From a close analysis of the materials and descriptions of their implementation (see Lyster, 2004b, for detailed analysis), it appears that the communication practice tasks used in Harley (1989b) and in Day and Shapson (1991) were simply too interesting and motivating for the learners; this caused them to revert to their more easily accessible, simplified interlanguage forms in oral activities. In contrast, controlled practice is much more apparent in the role-plays in Lyster (1994) and the games, songs, and rhymes described in Harley (1998). It can be argued that the greater amount of automaticity practice in these studies was a factor in the greater impact of the instructional treatment on learners' oral production.

The instructional treatment implemented in a recent classroom study by Lyster (2004a) illustrates the role of feedback in the Awareness-Practice-Feedback sequence. The instructional unit for Grade 5 immersion students was designed to draw their attention to word endings as predictors of grammatical gender. The form-focused activities were embedded in the children's regular curriculum – a commercially produced set of materials that integrated language arts, social studies, and science. The awareness and practice activities served to facilitate the students' comprehension of some otherwise very difficult texts that were intended for native speakers by providing students with simplified and shorter versions of each text. These short texts provided the pedagogical context into which a focus on form was integrated, primarily by highlighting in bold the endings of target nouns and asking students to fill in the missing definite or indefinite article before each noun. Built into these activities was considerable repetitiveness, although the activities were always related to the students' subject matter instruction. In addition, feedback provided by teachers in content-based lessons was a major focus in this pedagogical intervention. One teacher provided reformulation in the form of recasts, a second provided prompts that pushed her students to self-repair, and a third was asked to complete the instructional unit but without regularly providing any particular type of feedback.

Results revealed that the three treatment groups demonstrated significant long-term improvement on the two oral-production tasks and a binary-choice test at the time of delayed post-testing and showed short-term improvement on a text-completion task at the time of imme-diate post-testing. Prompts proved to be the most effective type of feed-back, with the prompt group distinguishing itself as the only group to significantly outperform the comparison group on all measures in both the short and long term. Form-focused instruction with recasts proved to be only marginally more effective than form-focused instruction with-out feedback. The superior performance of the prompt group may be attributed to the opportunities that the teacher's prompts provided stu-dents to practice and thereby proceduralize their knowledge of the rules for predicting grammatical gender.

Concluding remarks

This chapter has explored how a three-phase instructional sequence moti-vated by cognitive theory can provide a guide for developing instructional activities to address the problem of fluent but non-nativelike speaking skills among immersion program students. This sequence begins with an initial awareness phase aimed to help learners notice the gap and then emphasizes automaticity practice in order to make target-language forms accessible for use in spontaneous communication. The third phase places our previous work on feedback into an instructional design framework. When students are engaged in content-based activities, it is essential that teachers use forms of feedback which prompt learners to self-repair. It has been argued here that this approach is needed because learners in Canadian immersion programs typically have limited contact with native speaker peers who can provide them with idiomatic models and feedback on the comprehensibility of their speech. Although nativelike attainment is not necessarily the goal for most immersion students, it is clear that non-nativelike speech can seriously impede communication with native speakers (MacFarlane, 2001) who rely on conventionalized sequences for rapid processing in face-to-face communication (Wray, 1999). We recognize that the situation of French immersion in Canada is unique in many ways, thus limiting the generalizability of our discussion. That being said, it must also be recognized that the Canadian immersion model of second language education has been exported to other contexts (e.g., Pica, 2002) where similar issues are likely to be a concern to educators.

Note

1. The 1983 version of the model is known as ACT*; the more recent version is called ACT-R ("R" for *rational*). Most of the basic assumptions are the same in both versions.

References

Allen, P., Swain, M., Harley, B., & Cummins, J. (1990). Aspects of classroom treatment: Toward a more comprehensive view of second language education. In B. Harley, P. Allen, J. Cummins, & M. Swain (Eds.), *The development of second language proficiency* (pp. 57–81). Cambridge, UK: Cambridge University Press.

Anderson, J. R. (1983). *The architecture of cognition.* Cambridge, MA: Harvard University Press.

Anderson, J. R. (1993). *Rules of the mind.* Hillsdale, NJ: Lawrence Erlbaum.

Anderson, J. R., Corbett, A. T., Koedinger, K., & Pelletier, R. (1995). Cognitive tutors: Lessons learned. *The Journal of Learning Sciences, 4,* 167–207.

Annett, J. (1991). Skill acquisition. In J. Morrison (Ed.), *Training for performance* (pp. 13–51). Chichester, UK: John Wiley.

Chaudron, C. (1986). Teachers' priorities in correcting learners' errors in French immersion classes. In R. Day (Ed.), *Talking to learn: Conversations in second language acquisition* (pp. 64–84). Rowley, MA: Newbury House.

Cook, G. (1989). *Discourse.* Oxford: Oxford University Press.

Day, E., & Shapson, S. (1991). Integrating formal and functional approaches to language teaching in French immersion: An experimental study. *Language Learning, 41,* 25–58.

de Bot, K. (2000). Psycholinguistics in applied linguistics: Trends and perspectives. *Annual Review of Applied Linguistics, 20,* 224–37.

DeKeyser, R. (1997). Beyond explicit rule learning: Automatizing second language morphosyntax. *Studies in Second Language Acquisition, 19,* 195–222.

DeKeyser, R. (1998). Beyond focus on form: Cognitive perspectives on learning and practicing second language grammar. In C. Doughty & J. Williams (Eds.), *Focus on form in classroom second language acquisition* (pp. 42–63). Cambridge, UK: Cambridge University Press.

DeKeyser, R. (2001). Automaticity and automatization. In P. Robinson (Ed.), *Cognition and second language instruction* (pp. 125–51). Cambridge, UK: Cambridge University Press.

Dicks, J. (1992). Analytic and experiential features of three French immersion programs: Early, middle and late. *Canadian Modern Language Review, 49,* 37–59.

Doughty, C. (2001). Cognitive underpinnings of focus on form. In P. Robinson (Ed.), *Cognition and second language instruction* (pp. 206–57). Cambridge, UK: Cambridge University Press.

Doughty, C., & Varela, E. (1998). Communicative focus on form. In C. Doughty & J. Williams (Eds.), *Focus on form in classroom second language acquisition* (pp. 114–38). New York: Cambridge University Press.

Fazio, L., & Lyster, R. (1998). Immersion and submersion classrooms: A comparison of instructional practices in language arts. *Journal of Multilingual and Multicultural Development, 19,* 303–17.

Fitts, P. M. (1964). Perceptual-motor skill learning. In A. W. Melton (Ed.), *Categories of human learning.* New York: Academic Press.

Fotos, S. (1994). Integrating grammar instruction and communicative language use through grammar consciousness-raising tasks. *TESOL Quarterly, 28,* 323–51.

Gass, S., & Selinker, L. (1994). *Second language acquisition: An introductory course.* Hillsdale, NJ: Lawrence Erlbaum.

Gatbonton, E., & Segalowitz, N. (1988). Creative automatization: Principles for promoting fluency within a communicative framework. *TESOL Quarterly, 22,* 473–92.

Gatbonton, E., & Segalowitz, N. (2005). Rethinking communicative language teaching: A focus on access to fluency. *Canadian Modern Language Review, 61,* 325–53.

Genesee, F. (1978). A longitudinal evaluation of an early immersion school program. *Canadian Journal of Education, 3,* 31–50.

Genesee, F. (1987). *Learning through two languages: Studies of immersion and bilingual children.* Cambridge, MA: Newbury House.

Harley, B. (1979). French gender "rules" in the speech of English-dominant, French-dominant, and monolingual French-speaking children. *Working Papers in Bilingualism, 19,* 129–56.

Harley, B. (1980). Interlanguage units and their relations. *Interlanguage Studies Bulletin, 5,* 3–30.

Harley, B. (1989a). Transfer in the written compositions of French immersion students. In H. W. Dechert & M. Raupach (Eds.), *Transfer in language production* (pp. 3–19). New York: Ablex.

Harley, B. (1989b). Functional grammar in French immersion: A classroom experiment. *Applied Linguistics, 10,* 331–59.

Harley, B. (1992). Patterns of second language development in French immersion. *Journal of French Language Studies, 2,* 159–83.

Harley, B. (1994). Appealing to consciousness in the L2 classroom. *AILA Review, 11,* 57–68.

Harley, B. (1998). The role of form-focused tasks in promoting child L2 acquisition. In C. Doughty & J. Williams (Eds.), *Focus on form in classroom second language acquisition* (p. 156–74). Cambridge, UK: Cambridge University Press.

Harley, B., Allen P., Cummins, J., & Swain, M. (Eds.). (1990). *The development of second language proficiency.* Cambridge, UK: Cambridge University Press.

Harley, B., Cummins, J., Swain, M., & Allen, P. (1990). The nature of language proficiency. In B. Harley, P. Allen, J. Cummins, & M. Swain (Eds.), *The development of second language proficiency* (pp. 7–25). Cambridge, UK: Cambridge University Press.

Harley, B., & Swain, M. (1984). The interlanguage of immersion students and its implications for second language teaching. In A. Davies, C. Criper & A. Howatt (Eds.), *Interlanguage* (pp. 291–311). Edinburgh: Edinburgh University Press.

Haynes, K. (2001, Feb. 28). Francophone for a week in Montreal. *Edmonton Journal,* p. F3.

Hulstijn, J. (2001). Intentional and incidental second language vocabulary learning: A reappraisal of elaboration, rehearsal and automaticity. In P. Robinson (Ed.), *Cognition and second language instruction* (pp. 258–86). Cambridge, UK: Cambridge University Press.

Kowal, M., & Swain, M. (1994). Using collaborative language production tasks to promote students' language awareness. *Language Awareness, 3,* 73–93.

Kowal, M., & Swain, M. (1997). From semantic to syntactic processing: How can we promote metalinguistic awareness in the French immersion classroom? In R. K. Johnson & M. Swain (Eds.), *Immersion education: International perspectives* (pp. 284–309). Cambridge, UK: Cambridge University Press.

Krashen, S. (1984). Immersion: Why it works and what it has taught us. *Language and Society, 12* (Winter), 61–64.

Krashen, S. (1994). The input hypothesis and its rivals. In N. Ellis (Ed.), *Implicit and explicit learning of languages* (pp. 45–77). London: Academic Press.

Long, M. (1996). The role of the linguistic environment in second language acquisition. In W. C. Ritchie & T. K. Bhatia (Eds.), *Handbook of language acquisition. Vol. 2: Second language acquisition* (pp. 413–68). New York: Academic Press.

Lyster, R., (1987). Speaking immersion. *The Canadian Modern Language Review, 43,* 701–17.

Lyster, R. (1994). The effect of functional-analytic teaching on aspects of French immersion students' sociolinguistic competence. *Applied Linguistics, 15,* 263–87.

Lyster, R. (1998a). Recasts, repetition, and ambiguity in L2 classroom discourse. *Studies in Second Language Acquisition, 20,* 55–85.

Lyster, R. (1998b). Immersion pedagogy and implications for language teaching. In J. Cenoz & F. Genesee (Eds.), *Beyond bilingualism: Multilingualism and multilingual education* (pp. 64–95). Clevedon, UK: Multilingual Matters.

Lyster, R. (2002). Negotiation in immersion teacher-student interaction. *International Journal of Educational Research, 37,* 237–53.

Lyster, R. (2004a). Differential effects of prompts and recasts in form-focused instruction. *Studies in Second Language Acquisition, 26,* 399–432.

Lyster, R. (2004b). Research on form-focused instruction in immersion classrooms: Implications for theory and practice. *Journal of French Language Studies, 14,* 321–41.

Lyster, R., & Ranta, L. (1997). Corrective feedback and learner uptake: Negotiation of form in communicative classrooms. *Studies in Second Language Acquisition, 19,* 37–66.

Lyster, R., & Rebuffot, J. (2002). Acquisition des pronoms d'allocution en classe de français immersif. *Acquisition et Interaction en Langue Étrangère, 17,* 51–71.

MacFarlane, A. (2001). Are brief contact experiences and classroom language learning complementary? *Canadian Modern Language Review, 58,* 64–83.

McLaughlin, B. (1987). *Theories of second-language learning.* London: Edward Arnold.

McLaughlin, B., & Heredia, R. (1996). Information-processing approaches to research on second language acquisition and use. In W. C. Ritchie & T. K. Bhatia (Eds.), *Handbook of second language acquisition* (pp. 213–28). San Diego: Academic Press.

Met, M. (1994). Teaching content through a second language. In F. Genesee (Ed.), *Educating second language children* (pp. 159–82). Cambridge, UK: Cambridge University Press.

Mougeon, R., & Rehner, K. (2001). Acquisition of sociolinguistic variants by French immersion students: The case of restrictive expressions, and more. *The Modern Language Journal, 85,* 398–415.

Nation, P. (1989). Improving speaking fluency. *System, 17,* 377–84.

Pawley, C. (1985). How bilingual are French immersion students? *Canadian Modern Language Review, 41,* 865–76.

Pica, T. (1994). Research on negotiation: What does it reveal about second-language learning conditions, processes, and outcomes? *Language Learning, 44,* 493–527.

Pica, T. (2002). Subject-matter content: How does it assist the interactional and linguistic needs of classroom language learners? *Modern Language Journal, 86,* 1–19.

Rebuffot, J. (1993). *Le point sur l'immersion au Canada.* Montreal: Éditions CEC.

Rehner, K. (2002). *The development of aspects of linguistic and discourse competence by advanced second language learners of French.* Unpublished doctoral dissertation, University of Toronto.

Rehner, K., & Mougeon, R. (1999). Variation in the spoken French of immersion students: To "ne" or not to "ne," that is the sociolinguistic question. *The Canadian Modern Language Review, 56,* 124–54.

Robinson, P. (Ed.). (2001). *Cognition and second language instruction.* Cambridge, UK: Cambridge University Press.

Schmidt, R., & Frota, S. (1986). Developing basic conversational ability in a second language: A case study of an adult learner of Portuguese. In R. Day (Ed.), *Talking to learn* (pp. 237–326). Rowley, MA: Newbury House.

Segalowitz, N. (1997). Individual differences in second language acquisition. In A. de Groot & J. Kroll (Eds.), *Tutorials in bilingualism: Psycholinguistic perspectives* (pp. 85–112). Mahwah, NJ: Lawrence Erlbaum.

Segalowitz, N. (2000). Automaticity and attentional skill in fluent performance. In H. Riggenbach (Ed.), *Perspectives on fluency* (pp. 200–19). Ann Arbor, MI: University of Michigan Press.

Segalowitz, N. (2003). Automaticity and second language learning. In C. Doughty & M. Long (Eds.), *Handbook of second language acquisition* (pp. 382–408). Oxford: Blackwell.

Segalowitz, N., & Gatbonton, E. (1995). Automaticity and lexical skills in second language fluency: Implications for computer assisted language learning. *Computer Assisted Language Learning, 8,* 129–49.

Segalowitz, N., & Lightbown, P. M. (1999). Psycholinguistic approaches to SLA. *Annual Review of Applied Linguistics, 19,* 43–63.

Segalowitz, N., & Segalowitz, S. J. (1993). Skilled performance, practice, and the differentiation of speed-up from automatization effects: Evidence from second language word recognition. *Applied Psycholinguistics, 14,* 369–85.

Selinker, L., Swain, M., & Dumas, G. (1975). The interlanguage hypothesis extended to children. *Language Learning, 25,* 139–52.

Shiffrin, R. M., & Schneider, W. (1977). Controlled and automatic human information processing: II. Perceptual learning, automatic attending, and a general theory. *Psychological Review, 84,* 127–90.

Skehan, P. (1998). *A cognitive approach to language learning.* Oxford: Oxford University Press.

Snow, M. (1987). *Immersion teacher handbook.* Los Angeles: UCLA.

Spada, N. (1997). Form-focussed instruction and second language acquisition: A review of classroom and laboratory research. *Language Teaching, 29,* 73–87.

Swain, M. (1985). Communicative competence: some roles of comprehensible input and comprehensible output in its development In S. Gass & C. Madden (Eds.), *Input in second language acquisition* (pp. 235–53). Rowley, MA: Newbury House.

Swain, M. (1988). Manipulating and complementing content teaching to maximize second language learning. *TESL Canada Journal, 6,* 68–83.

Swain, M. (1995). Three functions of output in second language learning. In G. Cook & B. Seidlhfer (Eds.), *Principles and practice in applied linguistics: Studies in honour of H. G. Widdowson* (pp. 125–44). Oxford: Oxford University Press.

Swain, M. (1996). Integrating language and content in immersion classrooms: research perspectives. *The Canadian Modern Language Review, 52,* 529–48.

Swain, M. (2000). French immersion research in Canada: Recent contributions to SLA and Applied Linguistics. *Annual Review of Applied Linguistics, 20,* 199–212.

Swain, M., & Lapkin, S. (1982). *Evaluating bilingual education: A Canadian case study.* Clevedon, UK: Multilingual Matters.

Swain, M., & Lapkin, S. (1990). Aspects of the sociolinguistic performance of early and late French immersion students. In R. Scarcella, E. Anderson, & S. Krashen (Eds.), *Developing communicative competence in a second language* (pp. 41–54). New York: Newbury House.

Swain, M., & Lapkin, S. (1998). Interaction and second language learning: Two adolescent French immersion students working together. *Modern Language Journal, 82,* 320–37.

Swain, M., & Lapkin, S. (2001). Focus on form through collaborative dialogue: Exploring task effects. In M. Bygate, P. Skehan, & M. Swain (Eds.), *Researching pedagogic tasks* (pp. 99–118). Harlow, UK: Longman.

Tarone, E., & Swain, M. (1995). A sociolinguistic perspective on second language use in immersion classrooms. *Modern Language Journal, 79,* 166–78.

Vigil, L., & Oller, J. (1976). Rule fossilization: A tentative model. *Language Learning, 26,* 281–95.

Warden, M., Hart, D., Lapkin, S., & Swain, M. (1995). Adolescent language learners on a three-month exchange: Insights from their diaries. *Foreign Language Annals, 28,* 537–50.

Willis, J. (1996). *A framework for task-based learning.* Harlow, UK: Addison Wesley Longman.

Wong Fillmore, L. (1992). Learning a language from learners. In C. Kramsch & S. McConnell-Ginet (Eds.), *Text and context: Cross-disciplinary perspectives on language study* (pp. 46–66). Lexington, MA: D.C. Heath.

Wray, A. (1999). Formulaic language in learners and native speakers. *Language Teaching, 32,* 213–31.

6 Second language education: Practice in perfect learning conditions?

Kris Van den Branden

Introduction

In this chapter, second language acquisition (SLA) will be defined as the acquisition of a language other than the mother tongue that plays a prominent role in the environment of the language learner. Second language acquisition is commonly distinguished from foreign language learning (FLL), which takes place in settings where the target language plays no major role in the community, although the difference between the two is relative rather than absolute.

For second language learners, opportunities to learn the L2 and practice using it potentially arise in informal circumstances on the street as well as in the L2 classroom. This chapter will explore to what extent these two contexts give rise to different learning experiences in order to draw conclusions on how L2 classrooms may best serve the needs of L2 learners. The chapter will suggest that, even though the L2 classroom cannot offer L2 learners the opportunity to practice using the target language in "real operating conditions" (Johnson, 1988), it may offer the learners the opportunities for practice under perfect learning conditions, provided the L2 classroom (a) combines a focus on meaningful interaction with a focus on form, (b) allows opportunities for elaborate and repeated practice, and (c) allows the learners to use the L2 in an affectively "safe" environment.

Instructed and informal second language learning

Learning a second language outside a classroom, for instance while conversing with neighbors on the street or with colleagues in the workplace, is typically called "natural." It resembles the natural way young children learn their first language, i.e., by implicitly acquiring the language while attempting to use it in communicative contexts for real-world purposes (Wells, 1985; Gallaway & Richards, 1994). In general, instructed second language learning is believed to be different in nature, in that it draws more on conscious learning, explicit focus on form, and controlled practice. In this view, the SL learner faces the task of transferring what he or she learned in class to functional language use in real life.

Yet, the difference between noninstructed and instructed second language learning may not be as absolute. For one, some second language learners in natural settings have been found to deliberately seek out opportunities to practice specific linguistic items and to consciously analyze the target language (Lennon, 1989). Similarly, the kind of learning processes that are claimed to spontaneously arise in natural settings (such as negotiating for meaning, using language for meaningful purposes) constitute the core business of prevailing pedagogical approaches such as task-based second language teaching (Long, 1985; Long & Crookes, 1992; Van den Branden, 2006) and communicative language teaching (Wilkins, 1976; Krashen & Terrell, 1983). There is, as Ellis (1994) suggests, no necessary connection between setting and type of learning.

Nor is there a necessary connection between setting and ultimate level of attainment. Although a number of studies have shown that, when the two are compared, informal second language acquisition leads to higher levels of proficiency than instructed language learning (Gass, 1987; D'Anglejan, 1978), naturalistic learning does not necessarily lead to high levels of proficiency. In fact, many learners who have been living in a context where L2 is the majority language dominating social and institutional life have been shown to develop only basic levels of SL proficiency (Klein & Dittmar, 1979; Klatter-Folmer & Van Avermaet, 1997). This is further corroborated by the fact that there is no uniform linear relationship between SL learners' length of time of residence (LOR) and second language acquisition (Flege & Liu, 2001). Actually, this should come as no surprise. Adult SL learners may vary greatly in the extent to which they exploit the naturalistic L2 learning opportunities their environment potentially offers. Various personal, social, political, and economic factors, such as the opportunity to work in contexts where the SL is used, the learners' subjective language learning needs, their willingness to build up relations with native speakers of the L2, and the density of L1 networks, highly influence the quantity and quality of target language interaction that SL learners actually engage in (Oyama, 1982; Van Avermaet & Klatter-Folmer, 1998). Flege & Liu (2001) compared two groups of Chinese immigrants who had come to the United States: One group had received formal instruction in English and had wide opportunities to interact with native speakers, while the other group had received no instruction and had worked full time during their stay in settings that afforded little opportunity to interact with native speakers. Both groups included immigrants with a relatively high LOR and immigrants with a relatively low one. Within the first group, the immigrants with a relatively longer LOR obtained significantly higher scores on a range of language tests than immigrants with a relatively shorter LOR, whereas no such significant differences were found in the second group. In other words, for the latter, simply living in the United States did not, in itself, result in more nativelike performance in the L2.

Studies by Snow and Hoefnagel-Höhle (1982), Long (1988), and Flege, Yeni-Komshian and Liu (1999) suggest that learners who receive both education and input in informal environments may be at an advantage when compared to L2 learners who only receive the latter. In a similar vein, studies into the effectiveness of pedagogical approaches that focus on the meaningful use of language, such as the natural approach adopted in Canadian immersion education (Swain, 1985), suggest that even if learners develop high levels of receptive language proficiency, their productive skills lag behind in terms of accuracy and advanced grammatical competence. This finding can be tied to accumulating evidence that focus on form has positive effects on accuracy in SL production (Norris & Ortega, 2000; R. Ellis, 2002), leading N. Ellis (2002) to the conclusion that "without any focus on form or consciousness raising . . . formal accuracy is an unlikely result" (p. 175). Reviewing 11 studies on this topic, R. Ellis (2002) points out that:

(a) the effects of form-focused instruction have mainly been shown for advanced learners, not for beginners,
(b) form-focused instruction has more chance of success if the treatment is extensive rather than short,
(c) the form-focused instruction is targeted at simple morphological features rather than complex syntactic rules.

Muranoi's (2000) study further indicates that form-focused instruction works best when the SL learners have the chance, either inside or outside the classroom, to also use the form that was focused upon in meaningful interaction (communicative practice). If form-focused instruction on particular items of the target language involves only isolated, drill-like practice in noncommunicative contexts, the learner may not be able to transfer the explicit knowledge to authentic contexts that involve meaningful interaction.

All this is in line with theoretical models that have stressed that, in order to reach advanced levels of proficiency, language learners need to focus both on meaning and on form. Skehan (1998) emphasizes that:

Learners need to be led to engage in cycles of analysis and synthesis. In other words, if meaning primacy and communicational pressure make for exemplar-based learning, it is important that there should be continual pressure on learners to analyze the linguistic units they are using, so that they can access this same material as a rule-based system. Equally, it is important that when the material does become available as such a system, learners should engage in the complementary process of synthesizing such language so that it will then become available in exemplar, memory-based form as well (p. 91).

This strongly suggests that naturalistic learning and formal education may actually complement each other. It also suggests that, especially for second language learners who aim to achieve advanced levels of proficiency, second language classrooms that offer the learner a sound mix of focus on meaning and focus on form (analysis and synthesis) might constitute very powerful language learning environments.

Instructed second language learning: What kind of practice?

One of the crucial questions that arises when it comes to putting these principles to second language classroom practice is which meaningful tasks the students in a second language course should be confronted with, and which particular linguistic forms should be focused upon. In this respect, research shows that many adult second language learners have specific, and sometimes urgent, goals in mind when enrolling in a course. Acquiring the second language allows them to reach real-world purposes in their immediate surroundings. A series of needs analyses were conducted in Dutch-speaking Flanders (Schuurmans, 1994; Wijnants, 1997; De Groof, 2002; Berben, 2003) in which second language learners (mainly immigrant workers) were asked why they wanted to learn Dutch as a second language (DSL). These studies indicated that the great majority of the informants strongly related DSL learning to five domains in which they hoped to function better as a result of developing L2 proficiency:

(a) finding a job and using Dutch in the workplace;
(b) using Dutch for informal purposes (e.g., making conversations with their neighbors);
(c) using Dutch for formal purposes in society (e.g., communicating at the town hall, the bank, the police office);
(d) using Dutch for educational purposes (study);
(e) using Dutch in order to follow their children's education (at a Dutch-medium school) and communicate with the teachers and headmaster of their children's school.

These studies also showed that many second language learners do not aim to reach native-level language proficiency. They basically want to reach a level of proficiency that allows them to use the language in the domains that are relevant to their immediate needs. Communicative adequacy prevails over linguistic correctness.

In a similar vein, Berben (2003) researched the drop-out behavior of 469 adult L2 students of Dutch in Flanders. She found that 27 percent of the students quit the DSL course and interviewed these informants on their reasons. Her study showed that the students dropped out mainly for three reasons:

(a) Personal and practical concerns. For many second language students, it was difficult to combine the course with child care, with a full-time job or with applying for a job, especially when the courses were organized during work hours. Other students were residing illegally in Flanders and, although they had been enrolled, they did not risk actually taking the course;
(b) Features of the course. Some students who dropped out showed a relatively low assessment of the quality of the course. The course had not met their expectations, they had not learned the kind of Dutch they needed for their personal purposes, or they had not been given sufficient opportunity to develop speaking proficiency. In addition, the teacher had not been sufficiently able to tune into their personal language learning needs.
(c) Features of the L2 school. Drop-out rates were lower in courses for which relatively high entrance fees had to be paid and in schools that followed up on students who did not come to the lessons.

All these studies clearly indicate that second language learners who enroll in an L2 course highly expect it to be geared to developing functional communicative proficiency. On the basis of these studies, Van Avermaet and Gysen (2006) suggest that second language curricula should be derived from needs analyses (Richterich, 1972, 1980; van Ek, 1980; Brindley, 1984a, 1984b; Nunan, 1992; Long & Crookes, 1992; Long, 2005) that involve the following four steps:

(a) Establish broad domains (such as the five in the Flemish research) in which the second language learners say they want to function better (subjective needs) or should be able to function according to stakeholders (objective needs). The latter group of stakeholders may include (depending on the course) teachers, teacher trainers, future employers, citizens, administrators, and so on;
(b) Select relevant language use situations (e.g., formal meetings, lectures, shopping) that are predominant in these domains;
(c) Define language tasks that typically arise in these language use situations. Tasks are goal-oriented activities that the learner aims to perform and that require the meaningful use of language (e.g., making an appointment);
(d) Describe linguistic forms (words, idiomatic expressions, formulae, grammatical constructions, and so on) that are typically used when performing these tasks.

For second language learners, especially for those who aim to develop their second language proficiency in order to function better in society, curricula that are designed bottom-up, taking needs-based language use situations and tasks in relevant domains as the starting point for the design of second language lessons, have high face validity. They provide the SL learners with the idea that what they learn in the classroom will be useful in the real world. Furthermore, by deriving course content from needs analysis, relevant form-function mappings will be established: The

SL student will be confronted with meaningful, communicative tasks that necessitate, or naturally give rise to, the use of particular linguistic forms (Loschky & Bley-Vroman, 1993). The presence and practice of certain linguistic forms in the SL curriculum is then derived from the fact that they typically are featured in relevant tasks. Form follows function. Linguistic forms are dealt with, focused upon, and practiced not as a goal in their own right but because they are naturally entwined with functional language use in relevant tasks.

Loschky and Bley-Vroman, however, acknowledge that manipulating and controlling the use of particular linguistic forms is much easier for receptive tasks (that require reading and listening comprehension) than for productive tasks, which allow the learner much more freedom and the option to avoid using, or paying attention to, particular forms altogether. And even with receptive tasks, some learners may still prefer to focus exclusively on meaning and communicative adequacy and not spontaneously analyze the forms that are being used in the target language. Such exclusive focus on meaning has been shown to result for some SL students in only a pidgin-version of the SL (e.g., the Heidelberger Forschungsprojekt "Pidgin Deutsch," 1978) in which formal development is restricted to basic levels and the learner can communicate only with other SL learners or with a very limited sample of native speakers who are able and willing to richly interpret the learner's output and fine-tune their input to the learner's limited level of comprehension.

Therefore, since many SL learners will need to be able to function in situations that require language use at a higher than basic level of complexity and correctness, SL curricula should guarantee that the students will be stimulated to enter into the cycles of analysis and synthesis that Skehan proposes and analyze the forms they are using while performing the meaningful tasks they are confronted with. This is visualized in Figure 6.1.

In this SL curriculum, focus on form is task-based in the sense that the selection of the forms that are focused upon and the actual decision to focus on a particular form are inspired by their relevance for the actual performance of a particular meaningful task. The focus on form is task-oriented in that the analysis, and practice, of linguistic form culminates in the new relevant use in meaningful tasks of the forms that were focused upon.

Obviously, there are various ways to accomplish the switch from task performance to a temporary focus on form in the classroom. One particularly interesting way arises when learners ask for it during task performance, for instance when they notice a word in the input that they do not understand and explicitly ask for the meaning of it, or when they are struggling with a morphological or grammatical rule while producing output and interrupt the teacher to ask about it (Doughty, 2002; Long & Robinson, 2001; also see Ortega in this volume). Learners' explicit call

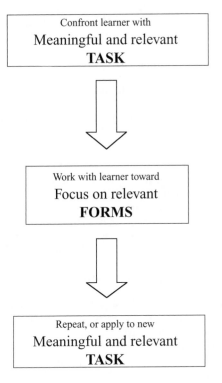

Figure 6.1 Task and form in SL curriculum design

for help not only indicates that they find a focus on a particular form relevant to task performance but also that they may be psycholinguistically ready to focus on that particular form, pay attention to the explicit information offered, and/or notice the gap between the explicit support and their own current interlanguage system.

Another way to draw the learners' attention to particular linguistic items while they are performing meaningful tasks is by providing the learners' target language use with feedback in which target forms are inserted. Various interactional devices can be used, ranging from implicit cues, through the use of recasts or clarification requests, to more explicit cues such as explicit corrections and negotiation of form. With regard to the more implicit devices, there now is extensive research that shows the strong potential of recasts to foster second language acquisition by alerting language learners to new forms in the language (Oliver, 1995; Tarone & Liu, 1995; Doughty & Varela, 1998; Long, Inagaki, & Ortega, 1998; Mackey & Philp, 1998; Mackey, Gass, & McDonough, 2000). Recasts, as illustrated in this example from Van den Branden (1995) allow the natural flow of meaningful communication to go on, thus catering for (semi-) real operating conditions, while alerting the language learners to new forms in the language and thus providing learners with salient, personalized input.

NNS: The policers came to the house
NS: You mean the police? And what did the police do?
NNS: Yes, they were searching the house

The above-mentioned research suggests that recasts optimally foster language acquisition when three conditions are met:

(a) Communicative salience: The target feature feeds into a high communicative need for the learner. In interaction contexts where second language learners need to handle input that their current interlanguage system cannot handle, they may be expected to pay close attention to the interactional help offered. Learners in search of the right word or structure are learners who are open to noticing such things in the input (Schmidt & Frota, 1985; Tarone & Liu, 1995; Van den Branden, 1997). In other words, especially when learners are experiencing difficulties in comprehending and using communicatively relevant target items, the use of implicit feedback to establish a focus on form may be particularly fruitful (Doughty & Williams, 1998; Long & Robinson, 2001; Doughty, 2002).
(b) Recycling: Uptake of recasts may be further enhanced when the meaningful task learners are confronted with begs for the re-use of the formal feature that was targeted in the recast (Crookes & Rulon, 1985);
(c) Awareness: The effectiveness of recasts appears to be higher when learners are made aware that the recast is a reaction to the accuracy of the form, not the content, of the original utterance (Nicholas, Lightbown & Spada, 2001).

Samuda (2001) provides another illustration of how focus on form and focus on meaning can be integrated within the same activity. In her study, she confronted SL learners with a task that stimulated meaningful communication and discussion. The learners were asked to speculate on a person's identity on the basis of the contents of his pockets. In their group interactions during the first phase of task performance, the SL learners were found not to use any modal verbs to express degrees of possibility, despite their high functional relevance for task performance. When the students presented their work to the rest of the class, the teacher first implicitly incorporated modal verbs in her feedback, but this did not lead to uptake by the students, probably because the students were focused entirely on meaning. The teacher then decided to briefly interrupt the meaning exchange and to explicitly focus on form. She explained in very simple terms when modals like *must* and *may* can be used to express degrees of probability. The learners actively participated in this focus on form episode. After this short explicit interlude, the focus on meaning was taken up again, giving the learners the chance to immediately make use of the forms they had been alerted to. In this phase of the lesson, the researcher did find spontaneous instances of uptake.

As Samuda's research illustrates, Task-Form-Task cycles (TFT) (cf. Figure 6.1) can be realized within one and the same lesson activity. This, however, need not always be the case. On the contrary, SL contexts offer the teacher and the learners rich opportunities to realize TFT cycles through a combination of outdoor and classroom performance. For one, the learners' actual L2 experiences in the outside world may constitute the contents of (parts of) the SL lesson, as when learners report on particular difficulties they faced when performing a language task in real life and these are taken up by the class or in individual interactions between the teacher and the learner. In a stronger version, the complete curriculum or syllabus can be negotiated with the students on the basis of their current needs or experiences. Another way of exploiting the practice opportunities the real world offers is to confront SL students with outdoor tasks, in which they are asked to perform communicative tasks in the real world, such as interviewing a native speaker, obtaining information on public transport, or making telephone calls, after these tasks were performed, prepared, and/or discussed in the classroom.

TFT cycles may also be completely realized outside the classroom, such as when learners are accompanied by their teacher or by other students while performing tasks in the outside world. For instance, while the SL learner is following a vocational training or working in a place where the target language is spoken, a language teacher or language coach may be present on the training floor or workfloor to provide linguistic support if the learners do not understand particular input or fail to make themselves clear. Periods of support on the spot may alternate with periods of sheltered instruction in the SL classroom, in which case the latter may function as preparatory practice, specifically focusing on the language tasks the student will be facing in the near future or the problems the learner met in the period before.

This might further be combined with support offered to the real-life interlocutors of the SL students, guiding these interlocutors to interact more efficiently with non-native speakers, both in terms of conducting successful conversations with SL learners and in promoting the latter's second language proficiency. Classic examples in this respect are the support of the vocational trainer or NS colleagues of adult SL learners in the workplace and the support of the headmaster or teacher of a school enrolling many NNS pupils.

Is practice rehearsal?

In more traditional views, practice in second language education tends to be associated with seemingly infinite rehearsal. In theoretical models that view language acquisition as skill building, repetition is believed to enhance automatization. In this respect, DeKeyser (2001) emphasizes that this need not imply a return to mechanical drill on isolated items, but that, in line with the previous section, forms that were noticed by the learner or were the focus of explicit instruction should return throughout the curriculum through sustained practice which ensures that:

> ...tasks are chosen and sequenced not only because of their non-linguistic content and their interactional demands, but also as a function of their potential for systematic, yet truly meaningful and context-embedded practice of forms that have previously been in focus. Such an integration of the task-based syllabus with attention to systematic skill development will ensure both a progression of real life communicative tasks with the range of forms they imply, and an equally natural progression of skillful use of these forms with the range of interactional uses that implies. (p. 146)

In theoretical models that view language acquisition as implicit learning, frequency is a necessary, yet not sufficient, component (N. Ellis, 2002), accounting for the gradual strengthening of associations between co-occurring elements in the input, which in turn underlies fluent language performance. To fully develop, language performance takes "tens of thousands of hours of practice" (N. Ellis, 2002, p. 175). Even if the implicit language learning process can be speeded up by explicit instruction and feedback, sufficient communicative practice is an essential ingredient of successful language learning, leading MacWhinney (1997) and N. Ellis to the conclusion that second language learners who have rich opportunities for communicative practice and, at the same time, can also receive some degree of form-focused instruction may have the best of both worlds.

One interesting way to enhance the recurrence of particular items is to have students in the classroom repeat the same task. A number of studies indicate that the repeated performance of the same tasks has beneficial effects on language acquisition. For instance, studies by Bygate (1996), Gass, Mackey, Alvarez-Torres, and Fernández-García (1999), and Van den Branden (1997) suggest that when learners are asked to perform the same task twice, their production shows clear improvement in terms of complexity of the output. While the learners tend to focus on meaning construction during their first performance, they can free processing space during the second performance, allowing them to focus more on the forms they are using.

This effect may further be enhanced when the learners are interactionally supported during the first performance and are given the chance to practice reusing the new forms they were offered. Van den Branden (1997) asked young second language learners of Dutch to perform an information-gap task. The subjects were asked to describe drawings that depicted what four suspects in a murder had done on the night of the crime. One group of subjects was asked to perform the task twice. On the second performance, the range of vocabulary they used (measured by the number of different words used) was significantly higher than on the first performance. However, these effects were much stronger when the subjects had been interactionally supported during the first performance, either by a peer or by a teacher. Qualitative analyses showed that the subjects during their second performance readily recycled new words they had been offered by their interlocutor during the first performance. Studies like these show that learners may exploit the repetition of tasks as the kind of context-embedded practice of formal items DeKeyser had in mind.

Affective factors

The fact that second language acquisition depends, at least partly, on the quantity of meaningful interactions and communicative practice SL learners engage in implies that to reach relatively high levels of language proficiency learners need to seek ample opportunities to use the L2 outside the classroom. After all, instructed SL learning, especially for adult learners, is bound by severe time limits. However, the extent to which SL learners will actually exploit the seemingly infinite opportunities for authentic L2 practice outside the classroom depends, at least partly, on affective factors.

MacIntyre, Clément, Dörnyei, and Noels (1998) have presented a theoretical model that proposes willingness to communicate as a construct that has a major impact on authentic L2 use. At the top of the model, which takes the shape of a pyramid, willingness to communicate in the L2 is most immediately influenced by two major factors:

(a) the learner's desire to communicate with a specific person, a desire which is mediated by affiliative measures (e.g., the desire to spend time with persons one likes) and control motives (e.g., the desire to influence other people's behavior);
(b) the learner's self-confidence, which is composed of perceived competence in the L2 and lack of anxiety.

This pyramid model adds an action motivation component to Gardner and Lambert's (1972) attitudinal motivation theory, emphasizing that language use is a highly dynamic process driven by motivations that are task specific and, throughout the process of task performance, open for change.

(Task) motivation is never static but is constantly increasing or decreasing depending on the various social influences surrounding action, the learner's appraisal of these influences and the action control operations the learner carries out on such motivational content. (Dörnyei, 2002, p. 156)

A number of studies indicate that speaking and listening tasks that involve authentic L2 use may arouse high anxiety levels because the process and outcome of communicative exchange is relatively unpredictable. In turn, this may negatively affect task motivation and task performance (Horwitz, Horwitz, & Cope, 1986; Matsumoto, 1989; MacIntyre & Gardner, 1991). SL learners might develop strong fears that they will not be able to meet the demands set by the task or their interlocutor's expectations in terms of clarity and fluency of output. In authentic L2 use outside the classroom, anxiety may be further aroused when the stakes may be high, as for instance when the learner is applying for a job or to purchase a house. As a result, L2 learners might be unwilling to signal nonunderstanding and elicit negotiation of meaning or to experiment with complex grammatical constructions at the edge of their current interlanguage because this potentially leads to more error-laden talk. A recent study by Dörnyei (2002) yielded significant positive correlations between SL students' attitudes toward a communicative task and their L2 use anxiety, indicating that "those learners who take the task more seriously experience more nervousness about speaking in the L2" (p. 148).

In addition, in real-life communicative practice, the interlocutors may further raise anxiety of L2 learners, for instance when the interlocutors are not willing to cooperate because of time constraints, negative attitudes they hold toward non-native speakers or high expectations (Deen, 1995; Van den Branden, 1995). As a result, learners may not fully exploit the rich opportunities for context-embedded practice in real operating conditions that the outside world potentially has to offer. MacIntyre, Gouthro, and Clément (1997) (quoted in MacIntyre et al. (1998)) asked Canadian ESL students to describe the situations in which they were most willing and least willing to communicate in the L2. Quite typically, the situations in which they were least willing to communicate tended to emphasize performance, error correction, and formal evaluation, while the situations in which they were most willing to communicate tended to emphasize solidarity and functional purpose (e.g., using the L2 as a secret code among friends). A study by MacIntyre, Baker, Clément, and Conrod (2001) stresses that for L2 learners who must expend additional effort to actively seek out communication opportunities for using the L2 outside the classroom (as in the case of very young immersion students or adult L2 learners who do not necessarily have to use the L2 in order to survive or function in society), the support by friends or close relatives would be beneficial. This study, then, indicates that when SL students are given outdoor tasks, especially tasks with which they are relatively unfamiliar, they might feel much safer and experience less L2 anxiety if they are allowed the opportunity to perform these tasks in pairs rather than individually.

In a similar vein, Plough and Gass (1993) report a study that shows that NNS dyads who are familiar with each other produce more clarification requests and confirmation requests (two interactional devices typically used in the negotiation for meaning) than when conversing with an interlocutor they are unfamiliar with. Varonis and Gass (1985) found significantly more negotiation routines in the interactions between NNS dyads than between NS-NNS dyads. Varonis and Gass claim that SL learners, when conversing with another learner, are probably less afraid to lose face because of a feeling of shared incompetence and may, therefore, be more inclined to display their nonunderstanding of L2 input, take risks when producing output, and practice their developing L2 skills in general.

A more recent, small-scale study by Dörnyei (2002) further corroborates these findings. In this study, 44 Hungarian ESL students were asked to perform an oral argumentative task and fill out self-report questionnaires that focused on various attitudinal/motivational issues, such as linguistic self-confidence, language use anxiety, willingness to communicate, and task attitudes. The study revealed significant correlations between the students' interactional behavior during task performance (as measured by the number of words and the number of speaking turns they produced) and their scores on the motivational scales, especially for the subjects who showed positive attitudes toward the task they were confronted with. In this latter group, students who showed high self-confidence in their L2 skills and an overall willingness to communicate in the L2 outperformed the others on the language measures. Significantly, in this study, the interlocutors' motivational disposition significantly correlated with the learners' task performance: If the learners were paired with a highly motivated or unmotivated partner, this affected their own disposition toward and interactional behavior during the task. Task motivation, in other words, tends to be co-constructed by task participants.

Although much more research is needed in this area, the above-mentioned studies suggest that, for some SL learners, SL classrooms might offer better and safer opportunities to practice their communicative skills and build up L2 confidence than the outside world. In addition, in the classroom, SL learners may also be offered more high-quality input, output opportunities, and feedback because of the way they themselves and their peer interlocutors behave in the interactions. Communicative interaction in small peer groups, as a rehearsal of real-life interaction with strangers in the outside world, should therefore be on the menu of the SL classroom at regular intervals and throughout the curriculum. In addition, the way the teacher handles the interaction with the students may be essential (Verhelst, 2006; Van Avermaet, Colpin, Van Gorp, Bogaert, & Van den Branden, 2006). One of the main challenges for second language teachers is to create a relatively safe learning environment in which L2 learners are offered rich opportunities for context-embedded practice and using the L2 in semi-real operating conditions, making sure that, at the same time, the learners' self-confidence is boosted, anxiety levels are held down, and ample opportunities for practicing specific items of the target language and negotiating for meaning become available. Teachers should balance negative feedback with positive feedback and appraisal, allow errors to occur and treat them as instances to learn from rather than to avoid, allow learners sufficient time to formulate their thoughts, and be supportive whenever learners are facing a communication breakdown. Learners must also be empowered to manipulate outside-world language learning conditions themselves. This can, for instance, be accomplished by training learners to ask for clarification, ask for repetitions, verbally indicate that they are not able to find the right word, use certain expressions that can save time or that can be used in many different communicative contexts, and interpret the interlocutors' nonverbal communicative behavior.

In this way, practice in the L2 classroom may constitute a rich scaffold for communication in the outside world. Context-embedded practice in the classroom in the shape of meaningful tasks in which focus on particular forms is functionally embedded may boost the L2 learners' self-confidence to perform the same tasks and use the L2 in the outside world. In turn, specific problems that the learner met while using the L2 in authentic situations in the outside world – whether it be problems understanding or producing specific items or problems performing certain tasks – may be taken up by the teacher in the L2 classroom and be integrated in the L2 classroom activities or curriculum. As a result, L2 practice in the classroom and L2 practice in the outside world will become more closely entwined, enhancing the chance of mutual enrichment and of SL learners ultimately developing the target language proficiency to perform the tasks that they need to be able to perform in the real world.

Conclusions

Figure 6.2 (Verhelst, 2006, based on Gysen, Rossenbacker, & Verhelst, 2000) summarizes the main ingredients for a powerful second language learning environment in the classroom.

In a safe, social climate in which learners are able to build up L2 self-confidence and are not afraid to experiment with new form-function mappings, learners are confronted with meaningful tasks that stimulate communicative practice. Before, while, and after performing these tasks, the learners are offered interactional support by the teacher and their fellow students. This support might range from implicit feedback on the learners' output and the negotiation for meaning of input that the

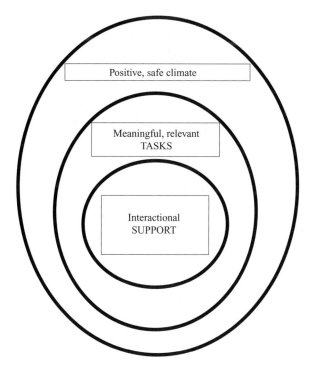

Figure 6.2 Powerful learning environments for language learning

learners fail to comprehend to more explicit kinds of support, such as form-focused instruction. As a result, the second language classroom, even if it cannot offer the learners communicative practice in real operating conditions because of physical and psychological barriers with the outside world, might offer the learner opportunities for communicative practice in optimal learning conditions.

References

Berben, M. (2003). *Uitval: waarom? Een analyse van omvang en oorzaken.* Leuven: Centrum voor Taal en Migratie.

Brindley, G. (1984a). The role of needs analysis in adult ESL programme design. In R. K. Johnson (Ed.). *The second language curriculum* (pp. 63–79). Cambridge, UK: Cambridge University Press.

Brindley, G. (1984b). *Needs analysis and objective setting in adult migration program.* Sydney: NSW Adult Migration Education Service.

Bygate, M. (1996). Effects of task repetition: Appraising the developing language of learners. In J. Willis & D. Willis (Eds.), *Challenge and change in language teaching* (pp. 136–46). Oxford: Heinemann.

Crookes, G., & S. Gass (Eds.) (1993). *Tasks in a pedagogical context: Integrating theory and practice.* Clevedon, UK: Multilingual Matters.

Crookes, G., & Rulon, K. (1985). *Incorporation of corrective feedback in native speaker/non-native speaker conversation.* Honolulu, HI: University of Hawai'i, Mānoa.

D' Anglejan, A. (1978). Language learning in and out of classrooms. In J. Richards (Ed.), *Understanding second and foreign language learning: Issues and approaches* (pp. 218–36). Rowley, MA: Newbury House.

Deen, J. (1995). *Dealing with problems in intercultural communication. A study of negotiation of meaning in native-non-native speaker interaction.* Unpublished doctoral dissertation, Catholic University, Tiburg.

De Groof, W. (2002). *Einddoelenonderzoek Nederlands als Tweede Taal in Brussel.* Leuven: Centrum voor Taal en Migratie.

DeKeyser, R. (2001). Automaticity and automatization. In Robinson, P. (Ed.), *Cognition and second language instruction* (pp. 125–51). Cambridge, UK: Cambridge University Press.

Dörnyei, Z. (2002). The motivational basis of language learning tasks. In P. Robinson (Ed.), *Individual differences and instructed language learning* (pp. 137–58). Amsterdam: John Benjamins.

Doughty, C. (2002). Cognitive underpinnings of focus on form. In P. Robinson (Ed.), *Cognition and second language instruction* (pp. 206–57). Cambridge, UK: Cambridge University Press.

Doughty, C., & Varela, E. (1998). Communicative focus on form. In C. Doughty, & J. Williams (Eds.), *Focus on form in classroom second language acquisition* (pp. 114–38). Cambridge, UK: Cambridge University Press.

Doughty, C., & Williams, J. (1998). *Focus on form in classroom second language acquisition.* Cambridge, UK: Cambridge University Press.

Ellis, N. (2002). Frequency effects in language processing: A review with implications for theories of implicit and explicit language acquisition. *Studies in Second Language Acquisition, 24,* 143–88.

Ellis, R. (1994). *The study of second language acquisition.* Oxford: Oxford University Press.

Ellis, R. (2002). Does form-focused instruction affect the acquisition of implicit knowledge? A review of the research. *Studies in Second Language Acquisition, 24,* 223–36.

Ellis, R. (2003). *Task-based language learning and teaching.* Oxford: Oxford University Press.

Flege, J., Yeni-Komshian, G., & Liu, S. (1999). Age constraints on second-language acquisition. *Journal of Memory and Language, 14,* 78–104.

Flege, J., & Liu, S. (2001). The effect of experience on adults' acquisition of a second language. *Studies in Second Language Acquisition, 23,* 527–52.

Gardner, R., & Lambert, W. (1972). *Attitudes and motivation in second language learning.* Rowley, MA: Newbury House.

Gallaway, C., & Richards, B. (Eds.). *Input and interaction in language acquisition.* Cambridge, UK: Cambridge University Press.

Gass, S. (1987). The resolution of conflicts among competing systems: A bi-directional perspective. *Applied Psycholinguistics, 8,* 329–50.

Gass, S., Mackey, A., Alvarez-Torres, M., Fernández-García, M. (1999). The effects of task repetition on linguistic output. *Language Learning, 49,* 549–80.

Gysen, S., Rossenbacker, K., & Verhelst, M. (2000). *Kleuterobservatie-Instrument Taalvaardigheid*. Leuven: Steunpunt NT2.

Heidelberger Forschungsprojekt "Pidgin Deutsch" (1978). The acquisition of German syntax by foreign migrant workers. In D. Sankoff (Ed.), *Linguistic variation: Model and methods*. New York: Academic Press.

Horwitz, E., Horwitz, M., & Cope, J. (1986). Foreign language classroom anxiety. *Modern Language Journal, 70*, 125–32.

Johnson, K. (1988). Mistake correction. *ELT Journal, 42*, 89–101.

Klatter-Folmer, J., & Van Avermaet, P. (1997). *Language shift amongst Italians in Flanders and Turks in the Netherlands*. Paper presented at the 1st International Symposium on Bilingualism, Vigo.

Klein, W., & Dittmar, N. (1979). *Developing grammars: The acquisition of German syntax by foreign workers*. Berlin: Springer.

Krashen, S., & Terrell, T. (1983). *The natural approach: Language acquisition in the classroom*. Oxford: Pergamon.

Lennon, P. (1989). Introspection and intentionality in advanced second language acquisition. *Language Learning, 39*, 375–95.

Long, M. (1985). A role for instruction in second language acquisition: Task-based language teaching. In K. Hylstenstam & M. Pienemann (Eds.), *Modelling and assessing second language acquisition* (pp. 77–99). Clevedon, UK: Multilingual Matters.

Long, M. (1988). Instructed interlanguage development. In L. Beebe (Ed.), *Issues in second language acquisition: Multiple perspectives*. Rowley, MA: Newbury House.

Long, M. (2005). *Second language needs analysis*. Cambridge, UK: Cambridge University Press.

Long, M., & Crookes, G. (1992). Three approaches to task-based syllabus design. *TESOL Quarterly, 26*, 27–56.

Long, M., Inagaki, S., & Ortega, L. (1998). The role of implicit negative feedback in SLA: Models and recasts in Japanese and Spanish. *Modern Language Journal, 82*, 357–71.

Long, M., & Robinson, P. (2001). Focus on form: Theory, research, and practice. In C. Doughty & J. Williams (Eds.), *Focus on form in classroom second language acquisition* (pp. 15–41). New York: Cambridge University Press.

Loschky, L., & Bley-Vroman, R. (1993). Grammar and task-based methodology. In G. Crookes & S. Gass (Eds.), *Tasks in a pedagogical context. Integrating theory and practice* (pp. 123–67). Clevedon, UK: Multilingual Matters.

Mackey, A., Gass, S., & McDonough, K. (2000). Do learners recognize implicit negative feedback? *Studies in Second Language Acquisition, 33*, 82–92.

Mackey, A., & Philp, J. (1998). Conversational interaction and second language development: Recasts, responses and red herrings. *Modern Language Journal, 82*, 338–56.

MacIntyre, P., Baker, S., Clément, R., & Conrod, S. (2001). Willingness to communicate, social support, and language learning orientations of immersion students. *Studies in Second Language Acquisition, 23*, 369–88.

MacIntyre, P., Clément, R., Dörnyei, Z., & Noels, K. (1998). Conceptualizing willingness to communicate in a L2: A situational model of L2 confidence and affiliation. *Modern Language Journal, 82*, 545–62.

MacIntyre, P., & Gardner, R. (1991). Methods and results in the study of anxiety in language learning: A review of the literature. *Language Learning, 44*, 283–305.

MacIntyre, P., Gouthro, M., & Clément, R. (1997). "I was talking to my aunt just fooling with head": Affective communication-related outcomes of junior high French immersion. Presented at the annual conference of the Canadian Psychological Association, Toronto, Ontario, June, 1997.

MacWhinney, B. (1997). Implicit and explicit processes: Commentary. *Studies in Second Language Acquisition, 19*, 227–82.

Matsumoto, K. (1989). Factors involved in the L2 learning process. *JALT Journal, 11*, 167–92.

Muranoi, H. (2000). Focus on form through interaction enhancement. *Language Learning, 50*, 617–73.

Nicholas, H., Lightbown, P., & Spada, N. (2001). Recasts as feedback to language learners. *Language Learning, 51*, 719–58.

Norris, J., & Ortega, L. (2000). Effectiveness of L2 instruction: A research synthesis and quantitative meta-analysis. *Language Learning, 50*, 417–528.

Nunan, D. (1992). *The learner-centred curriculum: A study in second language teaching*. Cambridge, UK: Cambridge University Press.

Oliver, R. (1995). Negative feedback in child NS-NNS conversation. *Studies in Second Language Acquisition, 17*, 459–81.

Oyama, S. (1982). A sensitive period in the acquisition of a non-native phonological system. *Journal of Psycholinguistic Research, 5*, 261–85.

Plough, I., & Gass, S. (1993). Interlocutor and task familiarity effects on interactional structure. In G. Crookes & S. Gass (Eds.), *Tasks in a pedagogical context: Integrating theory and practice* (pp. 35–56). Clevedon, UK: Multilingual Matters.

Richterich, R. (1972). *A model for the definition of language needs of adults learning a modern language*. Strasbourg: Council of Europe.

Richterich, R. (1980). *Identifying the needs of adults learning a foreign language*. Oxford: Pergamon Press.

Robinson, P. (2001). Task complexity, cognitive resources, and syllabus design: A triadic framework for examining task influence on SLA. In P. Robinson (Ed.), *Cognition and second language instruction* (pp. 287–318). Cambridge, UK: Cambridge University Press.

Samuda, V. (2001). Guiding relationships between form and meaning during task performance: The role of the teacher. In M. Bygate, P. Skehan, & M. Swain (Eds.), *Researching pedagogic tasks, second language learning, teaching and testing* (pp. 109–14). Harlow, UK: Longman.

Schmidt, R., & Frota, S. (1985). Developing basic conversational ability in a second language: A case study of an adult learner. In R. Day (Ed.). *Talking to learn: Conversation in second language acquisition* (pp. 237–326). Rowley, MA: Newbury House.

Schuurmans, I. (1994). *Behoeftenonderzoek Nederlands als Tweede Taal in Vlaanderen*. Leuven: Centrum voor Taal en Migratie.

Skehan, P. (1998). *A cognitive approach to language learning*. Oxford: Oxford University Press.

Snow, C., & Hoefnagel-Höhle, M. (1982). School age second language learners' access to simplified linguistic input. *Language Learning, 32*, 411–30.

Swain, M. (1985). Communicative competence: Some roles of comprehensible input and comprehensible output in its development. In S. Gass & C. Madden (Eds.), *Input in second language acquisition* (pp. 235–53). Rowley, MA: Newbury House.

Tarone, E., & Liu, G. (1995). Should interlanguage variation be accounted for in a theory of second-language acquisition? In G. Cook & B. Seidlhofer (Eds.), *Principle and practice in applied linguistics: Studies in honour of Henry G. Widdowson* (pp. 107–24). Oxford: Oxford University Press.

Van Avermaet, P., & Gysen, S. (2006). From needs to tasks: Language learning needs in a task-based approach. In Van den Branden, K. (Ed.), *Task-based language education: From theory to practice* (pp. 17–46). Cambridge, UK: Cambridge University Press.

Van Avermaet, P., Colpin, M., Van Gorp, K., Bogaert, N., & Van den Branden, K. (2006). The role of the teacher in TBLT. In Van den Branden, K. (Ed.), *Task-based language education: From theory to practice* (pp.175–96). Cambridge, UK: Cambridge University Press.

Van Avermaet, P., & Klatter-Folmer, J. (1998). The role of L2 self-assessment in language choice behaviour: Immigrant shift to Dutch in Flanders and the Netherlands. In *Te Reo (Journal of the Linguistic Society of New Zealand)*, Vol. 41, Special Issue: Proceedings of the sixth Language and Society Conference, 137–52.

Van den Branden, K. (1995). *Negotiation of meaning and second language acquisition. A study of primary school classes.* Unpublished doctoral dissertation, Catholic University, Leuven.

Van den Branden, K. (1997). Effects of negotiation on language learners' output. *Language Learning, 47,* 589–636.

Van den Branden, K. (Ed.) (2006). *Task-based language education: From theory to practice.* Cambridge, UK: Cambridge University Press.

Van Ek, J. (1980). *The threshold level.* Oxford: Pergamon Press.

Varonis, E., & Gass, S. (1985). Non-native/non-native conversations: A model for negotiation of meaning. *Applied Linguistics, 6,* 71–90.

Verhelst, M. (2006). A box full of feelings: Promoting infants' second language acquisition all day long. In Van den Branden, K. (Ed.), *Task-based language education: From theory to practice* (pp. 197–216). Cambridge, UK: Cambridge University Press.

Wells, G. (1985). *Language development in the pre-school years.* Cambridge, UK: Cambridge University Press.

Wijnants, L. (1997). *Behoeftenonderzoek Nederlands als Tweede Taal in de provincie Vlaams- Brabant.* Leuven: Centrum voor Taal en Migratie.

Wilkins, D. (1976). *Notional syllabuses.* Oxford: Oxford University Press.

7 Meaningful L2 practice in foreign language classrooms: A cognitive-interactionist SLA perspective

Lourdes Ortega

For many years now classroom-based SLA researchers have concerned themselves with how L2 practice contributes to L2 learning. In doing so they have produced a rich body of empirical evidence suggestive of certain qualities in practice that inherently call for the engagement of L2 competence-expanding processes within instructed contexts. The approach to L2 practice that this chapter presents rests on a number of cognitive-interactionist SLA theories that view language learning as arising from the interaction of multiple influences which are both learner-internal (e.g., attention to form) and learner-external (e.g., a task design that offers essential L2 input and feedback). Cognitive-interactionist SLA theories are also functionalist in that they assume L2 learning processes are activated in the course of engaging in meaning-making through language and action and as a result of functional requirements of specific things done with language. I draw on the assumption that meaningful use of the L2, and particularly the meaningful productive use afforded during communicative interactional practice, drives acquisition. This assumption is empirically grounded in the interaction hypothesis literature (Gass, 1997; Long, 1996; Pica, 1994; Swain, 2002) and in related cognitive approaches to L2 task performance (Robinson, 2001; Skehan, 1998).

This chapter first outlines three principles for L2 practice design gleaned from the accumulated empirical evidence contributed by cognitive-interactionist SLA studies. I then discuss some challenges and possibilities that FL teachers may want to consider when applying these SLA-based principles in foreign language classrooms, which naturally present particular constraints and potentials as contexts for formal L2 instruction.

A word about language teaching contexts

Before delving into considerations of L2 practice, it is important to acknowledge the true complexity of *context* and *foreign* as they pertain to language teaching. Although the traditional dichotomy between second and foreign language contexts for L2 learning is useful in abstract terms, in reality the distinction is anything but straightforward. At an individual level, persons who live abroad for an extended period of time in order to further their study of a language may still view themselves as foreign rather than second language speakers, since they have no plans to become permanent residents in the host country. At a broader, societal level, in many EFL contexts English has a currency close to that of a second language, owing to its international status as a lingua franca or to its postcolonial status. How comparable are such EFL contexts to those where the presence of English is truly foreign, as in, for example, China or Spain? Indeed, how comparable are EFL contexts abroad to U.S. contexts in which a language other than English is taught? Furthermore, a number of so-called foreign languages in the United States are spoken by large groups of people in communities readily accessible outside the classroom.[1]

The reader should therefore be advised that this chapter draws from an idealized understanding of FL context as (mostly college-level) foreign language teaching in the United States in prototypical settings where the L2 is not spoken by an immediate surrounding community. This choice is motivated by my familiarity with such contexts as an L2 teacher and an SLA researcher, and it should not be viewed as a legitimization of this particular abstraction over other FL settings. Readers will have to judge the applicability and usefulness of what this chapter proposes to their own foreign language teaching contexts.

Optimal L2 practice from a cognitive-interactionist SLA perspective: Three principles

The present chapter adopts Lightbown's (2000) definition of practice "as opportunities for meaningful language use (both receptive and productive) and for thoughtful, effortful practice of difficult linguistic features" (p. 443). Therefore, I will discuss principles for the design of meaningful practice in foreign language classrooms of the kind that enables peer collaboration and a purposefully selective but relatively unobtrusive focus on the language code within a wider context of communication. This emphasis is in alignment with largely germane proposals for L2 instruction made by Doughty and Williams (1998), Ellis (2003), Lightbown (2000), and Spada (1997). It also draws closely on the specific proposal for task-based language learning developed by Robinson (1995, 2001).

As an instructional component, *practice* is an umbrella term that encompasses widely different kinds of language-related performance, but a few general design choices can be considered basic.

MODALITY:	Spoken
	Written
LANGUAGE DOMAIN:	Word-level
	Sentence-level
	Discourse-level
MODE:	Comprehension < Interaction > Production
DEGREE OF MEANINGFULNESS:	Focus on meaning < Focus on form > Focus on forms
DEGREE OF TASK-INTEGRATION OF A FORM:	Natural > Useful > Essential

Figure 7.1 Some basic options in the design of L2 practice

As shown in Figure 7.1, learners may practice language in the oral or written *modalities*, even though, regrettably, the term *language practice* is most often associated with oral work in second and foreign language teaching (cf. Cumming, 1990; Valdés, Haro, & Echevarriarza, 1992). Whether L2 practice involves written or spoken language, learners may be asked to practice by thinking about, manipulating, and/or producing or comprehending language at different *language domain levels*. It should be noted that the choice of language domain which ought to define the scope of L2 practice is in no way dictated by the nature of the linguistic targets to be practiced. Indeed, most grammatical forms can be described by recourse to semantic and pragmatic characterizations (see Yule, 1998) and could potentially be practiced at the discourse domain level (Celce-Murcia, 2002).

The remaining three design options shown in Figure 7.1 (*mode, meaningfulness*, and *task-integration of a form*) are the main focus of this chapter. I argue that optimal L2 practice in the foreign language classroom should be interactive, truly meaningful, and with a built-in focus on selective aspects of the language code that are integral to the very nature of that practice. In sum, I advocate a task-based approach to practice which incorporates a systematic focus on form (see Doughty & Williams, 1998; Long & Robinson, 1998). In what follows, a theoretical rationale for each of the three principles is offered.

Principle 1: L2 practice should be interactive

Interactive practice during pair or group work presents several advantages over teacher-fronted activities. When afforded the opportunity to interact with peers rather than with the teacher, students talk more (Pica & Doughty, 1985a) and negotiate for meaning more often (Doughty & Pica, 1986; Rulon & McCreary, 1986). Even more importantly, learner-learner interaction affords better opportunities for the expression of a wider variety of meanings and functions than is typically possible with teacher-fronted interactions (see Chaudron, 1988; Hall & Walsh, 2002). This was documented by Long, Adams, Mclean, and Castaños (1976) in an early study of EFL in Mexico and was also found by Kern (1995) in a more recent study of college-level French. Incipient evidence also suggests that learners are more attentive to language in exchanges initiated by peers (Slimani, 1991; Williams, 1999) and in groups rather than in teacher-fronted exchanges (Nabei, 2002), and attention is posited to be a crucial prerequisite for language learning (Schmidt, 2001). Finally, interactive practice is superior to individual work because collaborative dialogue provides learners with L2 competence-expanding opportunities whenever they negotiate meaning during nonunderstanding episodes (Gass, 1997; Long, 1996; Pica, 1994) and whenever peers collaborate to identify language problems and negotiate language solutions (Swain, 2002; Swain, Brooks, & Tocalli-Beller, 2002).

In sum, L2 learning theories provide converging arguments for the central role that interactive practice among peers should play in formal L2 instruction, pointing at linguistic, psycholinguistic, and sociocognitive benefits that are thought to facilitate optimal L2 development.

Principle 2: L2 practice should be meaningful

The adjective *meaningful* is used here in connection to L2 practice in two distinct, complementary senses. In the cognitive-interactionist SLA sense, meaningful refers to the prerequisite of *focus on form*, or concurrent attention to meaning and form during processing (following Doughty & Williams, 1998; Long, 1997; Long & Robinson, 1998). Practice also needs to be meaningful in the sense of cognitive engagement or involvement with a task, a quality that arises from learners being personally committed to the practice event.

Although there are a number of differing functional views of language use and language learning in linguistics (e.g., Biber, Conrad, & Reppen, 1998; Gee, 1996; Givón, 1993; Halliday, 1994; Langacker, 1987; Tomasello, 1998) and second language acquisition (e.g., Ellis, 2002; Pienemann, 1998; Tomlin, 1990), all functional positions agree with the basic tenet that language is learned in and through performance. According to SLA functional accounts, in the course of engaging in meaning-making through language and action and as a consequence of functional requirements of specific things done with language, rich formal and semantic cues conspire to make form-function connections salient for the learner, and new grammar knowledge emerges (Robinson, 1995, 2001). It follows, then, that both form and meaning need to be closely interwoven into the design of L2 practice (Doughty & Williams, 1998). It also follows that, under a functional SLA view, tasks (understood as language-and-action events of meaning-making) are considered the optimal unit for the design of L2 practice (see Long & Crookes, 1992; Robinson, 2001; Skehan, 1998).

In defining the principle of focus on form, Doughty and Williams (1998) have gone so far as to claim that engagement with meaning is probably a cognitive prerequisite for learning new forms. In the same vein, Long and Robinson (1998) argue that a focus on the linguistic code is in many cases necessary but can only be used by the learner to promote development if it arises incidentally as a function of the demands of the task at hand. A specific model for how form-function mapping works psycholinguistically during meaningful performance has been advanced by Robinson (2001). Robinson contends that during task performance learners' attentional pools are deeply engaged, and attention needs to be paid to speech. The higher the cognitive demands of a task (relative to a learner's given L2 proficiency), the more cognitive resources a learner will expend on the language. Likewise, the more cognitively demanding a task is made, the more linguistically complex the L2 output is predicted to be (while fluency will obviously decrease). This is because if a task is made particularly complex so as to functionally require the use of complex language forms, learners will attempt to access and utilize those forms, if at all available in their developing interlanguage system, or they will try to obtain new forms. They may, for instance, search for new forms by paying attention to the L2 input available in the classroom, by requesting help from the teacher or from a peer, by consulting resources such as a dictionary, or often by transferring some relevant knowledge from the L1 or by hypothesizing a solution based on some previous knowledge about the L2. As a result of this pushed performance, accuracy may increase or decrease, depending on the type of task demands and the cognitive resources they tap, but for Robinson accurate performance is not of essential importance for optimal learning. More feedback (and more modification of one's own output) is likely to arise during complex task performance, since more problems are likely to occur. In all cases, heightened attentional and interactional processes during complex task-based performance will foster noticing (for instance, noticing gaps between the interlocutor's utterance and one's own, noticing holes in one's own L2 competence, and noticing new forms in the input) and will push and stretch the upper limits of the interlanguage, thereby fine-tuning existing form-function mappings and establishing incipient new ones. In a recent study, Izumi and Izumi (2004) found evidence that meaningful engagement in the psycholinguistic sense of focus on form may be crucial for L2 learning. They compared two practice tasks, one productive and the other receptive, both carefully designed to teach relative clauses to EFL learners. To their surprise, they found that the oral production task was less effective than the listening comprehension task because the former was mechanical rather than meaningful.

Meaningfulness, in the second sense of cognitive engagement or personal involvement with a task, is also crucial in L2 learning. It is held to be an optimal condition for learning in environmentalist theories of first language development (e.g., Gopnik, Meltzhoff, & Kuhl, 1999), in research on literacy development (e.g., Almasi, McKeown, & Beck, 1996), in schema theories of knowledge construction (see Alexander, Schallert, & Hare, 1991), and in motivation theories (Dörnyei, 1994). In SLA, some researchers have attempted to infer this second sense of task meaningfulness from learners' investment in the topic (Eisenstein & Starbuck, 1989) or their willingness to take risks (Beebe, 1983), but the concept remains largely unexplored, perhaps because of the difficult challenge of operationalizing it empirically. This difficulty notwithstanding, it should be clear that designing tasks that engage learners personally and cognitively in the practice event is crucial for optimal L2 learning (see, for instance, Dörnyei & Kormos, 2000).

Principle 3: There should be a focus on task-essential forms

Oftentimes, task-based practice seems to be interpreted as concomitant with the general practice of global L2 (mostly speaking) skills, without particular intensive practice of specific aspects of the target language (e.g., Schulz, 2002). However, as Loschky and Bley-Vroman (1993) pointed out, it is possible to design interactive tasks in which learners practice form-function connections in the L2 that the task makes particularly salient. This is because much of what learners are asked to "do" as part of their language practice in the classroom (i.e., whatever tasks) will require the use of some structures and forms that are relatively essential to doing the activity.[2] Indeed, much light has been shed on the linguistic demands of particular genres and registers by research on corpus linguistics (e.g., Biber et al., 1998) and systemic functional linguistics (e.g., Unsworth, 2000), and teachers can turn to this body of knowledge to match tasks to forms essential to them (see Biber & Reppen, 2002; Schleppegrell, 1998), although research in languages other than English is unfortunately less readily available.

For instance, Schleppegrell (1998) found that descriptions of animals required extensive use of expanded complements of several types (*the tiger's fur, that lives in the desert, with red spots*), with possessive constructions posing the most problems for her ESL learners. Thus, EFL teachers who wanted to give their students task-essential practice with possessives in English could be sure that an information-gap task in which students need to write and exchange animal descriptions would afford ample linguistic contexts for the use of the possessive construction and, by extension, numerous opportunities for the teacher to provide error correction on the same linguistic target. Tarone and Parrish (1988) discovered that a narrative and an interview task made very different linguistic demands on ESL students. Specifically, the English narratives involved mostly one form-function mapping (the use of the definite article for all subsequent mentions after the main characters are introduced), whereas the interviews required the use of both definite and indefinite articles in a wider range of functional contexts. If an EFL teacher's goal was to give students extensive practice with the use of the English article system, that teacher would know that an interview task is likely to be more appropriate for that goal than a narrative task. On the other hand, if the pedagogic goal at hand were to provide focused practice with the uses of the definite article alone, Tarone and Parrish's findings suggest that a narrative would be more beneficial than an interview task.

Moreover, knowledge about the linguistic requirements of tasks can be most fruitfully utilized in the design of practice if it is matched with knowledge about how learners of a given target language acquire certain grammatical systems. For instance, Bardovi-Harlig (1994) established that the acquisition of the past perfect by learners of English entails successive developmental stages. First, learners master the simple past tense morphology, then they begin to create contexts for the use of past perfect by deviating from the natural chronological order in narratives (that is, they create reverse-order reports of events), and finally past perfect tense morphology begins to emerge in these reverse-order report contexts. Knowing this, an EFL teacher whose learners have already mastered the use of the simple past tense can speed up the path toward attainment of the past perfect morphology by planning narrative tasks that naturally require that certain key events be reported in reverse rather than chronological order.

In sum, the meaningful interactive practice advocated in this chapter does not assume that learning tasks will involve ample use of any and all kinds of language, a so-called shotgun approach. Rather, in FL curricula, many of which have largely linguistic goals, a sound pedagogical principle is the matching of classroom tasks with essential form-function mappings. Using this strategy when designing meaningful practice allows FL teachers to move beyond the rather vague tenets that practice makes perfect and that speaking and writing in general are enough.

Meaningful L2 practice in foreign language contexts

How relevant are the proposed three principles for the design of L2 practice in FL contexts? Limited opportunity for L2 practice is the most salient characteristic of FL contexts. Outside the classroom, exposure to and involvement with the target language may be rare or impossible, and this limitation severely constrains the range of L2 functions and meanings available for learning. Inside the FL classroom, L2 practice is influenced by the fact that students (and, oftentimes, teacher and students) share the same L1. Last, but not least, overall amount and intensity of instruction is typically limited to up to five hours a week. In terms of second language development this all means that, by comparison with second and bilingual language instruction contexts, L2 instruction in foreign language contexts is likely to involve students who start at generally lower levels of L2 proficiency (in many cases at true beginning levels), who undergo a generally slower pace of development, and who achieve overall lower levels of ultimate attainment, particularly in areas of linguistic ability for use that go beyond grammar, such as pragmatic and sociolinguistic competence (Bardovi-Harlig & Dörnyei, 1998). Given these unique features of the FL learning context, teachers may raise a number of concerns for the design and implementation of interactive meaningful L2 practice in the classroom, three of which at last can be dispelled.

How good are FL students as sources of positive and negative input?

Most foreign language teachers readily recognize the beneficial impact of devoting classroom time to interactive practice, their two unquestioned arguments being that interactive activities promote fluency and are a source of learner motivation. However, in terms of L2 development, many teachers still wonder if there are also some dangers in asking students who share the same L1, and therefore may share essentially the same interlanguage grammar, to engage in (practically unsupervised) interactive L2 practice in the classroom. Unfortunately, evidence on this issue gleaned directly from FL contexts is scarce.

The evidence contributed from research in bilingual, immersion, or intensive contexts is discouraging (see review in Pica, 1994) and suggests that peer interaction can result in the development of "classroom dialects" (Long & Porter, 1985, p. 224; see also Tarone & Swain, 1995). However, these contexts are characterized not only by linguistic homogeneity (i.e., a shared L1 and similar interlanguages) but also by extensive contact hours (e.g., all school day in immersion settings and five hours a day for five months in intensive English programs in Canadian schools).

More directly relevant for FL classrooms are the findings gleaned from research in ESL contexts, in which hours of formal classroom instruction are typically more limited, and particularly from several ESL studies where interactions among students who shared the same L1 were investigated. Here the evidence is much more encouraging: The bulk of ESL studies suggests that learners are as capable as native speaking interlocutors of providing one another with comprehensible input and encouraging pushed output from one another (Gass & Varonis, 1985, 1986, 1989; Pica, Lincoln-Porter, Paninos, & Linnell, 1996; Ross, 1988; Shehadeh, 1999; Varonis & Gass, 1985). Indeed, some of these studies found learner-learner interactions to engender more negotiations than learner-native speaker interactions (Shehadeh, 1999; Varonis & Gass, 1985), a finding that was replicated by Ross (1988) in an EFL context in Japan. As an explanation, Varonis and Gass (1985) suggested that learners may feel a greater pressure to save face when the interlocutor is a native speaker of the L2 (or, I would argue, a noticeably more competent target-language user, whether native or not) but may feel freer to signal nonunderstanding when the interlocutors are other learners.

There is still the concern of just how targetlike students can be as input and output providers for each other. Porter's (1983) dissertation research (cited in Long & Porter, 1985, p. 216) revealed that L1 Spanish learners of ESL did not produce more errors when interacting with one another than when doing the same L2 tasks with native speakers. Pica et al. (1996) found that 10 (400 to 500 TOEFL-scoring) Japanese L1 learners of ESL provided one another with signals of nonunderstanding and modifications of output which were targetlike albeit simple (i.e., students mostly relied on segmenting rather than elaborating utterances). Another aspect related to accuracy levels exhibited during peer interactions is learners' self-correction behavior. Self-corrections appeared to be a pervasive feature in the interactions among first- and second-year college Spanish learners described by Buckwalter (2001). In fact, not only did the FL learners in these 29 dyads self-correct very frequently, but they monitored morphosyntactic accuracy as much as lexical aspects of their production.

Finally, do learners mislead each other? Much to the contrary, ESL research suggests that they are capable of providing peers with corrections, although in small amounts, and that they usually do not miscorrect (Bruton & Samuda, 1980, cited in Pica et al., 1996; Gass & Varonis, 1986, 1989; Jacobs, 1989; Pica & Doughty, 1985a, 1985b; Porter, 1986). The situation seems to be similar in FL classrooms, although the evidence is scant. For instance, in a Japanese as a foreign language context, Ohta (2001) found that seven adult learners incorporated each other's mistakes very rarely. Likewise, in a Spanish as a foreign language context, Pellettieri (2000) investigated the quality of negotiations by five dyads over five different collaborative tasks and found that of 31 peer feedback moves only six were non-targetlike and only two of these were incorporated by the other learner in the dyad.

In sum, FL teachers can be confident that, other things being equal, their students are capable of providing one another with comprehensible input and of encouraging pushed output and that they are likely to exhibit levels of accuracy and monitoring that are no worse or better when they interact with other students than under strict teacher supervision. Likewise, there is no reason to fear that students will mislead each other, as they are not likely to miscorrect or copy mistakes from each other.

Can FL learners handle meaningful practice, or will accuracy be compromised?

FL teachers often hold accuracy as a main goal of foreign language education, and much FL pedagogy, particularly in college-level instruction, seems to adopt a "one rule at a time," "simple before complex" approach to the presentation and practice of grammar. Partly because of this focus, it is not infrequent to hear concerns that practice needs to be kept simple to fit the limited linguistic resources of FL learners and to avoid the excessive use of the L1 (e.g., Buckwalter, 2001, p. 394). In conflict with this belief, however, SLA theories strongly indicate that both cognitive and linguistic complexity are crucial elements if learning is to be fostered through practice, whereas they also suggest that accuracy may play a less important role in acquisition processes. In short, a surprising but reasonable thought is that teachers may need to view accuracy as a desirable product of learning rather than as a catalyst for learning.

There is no evidence to support the misconception that errors should be avoided or that they stem from (much less cause) a failure to learn. On the contrary, certain "errors" are symptomatic of clear progress toward targetlike representations of the grammar (as in overgeneralization errors such as *goed* or *wented* or the creation of a reverse-order report context without yet supplying the required past perfect morphology, cf. Bardovi-Harlig, 1994). In addition, less-than-accurate production may be a necessary ingredient for learning to proceed to optimal advanced levels because it is precisely through repairs of nonunderstanding and feedback on errors that learners may obtain the necessary positive and negative input to push their interlanguage development (White, 1987).

In a mirror image of the famous i+1 metaphor (Krashen, 1985), one could encapsulate the crucial need for complexity in L2 production in an "o+1" metaphor: Practice needs to be facilitated at an output plus one level, slightly beyond what the learner currently can handle in writing or speaking. In Tarone's words, "interactional contexts where the learner needs to produce output that the current interlanguage system cannot handle" are the ones that have truly competence-expanding qualities (Tarone, 1993, p. 17, cited in Swain & Lapkin, 1995, p. 374). More precisely, practice which is meaningful in the two senses outlined earlier and whose demands exceed the learner's current abilities is the kind most likely to destabilize internal interlanguage representations because it encourages risk-full attempts by the learner to handle complex content beyond current competence; under such conditions, learning can happen. Naturally, a balance between the current level of L2 proficiency and task demands needs to be achieved (Skehan, 1998), but an element of challenge regarding cognitive and linguistic complexity of the practice ought to be engineered in that balance. The need to probe cognitive and linguistic complexity during L2 practice, even if accuracy seems compromised, cannot be overstated.

How can FL students' shared knowledge of their L1 aid L2 practice?

Many FL teachers (both those who share the L1 with their students and those who do not) are eager to motivate their students to make maximal use of the target language during practice time and to avoid the pitfall of lapsing into using the L1 (e.g., Polio & Duff, 1994). Yet, this shared L1 knowledge can also be exploited in fruitful ways.

An advantage afforded by linguistic homogeneity in FL classrooms is that it is possible to design practice building directly on L1 knowledge that all students share. A type of practice proposed in the SLA literature illustrates this point particularly well: VanPatten and Cadierno's (1993) input processing instruction. These researchers hypothesized that in order for students to internalize the use of the Spanish direct object pronoun system, it would be more beneficial to give them practice with comprehending the pronoun in Object-Verb-Subject sentences (such as *lo besa la mujer*, "him kisses the woman"), rather than to ask them to practice the pronouns in fill-in-the-gap exercises involving canonical word order sentences (such as *la mujer ___ besa*, "the woman kisses ___"), even though the latter is traditionally sanctioned practice in most Spanish FL classrooms. Since English assigns the first word in the sentence as the subject, VanPatten and Cadierno's rationale was that learners needed to be forced to process noncanonical word order examples in order for their internal grammar to attune itself to the fact that Spanish uses morphology rather than word order in the assignment of syntactic interpretation to sentences. VanPatten and Cadierno found evidence that in the course of practicing how to parse the string as object-verb-subject using morphological cues, students learn the form and the preverbal position of Spanish pronouns more efficiently. It is unlikely that this input processing activity would be equally effective in linguistically heterogeneous classrooms, since it is designed to address specific and crucial L1-L2 differences.

Recent studies of collaborative L2 learning from a sociocultural perspective have also provided evidence that the L1 takes on a cognitive tool function during task-based group work (Antón & DiCamilla, 1999; Brooks & Donato, 1994; Platt & Brooks, 1994). Essentially, by resorting to the L1 during collaborative L2 practice, FL learners avail themselves of a tool to engage in more negotiation of form and metatalk at earlier levels of proficiency than would be otherwise possible given their limited L2 resources. This is a way students use their shared L1 to enhance the learning potential of interactive L2 tasks.

Moreover, whether students share the same L1 with some or all peers in the classroom and whether the L1 is used overtly or covertly, all language learners actively employ and exploit their existing knowledge of additional languages (their mother tongue and/or other learned foreign languages) in order to form hypotheses about the target language and to selectively guide their attention to aspects of the L2 input (Bley-Vroman, 1989; VanPatten, 1998). This has been documented extensively in diary accounts of language learning (see, for example, the detailed introspections of Schmidt's learning of Portuguese presented in Schmidt & Frota, 1986), in introspective documentations of learning strategy use, and in process investigations of L2 writing. Thus, for instance, Cohen, Weaver, and Li (1996) found that both good and poor language learners used L1 translation as a strategy during L2 speaking tasks, albeit in different ways, and Roca de Larios, Murphy, and Manchón (1999) widely documented in an EFL setting how "writers expand, elaborate, and rehearse ideas through their L1 and also backtranslate at times into the mother tongue to verify that their intentions are being fulfilled" (p. 25).

In view of such varied and compelling evidence, FL teachers may want to reconceptualize the students' shared L1 as a resource they can capitalize on in order to improve their practice design. First, they may hone their focus on task-essential forms by productively using L1-related information about how students are likely to process the L2 input (VanPatten & Cadierno, 1993) and what they are likely to find difficult to learn (see Harley, 1993; Spada & Lightbown, 1999). Second, instead of trying to ban the use of the L1 in the linguistically homogeneous classroom, teachers may want to facilitate appropriate L1 uses during learner-learner collaborative practice. If learners are "on task," if the L1 is employed for functions that are thought to foster L2 development (for example, negotiating form through metatalk), and if the learners would otherwise be unable to handle such moves with limited L2 resources, then creating a regulated space for the use of strategic translation and code switching during L2 practice may be beneficial. Levine (2003) offers good advice on sensible use of the L1 in FL classrooms, and Liebscher and Dailey-O'Cain (2004) describe in depth how this was done successfully in a German classroom.

Challenges and possibilities for competence-expanding practice in FL Classrooms

Certain task design strategies have been found to be successful in creating conditions that foster L2 learning. Some parameters of the communicative situation seem to be particularly important, such as the existence of one correct solution to the task, the need for interlocutors to exchange information, and so on. A good summary of these parameters can be found in Pica, Kanagy, and Falodun (1993). Other recommendations for task design which are based on empirical evidence include:

- letting students plan aspects of the task and the language that goes with it before they engage in doing the task for real (Ortega, 2005)[3]
- giving students opportunities to rehearse and recycle activities (Bygate & Samuda, 2005; Gass, Mackey, Alvarez-Torres, & Fernández-García, 1999)
- asking students to strive for best performance by making them accountable to the rest of the class or by increasing the stakes (Skehan, 1998)
- getting students to negotiate by creating unexpected gaps in the information they share (Yule & Macdonald, 1990)

Good syntheses of communicative task design principles can be found in the two volumes by Crookes and Gass (1993) and, in chronological order, Yule (1996), Skehan (1998), and Ellis (2003). A recent volume entirely devoted to foreign language contexts is Leaver and Willis (2004). The remainder of the chapter turns to three issues related to meaningful L2 practice that seem particularly relevant in FL classrooms.

Realistic expectations for negotiation in FL classrooms

One consistent finding in negotiation-of-meaning ESL studies is that during meaningful interaction, learners overwhelmingly negotiate meaning and/or form related to lexical problems, and to some extent to phonological ones, while grammar proper seems to be more often ignored (Pica, 1994).[4] Findings from two FL studies, however, contradict this picture, and although the evidence is admittedly limited until more FL studies begin accumulating, these studies cast doubts on the validity of extending the "negotiate-over-lexis-first" principle to FL contexts.

In her study of fourth-semester Japanese learners (most of whom had 300 hours of college instruction when they were investigated), Iwashita (2001) found that "there were more syntactic modifications than lexical modifications across proficiency and tasks" (p. 278). Similarly, in her qualitative analysis of a corpus of task-based interactions by 29 dyads of college first- and second-year Spanish learners, Buckwalter (2001) reported that collaborative negotiation episodes (which she called other-repairs) focused on lexical problems almost exclusively but were very infrequent. Self-repairs, on the other hand, were very frequent in the corpus and often focused on morphosyntactic as well as lexical problems.

Why would FL learners negotiate surprisingly less often over lexical problems than ESL learners have been documented to do? This could be in part because FL learners may run into fewer nonunderstandings during peer interactions due to their more homogeneous backgrounds (resulting from sharing the same L1, developing similar interlanguages, and going through relatively similar formal language learning experiences), which may make idiosyncratic pronunciations more intelligible and linguistic repertoires more predictable than in ESL interactions (Buckwalter, 2001, p. 393). Another contributing factor may be that, given the limited vocabulary size associated with low levels of FL proficiency, learners may perceive as futile trying to negotiate over lexical gaps that neither partner could possibly know (Iwashita, 2001, p. 278). And why would FL learners engage in more frequent negotiation over morphosyntactic aspects of their production than ESL learners typically are found to do? This difference may arise from FL curriculum influences, from the very nature of the language learned, or from a combination of both. Much early FL instruction places a good deal of emphasis on the explicit learning of morphosyntax, making learners more aware of and possibly more resourceful with negotiating this aspect of the target language during pedagogical practice (Iwashita, 2001, p. 278). At the same time, L2 learners of English may not need to attend to morphology as much as learners of so-called strong-morphology languages (Buckwalter, 2001, p. 392) such as Japanese and Spanish.

Based on the accumulation of findings, FL teachers can expect the quality of interactions during L2 practice to evolve along with an instructional program, as proficiency gradually increases. Given that, in FL contexts, students are likely to start at lower proficiency levels and to progress at a slower pace than is typically the case in ESL contexts, we would expect pair and group practice in the beginning to be characterized by more reliance on simple segmentation of utterances in signals and modifications of output (Pica et al., 1996; Iwashita, 2001) and on negotiation over their available limited linguistic resources, perhaps with a predominance of negotiation of morphology, at least for morphology-strong L2s (Buckwalter, 2001; Iwashita, 2001). Negotiation of form, and more particularly metatalk, can be expected to be relatively frequent even in lower-proficiency interactions (and certainly more so than in ESL interactions), owing to the use of the L1 (e.g., Antón & DiCamilla, 1999). Only at intermediate and advanced levels of the language would FL learners start developing the ability to engage in extensive negotiation of meaning and form or in more frequent explicit peer correction (Williams, 1999), and they would probably be able to do so at this point using the L2 rather than the L1. The role of teachers as facilitators who make themselves available to the various groups and pairs during the interactions is all the more crucial in FL instruction, and particularly in lower-level classes, given that at low proficiency levels learners arguably prefer to request assistance from the teacher rather than from other learners (Williams, 1999).

This progression ought to be taken as tentative, since not much FL research exists comparing negotiation at various proficiency levels (or comparing negotiation of meaning versus negotiation of form, and so on), but it can nevertheless be useful in helping teachers develop realistic expectations for task-based, meaningful L2 practice in FL curricula.

The importance of mixed proficiency and cooperativeness

All language teachers are well aware of the importance of ensuring that their learners feel motivated to negotiate over meaning and form as much as possible and that they interact in a balanced fashion that favors equal participation by all group members. But how can this be achieved by design rather than leaving it up to the goodwill of our students?

In general, it appears that the less shared background interlocutors possess and the more heterogeneous the groupings are, the higher the amount of negotiation that can be expected in pair or group interactive practice (Varonis & Gass, 1985). In FL classrooms, where all students share the same L1 and have often gone through very similar experiences learning the language, mixed proficiency grouping seems to be the most important strategy to achieve that heterogeneity.

Iwashita (2001) investigated the opportunities for modified output that 24 fourth-semester learners of Japanese as a foreign language in an Australian university would provide each other if they were paired by the same proficiency level (low-low or high-high) versus a mixed proficiency level (high-low). As is common in many FL college-level programs, the students were all in the same class level, but real proficiency differences were noticeable due to differences in amounts of prior Japanese instruction during high school and/or naturalistic exposure through stay-abroad experiences. Iwashita found that the four mixed-level dyads produced substantially more language than either the four low-low or the four high-high level dyads and that the four low-level learners who interacted with a high-level interlocutor produced more output modifications than the low-level learners who interacted with same-proficiency interlocutors. Thus, this study provides some confirmation in an FL context that mixed proficiency groupings optimize the quality of L2 practice that lower-level learners are afforded during interaction.

In addition to ensuring mixed proficiency levels, teachers ought to give issues of control and cooperation careful consideration when deciding how to group students for L2 practice. Yule and Macdonald (1990) argue that "in task-based interactions, the more proficient learner should be given the less dominant role" (p. 553). These researchers proposed this grouping strategy based on their observation that ESL students negotiated more successfully the solutions to an L2 map task when the relatively lower proficiency students (with an average TOEFL score of 562) were the senders of the information and the relatively higher proficiency students (with an average TOEFL score of 625) were the receivers. In stark contrast, when given the more dominant role, 82.5 percent of the time the higher proficiency interlocutors tended to ignore nonunderstandings, gave up on solving them, or solved them arbitrarily by imposition rather than negotiation! As Yule and Macdonald remark, a more cooperative stance not only enhances the learning opportunities of the less proficient interlocutor (who receives more comprehensible input and produces more modified output), but it also challenges the more proficient speaker in the less dominant role, who is forced "to listen (as well as speak), to take one's interlocutor's perspective into account (rather than ignore it), and to tailor one's contributions to fit a particular interactive partner's knowledge (instead of only displaying one's own knowledge)" (Yule & Macdonald, 1990, p. 553). These are less obvious but important learning benefits in the development of conversational and pragmatic competence.

Interactional styles can also have a profound influence on the language learning benefits ultimately obtained through interaction, as shown recently by Storch (2004). Storch discerned four stable patterns of interaction among her 20 ESL students in an Australian pre-university class: collaborative, dominant-dominant, dominant-passive, and expert-novice. Storch observed that within each of three task cycles, the four students in the collaborative and the expert-novice dyads internalized or consolidated the forms they had negotiated collaboratively, as evidenced by their use of such forms in subsequent individual tasks. The four students who were in dominant-dominant or dominant-passive interactional relationships, on the other hand, engaged in a comparable amount of negotiation episodes during the three cycles of practice, but in their individual performance there was no trace of transfer of learning. Consequently, as Storch warns, it is advisable to monitor for patterns of interaction early in the semester and to encourage students to change partners if dominant-dominant or dominant-passive relationships are forged among particular students.

Technology-based strategies for expanding FL practice

For most foreign language contexts, the problem of the very limited number of instructional hours available is compounded by the lack of availability of L2 input in the outside world. In addition, one prominent feature of FL contexts is that many of the teachers, like their students, are non-native speakers of the target language. These FL teachers express concerns and wonder whether their students are at a disadvantage for obtaining high quality L2 input and for attaining nativelike competence.[5] Thus, a considerable challenge in foreign language education contexts is how to provide learners with rich and relevant opportunities to be exposed to and to use the target language across a range of topics, contexts, and communicative situations. The use of computer technology can be one powerful means to directly address this challenge. Indeed, technology applications are increasingly affecting how foreign language classrooms are conducted (see Blake, 1998; Chapelle, 2003, particularly chap. 5; Warschauer & Kern, 2000). In this section, I discuss three applications of computer-assisted language learning that can help stretch opportunities for meaningful L2 practice.

First, computer-based technologies can help secure high-quality practice through large-scale curricular collaborations with native-speaking students enrolled in a course in another country. Belz (2002) reports on such a networked collaboration between a fourth-semester German conversation and composition course at a university in the United States and a teacher education undergraduate course at a university in Germany. The learning purpose of the curriculum was to develop foreign language competence (in German for the U.S. students and in English for the German students) and intercultural awareness. The two groups completed a number of between-sites pair and group assignments involving reading literature or viewing films of parallel or similar content in both languages, such as the story of Cinderella in the original German fairy tale by the Brothers Grimm and in the English animation film version by Disney. These telecollaborative assignments were supported by the use of e-mail, chat, and Web construction, and the students were allowed to use both languages (German and English) in order for both groups to benefit linguistically from the course.

Meskill and Ranglova (2000) collaborated in creating a literature- and technology-based course for EFL in the University of Sofia in Bulgaria. The goal was to revamp the college-level Bulgarian EFL literature curriculum so as to make it more communicative and learner-centered (the authors do not specify what linguistic or cultural benefits were expected to be gained by the U.S. students involved in the project). The EFL students read contemporary U.S. and British short stories, and they discussed the readings with graduate students in Albany, NY, via e-mail. Other innovative uses of technology in this project included home production by the U.S. students of audiotaped excerpts from the readings that were used by the Bulgarian students to complete pronunciation-related activities and the use of concordancing programs that allowed the EFL students to investigate grammar issues in an inductive, learner-centered way.

Telecollaborations can also be achieved via simpler curricular components, such as asynchronous exchanges with electronic pen pals (e.g., in first- and second-semester Spanish classes at a university in Florida, reported by Stepp-Greany, 2002) or synchronous chat interactions for specific assignments to be completed outside of class time throughout a semester. Toyoda and Harrison (2002) report on such an exchange between undergraduate learners of Japanese in Australia and Japanese native speakers who were living in Australia and Japan. Students and native speakers used chat once a week over a semester in order to discuss ideas for a Web page creation project. The researchers documented how the computer-mediated interactions led to negotiation of nonunderstandings caused by lexical, grammatical, and discourse problems. For instance, Toyoda and Harrison observed that abbreviated sentences, which are typical of face-to-face conversational Japanese (e.g., using the word *toka*), consistently caused communication breakdowns. Without having engaged in chat, the students would not have realized that this particular aspect of Japanese oral communication existed, as this type of discourse is not typically reflected in Japanese FL textbooks.

A second way in which technology-based activities can stretch output practice beyond official instruction hours is in the form of e-mail assignments with teachers and with tutors. For example, González-Bueno (1998) investigated the use of teacher-student electronic journals via e-mail with 50 students of Spanish at a university in the U.S. Southwest. She found the students produced higher quantities of the L2 than did a comparison group in paper-and-pencil dialogue journals. They also deployed a wider variety of language functions in their electronic writing, including more questions and more discourse markers and initiated more messages and topics, including more personal and expressive content. The documentation of these language features in the e-mail dialogue journals is encouraging, particularly given that these students were at Novice and Intermediate-Low levels of L2 proficiency (ACTFL, 1998) (for similar findings in French, see Lamy and Goodfellow, 1999).

Finally, computer-mediated synchronous forums can maximize the benefits of collaborative L2 practice carried out not only outside but also inside the classroom, in that they seem to be powerful catalysts for high-quality interactive classroom practice. For one, there is evidence that computer-based interactive tasks accrue similar benefits to face-to-face, task-based interactions (e.g., negotiation over lexical nonunderstanding; see Blake, 2000; González-Lloret, 2003), but they also lead to interesting additional benefits. For instance, it is possible that computer-mediated interactions facilitate conditions of language awareness and enhanced noticing because of the writing and reading that mediates the interaction. This is suggested by Pellettieri (2000), who after inspecting the students' use of the backspacing key observed that "learners were doing a good deal of self-monitoring, as evidenced by their same-turn self-repair" and, moreover, that they "backspaced to make syntactic elaborations, thus pushing their utterances to a more advanced syntax" (p. 81). Writing-related activities can also be successfully carried out in electronic synchronous environments rather than face-to-face, with advantages also related to the quantity and, particularly, the quality of the discourse produced (see for example Abrams' [2001] study of group journal writing assignments in four third-semester German classes). Finally, the traditional discussion of readings can be greatly improved when carried out through computer-based synchronous discussions, as it has been shown that the computer-mediated environment allows learners to produce more quantity of L2 output and more varied and complex discourse than teacher-moderated discussions typically engender during the same amount of classroom time (e.g., Kern, 1995; see a review of the L2 learning potential of this kind of practice in Ortega, 1997).

These computer-assisted projects and assignments are suggestive of the many ways in which technology can be used to stretch the input and output limits of the FL classroom. The studies reviewed attest to the remarkable benefits of technology applications that provide high quality output and interaction opportunities that are meaningful, negotiated, reflective of authentic discourse, and culturally relevant. Further, such designs allow the FL teacher to take on a facilitator role rather than being the sole input provider and output arbiter.

Conclusion

From the cognitive-interactionist and functional perspective I have presented in this chapter, language learning happens as a consequence of the interaction of multiple influences. These influences, which are both learner-internal (e.g., attention to form) and learner-external (e.g., a task design that offers essential L2 input and feedback), are activated in the course of engaging in meaning-making through language and action, and as a result of functional requirements of specific things done with language. Accordingly, I have argued that optimal L2 practice in the foreign language classroom should be interactive, meaningful, and with a built-in focus on selective aspects of the language code that are integral to the very nature of that practice. FL teachers who are fully aware of constraints that FL contexts place on the quantity and quality of L2 practice opportunities should find ways to exploit the shared linguistic knowledge of their students instead of viewing the L1 as a hindrance to effective L2 practice. They should develop strategies for increasing learners' venues for FL practice beyond the confines of the classroom. Finally, and most critically, they should monitor the quality of L2 input and output that students are afforded during practice activities inside the classroom and enrich such practice by means of careful design. Naturally, teachers will need to evaluate the merits of the principles proposed and the issues raised not only against their knowledge of the constraints and possibilities for language teaching in their specific contexts but also in light of their own explicit theories of the goals of L2 practice. These goals can only be fully formulated relative to a personal choice of broader goals for foreign language education (cf. Kern, 2002; Reagan & Osborn, 2002; Schulz, 2002).

Optimal meaningful language practice is *not* a simple matter of letting students do communicative tasks in the hope that they will produce language and negotiate meaning and form, the more the merrier. Clearly, it is up to the teacher to provide students with the motivation to communicate in the target language (Dörnyei, 1994), the orientation towards learning language while doing a task (Williams, 1999), the need to engage in negotiation of meaning and pushed output through careful activity design (Robinson, 2001; Skehan, 1998), and the opportunity to generate complex meanings that truly challenge and expand current language competencies in productive ways. I hope this chapter has offered readers some new venues for thinking critically about how to work toward these goals for L2 practice in their own teaching contexts.

Notes

1. It is regrettable how invisible these U.S. communities of the target language are as a resource for the FL classroom and for society at large. Hornberger (2002, p. 47) eloquently contends that "we squander our ethnic language resources while lamenting our lack of foreign language resources." Reagan and Osborn (2002, p. 9) critically point out that "even where there are local opportunities for students to actually use the target language (Spanish in the Southwest, French in parts of the Northeast, and so forth) the language of the classroom tends to differ dramatically from the local variety, thus again emphasizing the Otherness of the classroom language and minimizing its actual usefulness for students." Some of these issues are examined in Ortega (1999).

2. Loschky and Bley-Vroman (1993) distinguished three degrees of integration of a form in a task (as shown in Figure 7.1): a form can be natural, useful, or essential to task performance. They noted that essential need of a form in a task may be difficult to achieve by design, although it is ideal for L2 learning.

3. Planning opportunity typically results in learners' pushing themselves to achieve higher levels of linguistic complexity during actual task performance. The benefits have been shown to hold true in a variety of foreign languages and FL contexts, such as EFL in Japan (Weaver, 2002; Wendel, 1997), Spanish in the U.S.A. (Ortega, 2005), German in the UK (Mehnert, 1998), and Chinese in Australia (Ting, 1996). Interestingly, the same benefits of planning also hold true for students in ESL contexts in the U.S.A. the UK, and Australia (see Ellis, 2005), even though ESL students arguably may be more used to speaking spontaneously than students in FL contexts. This shows that differences of context may not always lead to relevant differences in matters of learning, although admittedly they often do.

4. This has been found in conversational contexts outside the classroom (e.g., Chun, Day, Chenoweth, & Luppescu, 1982; Day, Chenoweth, Chun, &

Luppescu, 1984), in teacher-learner interaction in content-based classes (e.g., Lyster, 1998; Musumeci, 1996; Pica, 2002) in learner-learner collaborative work in ESL classrooms (e.g., Williams, 1999) and in FL computer-based interactive tasks (Blake, 2000; Pellettieri, 2000).

5. SLA insights into the learner-driven and environment-influenced nature of L2 acquisition lead to the conclusion that teachers can only be facilitators of external conditions that trigger and support L2 acquisition. Moreover, as I hope the range of issues discussed in this chapter shows, FL instruction would be severely impoverished if the teacher, native or not, were to function as the sole source of L2 input and the only legitimate interlocutor in the classroom.

References

Abrams, Z. I. (2001). Computer-mediated communication and group journals: Expanding the repertoire of participant roles. *System, 29*, 489–503.

Alexander, P. A., Schallert, D. L., & Hare, V. C. (1991). Coming to terms: How researchers in learning and literacy talk about knowledge. *Review of Educational Research, 61*, 315–43.

Almasi, J. F., McKeown, M. G., & Beck, I. (1996). The nature of engaged reading in classroom discussions of literature. *Journal of Literacy Research, 28*, 107–46.

American Council for the Teaching of Foreign Languages (ACTFL). (1998). *Proficiency guidelines revised*. Yonkers, NY: ACTFL.

Antón, M., & DiCamilla, F. J. (1999). Socio-cognitive functions of L1 collaborative interaction in the L2 classroom. *Modern Language Journal, 83*, 233–47.

Bardovi-Harlig, K. (1994). Reverse-order reports and the acquisition of tense: Beyond the principle of chronological order. *Language Learning, 44*, 243–82.

Bardovi-Harlig, K., & Dörnyei, Z. (1998). Do language learners recognize pragmatic violations? Pragmatic versus grammatical awareness in instructed L2 learning. *TESOL Quarterly, 32*, 233–62.

Beebe, L. (1983). Risk-taking and the language learner. In H. Seliger & M. H. Long (Eds.), *Classroom oriented research in second language acquisition* (pp. 39–66). Rowley, MA: Newbury House.

Belz, J. A. (2002). Social dimensions of telecollaborative foreign language study. *Language Learning and Technology, 6* (1), 60–81.

Biber, D., Conrad, S., & Reppen, R. (1998). *Corpus linguistics: Investigating language structure and use*. New York: Cambridge University Press.

Biber, D., Johansson, S., Leech, G., Conrad, S., & Finegan, E. (1999). *Longman grammar of spoken and written English*. New York: Longman.

Biber, D., & Reppen, R. (2002). What does frequency have to do with grammar teaching? *Studies in Second Language Acquisition, 24*, 199–208.

Blake, R. (1998). The role of technology in second language learning. In H. Byrnes (Ed.), *Learning foreign and second languages: Perspectives in research and scholarship* (pp. 209–37). New York: The Modern Language Association of America.

Blake, R. (2000). Computer mediated communication: A window on L2 Spanish interlanguage. *Language Learning and Technology, 4*(1), 120–136.

Bley-Vroman, R. (1989). What is the logical problem of foreign language acquisition? In S. M. Gass & J. Schachter (Eds.), *Linguistic perspectives on second language acquisition* (pp. 41–68). Cambridge, UK: Cambridge University Press.

Brooks, F. B., & Donato, R. (1994). Vygotskyan approaches to understanding foreign language learner discourse during communicative tasks. *Hispania, 77*, 262–74.

Bruton, A., & Samuda, V. (1980). Learner and teacher roles in the treatment of oral error in group work. *RELC Journal, 11*, 49–63.

Buckwalter, P. (2001). Repair sequences in Spanish L2 dyadic discourse: A descriptive study. *The Modern Language Journal, 85*, 380–97.

Bygate, M., & Samuda, V. (2005). Integrative planning through the use of task repetition. In R. Ellis (Ed.), *Planning and task performance in a second language* (pp. 37–74). Philadelphia: John Benjamins.

Celce-Murcia, M. (2002). Why it makes sense to teach grammar in context and through discourse. In E. Hinkel & S. Fotos (Eds.), *New perspectives on grammar teaching in second language classrooms* (pp. 119–33). Mahwah, NJ: Lawrence Erlbaum.

Chapelle, C. (2003). *English language learning and technology*. Philadelphia: John Benjamins.

Chaudron, C. (1988). *Second language classrooms: Research on teaching and learning*. New York: Cambridge University Press.

Chun, A., Day, R. R., Chenoweth, A., & Luppescu, S. (1982). Errors, interaction and correction: A study of native-nonnative conversations. *TESOL Quarterly, 16*, 537–47.

Cohen, A. D., Weaver, S. J., & Li, T.-Y. (1996). *The impact of strategies-based instruction on speaking a foreign language*. Minneapolis: University of Minnesota, Center for Advanced Research on Language Acquisition (CARLA).

Crookes, G., & Gass, S. M. (Eds.). (1993). *Tasks in a pedagogical context: Integrating theory and practice* (2 vols.). Philadelphia: Multilingual Matters.

Cumming, A. (1990). Metalinguistic and ideational thinking in second language composing. *Written Communication, 7*, 482–511.

Day, R., Chenoweth, N. A., Chun, A., & Luppescu, S. (1984). Corrective feedback in native-nonnative discourse. *Language Learning, 34*, 19–46.

Dörnyei, Z. (1994). Motivation and motivating in the foreign language classroom. *The Modern Language Journal, 78*, 273–84.

Dörnyei, Z., & Kormos, J. (2000). The role of individual and social variables in oral task performance. *Language Teaching Research, 4*, 275–300.

Doughty, C., & Pica, T. (1986). Information gap tasks: Do they facilitate second language acquisition? *TESOL Quarterly, 20*, 305–25.

Doughty, C., & Williams, J. (1998). Pedagogical choices in focus on form. In C. Doughty & J. Williams (Eds.), *Focus on form in classroom second language acquisition* (pp. 197–261). New York: Cambridge University Press.

Eisenstein, M., & Starbuck, R. (1989). The effect of emotional investment on L2 production. In S. Gass, C. Madden, D. Preston, & L. Selinker (Eds.), *Variation in second language acquisition* (pp. 125–37). Philadelphia: Multilingual Matters.

Ellis, N. (2002). Frequency effects in language processing: A review with implications for theories of implicit and explicit language acquisition. *Studies in Second Language Acquisition, 24*, 143–88.

Ellis, R. (2003). *Task-based language learning and teaching*. New York: Oxford University Press.

Ellis, R. (Ed.). (2005). *Planning and task performance in a second language*. Philadelphia: John Benjamins.

Gass, S. M. (1997). *Input, interaction, and the second language learner*. Mahwah, NJ: Lawrence Erlbaum.

Gass, S., Mackey, A., Alvarez-Torres, M. J., & Fernández-García, M. (1999). The effects of task repetition on linguistic output. *Language Learning, 49*, 549–81.

Gass, S. M., & Varonis, E. (1985). Task variation and nonnative/nonnative negotiation of meaning. In S. Gass & C. Madden (Eds.), *Input in second language acquisition* (pp. 149–61). Rowley, MA: Newbury House.

Gass, S. M., & Varonis, E. M. (1986). Sex differences in nonnative speaker-nonnative speaker interactions. In R. Day (Ed.), *Talking to learn: Conversation in second language acquisition* (pp. 327–52). Rowley, MA: Newbury House.

Gass, S. M., & Varonis, E. M. (1989). Incorporated repairs in nonnative discourse. In M. Eisenstein (Ed.), *The dynamic interlanguage* (pp. 71–86). New York: Plenum Press.

Gee, P. (1996). *Social linguistics and literacies: Ideology and discourses* (2nd ed.). London: Taylor and Francis.

Givón, T. (1993). *English grammar: A function-based approach*. Philadelphia: John Benjamins.

González-Bueno, M. (1998). The effects of electronic mail on Spanish L2 discourse. *Language Learning and Technology, 1* (2), 55–70.

González-Lloret, M. (2003). Designing task-based call to promote interaction: *En busca de esmeraldas*. *Language Learning & Technology, 7*, 86–104.

Gopnik, A., Meltzoff, A. N., & Kuhl, P. K. (1999). *The scientist in the crib: Minds, brains, and how children learn*. New York: William Morrow.

Hall, J. K., & Walsh, M. (2002). Teacher-student interaction and second language learning. *Annual Review of Applied Linguistics, 22*, 186–203.

Halliday, M. A. K. (1994). *An introduction to functional grammar* (2nd ed.). London: Edward Arnold.

Harley, B. (1993). Instructional strategies and SLA in early French immersion. *Studies in Second Language Acquisition, 15*, 245–60.

Hornberger, N. H. (2002). Multilingual language policies and the continua of biliteracy: An ecological approach. *Language Policy, 1*, 27–51.

Izumi, Y., & Izumi, S. (2004). Investigating the effects of oral output on the learning of relative clauses in English: Issues in the psycholinguistic requirements for effective output tasks. *The Canadian Modern Language Review, 60*, 587–609.

Iwashita, N. (2001). The effect of learner proficiency on interactional moves and modified output in nonnative-nonnative interaction in Japanese as a foreign language. *System, 29*, 267–87.

Jacobs, G. (1989). Miscorrection in peer feedack in writing class. *RELC Journal, 20*, 68–76.

Kern, R. G. (1995). Restructuring classroom interaction with network computers: Effects on quantity and characterisitcs of language production. *The Modern Language Journal, 79 (4)*, 457–76.

Kern, R. (2002). Reconciling the language-literature split through literacy. *ADFL Bulletin, 33 (3)*, 20–24.

Krashen, S. (1985). *The input hypothesis*. London: Longman.

Lamy, M.-N., & Goodfellow, R. (1999). "Reflective conversations" in the virtual language classroom. *Language Learning and Technology, 2(2)*, 43–61.

Langacker, R. W. (1987). *Foundations of cognitive grammar*. Vol. 1: *Theoretical prerequisites*. Stanford, CA: Stanford University Press.

Leaver, B. L., & Willis, J. R. (Eds.). (2004). *Task-based instruction in foreign language education practices and programs*. Washington, DC: Georgetown University Press.

Levine, G. S. (2003). Student and instructor beliefs and attitudes about target language use, first language use, and anxiety: Report of a questionnaire study. *The Modern Language Journal, 87*, 343–64.

Liebscher, G., & Dailey-O'Cain, J. (2004). Learner code-switching in the content-based foreign language classroom. *The Canadian Modern Language Review, 60*, 501–25.

Lightbown, P. M. (2000). Classroom SLA research and second language teaching. *Applied Linguistics, 21*, 431–62.

Long, M. H. (1996). The role of the linguistic environment in second language acquisition. In W. Ritchie & T. Bhatia (Eds.), *Handbook of second language acquisition* (pp. 413–68). New York: Academic Press.

Long, M. H. (1997). *Focus on form in task-based language teaching*. Presentation at the Annual McGraw-Hill Teleconference in Second Language Teaching. Available at: http://www.mhhe.com/socscience/foreignlang/top.htm.

Long, M. H., Adams, L., McLean, M., & Castaños, F. (1976). Doing things with words: Verbal interaction in lockstep and small group classroom situations. In J. F. Fanselow & R. Crymes (Eds.), *On TESOL '76* (pp. 137–53). Washington, DC: TESOL.

Long, M. H., & Crookes, G. (1992). Three approaches to task-based syllabus design. *TESOL Quarterly, 26*, 27–56.

Long, M. H., & Porter, P. A. (1985). Group work, interlanguage talk, and second language acquisition. *TESOL Quarterly, 19*, 207–28.

Long, M. H., & Robinson, P. (1998). Focus on form: Theory, research, and practice. In C. Doughty & J. Williams (Eds.), *Focus on form in classroom second language acquisition* (pp. 15–41). New York: Cambridge University Press.

Loschky, L., & Brey-Vroman, R. (1993). Grammar and task-based methodology. In G. Crookes & S. Gass (Eds.), *Tasks and language learning: Integrating theory and practice* (pp. 123–67). Philadelphia: Multilingual Matters.

Lyster, R. (1998). Negotiation of form, recasts, and explicit correction in relation to error types and learner repair in immersion classrooms. *Language Learning, 48*, 183–218.

McCarthy, M., & Carter, R. (2002). Ten criteria for a spoken grammar. In E. Hinkel & S. Fotos (Eds.), *New perspectives on grammar teaching in second language classrooms* (pp. 51–75). Mahwah, NJ: Lawrence Erlbaum.

Mehnert, U. (1998). The effects of different lengths of time for planning on second language performance. *Studies in Second Language Acquisition, 20*, 83–108.

Meskill, C., & Ranglova, K. (2000). Sociocollaborative language learning in Bulgaria. In M. Warschauer & R. Kern (Eds.), *Network-based language teaching: Concepts and practice* (pp. 20–40). New York: Cambridge University Press.

Musumeci, D. (1996). Teacher-learner negotiation in content-based instruction: Communication at cross-purposes? *Applied Linguistics, 17*, 286–325.

Nabei, T. (2002) *Recasts in classroom interaction: A teacher's intention, learners' attention, and second language learning.* Unpublished doctoral dissertation, University of Toronto.

Ohta, A. S. (2001). Peer interactive tasks and assisted performance in classroom language learning. In A. S. Ohta (Ed.), *Second language acquisition processes in the classroom: Learning Japanese* (pp. 73–128). Mahwah, NJ: Lawrence Erlbaum.

Ortega, L. (1997). Processes and outcomes in networked classroom interaction: Defining the research agenda for L2 computer-assisted classroom discussion. *Language Learning and Technology, 1*, 82–93.

Ortega, L. (1999). Language and equality: Ideological and structural constraints in foreign language education in the U.S. In T. Huebner & K. A. Davis (Eds.), *Sociopolitical perspectives in language policy and planning in the USA* (pp. 243–66). Philadelphia: John Benjamins.

Ortega, L. (2005). What do learners plan? Learner-driven attention to form during pre-task planning. In R. Ellis (Ed.), *Planning and task performance in a second language* (pp. 77–109). Philadelphia: John Benjamins.

Pellettieri, J. (2000). Negotiation in cyberspace: The role of chatting in the development of grammatical competence. In M. Warschauer & R. Kern (Eds.), *Network-based language teaching: Concepts and practice* (pp. 59–86). New York: Cambridge University Press.

Pica, T. (1994). Research on negotiation: What does it reveal about second-language learning condition, processes, and outcomes? *Language Learning, 44*, 493–527.

Pica, T. (2002). Subject matter content: How does it assist the interactional and linguistic needs of classroom language learners? *The Modern Language Journal, 86*, 1–19.

Pica, T., & Doughty, C. (1985a). Input and interaction in the communicative language classroom: A comparison of teacher-fronted and group activities. In S. M. Gass & C. G. Madden (Eds.), *Input in second language acquisition* (pp. 115–32). Rowley, MA: Newbury House.

Pica, T., & Doughty, C. (1985b). The role of group work in classroom second language acquisition. *Studies in Second Language Acquisition, 7*, 233–48.

Pica, T., Kanagy, R., & Falodun, J. (1993). Choosing and using communication tasks for second language instruction and research. In G. Crookes & S. Gass (Eds.), *Tasks and language learning: Integrating theory and practice* (pp. 9–34). Philadelphia: Multilingual Matters.

Pica, T., Lincoln-Porter, F., Paninos, D., & Linnell, J. (1996). Language learners' interaction: How does it address the input, output, and feedback needs of language learners? *TESOL Quarterly, 30*, 59–84.

Pienemann, M. (1998). *Language processing and second language development: Processability theory.* Philadelphia: John Benjamins.

Platt, E. J., & Brooks, F. (1994). The "acquisition-rich" environment revisited. *The Modern Language Journal, 78*, 497–511.

Polio, C. G., & Duff, P. A. (1994). Teachers' language use in university foreign language classrooms: A qualitative analysis of English and target language alternation. *The Modern Language Journal, 78*, 313–26.

Porter, P. A. (1983) *Variations in the conversations of adult learners of English as a function of the proficiency level of the participants*. Unpublished doctoral dissertation, Stanford University.

Porter, P. A. (1986). How learners talk to each other: Input and interaction in task-centered discussions. In R. Day (Ed.), *Talking to learn: Conversation in second language acquisition* (pp. 200–22). Rowley, MA: Newbury House.

Rabie, S. R. (1996) *Negative feedback, modeling, and vocabulary acquisition in task-based interaction*. Unpublished master's thesis, University of Hawai'i at Mānoa.

Reagan, T. G., & Osborn, T. A. (2002). *The foreign language educator in society*. Mahwah, NJ: Lawrence Erlbaum.

Robinson, P. (1995). Attention, memory, and the "noticing" hypothesis. *Language Learning, 45*, 283–331.

Robinson, P. (2001). Task complexity, cognitive resources, and syllabus design: A triadic theory of task influences on SLA. In P. Robinson (Ed.), *Cognition and second language instruction* (pp. 287–318). New York: Cambridge University Press.

Roca de Larios, J., Murphy, L., & Manchón, R. (1999). The use of restructuring strategies in EFL writing: A study of Spanish learners of English as a foreign language. *Journal of Second Language Writing, 8*, 13–44.

Ross, S. (1988). Accomodation in interlanguage discourse from an EFL perspective. *System, 16*, 347–54.

Rulon, K. A., & McCreary, J. (1986). Negotiation of content: Teacher-fronted and small-group interaction. In R. Day (Ed.), *Talking to learn: Conversation in second language acquisition* (pp. 182–99). Rowley, MA: Newbury House.

Schmidt, R. (2001). Attention. In P. Robinson (Ed.), *Cognition and second language instruction* (pp. 3–33). New York: Cambridge University Press.

Schmidt, R., & Frota, S. (1986). Developing basic conversational ability in a second language: A case study of an adult learner of Portuguese. In R. R. Day (Ed.), *Talking to learn: Conversation in second language acquisition* (pp. 237–322). Rowley, MA: Newbury House.

Schleppegrell, M. (1998). Grammar as a resource: Writing a description. *Research in the Teaching of English, 32*, 182–211.

Schulz, R. (2002). Changing perspectives in foreign language education: Where do we come from? Where are we going? *Foreign Language Annals, 35*, 285–92.

Shehadeh, A. (1999). Non-native speakers' production of modified comprehensible output and second language learning. *Language Learning, 49*, 627–75.

Skehan, P. (1998). *A cognitive approach to language learning*. New York: Oxford University Press.

Slimani, A. (1991). Evaluation of classroom interaction. In J. C. Alderson & A. Beretta (Eds.), *Evaluating second language education* (pp. 197–220). New York: Cambridge University Press.

Spada, N. (1997). Form-focussed instruction and second language acquisition: A review of classroom and laboratory research. *Language Teaching, 29*, 1–15.

Spada, N., & Lightbown, P. (1999). Instruction, first language influence, and developmental readiness in second language acquisition. *The Modern Language Journal, 83*, 1–22.

Stepp-Greany, J. (2002). Student perceptions on language learning in a technological environment: Implications for the new millennium. *Language Learning and Technology, 6* (1), 165–80.

Storch, N. (2004). Using activity theory to explain differences in patterns of dyadic interactions in an ESL class. *The Canadian Modern Language Review, 60*, 457–80.

Swain, M. (2002). The output hypothesis and beyond: Mediating acquisition through collaborative dialogue. In J. P. Lantolf (Ed.), *Sociocultural theory and second language learning* (pp. 97–114). New York: Oxford University Press.

Swain, M., Brooks, L., & Tocalli-Beller, A. (2002). Peer-peer dialogue as a means of second language learning. *Annual Review of Applied Linguistics, 22*, 171–85.

Swain, M., & Lapkin, S. (1995). Problems in output and the cognitive processes they generate: A step towards second language learning. *Applied Linguistics, 16*, 371–91.

Tarone, E. (1993). *Second language acquisition in a variationist framework.* Unpublished manuscript, University of Minnesota.

Tarone, E., & Parrish, B. (1988). Task-related variation in interlanguage: The case of articles. *Language Learning, 38*, 21–44.

Tarone, E., & Swain, M. (1995). A sociolinguistic perspective on second-language use in immersion classrooms. *The Modern Language Journal, 79*, 24–46.

Ting, S. C. (1996). Planning time, modality and second language task performance: Accuracy and fluency in the acquisition of Chinese as a second language. *The University of Queensland Working Papers in Language and Linguistics, 1*, 31–64.

Tomasello, M. (Ed.). (1998). *The new psychology of language: Cognitive and functional approaches to language structure.* Mahwah, NJ: Lawrence Erlbaum.

Tomlin, R. (1990). Functionalism in second language acquisition. *Studies in Second Language Acquisition, 12*, 155–77.

Toyoda, E., & Harrison, R. (2002). Categorization of text chat communication between learners and native speakers of Japanese. *Language Learning and Technology, 6* (1), 82–99.

Unsworth, L. (Ed.). (2000). *Researching language in schools and communities.* New York: Cassell.

Valdés, G., Haro, P., & Echevarriarza, M. P. (1992). The development of writing abilities in a foreign language: Contributions toward a general theory of L2 writing. *The Modern Language Journal, 76*, 333–52.

VanPatten, B. (1998). Cognitive characteristics of adult second language learners. In H. Byrnes (Ed.), *Learning foreign and second languages* (pp. 105–27). New York: The Modern Language Association of America.

VanPatten, B., & Cadierno, T. (1993). Explicit instruction and input processing. *Studies in Second Language Acquisition, 15*, 225–41.

Varonis, E., & Gass, S. (1985). Non-native/non-native conversations: A model for negotiation of meaning. *Applied Linguistics, 6*, 71–90.

Warschauer, M., & Kern, R. (Eds.). (2000). *Network-based language teaching: Concepts and practice.* New York: Cambridge University Press.

Weaver, C. (2002, April). *Pre-task planning: Does practice make perfect?* Paper presented at the AAAL conference, Salt Lake City, UT.

Wendel, J. N. (1997). *Planning and second-language narrative production.* Unpublished doctoral dissertation, Temple University.

White, L. (1987). Against comprehensible input: The Input Hypothesis and the development of L2 competence. *Applied Linguistics, 8,* 95–110.

Williams, J. (1999). Learner-generated attention to form. *Language Learning, 49,* 583–625.

Yule, G. (1996). *Referential communication tasks.* Mahwah, NJ: Lawrence Erlbaum.

Yule, G. (1998). *Explaining English grammar.* Oxford: Oxford University Press.

Yule, G., & Macdonald, D. (1990). Resolving referential conflicts in L2 interaction: The effect of proficiency and interactive role. *Language Learning, 40,* 539–56.

8 Study abroad as foreign language practice

Robert M. DeKeyser

A semester abroad is often seen as the ultimate opportunity to practice a foreign language, in terms of both quantity and quality of input and interaction. For some students, parents, teachers, administrators, and prospective employers, study abroad is not only the best form of practice, sometimes it is the only form they consider to be useful. Yet, the literature shows that many students come back from abroad with a certain level of disappointment about their progress, and that even those who feel that they made substantial progress have not improved much on objective measures, especially with respect to accuracy. This chapter describes how students typically practice their language skills abroad and how this influences their proficiency gains. It then compares this typical practice abroad with what SLA theory and the relevant literature in cognitive psychology, specifically skill acquisition theory, have to say about good practice. Finally it argues that the linguistic benefits of study abroad could be greatly enhanced by planning systematically for a continuum of practice from basic classroom instruction to pre-departure training, on-site observation and guidance, and courses for students returning home.

What is typically achieved as a result of study abroad?

This first section provides an assessment of what progress is typically made in the four skills during study abroad. A few studies report on various skills; they will be discussed here first. Research focusing more narrowly on one or two skills will be dealt with next. The emphasis will be on speaking, because that is the skill for which most documentation is available; this probably reflects the fact that improvement in this area is usually seen as the main goal of study abroad. Only studies with a minimum of four participants will be discussed.

Progress on multiple-skill assessments

The largest study of this kind (n = 3,212) was conducted by Teichler and Maiworm (1997). It found that progress in speaking (and other skills) in most cases meant improving from a 4 to a 2 on a 7-point self-rating scale (where 7 = extremely limited and 1 = very good) and that the percentage of students reporting substantial L2 proficiency improved from 15 percent before the stay abroad to 67 percent after. Meara (1994) reported substantial improvement for a sample of 586 British students going abroad, especially in listening and speaking, less so in reading and writing. The figures in these two studies are hard to interpret, given the number of L2s involved, along with the varying levels of preparation and the widely differing length and nature of the experience abroad. More narrowly focused studies such as Lapkin, Hart, and Swain (1995), based on 116 English-speaking students of French, and Mizuno (1998), with 51 American learners of Japanese, also report substantial progress on all skills. Any evaluation based on self-assessments in the study abroad context should be treated with extreme caution, however. All the studies that compared self-assessments from students overseas with actual objective tests found a distressingly low correlation (Allen, 2002; Carlson, Burn, Useem, & Yachimowicz 1991; Lapkin et al. 1995) not only for the pre-test when students had not really had a chance to assess their own communicative skills yet but even for the post-test.

Objective, multiple-skill assessments are hard to come by for obvious practical reasons. The oldest, best-known, and also the largest (n = 2,782) study to include them is Carroll (1967). He found that the amount of study abroad was a more important predictor of proficiency than language learning aptitude or years of language study in school. Detailed results were presented for listening only, but he stated that "the patterns of results are for the most part very similar to those for the listening test score" (p. 136). Gomes da Costa, Smith, and Whiteley (1975), a study modeled after Carroll's but conducted exclusively with British students of German, found similar results in the sense that the length of study abroad was the best predictor of proficiency; it was a significant predictor for speaking, listening, and writing, but not reading. Brecht, Davidson, and Ginsberg (1995) also obtained objective measures for multiple skills (speaking, listening, and reading) for a large number of students (n = 658), in this case, American learners of Russian. Speaking skills typically went up by one level on the Oral Proficiency Interview (OPI) scale. Scores for the other skills are discussed in terms of predictors, but sizes of gains are not given.

Progress in speaking

Popular wisdom is very clear on this point: Students who go abroad make spectacular progress in L2 speaking skills. The picture that emerges from the empirical literature, however, is more complex. While some researchers do document large gains, others find little or no progress or progress that is very narrowly delimited. Substantial effects of a stay abroad on speaking proficiency were documented by Carlson et al. (1991) in the sense of average progress from intermediate + to advanced + on the ACTFL scale, but only for a subsample of 20 learners from a much larger study and for learners who had usually spent a year or more abroad. Golonka (2001), using the same measure and a similar analysis, found that about half of her learners had advanced from intermediate + to advanced or advanced + after one semester. Yager (1998) reported that 22 out of 30 students in his study improved significantly, 19 of them in all three areas assessed (grammar, pronunciation, global). Others found smaller effects, i.e., intermediate–high OPI ratings for a group that went abroad versus intermediate–mid for a group that stayed at home (Huebner, 1995), or no relationship at all between time spent abroad and speaking proficiency (Magnan, 1986).

Several studies provide a more detailed qualitative assessment of progress in speaking skills. Allen (2002) found large and comparable effect sizes for fluency, comprehensibility, and amount of communication after six weeks abroad, and a medium effect for quality of communication. Davie (1996), using self-assessments only, found some to great progress in colloquial Russian, some in vocabulary, and little to some in grammar and formal Russian. Freed (1995), using OPIs, found little difference in overall gains for a group abroad compared with a group at home but higher fluency gains for the group abroad, especially for rate of speech and especially for those with lower initial fluency. Segalowitz and Freed (2004) again found a significant difference for rate of speech and also for length of the longest turn, length of the longest fluent run, and length of filler-free runs. Likewise, Towell, Hawkins, and Bazergui (1996) found significant improvement in fluency, mainly due to increase in length of runs. After one year abroad, their subjects had bridged almost half of the gap between their L1 and initial L2 measures of fluency. Isabelli (2002) found improvement in fluency for all students and in discourse skills for some. Freed, Segalowitz, and Dewey (2004) found improvement in various aspects of fluency for students in an overseas program in France (and not for comparable students in regular instruction at home), but this improvement was far less substantial than for a third group in a domestic immersion program. Marriott (1995) found that politeness markers improved but mostly only formulaically, far less in verb forms or in choice of noun/pronoun for third-person referent. Regan (1995) was the most focused of all and documented more nativelike *ne*-deletion in French L2 negative constructions, especially in formulas.

Progress in listening

The only study that assessed listening skills and that is not previously mentioned is Allen (2002), which documented a medium-effect size in listening skill gains for 25 English-speaking learners of L2 French after six weeks abroad.

Progress in reading

Most studies that have investigated progress in reading during study abroad are multiple-skill studies and have been mentioned. One recent study that dealt exclusively with reading development abroad is Dewey (2004). Comparing American students of Japanese in Japan and at home (both groups being in intensive immersion programs), he found no difference for a vocabulary test or free recall measures, but self-assessments showed more confidence, and think-aloud protocols showed more monitoring for the group that spent time in Japan.

Progress in writing

Here again, very few studies exist that look only at this skill in study abroad. The only recent example found is Freed, So, and Lazar (2003). Contrary to what was reported for oral fluency in Freed (1995), no significant progress in written fluency during a semester abroad was found. It is hard to interpret this lack of progress, however, because the comparison group at home declined, and the number of subjects in both groups was small (15 each).

Conclusion: How much skill is acquired abroad?

While the evidence on listening, reading, and writing skills is extremely scarce, the findings on speaking proficiency show a number of relatively clear tendencies: A majority of students make measurable progress in speaking, especially in terms of fluency, at least in the programs of longer duration. Documentation of substantial improvement on accuracy[1] or in programs of less than one semester is scarce. While some researchers have documented more progress for students with lower initial proficiency than for the more advanced students (Freed, 1995; Klapper & Rees, 2003; Lapkin et al., 1995; Teichler & Maiworm, 1997; Yager, 1998), there is also evidence showing the opposite (Brecht et al., 1995; Rivers, 1998).

Several researchers have offered explanations for why the more advanced students may learn more: They interact more (Brecht & Robinson, 1993), they take more frequent advantage of "extracurricular listening" (e.g., to radio, films, television) (Segalowitz & Freed, 2004, p. 195), and they are "more adept at managing the ceaseless flow of TL [target language] input" (Rivers, 1998, p. 492) during such exposure and interaction. It may very well be that the more advanced students are indeed the ones that are learning more in the long run and that the weaker students make the quickest progress at the beginning, catching up on conversational routines and such, and also that their subsequent gains are better reflected on instruments such as the OPI than those of the more advanced students. The transition from intermediate-high to advanced on the ACTL OPI is notoriously hard to bring about (see various contributions in Leaver and Shekhtman, 2002).

Finally, it is important to keep in mind that the skills that students have acquired abroad may be both overestimated and underestimated, depending on what is assessed and how. Many cognitive and educational psychologists have stressed that consistent task environments are necessary to show transfer of training (e.g., Bransford, Brown, & Cocking, 1999; Whittlesea & Dorken, 1993). Students abroad often overestimate the gains they have made because they do not realize how these gains are limited to use in the overseas program or, even more specifically, the homestay environment and do little to improve, say, accuracy in writing or even fluency in a formal context such as a job interview. On the other hand, applied linguists and educators may underestimate what students have learned if they assess their gains only by means of paper-and-pencil tests and OPI-type interviews.

What kinds of practice lead to these outcomes?

Not only the outcome but also the process of language study abroad is often rather different from the corresponding myth. Even in terms of sheer quantity, many students do not receive the amounts of practice that one could naively expect. Even in programs of relatively long duration, say a semester or more, the quantity of actual practice is limited by a variety of factors. For many students, especially for native speakers of English, particularly for those at the lower levels of proficiency and most particularly for those in more or less sheltered programs, the temptation to speak their native language is great. Not only does speaking the L1 take less effort, it conveys many other advantages as well. It may allow for more precise and more rapid communication, it may allow students to say things they do not want the native speakers of the second language in question to understand, and it may create a bond with other students and their shared (sub)culture (e.g., Levin, 2001). The importance of the latter factor is not to be underestimated at a time when students may be experiencing something between mild homesickness and severe culture shock. The native language thus becomes a protective capsule, a symbolic withdrawal from a cultural context they cannot withdraw from physically (Wilkinson, 1998). DeKeyser (forthcoming), for instance, documents how American students in a study abroad program in Argentina doggedly stuck to Spanish during the first three weeks of their stay, only to revert to English after that, when many of them became increasingly unhappy with the program and their hosts or the host culture.

The quality of L2 practice often leaves even more to be desired. A large part of it may be entirely passive: listening to university lectures, watching television, listening to tour guides, eavesdropping on conversations (see esp. Brecht & Robinson, 1993; Levin, 2001; Rivers, 1998; Wilkinson, 1998, 2002). Situations like these obviously do not provide practice in output/interaction and are severely limited even in terms of input because it may be either very repetitive or very hard to comprehend. In neither case does the student get good comprehensible input. More importantly, even when practice is truly interactive, it may do little to stretch the limits of the student's interlanguage because it is almost formulaic in nature: politeness formulas, routine requests, and routine inquiries, such as "how are you?" "could you pass me the bread?" and "how was your day?" (cf. Wilkinson, 1998).

From a psycholinguistic point of view, however, the most important limitation on quantity and quality of practice is probably that skill acquisition theory usually distinguishes three stages, i.e., declarative knowledge, proceduralization, and automatization (see the introductory chapter for explanation), and a stay abroad should be most conducive to the third stage. It can – at least for some students – provide the large amount of practice necessary for the gradual reduction of reaction time, error rate, and interference with other tasks that characterize the automatization process (cf. e.g., DeKeyser 2001; Segalowitz, 2003). In reality, however, students often plateau because they are never provided with ideal circumstances for proceduralization and therefore never get to the automatization of rules. Often information about grammar rules was provided years before the stay overseas; students' memory of it may be shaky at best. In other cases, while available in declarative form in such a way that it can be drawn on for fill-in-the-blanks tests and other paper-and-pencil activities, this knowledge has (almost) never been drawn on for actual communication and has therefore not been proceduralized.

When students begin their stay overseas, they are so overwhelmed by the communicative demands on them that they try to skip the proceduralization stage. They try to do the best they can to communicate, i.e., transmit reasonably accurate and relevant information at an acceptable speed, and that leaves them no time to draw on their hard-to-access declarative knowledge. As a result, the automatization that eventually takes place as a result of many encounters of this kind leads to automatic use of formulas only, not automaticity of rule use. Only behaviors can be automatized, not knowledge, and if students are seldom able to engage in the behavior of communicating while drawing on declarative knowledge of a rule (proceduralization), then rule automatization is impossible. Students, therefore, may quickly improve their ability to handle routine exchanges and initially feel that they are making good progress in learning the L2, but they stall when more extensive conversations about more involved topics require the use of rules in some form.

The lack of sufficiently developed classroom knowledge has two paradoxical effects. On the one hand, there are the well-known claims along the lines of "I learned more in a month abroad than in a year in the classroom." On the other hand, however, as students have not had a chance to proceduralize the basic grammar, let alone to develop the most minimal discourse skills in the classroom, they very much feel the need for classroom(-like) instruction, which leads them to treat native speakers like teachers, to ask for more classroom explanations while abroad, and to focus their attention during their stay overseas on the discrete items of grammar and vocabulary that can equally well be learned at home, while being unable to acquire the idioms, discourse skills, and elements of strategic competence that study abroad is ideally suited for (Miller & Ginsberg, 1995; cf. also Brecht & Robinson, 1995; Pellegrino, 1998). "In spite of the fact that students denigrate formal instruction, their views of language and their views of learning lead them to recreate classroom situations in interactions with native speakers outside of class" (Miller & Ginsberg, 1995, p. 295). This, along with their lack of insight into the processes of language acquisition and use, makes them miss many opportunities to learn from the input provided overseas. "To a large extent students' views of language exclude many of the features of language for which study abroad is particularly advantageous" (ibid.).

Finally, students tend to receive little appropriate feedback when they do produce nonformulaic output. Native speakers may be reluctant to correct them, especially if the students are at such a low level that they make mistakes all the time; on the other hand, if only small mistakes are made occasionally that do not interfere with communication, native speakers may not be inclined to correct because they feel that is simply how foreigners talk. At other times, they may not even be able to correct because a whole sentence is incomprehensible, or it is clear something is wrong with the sentence but not which element should be changed. Therefore, the same error can be repeated often without being corrected so that it becomes a permanent feature of the student's interlanguage, not only in terms of performance but even in terms of students' explicit (declarative) knowledge. Students may stubbornly insist that something is correct when that kind of error is pointed out to them explicitly at the end of or after their study abroad.

In sum, foreign language practice during study abroad is more limited than one may assume, in terms of quantity as well as quality and in terms of input, output, interaction, and feedback. And yet it is precisely the nature of the interactive practice that may be the most important determiner of proficiency gains, as documented in several recent dissertations. Mizuno (1998) showed how "can-do ratings" for very specific subskills varied dramatically, depending, of course, on what specifically was practiced. Isabelli (2000) found that the key predictor for achievement was amount of interaction in the target language, itself a function of motivation. Golonka (2001) found that self-correcting behaviors during interaction with native speakers are a more important predictor of gains than knowledge of grammar. On a larger scale, Meara (1994) reported that the estimated amount of time spent speaking the L2 was the best predictor of estimated gains in all four skills. Brecht and Robinson (1993) found that students with the same level of speaking proficiency gained more if they used the L2 more. They also found that the students who started with a relatively high level of proficiency gained more *and* interacted more than those of lower levels of proficiency. The combination of the two findings suggests that higher-proficiency students gain more because they interact more, which implies that it is very important to make sure that participants in study abroad programs be at a high enough level of speaking/listening proficiency to ensure they can engage in interaction of sufficient quality and with sufficient frequency to make meaningful progress.

What would constitute good practice?

The state of affairs described in the previous section contrasts sharply with what both psychological theories of skill acquisition and second language acquisition theories would consider to be good practice. Yet, in spite of ongoing controversies about various points in both of these areas, it is widely agreed that they are all of central relevance.

Skill acquisition theory first of all teaches us that considerable practice is required to automatize a skill. One famous early study even documented continued improvement in performance in making cigars after rolling up to 20 million exemplars (Crossman, 1959, quoted in Newell and Rosenbloom, 1981). This theory also teaches us that practice is very skill-specific: Practice in writing computer programs improves performance in writing them, not necessarily in reading them and vice versa (see e.g., Anderson, 1993; Anderson, Fincham, and Douglass, 1997; Singley & Anderson, 1989). In second language learning, the same phenomenon was demonstrated in DeKeyser (1997). Having practiced both comprehension and production and having practiced all rules were not enough for students to do well on post-treatment tests. They had to have practiced the specific rule in the specific skill in order to do well in terms of both speed and accuracy.

Second, procedural knowledge can also be developed by working through examples of the behavior required – be it solving a math problem or producing a specific syntactic structure to express a specific meaning – while keeping in mind how the example is an instance of the rule (cf. Anderson & Fincham, 1994). This proceduralization can happen rather quickly through a small set of instances. Automatization, however, of the behavior/procedural knowledge (so that it takes minimal time and effort, has a very low error rate, and interferes minimally with other tasks) requires processing a great many instances. Automaticity can be gradually increased under pressure; the initial stages of proceduralization, on the contrary, require careful, deliberate use of the relevant declarative knowledge in the execution of the target task.

Third, it is important to receive explicit feedback immediately after making a mistake during the proceduralization stage so that it becomes clear what went wrong in the application of the declarative knowledge to the behavioral task (see the first section of the introductory chapter).

Second language acquisition theory has made a different set of contributions, which are focused more on conditions for acquiring knowledge than for practicing it. It is now generally accepted that comprehensible input is an important part of successful second language acquisition (see e.g., Carroll, 2001; Gass, 1997, 2003; Krashen 1982; Leow, this volume; Long, 1996; VanPatten 2003), and that practice in the processing of form-meaning relationships in the input ("processing instruction") is important for developing competence (see esp. VanPatten, 1996, 2003). The role of "comprehensible output" (Swain, 1985) is also considered important, even though debate continues about whether its main function is to make students "notice the gap" (Doughty, 2001; Izumi, 2002, 2003; Swain, 1985, 1998; Swain & Lapkin, 1995) and thus improve their competence or merely to improve fluency, i.e., performance (for discussion see e.g., DeKeyser, Salaberry, Robinson, & Harrington, 2002; R. Ellis, 2003; Muranoi, this volume; Shehadeh, 2002; VanPatten, 2002a, 2002b).

The role of interaction has also received ample attention (e.g., Gass, 1997, 2003; Long, 1983, 1996; Lyster, 1998a; Mackey, this volume). It is widely accepted that interaction between native and non-native speakers leads to negotiation of meaning, which certainly improves comprehensible input and, possibly, uptake.

Feedback remains a more controversial issue (cf. esp. Leeman, 2003, this volume; Nicholas, Lightbown, & Spada, 2001), but most researchers agree that explicit negative feedback is necessary for some elements of L2 (see esp. White, 1991) and that it is important for learners to be aware of what is being corrected (cf. Philp, 2003).

Taken together then, the fields of skill acquisition theory and second language acquisition theory have established a series of conditions for the acquisition of knowledge and development of skill which, more often than not, study abroad conditions fail to meet. Even during a stay overseas, students experience a lack of real practice time, of opportunities for proceduralization, of immediate and explicit feedback, and of active negotiation of meaning in challenging conversations. Sometimes, even conditions for ample comprehensible input are not met.

Given that the requirements for L2 skill acquisition as described in this section are often not met under the conditions described in the previous section, it is no surprise that one finds the rather disappointing outcomes described in the first section of this chapter.

What can be done to improve foreign language practice during study abroad?

The previous sections put heavy emphasis on the relative failure of study abroad experiences and tried to explain this phenomenon by pointing out how impoverished L2 language practice overseas often is, compared with what it could be. Clearly, however, some students do make spectacular progress, especially in terms of fluency (see esp. Towell, Hawkins, & Bazergui, 1996). The question, then, is how to ensure that more students experience the kind of L2 practice overseas that leads to such progress.

First of all, the quality of the students' learning experience abroad depends to a large extent on their preparation at home. Specifically, when it comes to improving fluency, probably the main goal of most language students who go overseas, it is important that the students be ready for fluency improvement in the sense of automatization. That means that they should have gone through some minimal proceduralization in the classroom. If they know how to use rules for communication, however haltingly, they will become much better at using them through repeated practice abroad. If not, they will spend their time practicing formulaic knowledge and gathering new declarative knowledge, not automatizing proceduralized rule knowledge. The problem, then, is that the transition from the classroom to the study abroad context coincides with the transition from declarative to procedural knowledge, a transition much harder to make under the social and time pressures that characterize this environment. The transition in skill acquisition that *should* coincide with going abroad is automatization. As this process requires a very large amount of varied practice, the native-speaking environment is a much better context for it than the classroom. The implications of this are quite clear. Students should have *functional* knowledge of the grammar that is assumed to be known at an intermediate level. Only then can they spend their time abroad doing what is very hard to do in the classroom, much easier during prolonged practice abroad, and essential for fluent production of L2 in a wide variety of contexts: completing the process of proceduralization and making substantial progress towards automaticity.

Therefore, as Davie (1996, p. 75) put it, "If we are to produce students who are well prepared to meet the demands of the *stazhirovka* [internship] and consequently survive in the language, they must be comfortable in using their Russian, both productively and receptively, in the context of each of the four skills."

Second, along with the language training, students could benefit from specific preparation in handling problems with input and output in interaction with native speakers. All too often, learners do not seem to realize that some communication strategies that work in the classroom do not work well with native speakers in the host country because the latter do not understand the specific nature of the students' misunderstandings, errors, hesitations, or implicit metalinguistic questions (see DeKeyser, 1990).

Paige, Cohen, Kappler, Chi, and Lassegard (2002) provide many suggestions, intended for pre-departure preparation, about how to use better strategies in the learning of all four skills before, during, and after the actual stay abroad. Many of these suggestions are at a macro-level, i.e., how to foster opportunities for interaction (being careful in choosing housing, going to the same stores repeatedly in order to get to know people, making an effort to make real friends among the locals). Some suggestions focus on the interaction itself (overcoming the fear to speak, finding a comfortable balance between planning and correcting, becoming comfortable with not understanding everything) or on how to maximize learning from the interaction (requesting that NSs correct but without interrupting and only after giving a chance at self-correction; asking for explicit information about how to carry out certain speech acts like apologies and compliments with various kinds of people under various circumstances). Few suggestions are very specific, such as "record segments of fast speech (. . .) and replay it several times (. . .) understanding more each time you listen to it" (p. 170), or "learn culturally appropriate ways to indicate that you are not following the conversation" (p. 174).

Paige et al. (2002) quote a student as saying she did not even realize how bad she was at comprehending spontaneous L2 speech till she was overseas. That was also one of the findings in DeKeyser (forthcoming). Several students in the group he observed in Argentina stated (1) that they thought they knew Spanish well before they arrived in Argentina but once there realized that was not the case at all, and (2) that they had hoped to be completely fluent by the end of their six-week stay but realized after a couple of weeks that that was out of the question. Findings such as these clearly show that realistic listening practice is often lacking completely in the stateside curriculum so that students who arrive overseas still need to learn how to practice before they can start learning from practice.

Once the students are on site, perhaps the most crucial intervention is to give them assignments that force them to interact meaningfully with NSs and overcome their fear of speaking. Archangeli (1999) describes a positive experience sending students out to interview different kinds of native speakers with a specific list of questions and debriefing them afterward. Giving assignments like that, at increasing levels of difficulty, along with making every effort to assign students to compatible families or roommates can help students to hit the ground running. Following an assignment up with classroom discussion under the guidance of an experienced teacher (perhaps on the basis of stimulated recall) can also be a privileged opportunity for proceduralization of rules. The availability of (the teacher's) rule knowledge during (a replay of) the execution of a very realistic target task provides ideal circumstances for transformation of that knowledge during the execution of that task.

Stimulated recall could be particularly useful also to force students to pay attention to recasts provided by NSs. The theoretical and empirical literature on corrective feedback shows that recasts make sense from a theoretical point of view (Leeman, this volume; Nicholas, Spada, & Lightbown, 2001) and can work well in practice (e.g., Ayoun, 2001; Han, 2002; Iwashita, 2003; Leeman, 2003; Long, Inagaki, & Ortega, 1998). It also shows, however, that students often do not notice recasts, or do not show uptake (e.g., Morris & Tarone, 2003; Lyster, 1998b), and that a variety of factors can influence the degree to which students become aware of them and benefit from them (Han, 2002; Philp, 2003). Teacher-guided stimulated-recall sessions of NS-NNS interactions should help students learn to distinguish what is a recast and what is a mere noncorrective reformulation.

The most universally neglected part of all, when it comes to maximizing the practice effect of study abroad, is what happens after re-entry into the home institution. Virtually without exception, returning students are in the same classrooms along with others who have not been abroad, exposed to the same teaching of declarative knowledge that they may or may not have proceduralized and automatized already, the same artificial communicative activities, even the same meaningless drills.[2] Clearly, students at this (or even a somewhat lower) level would benefit more from truly communicative activities (possibly task-based focus on form) specifically designed to build on and expand on the (often very narrow and specific) interactional skills they have acquired abroad.

Conclusions

Although students typically make substantial gains in fluency during study abroad, at least in the case of more extended stays, they typically do not gain all that much in accuracy. Even for fluency the gains are far from universal, and for the other three skills, including listening, there is very little information that can be considered both valid and reliable.

Proficiency gains during a semester overseas, then, appear rather modest compared with the investment of time and money and with the almost magical language learning powers often ascribed to the overseas experience. This lack of efficiency can be attributed to a variety of factors that, taken together, very seriously diminish both quantity and quality of verbal interaction with native speakers. They range from inadequate preparation in terms of language knowledge and language learning strategies to living conditions that are not conducive to creative practice and a variety of sociocultural factors. While program directors, counselors and teachers cannot do much about students' aptitude, personality, and motivation, they play a large role in the language learning experiences that prepare students for their stay abroad, in the selection of living conditions and other aspects of how the program is set up and even in determining at what point in the curriculum the student goes overseas. Together they can and should work on a much better integration of the stateside language curriculum with the overseas experience so that students can approach the combination of basic courses, overseas practice, and advanced courses as a long-term process of skill acquisition instead of a series of disjoint experiences that lead to a juxtaposition of automatized routines and merely declarative rule knowledge.

Recommendations for future research

Whatever the impact of program characteristics or initial proficiency may be on the extent of students' progress overseas, there is little doubt that the strongest determinant of success, besides aptitude, is the students' behavior as learners (which, of course, is determined in turn by program context and proficiency level as well as aptitude and motivation). If we are to be able to make better recommendations to students about who would benefit most from going overseas, and more particularly to what kind of program at what point in the home curriculum, we need to know better how exactly the interaction between specific aptitudes, specific behaviors, and specific contexts leads to specific changes in proficiency.

Very few semester overseas studies document individual students' behaviors in great detail, and even fewer relate them to these individuals' learning. Mizuno (1998) stands out as a valiant attempt in that direction, in the sense that her research includes both detailed proficiency ratings (a very wide variety of can-do scales) and details about individuals' backgrounds and interactions. The drawback in this study is that it is based on self-assessments only, not micro-level participant observation. Segalowitz and Freed (2004) provide a different part of the puzzle by studying aptitude profiles at a micro-level and linking them with progress. They did not, however, look at behaviors as an intervening variable.

Future research should include a fine-grained analysis of individual students' behavior as intervening variable between aptitude and initial proficiency, on the one hand, and language learning success, on the other. We need to get into the student's head rather than conduct black-box research that links student or program characteristics with outcomes. That can only be achieved by combining qualitative methodologies such as participant observation and protocol analysis (including stimulated recall) with quantitative methodologies more typically used in psycholinguistics, educational psychology, and the psychology of individual differences. This implies that both intensive participant observation and substantial amounts of quantification for sizeable numbers of students will be necessary. Such studies are inevitably very time-consuming and expensive. Only that kind of research, however, can provide the best scientific basis for recommending program choices to students and for providing pre-departure training adapted to their aptitudes, proficiency levels, and goals.

Notes

1. Klapper and Rees (2003) do report substantial progress on a broad discrete-item grammar test for German as a foreign language after a six-month stay abroad. They also point out, however, that for many elements of grammar, progress during preceding instruction at home, at least for their Focus on Forms group, was greater than during the stay in Germany. This study is not mentioned in the overview of empirical studies because it does not deal with one of the four skills, only with grammar knowledge as shown on a grammar test.
2. A few years ago, I observed a particularly poignant example of how a student who had returned from abroad (Ecuador) was not getting appropriate practice in the classroom. His year-long stay abroad had been particularly successful, and he spoke with a level of accuracy and fluency comparable to that of a native speaker. When the class was engaged in a mechanical drill on the Spanish imperative, however, he made the most absurd kind of mistake. Instead of replacing *debe hacer esto* ("you have to do this") with *haga esto* ("do this!" – the targeted imperative form), he said *deba hacer esto* ("have to do this!"). This mistake was clearly induced by the mechanical nature of the exercise and was something that somebody at this level of proficiency would never say outside of this very artificial context of the mechanical drill.

References

Allen, H. (2002). *Does study abroad make a difference? An investigation of linguistic and motivational outcomes.* Unpublished doctoral dissertation, Emory University.
Anderson, J. R. (1993). *Rules of the mind.* Hillsdale, NJ: Lawrence Erlbaum.

Anderson, J. R., & Fincham, J. M. (1994). Acquisition of procedural skills from examples. *Journal of Experimental Psychology: Learning, Memory and Cognition, 20*(6), 1322–40.

Anderson, J. R., Fincham, J. M., & Douglass, S. (1997). The role of examples and rules in the acquisition of a cognitive skill. *Journal of Experimental Psychology: Learning, Memory and Cognition, 23*(4), 932–45.

Archangeli, M. (1999). Study abroad and experiential learning in Salzburg, Austria. *Foreign Language Annals, 32*(1), 115–24.

Ayoun, D. (2001). The role of negative and positive feedback in the second language acquisition of the *passé composé* and the *imparfait*. *The Modern Language Journal, 85*(2), 226–43.

Bransford, J. D., Brown, A. L., & Cocking, R. R. (1999). *How people learn. Brain, mind, experience, and school*. Washington, DC: National Academy Press.

Brecht, R. D., Davidson, D. E., & Ginsberg, R. B. (1995). Predictors of foreign language gain during study abroad. In B. Freed (Ed.), *Second language acquisition in a study abroad context* (pp. 37–66). Amsterdam/ Philadelphia: John Benjamins.

Brecht, R. D., & Robinson, J. L. (1993). *Qualitative analysis of second language acquisition in study abroad: The ACTR/NFLC project*. National Foreign Language Center.

Brecht, R. D., & Robinson, J. L. (1995). On the value of formal instruction in study abroad. Student reactions in context. In B. F. Freed (Ed.), *Second language acquisition in a study abroad context* (pp. 317–34). Amsterdam/ Philadelphia: John Benjamins.

Carlson, J. S., Burn, B. B., Useem, J., & Yachimowicz, D. (1991). *Study abroad: The experience of American undergraduates in Western Europe and the United States*. Council on International Educational Exchange.

Carroll, J. B. (1967). Foreign language proficiency levels attained by language majors near graduation from college. *Foreign Language Annals, 1*, 131–151.

Carroll, S. E. (2001). *Input and evidence*. Amsterdam: John Benjamins.

Crossman, E. R. F. W. (1959). A theory of the acquisition of speed-skill. *Ergonomics, 2*, 153–66.

Davie, J. (1996). Language skills, course development, and the year abroad. *Language Learning Journal, 13*, 73–6.

DeKeyser, R. M. (1990). Foreign language development during a semester abroad. In B. Freed (Ed.), *Foreign language acquisition research and the classroom* (pp. 104–19). Lexington, KY: Heath.

DeKeyser, R. M. (1997). Beyond explicit rule learning: Automatizing second language morphosyntax. *Studies in Second Language Acquisition, 19*(2), 195–221.

DeKeyser, R. M. (2001). Automaticity and automatization. In P. Robinson (Ed.), *Cognition and second language instruction* (pp. 125–51). New York: Cambridge University Press.

DeKeyser, R. M. (forthcoming). Monitoring processes in Spanish as a second language during a study abroad program.

DeKeyser, R. M., Salaberry, R., Robinson, P., & Harrington, M. (2002). What gets processed in processing instruction? A commentary on Bill VanPatten's

"Processing instruction: An update." *Language Learning, 52*(4), 805–23.

Dewey, D. P. (2004). A comparison of reading development by learners of Japanese in intensive domestic immersion and study abroad contexts. *Studies in Second Language Acquisition, 26*(2), 303–27.

Doughty, C. (2001). Cognitive underpinnings of focus on form. In P. Robinson (Ed.), *Cognition and second language instruction* (pp. 206–57). Cambridge, UK: Cambridge University Press.

Ellis, R. (2003). *Task-based language learning and teaching.* Oxford: Oxford University Press.

Freed, B. (1995). What makes us think that students who study abroad become fluent? In B. Freed (Ed.), *Second language acquisition in a study abroad context* (pp. 123–48). Amsterdam/Philadelphia: John Benjamins.

Freed, B., Segalowitz, N., & Dewey, D. P. (2004). Context of learning and second language fluency in French: Comparing regular classroom, study abroad and intensive domestic immersion programs. *Studies in Second Language Acquisition, 26*(2), 275–301.

Freed, B., So, S., & Lazar, N. A. (2003). Language learning abroad: how do gains in written fluency compare with oral fluency in French as a second language? *ADFL Bulletin, 34*(3), 34–40.

Gass, S. (1997). *Input, interaction, and the second language learner.* Mahwah, NJ: Lawrence Erlbaum.

Gass, S. (2003). Input and interaction. In C. J. Doughty & M. H. Long (Eds.), *Handbook of second language acquisition* (pp. 224–55). Oxford: Blackwell.

Golonka, E. (2001). *Identification of salient linguistic and metalinguistic variables in the prediction of oral proficiency gain at the advanced-level threshold among adult learners of Russian.* Unpublished doctoral dissertation, Bryn Mawr College.

Gomes da Costa, B., Smith, T. M. F., & Whiteley, D. (1975). *German language attainment. A sample survey of universities and colleges in the UK.* Heidelberg: Julius Groos.

Han, Z. (2002). A study of the impact of recasts on tense consistency in L2 output. *TESOL Quarterly, 36*(4), 543–72.

Huebner, T. (1995). The effects of overseas language programs: Report on a case study of an intensive Japanese course. In B. F. Freed (Ed.), *Second Language Acquisition in a Study Abroad Context* (pp. 171–93). Amsterdam/Philadelphia: John Benjamins.

Isabelli, C. L. (2000). *Motivation and extended interaction in the study abroad context: Factors in the development of Spanish language accuracy and communication skills.* Unpublished doctoral dissertation, University of Texas at Austin.

Iwashita, N. (2003). Negative feedback and positive evidence in task-based interaction: Differential effects on L2 developments. *Studies in Second Language Acquisition, 25*(1), 1–36.

Izumi, S. (2002). Output, input enhancement, and the noticing hypothesis: An experimental study on ESL relativization. *Studies in Second Language Acquisition, 24*(4), 541–77.

Izumi, S. (2003). Comprehension and production processes in second language learning: In search of the psycholinguistic rationale of the output hypothesis. *Applied Linguistics, 24*(2), 168–96.

Klapper, J., & Rees, J. (2003). Reviewing the case for explicit grammar instruction in the university foreign language learning context. *Language Teaching Research, 7*(3), 285–314.

Krashen, S. D. (1982). *Principles and practice in second language acquisition.* Englewood Cliffs, NJ: Prentice-Hall.

Lapkin, S., Hart, D., & Swain, M. (1995). A Canadian interprovincial exchange: Evaluating the linguistic impact of a three-month stay in Quebec. In B. F. Freed (Ed.), *Second language acquisition in the study abroad context* (pp. 67–94). Amsterdam/Philadelphia: John Benjamins.

Leaver, B. L., & Shekhtman, B. (Eds.). (2002). *Developing professional-level language proficiency.* New York: Cambridge University Press.

Leeman, J. (2003). Recasts and second language development: Beyond negative evidence. *Studies in Second Language Acquisition, 25*(1), 37–63.

Levin, D. M. (2001). *Language learners' sociocultural interaction in a study abroad context.* Unpublished doctoral dissertation, Indiana University.

Long, M. H. (1983). Native speaker/non-native speaker conversation and the negotiation of comprehensible input. *Applied Linguistics, 4*(2), 126–41.

Long, M. H. (1996). The role of the linguistic environment in second language acquisition. In W. C. Ritchie & T. K. Bhatia (Eds.), *Handbook of second language acquisition* (pp. 413–68). San Diego, CA: Academic Press.

Long, M. H., Inagaki, S., & Ortega, L. (1998). The role of implicit negative feedback in SLA: Models and recasts in Japanese and Spanish. *The Modern Language Journal, 82*(3), 357–71.

Lyster, R. (1998a). Negotiation of form, recasts, and explicit correction in relation to error types and learner repair in immersion classrooms. *Language Learning, 48*(2), 183–218.

Lyster, R. (1998b). Recasts, repetition, and ambiguity in L2 classroom discourse. *Studies in Second Language Acquisition, 20*(1), 51–81.

Magnan, S. S. (1986). Assessing speaking proficiency in the undergraduate curriculum: Data from French. *Foreign Language Annals, 19*(5), 429–37.

Marriott, H. (1995). The acquisition of politeness patterns by exchange students in Japan. In B. F. Freed (Ed.), *Second language acquisition in a study abroad context* (pp. 197–224). Amsterdam/Philadelphia: John Benjamins.

Meara, P. (1994). The year abroad and its effects. *Language Learning Journal, 10,* 32–38.

Miller, L., & Ginsberg, R. (1995). Folklinguistic theories of language learning. In B. Freed (Ed.), *Second language acquisition in a study abroad context* (pp. 293–315). Amsterdam/Philadelphia: John Benjamins.

Mizuno, N. (1998). *The impact of study abroad experience on American college students who studied in Japan.* Unpublished doctoral dissertation, University of Southern California.

Morris, F. A., & Tarone, E. E. (2003). Impact of classroom dynamics on the effectiveness of recasts in second language acquisition. *Language Learning, 53*(2), 325–68.

Newell, A., & Rosenbloom, P. S. (1981). Mechanisms of skill acquisition and the law of practice. In J. R. Anderson (Ed.), *Cognitive skills and their acquisition* (pp. 1–55). Hillsdale, NJ: Lawrence Erlbaum.

Nicholas, H., Lightbown, P. M., & Spada, N. (2001). Recasts as feedback to language learners. *Language Learning, 51*(4), 719–758.

Paige, R. M., Cohen, A. D., Kappler, B., Chi, J. C., & Lassegard, J. P. (2002). *Maximizing study abroad. A students' guide to strategies for language and culture learning and use.* Minneapolis: University of Minnesota Center for Advanced Research on Language Acquisition.

Pellegrino, V. A. (1998). Student perspectives on language learning in a study abroad context. *Frontiers: The Interdisciplinary Journal to Study Abroad,* 91–120.

Philp, J. (2003). Constraints on "Noticing the Gap": Nonnative speakers' noticing of recasts in NS-NNS interaction. *Studies in Second Language Acquisition, 25*(1), 99–126.

Raupach, M. (1987). *Procedural learning in advanced learners of a foreign language.* Duisburg, Germany: Universität Duisburg Gesamthochschule.

Regan, V. (1995). The acquisition of sociolinguistic native speech norms: Effects of a year abroad on second language learners of French. In B. F. Freed (Ed.), *Second language acquisition in a study abroad context* (pp. 245–267). Amsterdam / Philadelphia: John Benjamins.

Rivers, W. P. (1998). Is being there enough? The effects of homestay placements on language gain during study abroad. *Foreign Language Annals, 31*(4), 492–500.

Segalowitz, N. (2003). Automaticity and second languages. In C. Doughty & M. H. Long (Eds.), *Handbook of second language acquisition* (pp. 382–408). Oxford: Blackwell.

Segalowitz, N., & Freed, B. (2004). Context, contact and cognition in oral fluency acquisition: Learning Spanish in at home and study abroad contexts. *Studies in Second Language Acquisition, 26*(2), 173–99.

Shehadeh, A. (2002). Comprehensible output, from occurrence to acquisition: An agenda for acquisitional research. *Language Learning, 52*(3), 597–647.

Singley, M. K., & Anderson, J. R. (1989). *The transfer of cognitive skill.* Cambridge, MA: Harvard University Press.

Swain, M. (1985). Communicative competence: some roles of comprehensible input and comprehensible output in its development. In S. M. Gass & C. G. Madden (Eds.), *Input in second language acquisition* (pp. 235–53). Rowley, MA: Newbury House.

Swain, M. (1998). Focus on form through conscious reflection. In C. Doughty & J. Williams (Eds.), *Focus on form in classroom second language acquisition* (pp. 64–81). New York: Cambridge University Press.

Swain, M., & Lapkin, S. (1995). Problems in output and the cognitive processes they generate: A step towards second language learning. *Applied Linguistics, 16*(3), 371–91.

Teichler, U., & Maiworm, F. (1997). *The ERASMUS experience. Major findings of the Erasmus evaluation research project.* European Commission.

Towell, R., Hawkins, R., & Bazergui, N. (1996). The development of fluency in advanced learners of French. *Applied Linguistics, 17*(1), 84–119.

VanPatten, B. (1996). *Input processing and grammar instruction. Theory and research.* Norwood, NJ: Ablex.

VanPatten, B. (2002a). Processing instruction: An update. *Language Learning, 52*(4), 755–803.

VanPatten, B. (2002b). Processing the content of input-processing and processing instruction research: A response to DeKeyser, Salaberry, Robinson, and Harrington. *Language Learning, 52*(4), 825–31.

VanPatten, B. (Ed.). (2003). *Processing instruction. Theory, research, and commentary.* Mahwah, NJ: Lawrence Erlbaum.

White, L. (1991). Adverb placement in second language acquisition. Some effects of positive and negative evidence in the classroom. *Second Language Research, 7,* 133–61.

Whittlesea, B. W. A., & Dorken, M. D. (1993). Incidentally, things in general are particularly determined: An episodic-processing account of implicit learning. *Journal of Experimental Psychology: General, 122,* 227–48.

Wilkinson, S. (1998). Study abroad from the participants' perspective: A challenge to common beliefs. *Foreign Language Annals, 31*(1), 23–39.

Wilkinson, S. (2002). The omnipresent classroom during summer study abroad: American students in conversation with their French hosts. *The Modern Language Journal, 86*(2), 157–73.

Yager, K. (1998). Learning Spanish in Mexico: The effect of informal contact and student attitudes on language gain. *Hispania, 81,* 898–913.

PART III:
INDIVIDUAL DIFFERENCES

This section deals with two of the individual learner differences that are most likely to affect various aspects of language learning in general and to determine what practice activities are optimal for learners characterized by these differences in particular. The most obvious difference is age, a factor that is widely considered to have dramatic effects on language learning success. In her chapter on age differences and their implications for practice, however, Carmen Muñoz presents evidence that the difference between young children on the one hand and adolescents or adults on the other is qualitative rather than quantitative. Older learners learn largely explicitly, using their ability to reason abstractly, while children learn largely implicitly, using their memory for concrete instances of language use. As a result, given the same amount of classroom exposure and practice, adolescents and adults actually make more progress than children because the traditional classroom context allows these older learners to draw on their superior analytical skills. As Muñoz illustrates in detail, it is important that classroom practice activities capitalize on the very different strengths in memory and analytical ability of children and adults by being adaptive to their age.

As older learners draw more on their analytical skills, individual differences in these skills will play an important role, as long as the learning conditions allow for these skills to come into play. Peter Robinson shows how various forms of aptitude, including both analytical skills and working memory, play an important role in a variety of learning conditions, except under conditions of completely incidental learning. He argues for the importance of adapting practice activities to the strengths and weaknesses of individual learners, taking into account their learning profiles, i.e., their various combinations of aptitudes, of which the combination of high and low levels of working memory with high and low levels of analytical ability are but one example. Drawing on Richard Snow's work in educational psychology and Peter Skehan's work in applied linguistics, Peter Robinson argues that aptitude complexes play different roles at different stages of the learning process and, therefore, that the extent to which they need to be taken into account depends on the kind of practice that is characteristic of these different stages.

9 Age-related differences and second language learning practice

Carmen Muñoz

Introduction

The aim of this chapter is to bring together information about age-related differences from the fields of psychology and second language (L2) acquisition research that may allow the identification of relevant characteristics of L2 learning practice activities appropriate to various ages.

It is assumed here that practice, understood in the sense of "engaging in an activity with the goal of becoming better at it" (DeKeyser, 1998, p. 50), has an important role to play in language learning and hence in the language classroom. This definition is sufficiently neutral to encompass the different views that assign various roles to practice in language acquisition: from item learning and the improvement of fluency (e.g., Ellis, 1997) to gradually bridging the gap between explicit knowledge and use (see DeKeyser, 2003). Further, research seems to provide increasing evidence of the importance of skill-specific practice; for example, input practice seems necessary in order to build comprehension skills and output practice to build production skills (DeKeyser & Sokalski, 1996; DeKeyser, 1997; Salaberry, 1997). In sum, practice may not make *perfect* (Ellis & Laporte, 1997), but it does make *better*.

It is also assumed here that good language learning practice activities present an adequate balance between demands and support.[1] An example of the importance of demands on learners is provided by the lack of accuracy observed in learners exposed only to comprehensible input, whose language learning resources are not "stretched" enough by the need to produce accurate L2 output (Swain, 1985, 1995). An example of support can be seen in the teacher's directing the learners' attention to the input, either to support young learners' limited attentional and memory capacity when they are required to attend to what is important and keep in mind the whole thing (Cameron, 2001, p. 9), or to help older learners "notice" the relevant features in the input or the gap between their interlanguage and the target language (e.g. Schmidt, 1990). On the other hand, to assess the type and amount of support that learners need and that should therefore be incorporated into a given activity, knowledge about learners' characteristics is essential: for example, knowledge about their state of cognitive maturation and its relevance to L2 learning, knowledge about affective and social characteristics typical of their age group, and knowledge about the ways in which age influences L2 outcomes in an instructed environment. The following sections are concerned with these areas. Each section ends with a table that identifies characteristics of language learning practice activities that are well-suited to the examined learners' traits.

Learner characteristics

Cognitive development and second language learning

Piaget and neo-Piagetian scholars have characterized children's development in a sequence of stages and substages. A first substage, extending from 18 months to 7 years of age, is said to prepare the "concrete operations" and to consist of a first period of preconceptual and symbolic thought up to age 4, followed by a period of intuitive thought which lasts until around the age of 7, and a period of consolidation of concrete operations up to age 11 or 12. These operations are conceived of as actions that are carried out in the mind, such as combining, ordering, separating, and recombining things, but which have a physical origin. These symbolic acts are still closely tied to the concrete things on which the original physical acts were performed; that is, the child is still mainly thinking about doing things with physical objects, such as ordering or separating building blocks, hence the term *concrete* operational period. Later research has shown that children under 11 are not as limited in the ability to reason deductively as previous experiments seemed to show and that they perform much better when they can make sense of situations and use this kind of understanding to help them to make sense of what is said to them (Donaldson, 1978).

At the age of 11 or 12, thinking becomes formal or abstract. Once it has been consolidated, this is the thinking of the intelligent adult. Its most marked feature is the ability to reason logically, from premises to conclusions. The formal operational thinker can entertain hypotheses, deduce consequences, and use these deductions to test hypotheses (Piaget, 1950). Donaldson (1978) prefers to refer to this kind of thinking as "disembedded" because it can operate without the supportive context of meaningful events that is required by younger children's thought.

From the perspective of information processing theory, differences in problem-solving abilities have been identified as one of the main explanations for the difference between second language learning by younger and older learners. One of the elements that is considered to contribute most to the development of problem-solving skills is memory, and this is why it deserves much more attention than in Piaget's theories. A very well-known theory is Case's (1985), which distributes problem-solving resources available to the child into two components: operative space and short-term storage space. In this view, only by age 9 or 10 does the child have enough short-term storage space to combine the results of all the cognitive operations needed to solve classical problems in child psychology research (e.g., those involving proportional reasoning). This increase in memory storage is seen as an effect of a decrease of the space needed for performing cognitive operations. In other words, developmental changes in storage result from an increase in operative efficiency: With development, the child becomes increasingly able to perform cognitive operations and has more space for memory storage.

Two elements are seen to contribute to improving operative efficiency: practice and biological maturation. With practice, what previously required effort and attention may finally become automatized and routine-like. With biological maturation, aspects such as rate of information processing increase regularly from childhood to adulthood.

In spite of the evident improvement that problem-solving abilities entail for cognitive development, problem solving has been considered by some researchers in the second language acquisition literature as negative. For example, Felix (1985) defended the idea that problem-solving cognitive structures compete in adult L2 learning with the language-specific cognitive structures employed by children. For Felix, as for others such as Krashen (1982) or Schwartz (1993), intellectual, analytical language abilities are not viewed as promoting L2 success but as interfering with it. However, abundant evidence has been found of a positive relationship between analytical language abilities and L2 learning outcomes, which appears to cast doubt on this position. Studies that have found a relationship between different components of language aptitude and age will be reviewed next. To conclude this section, Table 9.1 presents implications for L2 learning practice that can be derived from learners' cognitive characteristics at various ages.

Language aptitude and second language learning

Research has shown the components of language aptitude to have differential strengths in young children and older learners. Young children have been seen to rely more on memory than on analysis, adopting a holistic, memory-oriented approach to language processing. The holistic mode of processing information seems to precede the analytic mode in cognitive development (Kemler Nelson & Smith, 1989), although a memory-oriented approach may remain a characteristic of fluent native speakers (Pawley & Syder, 1983). Both in first and second language acquisition,

TABLE 9.1 IMPLICATIONS OF COGNITIVE DEVELOPMENT FOR
L2 LEARNING PRACTICE

Characteristics of adequate L2 learning practice activities for young children:
• they involve "doing things"
• they involve simple actions that do not require multiple cognitive operations
• they can "stretch" children's performance when they are embedded in a
  familiar context and children can make sense of them

Characteristics of adequate L2 learning practice activities for older learners:
• they may involve logical reasoning
• they may involve multiple cognitive operations
• they can be disembedded from the immediate context

---

children have been observed to extract and use meaningful chunks of
memorized language that are not internally analyzed (Hakuta, 1974;
Peters, 1983; Wray, 2000). On the other hand, older children (11- to
13-year-olds) in an instructed environment have been seen to deconstruct and analyze memorized chunks (Weinert, 1994; Myles, Hooper, &
Mitchell, 1998; Myles, Mitchell, & Hooper, 1999). For example, Myles
et al. (1998) observed two stages in the process of breaking down chunks.
In a first stage, learners "tag on" an element to the unchanged formula,
while in a second stage the segmentation process itself begins and chunks
are deconstructed. The authors also observed the "scaffolding" provided
by conversational interaction with a more competent target language
speaker that enabled learners to compare their own formulas to incoming input in order to tackle the process of analysis (1998, p. 360). That is,
the analytic mode on which older learners increasingly rely allows these
learners to take apart the components of the whole.

The importance of memory in younger learners and of analytic abilities in older learners has been observed among early immersion and
late immersion students, respectively (Harley & Hart, 1997). Among the
former, the measure of memory for text was the strongest predictor of
L2 proficiency scores, whereas among the latter the measure of analytical language ability was the only statistically significant predictor. This
finding – a holistic memory orientation among early immersion learners
and a language-analytical orientation among late immersion learners –
was given two possible interpretations by these researchers. First, the
difference may be due to maturational differences, which would make
language learning around adolescence depend on different cognitive abilities, mainly analytical language ability, when learning begins. Alternatively, the results could be the outcome of the different experience learners
had in the two programs. While instruction in early immersion programs
is oriented initially toward incidental learning and holistic processing of
meaning in context, instruction in late immersion involves, according

to Harley and Hart, a heavier initial focus on the second language as a code to be taken apart and intentionally mastered (1997, p. 395).

Furthermore, analytical abilities may also be enhanced by adult learners in order to compensate for memory shortcomings. This was the interpretation given by Skehan (1986) to his finding of two different subgroups in terms of strengths and weaknesses in different components of language aptitude among adult foreign language learners. One of the subgroups showed a strong relationship between younger age and good memory but a not-so-strong grammatical sensitivity. The other subgroup showed a strong relationship between older age and high grammatical sensitivity, but the group was only average in memory. Furthermore, memory seems to be strongly connected with rather passive, implicit, "data-driven processes" in the study by Williams (1999), in which he found a strong correlation between the learning of semantically redundant morphological agreement rules and various measures of memory and no correlation between semantically nonredundant rules (for marking plural on the noun or person on the verb) and those memory measures.

Research has also shown a weaker relationship between aptitude and L2 learning among children than among adults. In particular, the study by DeKeyser (2000) on the interaction between age and aptitude among Hungarian immigrants to the United States showed age to be a significant predictor of proficiency for lower- but not for higher-aptitude learners, and aptitude to be a significant predictor for older, but not for younger learners. According to DeKeyser, such age differences in predictive validity of aptitude fit with his hypothesis that adults learn largely explicitly (consciously), while children learn implicitly (unconsciously),[2] in line with Bley-Vroman's (1988) proposal of a fundamental difference between the learning mechanisms used by children and adults to explain the differential success in second language learning outcomes. Also Ulman (2001), on the basis of neurolinguistic evidence, relates implicit/procedural learning to younger learners and explicit/declarative learning to older learners.

To summarize, the evidence that language aptitude has different strengths in young children and older learners leads to the identification of certain characteristics of L2 learning practice activities that are suitable to the different age groups (see Table 9.2). Further differences between younger and older learners include different perceptual learning styles as well as a different repertoire and use of learning strategies, to which we turn in the next section.

Language learning style and strategies

Language learning resources also include perceptual abilities and preferences, which have been shown to vary in learners of different age as well. Thus, research on perceptual learning styles has characterized young

TABLE 9.2 IMPLICATIONS OF LANGUAGE APTITUDE FOR
L2 LEARNING PRACTICE

Characteristics of adequate L2 learning practice activities for young children:
• they use meaningful chunks and routines
• they are essentially communicative activities that involve holistic use of
  language
• they provide massive amounts of input to guarantee incidental learning

Characteristics of adequate L2 learning practice activities for older learners:
• they can help deconstruct and analyze memorized chunks
• they may involve language analysis
• they involve both implicit and explicit learning

---

children as haptic (i.e., depending upon touch and kinesthesis) and manual. They do better if they respond to verbal stimuli with body movements, accompany their words with actions, and do things with their
hands. As they age, learners develop a preference for a visual and/or
auditory learning style. A preference for either of these styles may, however, be influenced by cultural and environmental factors rather than by
age (Reid, 1987).

Children's use of strategies begins at around age 6 with the emergence
of memorization strategies. The first to appear is usually repetition, followed by organization (grouping elements into conceptual categories)
and, later, by elaboration (relating elements to an image or a story). In
general, older children are observed to generate more complex strategies,
to accommodate a specific strategy to a specific task, and to be more capable in the execution of strategies, all of which improves memory results
(Vasta, Haith, & Miller, 1999).

Similarly, in a study of the development of verbal analogical reasoning
(Sternberg & Nigro, 1980) it was found that, as children grew older, their
strategies shifted so that they relied on word association less and abstract
relations more, an indication of better reasoning abilities. Sternberg sees
this as evidence that older children are typically at an advantage over
younger children in being able to turn their superior abstract-thinking
abilities to their advantage in understanding the structure of the new
language (2002, p. 25).

Studies on school learners have shown that vocabulary learning strategies change with age and that successful and less successful learners vary with respect to which strategies they use and how they use
them (Schouten-van Parreren, 1992). Comparisons of secondary school
learners with older learners also show changes in vocabulary learning
strategies with age, although learners seem to be affected by culturally
determined educational practices, such as the use of monolingual or bilingual dictionaries (Ahmed, 1988; Schmitt, 1997).

On the other hand, not many studies have examined strategy use from the point of view of its development in learners over time. Chesterfield and Chesterfield (1985) observed young Mexican-American children in preschool and first grade over a two-year period and suggested a natural order in the acquisition of learning strategies. The authors found that at the initial stages, learners did not use any strategies with regularity and that the first strategies students were observed to use, such as repetition, were not very demanding from a linguistic point of view. Later on, learners were observed to use a wider variety of strategies, such as formulaic expressions and verbal *attention getters*, which allowed them to initiate and sustain conversation. In the last stages, learners were using strategies that allowed them to extend conversation over a number of turns, such as clarification requests, and which required some degree of metalinguistic awareness, such as monitoring.

Other studies that have attempted to explore the existence of a developmental trend in the use of learning strategies have generally extended over short periods of time, and results are mixed (O'Malley & Chamot, 1990; Takeuchi, 2003; Yamamori, Takamichi, Tomohito, & Oxford 2003). An exception is the work by Victori and Tragant (2003), who used a semi-open questionnaire (consisting of short-answer questions to specific issues) to carry out a study which involved cross-sectional data from 766 children and adolescents who were more than three years apart, as well as longitudinal data coming from 38 learners (from 12 to 14 years old) who were traced over a period of two years. In general, the complexity of the type of cognitive strategies that these EFL students reported increased with age and proficiency level, from mere repetition to memorization strategies, mnemonic techniques, inferencing, and more creative practice strategies. In the longitudinal study, common trends of development were identified, but there was also evidence of individual variability.

In a recent follow-up study, Tragant and Victori (2006) explored differences between the strategies reported in the same semi-open questionnaire by 703 EFL learners of different ages, including children, teenagers and adults, but this time isolating the effects of age from those of length of instruction. Longitudinal data from 86 learners were also analyzed. Results indicated that for a considerable number of learners there is an observable progress in reported strategy use, either in the nature or in the number of strategies reported or in both. Regarding the nature of the strategies reported, as age increases, strategies tend to be more sophisticated, going from repetition, use of the dictionary, or asking others, to a wider range, involving mostly cognitive strategies such as analysis, practice, exposure to the L2, but also some metacognitive strategies such as revision. Regarding number, as these learners grow older, they are able to report more strategies, showing an increase in metacognitive awareness.

TABLE 9.3 IMPLICATIONS OF AGE-RELATED STYLES AND STRATEGIES FOR L2
LEARNING PRACTICE

Characteristics of adequate L2 learning practice activities for young children:
• they involve physical and manual movements
• they make use of repetition

Characteristics of adequate L2 learning practice activities for older learners:
• they are varied to accommodate to different learning styles
• they may involve metalinguistic awareness and reflection
• they can be planned by learners based on their superior metacognitive
  knowledge

These findings reveal not only the evolution over time of strategic behavior but also the increase of strategic knowledge, that is, of reflection about strategic behavior. Strategic knowledge has been considered a component of metacognitive knowledge, together with person knowledge and task knowledge (which can be seen as related to language awareness) (Flavell, 1979).

Research conducted in the context of L1 learning has concluded that metacognitve knowledge and planned strategic behavior are products of adolescent thinking rather than childhood thinking (Brown & Sullivan Palincsar, 1982). Furthermore, metacognitive knowledge does not automatically increase with age but develops over time with increased experience, cognitive maturation, and self-reflection (Brown, 1980).

Closely related to the growth of metacognitive knowledge, the evolution of self-consciousness is associated with affective, personality, and social factors, to which we turn next. To conclude this section, Table 9.3 displays relevant implications for L2 learning practice of the differences in learning styles and strategies that are characteristic of young children and older learners.

Affective, personality, and social factors

From a developmental cognitive perspective, self-consciousness evolves when children improve in taking account of other people's point of view during the concrete operational period. Self-consciousness causes children to worry about other people's perceptions and leads to increasingly critical self-evaluations, which, in turn, reduce self-esteem. Self-esteem is one of the psychological traits that evolves with age: Children younger than 8 do not have a well-developed sense of global self-evaluation (Harter, 1988). Between 8 and 11 years of age, self-esteem is generally stable with a slight tendency to improvement (Dunn 1994). However, by age 11 or 12 self-esteem is observed to decrease and not to increase again till the mid teens. In addition, biological changes occurring during puberty entail physical and psychological tensions that may lead to negative emotional states.

The generally low self-esteem observed around the puberty years is expected to affect academic self-concept as well (Vasta, Haith, & Miller, 1999). This, in turn, may be associated with lower levels of motivation toward school, school learning in general, and foreign language learning. In fact, in a study on attitudes toward foreign language learning by students from different age groups, learners in the puberty years were observed to have lower levels of motivation toward English than older, adolescent learners (Muñoz & Tragant, 2001). An interesting result of this study, which compares 10-, 12-, 14-, and 17-year-old learners, is the finding that the youngest learners expressed motivational orientations that were markedly different from those of the other age groups. For example, the younger learners made more references to the less tangible and more intrinsic types of orientation (such as interest in English or having a positive attitude toward the language and the teacher) than the older students. On the other hand, the older groups showed a clear orientation toward an instrumental motivation (i.e., being concerned with the practical value of learning English) of a generally extrinsic type, in line with previous studies (e.g., Schmidt, Boraie, & Kassabgy, 1996).

Several studies have shown that the motivation of children prior to age 10 or 11 is of a clearly intrinsic nature and that it is strongly affected by the language learning environment (see Hawkins, 1996; Blondin, Candelier, Edelenbos, Johnstone, Kubanek-German, & Taeschner, 1998). Given that young children are mainly concerned with the here and now, they are inclined to have a positive attitude toward learning a second or foreign language if they enjoy the activities they engage in in the classroom, the teacher, and the general atmosphere in class. In contrast, older learners may be less influenced by these factors and develop a positive attitude toward the foreign language if they are very certain about the benefits that language learning may bring them or their future career.

Another important trait for which changes have been observed during childhood and adolescence concerns social relationships with adults and with peers. Importantly, the relationship of children, particularly in the first and middle grades of primary school, with an adult tends not to be confrontational because young children are eager to please the adult. However, a negative side effect may be that the child will not tell the adult teacher when he or she does not understand, and the teacher may not easily notice that some learning has gone undone (Cameron, 2001). In contrast, older children and adolescents may be more confrontational and will require the adult to be aware of their need for self-affirmation.

As far as peer relationships are concerned, psychologists have observed that older children tend to cooperate further than younger children and that differences seem to be clearly based on differences in cognitive abilities and emotional development. Thus, older children find it easier to take account of other people's social, physical, or emotional point of view and hence understand the situation from another's viewpoint. The ways in which children participate in a group also differ with age. Older children can better accommodate their behavior to the group's interests, choosing cooperative strategies, while younger children tend to choose self-centered competitive strategies (Schmidt, Ollendick, & Stanowicz, 1988).

A number of studies have looked at age differences in relation to interactional skills in a second language. The pioneer work by Scarcella and Higa (1982) compared child and adolescent learners and found the latter to have a more active involvement in negotiating, understanding, and sustaining conversations than the younger learners. Their NS interlocutors, in turn, modified their utterances accordingly, and these modifications provided the learners with finely tuned input precisely when it was more relevant for them. In contrast, the younger learners received comprehensible input that included different types of adjustments but that was not similarly directed to problematic items. Also, Muñoz (2002, 2003a) found differences between children and adolescents (aged between 10 and 17) in oral semi-structured interviews in a foreign language situation. She observed that when the adolescent learners ran into production or comprehension problems, they avoided silences to a greater extent than the younger learners and resorted to code switching (interviewers shared the learners' L1) in order to sustain the conversation. This had an effect as well on the performance of the interviewers, who tended to drop the topics in front of the younger learners' silences and to maintain them in front of the older learners' code switching.

In another study with learners from the same groups as in the previous study, Grañena (in press) focused on breakdowns in interaction arising from production problems. In particular, she analyzed the use of appeals of assistance by children, adolescents, and a group of young adults in a picture story narration task in which the expert interviewer was actively involved in the interaction. The findings showed that older learners and adolescents used proportionally a greater amount of direct and explicit indirect signals than the youngest learners and that the latter showed a clear preference for implicit signals such as hesitation pauses and silence when they encountered a production problem. Adult learners also had a higher proportion of implicit signals than the adolescents, but their overall behavior was proportionally more explicit. The degree of explicitness of the appeals had an effect on the type of feedback the learners obtained from the interviewers. Thus, the more explicit behavior of the older learners resulted in the provision of the language items required by the learners with greater frequency than the more implicit behavior.

TABLE 9.4 IMPLICATIONS OF AFFECTIVE, PERSONALITY, AND SOCIAL
CHARACTERISTICS FOR L2 LEARNING PRACTICE

Characteristics of adequate L2 learning practice activities for young children:
• they are enjoyable in themselves to stimulate motivation
• in group tasks, the share of each member is clear from the start
• in L2 oral activities, children are provided with an interactional scaffold

Characteristics of adequate L2 learning practice activities for older learners:
• they may refer to topics connected with learners' interests and professional concerns to stimulate motivation
• in group tasks, learners can cooperate efficiently and make decisions about who does what
• they do not expose learners to their peers in ways that may threaten learners' self-image

---

Research has also found differences in the process of negotiation for meaning between learner dyads of different ages. For example, Oliver (1998) found that children and adults used different types of interactional strategies with different relative frequency. When comparing the interactional behavior of the child dyads in her study with that of adult dyads, as reported by Long (1983), Oliver observed that the younger acquirers made more frequent use of other-repetitions while adults used clarification requests and confirmation checks with higher frequency than children.

Other studies have examined differences in the use of negative feedback by child and adult learners, with mixed results. Mackey, Oliver, and Philp (1997) compared learners of different ages in NNS-NNS dyadic conversation and found both similarities and differences. While both age groups responded to non-targetlike utterances with implicit negative feedback about one-third of the time, children used the negative feedback provided more often than adults did. In contrast, Oliver (2000) compared child and adult NNS-NS interactions and found no significant differences in uptake of negative feedback according to learners' age in either teacher-fronted lessons or in tasks involving pairs. But she found that age affected the pattern of interaction significantly. For example, adults received a larger proportion of negative feedback than children did both in teacher-fronted lessons and in paired tasks. In addition, the feedback that adults received from their teachers was more likely to be in the form of a negotiation strategy than that received by children from their teachers.

In this section, various learner characteristics have been examined that have evident educational implications. These characteristics can be incorporated both into the specific actions demanded by the learning tasks and into the conditions under which the learning process takes place, as illustrated in Table 9.4.

Second language outcomes and age

After the review of relevant learner characteristics in the previous sections, the focus will now be on research that has looked into age-related differences in second language acquisition outcomes. While the issue has typically been addressed from the perspective of the age factor in language acquisition, that is, of the maturational constraints that may prevent nativelike ultimate attainment, the specific effects of age on the learning processes in an instructed environment may be of greater concern for the classroom.

Age of onset and ultimate attainment

The effects of age on L2 learning have usually been studied in relation to the issue of the existence of a critical period in second language acquisition, that is, a biologically determined period during which language acquisition is both effortless and successful. Originally, the period in which nativelike acquisition was claimed to take place extended from roughly two years of age till puberty (Lenneberg, 1967). However, age has also been observed to influence the rate of acquisition. More than two decades ago, Krashen, Long, and Scarcella (1982, p. 159) drew three generalizations out of the existing findings from research studies:

(i) adults proceed through early stages of morphological and syntactic development faster than children
(ii) older children acquire faster than younger children in early stages of morphological and syntactic development
(iii) child starters outperform adult starters in the long run.

This provided a clarification to the apparent contradictory findings obtained by different studies. On the one hand, studies of learners in a naturalistic environment but with a relatively short length of residence in the target language community, as well as studies of learners in an instructed environment, had shown older starters to obtain higher results than younger starters. On the other hand, studies of learners in a naturalistic environment but with an extended length of residence had shown younger starters to attain higher levels of second language proficiency. Thus, ultimate attainment of young starters in the long run often appeared nativelike, which seemed to provide evidence for a critical period in second language acquisition. Furthermore, the study by Snow and Hoefnagel-Höhle (1978) with learners in a naturalistic situation examined at intervals of several weeks for a period of 12 months was able to capture the process by which younger learners were able to catch up with older learners. The distinction between rate (initially faster in older learners) and ultimate attainment (ultimately higher in younger learners) solved the apparent contradiction in the findings.

Ultimate attainment studies have focused on various language skills with heterogeneous results regarding the end point for attaining native-like levels. For example, Patkowski (1980) compared the morphosyntactic performance of a group of immigrants to the United States who had started to acquire English before the age of 15 with another group who had started after that age. The results showed a strong effect for age of onset, that is, initial age of learning, but not for length of residence. Furthermore, results were found to follow a normal distribution above age 15, showing no effects for age of arrival among the older group, while the curve was skewed to the right below age 15, showing that among the younger group the higher scores corresponded to those with an earlier age of arrival. Oyama (1976) analyzed the pronunciation and listening comprehension of two groups of immigrants and found that learners with age of onset under 12 performed in the range of native speaker controls but learners above that age did not.

Other studies have placed the end point of the critical period before puberty. Hyltenstam (1992) investigated L2 learners of Swedish with age of onset between 3 and 12 and compared their grammatical and lexical error rates with those of native speakers. He found significantly higher error rates among the L2 speakers and a clear-cut division at age 7. Below this age, some learners performed as well as natives, but above 7 no learner did. The author concluded that nativelike performance seemed possible if learning starts before the age of 7, specifying a lower offset age, or chronological limit, for the critical period, although even such an early start did not seem to guarantee a nativelike ultimate attainment in all cases.

More recently, some researchers have argued that age effects are not linked to any specific age span, ultimate attainment showing a linear decline with increasing age of onset (e.g., Birdsong & Molis, 2001). Birdsong (1999, p. 12) has argued in favor of an interaction of factors: developmental factors up to the end of maturation (that is, before the mid to late teens) and nondevelopmental factors thereafter. Similarly, Hyltenstam and Abrahamsson (2000, p. 157) have developed an explanation in terms of maturational constraints up to the end of maturation and socio-psychological factors after that point. Further, Hyltenstam and Abrahamsson (2000, 2003) see no guarantee of reaching nativelike proficiency in a second language even when learning begins at an early age, underscoring the very early onset of an age-related decline.

In the field of L2 pronunciation, Flege also argues against an offset age around puberty for the acquisition of L2 vowels and consonants. Moreover, while in earlier writings he noted the age of 5 or 7 as a cutoff point (e.g., Flege, 1992), in his more recent work he posits a general linear decline with age (e.g., Flege, 1999). Flege argues that the younger L2 learning starts, the easier it is to perceive phonetic differences that trigger the creation of new phonetic categories, while with increasing age, learners tend to assimilate the new sounds to their L1 categories, observing the paradox that at an age when children's sensorimotor abilities are generally improving, they seem to lose the ability to learn the vowels and consonants of an L2. However, he argues that the root cause of foreign accent is not motoric difficulty, in contrast with L1 segmental production errors, but rather is to be found at a "mentalistic level of linguistic organization."

Moreover, Flege and his associates argue that foreign accents are not inevitable and that non-native perception of L2 sounds does not remain constant. On the contrary, the perceived relation of L1 and L2 sounds may change as a function of L2 experience and proficiency. In sum, Flege assumes that the phonetic systems used in the production and perception of vowels and consonants *remain adaptive over the life span* (Flege's emphasis) and that phonetic systems reorganize in response to sounds encountered in an L2 through the addition of new phonetic categories or through the modification of old ones (Flege, 1995, p. 233). The reorganization of phonetic systems may need, in addition to continued access to massive L2 input, intensive training in the perception and production of L2 speech sounds. Massive input and intensive training together with very high motivation have been proposed as the factors that could explain the nativelike performance in pronunciation tasks of exceptional adult learners (see research by Bongaerts and his colleagues, e.g., Bongaerts, 1999). Notwithstanding the constrained nature of the sentence reading task in those experiments, which may weaken the claim that these advanced learners' underlying competence is nativelike, the studies underscore the value of focused training for improving adult learners' foreign accents. Similarly, prominent experience-based perception models agree that perceptual discrimination of non-native contrasts can be "recovered" if attention is directed to those contrasts (see Bongaerts, 2003).

Age and formal language learning

Other studies have examined L2 outcomes in instructional settings. These have generally shown a rate advantage on the part of older learners and have often been conducted in contexts in which the target language is a foreign language, and hence the exposure to the language is less than in a naturalistic setting. In such conditions of very little exposure to the target language, the prevalence of a second language learning advantage for older learners has been discussed recently from different perspectives.

For example, DeKeyser (2000) has claimed, within the perspective of the *fundamental difference hypothesis* (Bley-Vroman, 1988), that children need massive exposure to the language for their implicit learning mechanisms to be activated and that they cannot find this type of exposure in a foreign language classroom. Under his view, the critical period hypothesis is restricted to naturalistic language acquisition and would therefore not apply to instructional settings. In contrast, Singleton (1995) has argued that the long-term advantage of the younger starters requires a longer period of time to show up than is needed in a naturalistic environment. According to him, longer studies than have been conducted to date are needed in order to show the alleged advantage of younger starters in an instructed environment.

The most well-known study of this type was conducted in England and Wales following the introduction of French for pupils from the age of 8 during the period 1964–74. The study monitored the progress of some 17,000 pupils over five years and compared learners who had begun school instruction in French at the age of 8 with learners who had begun at the age of 11. The latter were observed to catch up with the former on all skills, with the exception of listening comprehension (Burstall, Jamieson, Cohen, and Hargreave, 1974). The research was criticized on methodological grounds because, as happened in the study conducted in Japan around the same time by Oller and Nagato (1974), younger starters had been mixed in the same classes with older starters at some point, and therefore results might have been influenced by the blurring effect of mixing experimental and control groups in the same classes (Singleton, 1989, p. 236). However, studies conducted in different educational systems corroborate the finding that early starters do not maintain a clear advantage for more than a relatively short period over late starters (e.g., Holmstrand [1980] in Sweden; Stankowski Gratton [1980] in Italy). Furthermore, no parallel studies are known to exist which show empirical evidence that younger starters in a foreign language context consistently outscore older starters after the same amount of instruction and exposure.

On the contrary, the Barcelona Age Factor (BAF) project, conducted in a period of a national curriculum change, with pupils that were never mixed in the same classes, has shown later starters outscoring earlier starters in different skills after the same number of instructional hours. In addition, the study has shown age-related differences in skill development that have an evident applied interest. The BAF project has examined over 2,000 EFL pupils distributed in five groups with different starting ages: younger than 6, 8, 11, and 14, and older than 18. The two main groups, those with an onset age of 8 and those with an onset age of 11, were compared after 200, 416, and 726 instructional hours (that is, after almost two years and one year, respectively; four years and three years, respectively; and eight years and seven years, respectively). In all comparisons, older starters generally obtain higher scores than younger starters on a variety of tests tapping morphosyntactic, lexical, narrative, and communicative skills (e.g., Muñoz, 2001, 2003a, 2003b; Pérez-Vidal, Torras, & Celaya, 2000; Celaya, Torras, & Pérez-Vidal, 2001).

Listening comprehension and phonetic tests do not show a consistent advantage of older learners over younger learners (Muñoz, 2003a; Fullana, 2005). In fact, these are the areas in which the latter are typically expected to show a clear superiority over the former. In contrast, the fact that the younger starters in the study do not outscore older starters may have been influenced by the lack of an accurate or nativelike phonetic model in the input. In his comparison of earlier starters and later starters in an instructional setting in Sweden, Holmstrand (1980) finds that the latter are indistinguishable from the former after three years and claims that early foreign language instruction that lacks native teacher models cannot benefit from younger children's special pronunciation ability (see also Flege's (1991) discussion of "accented L2 input" in foreign language learning).

A different research project also conducted in Spain following the curriculum change that mandated an earlier start of foreign language teaching (from age 11 to age 8) has provided similar findings. After the same number of instructional hours (594), extended over six years, older starters outscore younger starters in morphosyntactic development (Lázaro, 2002). Similarly, a group of 30 older starters obtained significantly higher scores than a parallel group of 30 younger starters in written composition, grammar and cloze tests, and in overall oral proficiency, although younger starters are seen to outscore older starters in pronunciation (Cenoz, 2002).

It is clear from this review that the context of language acquisition, naturalistic as in a second language or formal as in a foreign language, has a strong influence on the effects of age on language acquisition in terms of both processes and product or ultimate attainment. Although in the latter context a learner's eventual attainment typically falls short of native speaker status, there is still much work to be done to help learners on their way toward fluent and accurate language use, as illustrated in Table 9.5.

An analysis of common practice activities

The previous sections have concluded with a number of characteristics that may identify good language learning practice activities that are adequate for younger and older learners and one drawn from psychological and L2 acquisition research. Consideration of these general characteristics may be helpful at different levels when designing teaching

TABLE 9.5 IMPLICATIONS OF AGE EFFECTS ON LANGUAGE OUTCOMES FOR L2
LEARNING PRACTICE

Characteristics of adequate L2 learning practice activities for young children:[3]
- they are mostly oral so that learners can benefit from their enhanced perceptive receptiveness
- they avoid heavily accented L2 input
- they involve great amounts of listening comprehension that do not make very high cognitive demands
- they provide massive amounts of L2 exposure for learners to capitalize on their implicit learning mechanisms

Characteristics of adequate L2 learning practice activities for older learners:
- they involve focused phonetic training and practice to allow the potential reorganization of the L2 learners' phonetic system
- they integrate attention to meaning and attention to form to foster accuracy, on the basis of learners' superior explicit learning mechanisms and metalinguistic awareness[4]

---

tasks and material for specific ages as well as when assessing learners' difficulties on certain tasks.

In this section, by way of illustration, some of the activities that are commonly offered by textbooks addressed to learners of various ages will be briefly analyzed in the light of the previously presented general characteristics. The activities chosen are not intended to constitute the best or even most frequently used activities for each age group, but they were found to be the most suitable for different age groups from a (nonexhaustive) list used in a teachers' survey (Muñoz, Castañé, & Corretja, 2002). The survey was also limited in that it did not include teachers of adult learners.

The survey was conducted with 88 foreign language teachers who had more than five years of teaching experience (a mean of 13.6 years) with preschool, primary, and/or secondary school learners (ages 3 to 18). Teachers were asked to grade activities listed in a questionnaire as "more" or "less" suitable for the age groups they had ever taught, on a scale from 1 (least suitable) to 4 (most suitable). Table 9.6 shows only those activities that 50 percent of teachers ranked as "very suitable."

Although the activities in the list did not reflect all the dimensions to be considered (i.e., affective and social factors), many of the characteristics of younger and older learners presented above can be recognized in the activities that are deemed to be very suitable for each age group by experienced teachers.

To begin with, listening is considered the most suitable activity for younger children: A large number of listening activities are deemed "very suitable" for both preschool and primary school children. These activities rely mostly on listening and then reacting by doing things such as

TABLE 9.6 A TEACHERS' SELECTION OF SUITABLE ACTIVITIES FOR DIFFERENT
LEARNER GROUPS (PRESCHOOL, PRIMARY, AND SECONDARY)

Listening	*Speaking*	*Reading*	*Writing*
	Preschool		
Listen and repeat (words)	Flashcards		
Listen and repeat (chanting)	Say and point / tick		
Listen and circle / draw / number / point / mark, etc.	Listen and repeat		
	Listen point, and say		
Listen and sing along	Look and say		
	Chant and act		
	Primary		
Listen and circle, etc.	Flashcards	Puzzles (cross- words, etc.)	Draw, match, and write
Listen and repeat (chanting)	Listen and repeat	Read and draw, guess, match	Reorganize the picture and write
Listen and repeat (words)	Say and point / mark		
Listen and act out	Listen, point, and say		
Listen and respond	Chant and act		
	Look and say		
	Secondary		
Listen and complete	Listen and act out / Role play	Read and respond (true / false)	Make up a story
Listen and respond	Discuss ideas	Read and respond (full answers)	Fill in the gaps
Listen and identify	Invent	Predict from the title and anti- cipate what the text contains	
		Read in detail and try to guess meaning of unfamiliar words by context	
		Skimming	
		Reorganize a text	
		Scanning	

circling and drawing and on repetition (the only exception is "listen and respond," which is considered suitable only for primary school not for preschool children). And, in fact, L2 learning practice activities that are cognitively adequate for young children, as summarized in Table 9.1, involve "doing things." Likewise, practice activities suited to young learners' preferred perceptual learning styles, as summarized in Table 9.3, involve physical and manual movements and make use of repetition.

In contrast, listening activities for secondary school pupils involve nonrepetitive responses and engage other cognitive operations (in completing and verbally responding) and logical reasoning (in identifying), as pointed out in Table 9.1.

Speaking activities for the younger pupils, both preschool and primary school learners, rely mostly on repetition and make abundant use of chunks. As seen earlier in this chapter, repetition is the first memorization strategy to appear, and the use of chunks suits young learners' memory orientation. Oral production is prompted by visual stimuli (flashcards, say, and point / mark) or auditory stimuli (listen and repeat), present in the immediate context (see Table 9.1). Often, stimuli are visually attractive, and activities are carried out in a playful manner, which promotes learners' intrinsic motivation (see Table 9.4).

On the other hand, speaking activities for the older pupils involve semi-controlled or free production in imaginary contexts (role-plays, invent), that is, disembedded from the immediate context. Speaking activities for this age group also involve logical reasoning, as when learners are required to discuss ideas. As presented earlier in this chapter, these are characteristics of cognitively adequate learning activities for older pupils (see Table 9.1). Moreover, oral production in role-plays may prompt the use of memorized chunks and the subsequent analysis of those chunks to adapt to new situational conditions (see Table 9.2). Learners' previous planning of these speaking activities is usually deemed necessary and effective, as corresponds to their strategic and social development (see Tables 9.3 and 9.4).[5]

Reading activities that are considered suitable for primary school pupils are limited to brief reading matter, such as crosswords, and which require children to do things such as draw or match. These are cognitively simple and can be joyfully played as games, which makes them motivating activities in themselves, according to the affective characteristics of young children, as seen above.

In contrast, reading is considered a very suitable activity for older children: A large number of reading activities are deemed "very suitable." They involve other skills as well (e.g., textual, contextual, inferencing), which reveals that learners' cognitive development allows them to be involved in multiple cognitive operations simultaneously (see Table 9.1) and that learners can analyze a text and reflect upon it.

Finally, according to this survey, writing activities in primary school are linked to a visual stimulus, that is, they are contextually supported, which puts them within reach of young children. Writing activities for this age group also involve doing things with the hands. Hence, they are suited to the cognitive development and perceptual learning style of young children (see Tables 9.1 and 9.3).

In contrast, writing activities for secondary school pupils involve free production with some planning requirement (make up a story), and lexical precision and morphosyntactic accuracy (fill in the gaps). These are all characteristics of secondary school pupils' more advanced cognitive and strategic development, as summarized in Tables 9.2 and 9.3.

Conclusions

Age has often been seen as a drawback for language learning, an impediment for adults to attain nativelike command of a language. Certainly, childhood can be considered a privileged time in which to learn a second language in a naturalistic environment. However, research on instructed second language learning has shown older children and adolescents to be more efficient learners, revealing the importance of their superior cognitive development. In addition, classroom research has shown that adults' language learning outcomes can be improved through focusing on form while learning the language for communication (see Doughty & Williams, 1998).

Arguably, the question that needs to be asked with respect to instructed learners' age is not whether older learners can ever attain nativelike proficiency. For one thing, this may be unrealistic in most circumstances and may not even be the learners's own goal. Rather, in a situation of instructed language learning, more important questions are which goals are suitable for the cognitive, personality, and social characteristics of learners of various ages, which conditions lead to greater success in learning specific parts of a second language at various ages, and which activities can help attain those goals under specific conditions; that is, what constitutes good practice at various ages.

Notes

1. Cameron (2001) elaborates on the relationship between demands and support in reference to teaching young children. For Cameron, the difference between demands and support creates the space of language growth (Bruner, 1983) and produces opportunities for learning. Too little support may not make the task accessible, while too much support may not leave space for language growth. Demands on pupils (and the corresponding support) can be of different types: mainly cognitive and language, but also interactional, metalinguistic, involvement, and physical.

2. Implicit learning is understood as learning without awareness of what is being learned, either inductively, through learning from the input, or deductively, through the use of parameters (DeKeyser, 2003).
3. Although input practice is emphasized here, practice for building production skills and stretching learners' language resources (Swain, 1985, 1995) is adequate for both young and older learners.
4. See Doughty and Williams (1998) for proposals on ways to incorporate focus on form in lessons whose overriding focus is on meaning or communication (Long, 1991, pp. 45–6).
5. Although included in the list, "negotiate for meaning" was not among those activities considered as very suitable by most teachers (50 percent or more), in spite of the importance it has gained in the fields of language learning and teaching in recent years. In fact, only 21.4 percent of secondary teachers ranked it as very suitable, while 57.1 percent ranked it as (3), suitable. This agrees with Oliver's findings (2000) that teachers of children are less likely to provide negative feedback in the form of negotiation than teachers of adults.

References

Ahmed, M. O. (1988). Vocabulary learning strategies. In P. Meara (Ed.), *Beyond words*. London: CILT.

Birdsong, D. (1999). Introduction: Whys and why nots of the critical period hypothesis for second language acquisition. In D. Birdsong (Ed.), *Second language acquisition and the critical period hypothesis* (pp. 1–22). Mawhwah, NJ: Lawrence Earlbaum.

Birdsong, D., & Molis, M. (2001). On the evidence for maturational constraints in second language acquisition. *Journal of Memory and Language, 44,* 235–49.

Bley-Vroman, R. (1988). The fundamental character of foreign language learning. In W. Rutherford and M. Sharwood Smith (Eds.), *Grammar and second language teaching: A book of readings* (pp. 19–30). New York: Newbury House.

Blondin, C., Candelier, M., Edelenbos, P., Johnstone R., Kubanek-German, A., & Taeschner, T. (1998). *Foreign languages in primary and pre-school education*. London: CILT.

Bongaerts, T. (1999). Ultimate attainment in L2 pronunciation: The case of very advanced late L2 learners. In D. Birdsong (Ed.), *Second language acquisition and the critical period hypothesis* (pp. 133–59), Mawhwah, NJ: Lawrence Earlbaum.

Bongaerts, T. (2003). *Effets de l'âge sur l'acquisition de la prononciation d'une seconde langue. Acquisition et interaction en langue étrangère (AILE), 18,* 79–98.

Brown, A. L. (1980). Metacognitive development and reading. In R. J. Spiro, B. C. Bruce, & W. F. Brewer (Eds.), *Theoretical issues in reading comprehension: perspectives and cognitive psychology, linguistics, artificial intelligence, and education* (pp. 453–81). Hillsdale, NJ: Lawrence Erlbaum.

250   *Carmen Muñoz*

Brown, A. L., & Sullivan Palincsar, A. (1982). Inducing strategic learning from texts by means of informed, self-control training. In D. K. Reid & W. P. Hresko (Eds.), *TL&LD. Metacognition and learning disabilities* 2(1), (pp. 1–18). Rockville, MD: Aspen Publication.

Bruner, J. (1983). *Child's talk: Learning to use language.* New York: Norton.

Burstall, C., Jamieson, M., Cohen, S., & Hargreaves, M. (1974). *Primary French in the balance.* Windsor, UK: NFER Publishing Company.

Cameron, L. (2001). *Teaching languages to young learners.* Cambridge, UK: Cambridge University Press.

Case, R. (1985). *Intellectual development.* New York: Academic Press.

Celaya, M. L., Torras, M. R., & Pérez-Vidal, C. (2001). Short and mid-term effects of an earlier start: An analysis of EFL written production. In S. Foster-Cohen & A. Nizegorodcew (Eds.), *EUROSLA Yearbook 2001:* 195–210. Amsterdam: John Benjamins.

Cenoz, J. (2002). Age differences in foreign language learning. *I.T.L. Review of applied linguistics, 135–136,* 125–42.

Chesterfield, R., & Chesterfield, K. (1985). Natural order in children's use of second language learning strategies. *Applied Linguistics,* 6(1), 45–59.

DeKeyser, R. (1997). Beyond explicit rule learning: Automatizing second language morphosyntax. *Studies in Second Language Acquisition, 19*(2), 195–221.

DeKeyser, R. (1998). Beyond focus on form: Cognitive perspectives on learning and practicing second language grammar. In C. Doughty & J. Williams (Eds.), *Focus on form in classroom second language acquisition* (pp. 42–63). Cambridge, UK: Cambridge University Press.

DeKeyser, R. (2000). The robustness of critical period effects in second language acquisition. *Studies in Second Language Acquisition, 22*(4), 499–533.

DeKeyser, R. (2003). Implicit and explicit learning. In C. Doughty & M. H. Long (Eds.), *The handbook of second language acquisition* (pp. 313–48) Malden, MA: Blackwell.

DeKeyser, R., & Sokalski, K. (1996). The differential role of comprehension and production practice. *Language Learning, 46*(4), 613–42.

Donaldson, M. (1978). *Children's minds.* London: Fontana.

Doughty, C., & Williams, J. (Eds.) (1998). *Focus on form in classroom second language acquisition.* Cambridge, UK: Cambridge University Press.

Dunn, J. (1994). Sibling relationships and perceived self-competence: Patterns of stability between childhood and early adolescence. In A. Sameroff & M. M. Haith (Eds.), *Reason and responsibility: The passage through childhood.* Chicago: University of Chicago Press.

Ellis, N. C., & Laporte, N. (1997). Contexts of acquisition: Effects of formal instruction and naturalistic exposure on second language acquisition. In A. M. B. de Groot & J. F. Kroll (Eds.), *Tutorials in bilingualism: Psycholinguistic perspectives* (pp. 53–83). Hillsdale, NJ: Lawrence Erlbaum.

Ellis, R. (1997). *SLA research and language teaching.* Oxford: Oxford University Press.

Felix, S. (1985). More evidence on competing cognitive systems. *Second Language Research, 1,* 47–72.

Flavell, J. H. (1979). Metacognition and cognitive monitoring. *American Psychologist, 34* (10 Special Issue), 906–11.

Flege, J. E. (1991). Perception and production: The relevance of phonetic input to L2 phonological learning. In T. Heubner & C. Ferguson (Eds.), *Cross-currents in second language acquisition and linguistic theory.* Philadelphia: John Benjamins.

Flege, J. E. (1992). Speech learning in a second language. In C. A. Ferguson, L. Menn, & C. Stoel-Gammon (Eds.), *Phonological development: Models, research, implications* (pp. 565–604). Timonium, MD: York Press.

Flege, J. E. (1995). Second language speech learning: Theory, findings, and problems. In W. Strange (Ed.), *Speech perception and linguistic experience: Issues in cross-language research* (pp. 233–77). Baltimore: York Press.

Flege, J. E. (1999). Age of learning and second language speech. In D. Birdsong (Ed.), *Second language acquisition and the critical period hypothesis,* (pp. 101–32). Mawhwah, NJ: Lawrence Earlbaum.

Fullana, N. (2005). *Second language phonological acquisition in a formal setting.* Unpublished doctoral dissertation, Universitat de Barcelona.

Grañena, G. (in press). Age, input and interactional skills. In C. Muñoz (Ed.), *Age and the rate of foreign language learning.* Clevedon, UK: Multilingual Matters.

Hakuta, K. (1974). Prefabricated patterns and the emergence of structure in second language acquisition. *Language Learning, 24,* 287–97.

Harley, B., & Hart, D. (1997). Aptitude, proficiency, and starting age for SLA. *Studies in Second Language Acquisition, 19,* 379–400.

Harter, S. (1988). Developmental processes in the construction of the self. In T. D. Yawkey & J. E. Johnson (Eds.), *Integration processes and socialization: Early to middle childhood* (pp. 45–78). Hillsdale, NJ: Lawrence Erlbaum.

Hawkins, E. (1996). The early teaching of modern languages: A pilot scheme. In E. Hawkins (Ed.), *Thirty years of language teaching* (pp. 155–64). London: CILT.

Holmstrand, L. (1980). *Effekterna på kunskaper, färdigheter och attityder av tidigt påbörjad undervisning I engelska. En delstudie inom EPÅL-projektet* [Early English teaching: Effects on knowledge, proficiency and attitudes] (Pedagogisk forkning i Uppsala 18). Uppsala, Sweden: Uppsala universitet, Pedagogiska institutionen.

Hyltenstam, K. (1992). Non-native features of near-native speakers. On the ultimate attainment of childhood L2 learners. In R. Harris (Ed.), *Cognitive processing in bilinguals* (pp. 351–68). Amsterdam: Elsevier.

Hyltenstam, K., & Abrahamsson, N. (2000). Who can become native-like in a second language? All, some, or none?. On the maturational controversy in second langauge acquisition. *Studia Linguistica, 54*(2), 150–66.

Hyltenstam, K., & Abrahamsson, N. (2001). Age and L2 learning: The hazards of matching practical "implications" with theoretical "facts." Comments on Stefka H. Marinova-Todd, D. Bradford Marshall, & Catherine E. Snow's Three misconceptions about age and L2 learning. *TESOL Quarterly, 35*(1), 151–70.

Hyltenstam, K., & Abrahamsson, N. (2003). Maturational constraints in SLA. In C. J. Doughty & M. H. Long (Eds.), *The handbook of second language acquisition* (pp. 539–88). Malden, MA: Blackwell.

Kemler Nelson, D. G., & Smith, J. D. (1989). Analytic and holistic processing in reflection-impulsivity and cognitive development. In T. Globerson & T. Zelniker (Eds.), *Cognitive style and cognitive development* (pp. 116–40). Norwood, NJ: Ablex.

Krashen, S. (1982). Accounting for child-adult differences in second language rate and attainment. In S. D. Krashen, R. C. Scarcella & M. H. Long (Eds.), *Child-adult differences in second language acquisition* (pp. 202–26). Rowley, MA: Newbury House.

Krashen, S. D., Long, M. H. & Scarcella, R. C. (1982). Age, rate and eventual attainment in second language acquisition. In S. D. Krashen, R. C. Scarcella & M. H. Long (Eds.), *Child-adult differences in second language acquisition* (pp. 161–72). Rowley, MA: Newbury House.

Lázaro, A. (2002). *La adquisición de la morfosintaxis del inglés por niños bilingües Euskera-Castellano: Una perspectiva minimalista*. Doctoral dissertation, Universidad del País Vasco.

Lenneberg, E. H. (1967). *Biological foundations of language*. New York: Wiley.

Long, M. H. (1983). Native speaker/non-native speaker conversation and the negotiation of comprehensible input. *Applied Linguistics, 4*, 126–41.

Long, M. H. (1991). Focus on form: A design feature in language teaching methodology. In K. de Bot, R. Ginsberg, & C. Kramsch (Eds.), *Foreign language research in cross-cultural perspective* (pp. 39–52). Amsterdam: John Benjamins.

Mackey, A., Oliver, R., & Philp, J. (October, 1997). *Patterns of interaction in NNS-NNS conversation*. Paper presented at Second Language Research Forum, East Lancing, MI.

Muñoz, C. (2001). *Factores escolares e individuales en el aprendizaje formal de un idioma extranjero*. In S. Pastor & V. Salazar (Eds.), *Tendencias y líneas de investigación en adquisición de segundas lenguas*. Monográfico Revista de Lingüística (pp. 247–68). Universidad de Alicante.

Muñoz, C. (2002). Speech adjustments in L3 interviews. *Anuari de Filologia,* Vol. XXIV, A (11), 69–80.

Muñoz, C. (2003a). Variation in oral skills development and age of onset. In M. P. García Mayo & M. L. García Lecumberri (Eds.), *Age and the acquisition of English as a foreign language: Theoretical issues and fieldwork* (pp. 161–81). Clevedon, UK: Multilingual Matters.

Muñoz, C. (2003b). *Le rythme d'acquisition des savoirs communicationnels chez des apprenants guidés. L'influence de l'âge. Acquisition et interaction en langue étrangère (AILE), 18*, 53–77.

Muñoz, C., Corretja, D., & Castañé, M. (2002). A survey of foreign language teachers' age-related beliefs and opinions. Unpublished manuscript, Universitat de Barcelona.

Muñoz, C., & Tragant, E. (2001). Motivation and attitudes towards L2: Some effects of age and instruction. In S. Foster-Cohen & A. Nizegorodcew (Eds.), *EUROSLA Yearbook 1* (pp. 211–24). Amsterdam: John Benjamins.

Myles, F., Hooper, J., & Mitchell, R. (1998). Rote or rule? Exploring the role of formulaic language in classroom foreign language learning. *Language Learning, 48*(3), 323–63.

Myles, F., Mitchell, R., & Hooper, J. (1999). Interrogative chunks in French L2: A basis for creative construction? *Studies in Second Language Acquisition, 21*, 49–80.

O'Malley, J. M., & Chamot, A. U. (1990). *Learning strategies in second language acquisition.* New York: Cambridge University Press.

Oliver, R. (1998). Negotiation of meaning in child interactions. *The Modern Language Journal, 82*, 372–86.

Oliver, R. (2000). Age differences in negotiation and feedback in classroom and pairwork. *Language Learning, 50*, 119–51.

Oller, J., & Nagato, N. (1974). The long-term effect of FLES: An experiment. *Modern Language Journal, 58*, 15–19.

Oyama, S. (1976). A sensitive period for the acquisition of a nonnative phonological system. *Journal of Psycholinguistic Research, 5*, 261–85. Reprinted in S. D. Krashen, R. C. Scarcella, and M. H. Long (Eds.), (1982). *Child-adult differences in second language acquisition* (pp. 20–38). Rowley, MA: Newbury House.

Patkowski, M. S. (1980). The sensitive period for the acquisition of syntax in a second language. *Language Learning, 30*, 449–72.

Pawley, A., & Syder, F. H. (1983). Two puzzles for linguistic theory: Nativelike selection and nativelike fluency. In J. C. Richards & R. W. Schmidt (Eds.), *Language and communication* (pp. 191–226). London: Longman.

Pérez-Vidal, C., Torras, M. R., & Celaya, M. L. (2000). Age and EFL written performance by Catalan/Spanish bilinguals. *Spanish Applied Linguistics, 4–2*, 267–90.

Peters, A. M. (1983). *The units of language acquisition.* Cambridge, UK: Cambridge University Press.

Piaget, J. (1950). *The psychology of intelligence.* London: Routledge & Kegan Paul.

Reid, J. (1987). The learning style preferences of ESL students. *TESOL Quarterly, 21*, 87–111.

Salaberry, M. R. (1997). The role of input and output practice in second language acquisition. *Canadian Modern Language Review, 53*(2), 422–51.

Scarcella, R., & Higa, C. (1982). Input and age differences in second language acquisition. In S. Krashen, M. Long, & R. Scarcella (Eds.), *Child-adult differences in second language acquisition* (pp. 175–200). Rowley, MA: Newbury House.

Schmidt, C. R., Ollendick, T. H., & Stanowicz, L. B. (1988). Developmental changes in the influence of assigned goals on cooperation and competition. *Developmental Psychology, 24*, 574–79.

Schmidt, R. (1990). The role of consciousness in second language learning. *Applied Linguistics, 11*(2), 17–46.

Schmidt, R., Boraie, D., & Kassabgy, O. (1996). Foreign language motivation: internal structure and external connections. *University of Hawai'i Working Papers in ESL, 14*(2), 1–72.

Schmitt, N. (1997). Vocabulary learning strategies. In N. Schmitt & M. McCarthy (Eds.), *Vocabulary: Description, acquisition and pedagogy.* Cambridge, UK: Cambridge University Press.

Schouten-van Parreren, C. (1992). Individual differences in vocabulary acquisition: A qualitative experiment in the first phase of secondary education. In P. Arnaud & H. Bejoint (Eds.), *Vocabulary and applied linguistics* (pp. 94–101). London: Macmillan.

Schwartz, B. (1993). On explicit and negative data effecting and affecting competence and linguistic behavior. *Studies in Second Language Acquisition, 15*, 147–63.

Singleton, D. (1989). *Language acquisition: The age factor*. Clevedon, UK: Multilingual Matters.

Singleton, D. (1995). Introduction: A critical look at the critical period hypothesis in second language acquisition research. In D. Singleton & Z. Lengyel (Eds.), *The age factor in second language acquisition* (pp. 1–29). Clevedon, UK: Multilingual Matters.

Singleton, D. (1997). Age and second language learning. In G. R. Tucker & D. Corson (Eds.), *Encyclopedia of language and education. Vol. 4. Second language education*, pp. 43–50. Kluwer Academic Publishers.

Skehan, P. (1986). Cluster analysis and the identification of learner types. In V. Cook (Ed.), *Experimental approaches to second language learning* (pp. 81–94). Oxford: Pergamon Press.

Snow, C., & Hoefnagel-Höhle, M. (1978). The critical period for language acquisition: Evidence from second language learning. *Child Development, 49*, 1114–28.

Stankowski Gratton, R. (1980). Una ricerca sperimentale sull'insegnamento del tedesco dalla prima classe elementare, *Rassegna Italiana di Linguistica Applicata, 12*(3), 119–41.

Sternberg, R. J. (2002). The theory of successful intelligence and its implications for language aptitude testing. In P. Robinson (Ed.), *Individual differences and instructed language learning*. Amsterdam/Philadelphia: John Benjamins.

Sternberg, R. J., & Nigro, G. (1980). Developmental patterns in the solution of verbal analogies. *Child Developments, 51*, 27–38.

Swain, M. (1985). Communicative competence: Some roles of comprehensible input and comprehensible output in its development. In S. Gass & C. Madden (Eds.), *Input in second language acquisition* (pp. 235–53). Rowley, MA: Newbury House.

Swain, M. (1995). Three functions of output in second language learning. In G. Cook & D. Seidlhofer (Eds.), *Principle and practice in applied linguistics* (pp. 125–44). Oxford: Oxford University Press.

Takeuchi, O. (2003). What can we learn from good foreign language learners? A qualitative study in the Japanese foreign language context. *System, 31*, 385–92.

Tragant, E., & Victori, M. (2006). Reported strategy use and age. In C. Muñoz (Ed.), *Age and the rate of foreign language learning* (pp. 208–36). Clevedon, UK: Multilingual Matters.

Ulman, M. T. (2001). The neural basis of lexicon and grammar in first and second language: The declarative/procedural model. *Bilingualism: Language and Cognition, 4*, 105–22.

Vasta, R., Haith, M. M., and Miller, S. A. (1999). *Child psychology: The modern science*, 3rd ed., New York: John Wiley & Sons.

Victori, M., & Tragant, E. (2003). Learner strategies: A cross-sectional and longitudinal study of primary and high-school EFL learners. In M. P. García Mayo & M. L. García Lecumberri (Eds.), *Age and the acquisition of english as a foreign language: Theoretical issues and fieldwork* (pp. 182–209). Clevedon, UK: Multilingual Matters.

Weinert, R. (1994). Some effects of a foreign language classroom on the development of German negation. *Applied Linguistics, 15*, 76–101.

Williams, J. N. (1999). Memory, attention, and inductive learning. *Studies in Second Language Acquisition, 21*(1), 1–48.

Wray, A. (2000). Formulaic sequences in second language teaching: Principle and practice. *Applied Linguistics, 21*(4), 463–89.

Yamamori, K., Takamichi, I., Tomohito, H., & Oxford, R. L. (2003). Using cluster analysis to uncover L2 learner differences in strategy use, will to learn and achievement over time. *IRAL, 41*, 381–409.

10 Aptitudes, abilities, contexts, and practice

Peter Robinson

Introduction: Aptitude – the once and future concept

This chapter is concerned with second language (L2) learning aptitude and the cognitive demands of practice in various instructional contexts. Specifically, it describes recent theories of and research into the structure of cognitive abilities that underlie aptitude. It also describes findings from recent empirical research into the extent to which these abilities are drawn on during practice in performing types of pedagogic tasks, in processing L2 input under conditions of practice that manipulate the focus of attention and intention and in uptake of focus on form delivered during practice on these tasks and under these conditions. Broadly conceived, aptitude for learning from opportunities for practice draws on more than cognitive abilities and involves affective and conative factors which may also be consistent determinants of an individual's engagement with the L2 (Ackerman, 2003; Dörnyei, 2002, 2005; MacIntyre, 2002; Robinson, 2005a; Snow & Farr, 1987). This said, this chapter addresses in detail only cognitive aspects of what Richard Snow (1994) called the cognitive-affective-conative triad of factors contributing to aptitude – focusing on these and their *interaction* with learning contexts.

Task and situation specificity

Aptitude, Snow argued, "should refer to being equipped to work at a particular kind of task or in a particular kind of situation" (Corno, Cronbach, Kupermintz, Lohman, Mandinach, Porteus, & Talbert, 2002, p. 3). The situation specificity of aptitude was an important aspect of Snow's thinking and that of others (see e.g., Sternberg & Wagner, 1994) and leads to the conclusion, explored in Snow's work (and this chapter), that aptitude is variegated but not so variegated as to be infinite. It must be constrained by a theory of the demands made by academic tasks, by treatments or a series of tasks, and by the situational context or academic setting for instruction (Snow, 1994, p. 12). Together, these amount to the opportunities a context affords for learning processes. Aptitude, in Snow's view, describes clusters of person variables, or what he called

256

"aptitude complexes" (1994, p. 8; cf. Robinson, 2001c, 2002a), which interact with and facilitate the adaptive processes that practice on tasks stimulates, resulting in short- and longer-term learning across a variety of educational domains. If aptitudes and tasks are well-matched, such practice and learning should lead eventually to the degree of mastery that is needed to accomplish lifetime pursuits in those domains.

As Corno et al. point out in discussing Snow's work, his "concept of aptitude is especially close to that of readiness . . . a latent quality that enables the development, or production, given specified conditions, of some more advanced performance"(2002, p. 3). Theorizing and researching the relationship of learner variables to L2 learning contexts, I will argue – adopting many of the positions Snow took – therefore requires specifying the combinations of such cognitive variables that contribute to this "readiness" or "latent quality" for success in L2 learning as well as a detailed accounting of their contribution to performance on specific tasks or in more broadly defined situations or learning conditions in which tasks and the language skills they implicate are practiced.

The turn away from L2 aptitude

In the previously described view, aptitude and the classroom learning situation are analyzed, and multicomponential concepts and specific aptitudes must be matched to specific tasks and learning conditions to ensure optimum development, performance, and transferability of classroom learning. However, in the 1960s, 1970s, and to some extent also the 1980s, L2 learning conditions were described at a very coarse-grained level, in terms of instructional methods such as audiolingualism, cognitive code, and communicative language teaching, with little direct connection made to the details of processing for SLA that cause the effects of methods on L2 learning outcomes. Aptitude, too, was relatively unanalyzed and viewed as a monolithic, static trait measured parsimoniously by inherited tests such as the Modern Language Aptitude Test (MLAT) (Carroll & Sapon, 1959) or Pimsleur's Language Aptitude Battery (PLAB) (Pimsleur, 1966) developed in the 1950s and 1960s and consisting of few subtests so as to ensure optimum administrative convenience. Some research showed, however (and quite understandably if Snow's views were correct), that while these tests predicted instructed L2 learning in audiolingual classrooms in the 1960s relatively well (the learning context they were developed to predict success in), they appeared to be less successful at predicting learning in the communicative L2 classrooms that became popular in the 1970s. They had low "treatment validity." Consequently, Cook argued, "Predictions about success need to take into account the kind of classroom that is involved rather than being biased towards one kind or assuming there is a single factor of aptitude which applies regardless of situation" (1996, p. 101). Going even further, the very different conclusion drawn by Krashen (1982) was not to inquire further into aptitude for L2 learning and its components and their relation to conditions of instruction but simply to argue that aptitude predicted only conscious learning, not unconscious acquisition during communicative exposure. For Krashen, aptitude was largely unimportant since, he argued, unconscious acquisition following the "natural order" was the process of widest influence on levels of ultimate L2 attainment and the stages of communicative ability that led to them. And so aptitude dropped out of focus in SLA theory and pedagogy.

Returning to L2 aptitude

This simple dismissal of the relevance of aptitude to instructed L2 learning is now questioned. In particular, two developments in the mid- to late-1990s made it possible to reopen the debate about how aptitude(s) interact with L2 learning conditions to affect instructed language development. First, conditions of L2 learning were studied at a much more fine-grained level of resolution than they had been before, enabling, as Snow argued was necessary, theories of learning at fairly specific contextual levels – that mapped onto cognitive processes in identifiable ways – to be developed and researched. Sometimes this research used computerized delivery of L2 learning conditions and assessment of L2 learning outcomes, as in the laboratory studies described in Hulstijn and DeKeyser (1997). At other times it has analyzed the information-processing demands of tasks and related them to features of task design (e.g., Bygate, 2001; Ellis, 2005; Robinson, 1995a, 1996c, 2001a, 2005b; Skehan, 1998). Research has also begun to look at the effect of specific interventionist options for giving feedback (Mackey, Philp, Egi, Fujii, & Tatsumi, 2002) or focusing learner attention on L2 form (Doughty & Williams, 1998) and their relationship to cognitive processes thought to contribute to instructed SLA (e.g., DeKeyser, 2001; Robinson, 1996b, 2001d; Schmidt, 2001; Skehan, 1998; VanPatten, 2004).

Second, aptitude also recently began to be retheorized as a dynamic (Sternberg & Grigorenko, 2000), potentially trainable concept (Sternberg, 2002). Such theories propose that abilities contributing to aptitude have their effects in interaction with the processing demands of real-world and instructional classroom contexts to which learners must adapt (Corno et al. 2002; Grigorenko, Sternberg, & Ehrman, 2000; Kyllonen & Lajoie, 2003; Robinson, 2001c, 2002a, 2002c; Snow, 1987, 1994). Complementary to these theories, multicomponential batteries of abilities, personality, and motivational traits have been proposed to assess potential for adaptation to learning contexts (see e.g., Ackerman, 2003; Dörnyei, 2002; Matthews & Zeidner, 2004; Robinson, 2005a;

Shavelson & Roeser, 2002), prompting much richer investigations of the relationships of L2 exposure to individual differences (IDs) and their influence on SLA processes.

In this dynamic view – as Snow and Sternberg have long argued – learning and adaptation to the learning environment, or classroom context for practice, is a result of the interaction of context with learners' patterns of abilities. With this basic principle in mind, the following section of this chapter reviews findings for L2 learning context-ability interactions at the levels of context described above – L2 learning condition, focus on form (FonF) technique, and pedagogic task. However, before reviewing these findings and the theoretical models of aptitude that draw on them, some brief discussion of the relationship of learning to practice is appropriate.

Learning and practice

Many of the studies to be described here, particularly the laboratory studies of L2 learning conditions and the FonF studies, have been concerned with the effects of different conditions of exposure on acquiring new (phonological, morphological, syntactic, lexical, or pragmatic) L2 knowledge. Second language learning is often distinguished from L2 practice in the sense that learning involves initial registration of the L2 input, whether this takes place at the level of unaware detection or with some degree of awareness or noticing (see Robinson, 1995b, 2003a; Schmidt, 1990, 2001; Tomlin & Villa, 1994), which can subsequently lead to longer-term retention and representational change (via mechanisms such as triggering in Universal Grammar, or associative learning in connectionist models, or memory rehearsal and elaboration in other cognitive models). However, in this simple account, L2 practice can be described as access to and subsequent elaboration of existing knowledge.

There is merit in this conceptual distinction, but in the time course of exposure to language input, it is hard to draw the distinction with any clarity. In Bialystok's (1994) terms, often greater "control" of existing L2 knowledge as a result of comprehension practice, or language use, leads to further "analysis" of the input, and so to more detection, noticing, rehearsal, and intake. In an important sense, then, in the studies to be described, learning occurs during dynamic exposure to and practice in processing L2 input presented under different learning conditions, classroom activities, or on different kinds of tasks. None of the following laboratory studies provide one-shot exposure to a form or lexical item – all provide for lengthy, experimentally controlled exposure. Similarly, studies of the effectiveness of FonF techniques, such as input enhancement or sustained and targeted recasts, take place over periods of instructional exposure. These task studies also invariably involve what may be new, previously unknown, undetected, or unnoticed L2 input being subsequently processed and reprocessed over the time course of task completion and often recycled on subsequent planned versus unplanned, or simple versus complex, versions of the task.

So in an important sense, the following summarized studies speak to how new L2 knowledge can be acquired (detected or noticed and registered) and also consolidated during the exposure and practice that the condition, technique, or L2 task involves. Such consolidation is also sometimes called learning, in the sense of "cue strengthening" (MacWhinney, 2001) or "instance strengthening" (Logan, 1988). The point is that while these forms of consolidation may be distinguishable from L2 input detection and noticing, they occur together during the time frame of exposure to L2 input, as does a further kind of learning that is intricately related to practice, i.e., restructuring of internal representations, resulting in developmental shifts (Mackey, 1999; Pienemann, 1998), perhaps as a result of mechanisms such as knowledge compilation and proceduralization (Anderson, 1993; DeKeyser, 2001). As Schmidt notes in discussing whether attention to and awareness of input is necessary for learning, "it is clear that successful L2 learning goes beyond what is present in input" (2001, p. 23) and that such learning is intricately related to practice, for some of the reasons just given.

Instructional contexts, individual differences, and learning

Laboratory research, attention, and awareness

In recent years, experimental laboratory SLA research has investigated the effects of learning under different conditions of exposure with the aim of relating the information-processing demands of different instructional sets to the L2 targets to the extent and duration of learning. Often, these instructional sets differ with respect to whether they promote awareness of the L2 targets, intention to learn the targets, and explicit metalinguistic knowledge about the form of the targets (e.g., de Graaff, 1997; DeKeyser, 1995, 1997; Ellis, 1993; Hulstijn, 1989; Robinson, 1996a, 1997b, 2002b, 2004, 2005c; Robinson & Ha, 1993; Williams, 1999). Contrary to theoretical claims, such as those of Krashen (1982) and Reber (1993) that implicit (unaware and unintentional) learning is more effective than explicit learning, especially where the stimulus domain is complex, DeKeyser (1995), Robinson (1996a), and de Graaff (1997) all found that L2 learning in explicit conditions, involving some degree of metalinguistic awareness and instruction, was at least as effective as learning in implicit conditions where the stimulus domain was complex and was, on the whole, much more effective where the L2 stimulus domain was simple.

In fact, there is evidence that learning in the implicit conditions of these studies, as in the explicit conditions, is a conscious process and does not result from qualitatively different, nonconscious, implicit learning mechanisms. De Graaff (1997), Robinson (1997a), and Williams (1999) all found IDs in aptitude (measured by subtests of conventional aptitude batteries such as MLAT) and memory ability influenced learning across implicit *and* explicit conditions, suggesting that adult L2 learning under all conditions of exposure is Fundamentally Similar (Robinson, 1996b, 1997a), since differences in the extent of learning in these conditions were affected by IDs in the conscious, information-processing abilities measured by the aptitude and memory tests.[1]

To examine the relationship between aptitude and awareness during L2 learning, Robinson (1995c, 1996b, 1997a) studied the effects of four conditions of exposure on the acquisition of simple versus complex L2 structures. These were an implicit condition, in which participants memorized examples; an incidental condition, in which participants processed examples for meaning; a rule-search condition, in which participants tried to find grammatical rules distinguishing examples presented; and an instructed condition, in which participants were taught and then applied a pedagogic rule explanation to examples. Implicit learners in the study, in general, learned poorly. However, for implicit learners in particular, there was a strong link between one of the abilities measured by a conventional measure of L2 learning aptitude (the grammatical sensitivity subtest of the MLAT), post-test L2 learning success, and – following experimental exposure and immediate post-test performance – awareness (at the levels of self-reported looking for regularities in the input and ability to verbalize partial rules about the structure of the input). Learners in the implicit L2 learning condition with high L2 aptitude were found to be those most likely to attest to having looked for structural regularities in the L2 input during implicit exposure and were also found to be able to verbalize rules about structural regularities following exposure.

Table 10.1 shows the results of planned comparisons of aptitude scores for those classified (on the basis of responses to a post-experimental questionnaire) as having *looked for rules*, versus those who did not, and being able to *verbalize rules*, versus those who could not. In each case, the grammatical sensitivity (GS) aptitude scores of the aware, implicit learners (who looked for and could verbalize rules) were significantly higher than those of their unaware counterparts. One can infer, then, that this aptitude subtest positively affects the potential to become aware during implicit L2 exposure. And awareness led to more learning for those implicit learners. As Table 10.2 shows, learners who looked for rules or could verbalize them were significantly different from and more

TABLE 10.1 PROBABILITY THAT APTITUDE SUBTEST SCORES DIFFERED
FOR IMPLICIT LEARNERS DEMONSTRATING TWO LEVELS OF AWARENESS
(ADAPTED FROM ROBINSON, 1997a)

MLAT aptitude subtest	Looked for rules	Verbalized rules
Grammatical sensitivity	$p = .016$	$p = .002$
Rote memory	ns.	ns.

TABLE 10.2 PROBABILITY THAT TWO LEVELS OF
AWARENESS ENCOURAGED SUCCESS IN IMPLICIT LEARNERS
(ADAPTED FROM ROBINSON, 1997a)

Rule	Looked for rules	Verbalized rules
Easy	$p = .03$	$p = .01$
Complex	$p = .02$	$p = .005$

successful than their unaware counterparts in learning both simple and complex rules.

The full pattern of correlations between the scores on the aptitude subtests and learning in each of the four conditions studied can be seen in Table 10.3, which shows that aptitude correlated significantly and positively with learning in all conditions, except the incidental processing-input-for-meaning condition. This finding appears to support Krashen's (1982) claim that acquisition occurring during processing for meaning (not form) is insensitive to IDs in aptitude. However, the two aptitude subtests used (rote memory for pairs of words and GS) were less likely to have matched the specific processing demands of this condition than the other conditions (memorize examples, search for rules, or apply previously learned metalinguistic explanations to examples). Subsequently (Robinson, 2002b, 2005c), these measures of aptitude were similarly found to be poor predictors of incidental learning, but a measure of working memory (WM) for text, based on Daneman and Carpenter's (1980) reading span test, was significantly and positively correlated with incidental learning. This is understandable, since processing input for meaning during incidental learning does not create opportunities for rote memorization of examples encountered or for the intentional application of explicit metalinguistic knowledge to input. However, processing for meaning does draw on the ability to simultaneously switch attention to form during problems in semantic processing, and fast switching between the attentional demands of tasks has recently been shown to be an ability that is strongly related to WM capacity (Logan, 2004).

One conclusion to be drawn from these studies of different learning conditions and their relationship to aptitude is that, while conventional

TABLE 10.3 CORRELATIONS OF SCORES ON APTITUDE SUBTESTS WITH LEARNING
EASY AND HARD RULES IN ALL CONDITIONS OF ROBINSON (1997a)

Condition/rule	MLAT grammatical sensitivity	MLAT rote memory	Total aptitude
Implicit			
easy	.69*	.3	.52*
hard	.75*	.25	.52*
Incidental			
easy	.35	.31	.39
hard	.28	.14	.23
Rule-search			
easy	.6*	.42	.56*
hard	.37	.51*	.5*
Instructed			
easy	.54*	.49*	.63*
hard	.56*	.46*	.62*

$* = p < .05$

measures of aptitude are suitable for predicting successful learning during some conditions of exposure and practice, they also need to be supplemented by other measures (such as WM), especially where the instructional condition involves processing for meaning alone with no intentional focus on form. Clearly, this research has begun to uncover relationships between IDs in aptitude (even using only subtests of conventional aptitude batteries, such as MLAT) with awareness and with subsequent L2 learning under a variety of closely controlled, experimental learning conditions. Such learning conditions are specified, delivered, and observed at a sufficient level of contextual and temporal granularity that one can, I think, make valid inferential claims about their relationship to IDs and also to the causal interactions of both with SLA processes (such as awareness resulting from noticing and intentional rule-search) and subsequent L2 learning success. The findings reported here, then, for ID correlates of implicit, incidental, rule-search, and instructed learning are drawn on later in this chapter to motivate one proposal for an aptitude battery that can be used to match learners to instructional options that provide optimum contexts for L2 practice and learning.

Classroom research, attention, and awareness

Research into the roles of attention and awareness has also studied the effects of different kinds of intervention that aim to direct learner attention to L2 form during classroom activities which have a primary focus on meaning and the achievement of communicative goals (see Doughty & Williams, 1998). Learning outcomes assessed in this research have been memory for and long-term retention of the L2 input encountered during instructional exposure as well as generalizability of the L2 knowledge base established during exposure to new contexts and novel L2 material. The degree of attention to and awareness of form during classroom L2 processing has been manipulated via use of various FonF techniques such as input flooding (see e.g., White, 1998), input enhancement (see Leeman, Arteagoitia, Fridman, & Doughty, 1995), recasting (Doughty & Varela, 1998), and input processing and rule explanation (VanPatten, 2004). Findings for this research have produced mixed results, with some but not all studies showing input enhancement and recasting to have an effect on subsequent L2 learning. In contrast, input-processing research has been claimed to show quite consistently positive effects for this technique (VanPatten, 2004; but cf. DeKeyser, Salaberry, Robinson, & Harrington, 2002). However, FonF research has not so far (with the partial exception of two studies reported below) examined the interaction of L2 learning via such techniques with IDs in patterns of cognitive abilities, and this could be an important explanation for the lack of overall significant gain by groups in some studies – especially those adopting less intrusive, and also less metalinguistic ability-dependent, FonF techniques such as input flooding and recasting. That is, the abilities necessary for learning from these two techniques may not be as homogeneously high in the usual studied population of learners (university-level students) as the abilities necessary for learning from input-processing instruction. These latter abilities are likely largely metalinguistic and analytic. University-level language majors can be expected to have strengths in such abilities since schooled success in traditional, formal, instructed contexts usually demands them (Sternberg, 2002). Consequently, there may be more variation in L2 learning from input flooding or recasting and smaller group effects for learning from these FonF techniques than for techniques such as input-processing instruction, which draws on a common groupwide (because schooled) set of analytic, metalinguistic abilities.

Nonetheless, the larger issue for instructed SLA research is that in any studied population of L2 learners, some learners' aptitudes may be more suited to one FonF technique versus another during the exposure that practice entails. The two studies to date that indicate this have both investigated the effects of IDs on learning from FonF delivered via recasting during classroom practice. Robinson and Yamaguchi (Robinson, 1999; Robinson & Yamaguchi, 1999) found that Japanese L1-speaking, university-level, nonlanguage majors showed significantly positive correlations (see Table 10.4) of measures of phonetic sensitivity and rote memory (using Sasaki's Language Aptitude Battery for the Japanese, LABJ) with learning from recasts during task-based interaction in English over a five-week period. Learning was measured by pre- and

TABLE 10.4 CORRELATIONS OF APTITUDE WITH GAIN SCORES ON ELICITED
IMITATION MEASURES OF RELATIVE CLAUSE LEARNING FROM RECASTS IN
ROBINSON AND YAMAGUCHI (1999) USING LABJ

Grammatical sensitivity	Rote memory	Phonetic sensitivity	Total aptitude
−.09	.51*	.5*	.44

* = p < .05

post-test gain scores on an elicited imitation measure of the form targeted
in the study, i.e., English relative clause production. Similarly, Mackey
et al. (2002) found that students at a range of levels from a variety
of L1-speaking backgrounds in a foreign language EFL program also
showed significantly positive relationships between measures of phonological WM capacity, noticing of information targeted by recasts (features
of *wh*-question formation) delivered over three days of communicative
L2 interaction, and subsequent interlanguage development. This was so,
however, only for those learners who were at a relatively lower developmental level at the beginning of the instructional intervention; the WM
capacity of learners at higher developmental levels who took part in the
brief treatment was not significantly related to uptake of information
targeted by recasts.

Taken together, the findings for a positive relationship between phonetic sensitivity, memory ability, learning from recasts in Robinson and
Yamaguchi's (1999) study and phonological WM, noticing of recast
information, and subsequent L2 development in Mackey et al. (2002)
suggests that these very similar abilities are positively implicated in aptitude for learning from the recasting FonF technique. However, as with
the finding for incidental learning in Robinson (1997a) (see Table 10.3),
in Robinson and Yamaguchi (1999) there were low, nonsignificant correlations of learning of relative clauses during task-based, meaning-focused
interaction (supplemented by targeted recasts) and the GS aptitude subtest (see Table 10.4). Therefore, the findings of Robinson (1997a) and
Robinson and Yamaguchi (1999) also constitute evidence for a possible
inference across contexts (laboratory studies of incidental learning and
classroom studies of focus on form during task-based learning) about the
noninfluence of IDs in grammatical sensitivity on aptitude for incidental
learning during processing for meaning. As with the laboratory research
described above, these findings suggest that learners may differ in their
aptitude(s) for learning from one FonF technique versus another during
opportunities for communicative practice – an issue addressed again in
the section on contemporary approaches to aptitude and their implications for matching L2 learners to optimum conditions of instructional
exposure.

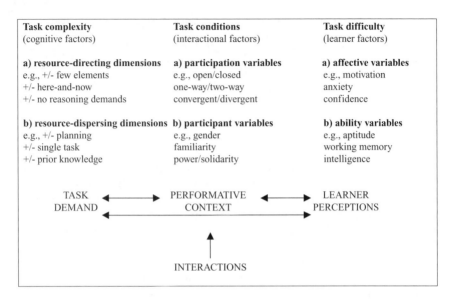

Task complexity (cognitive factors)	Task conditions (interactional factors)	Task difficulty (learner factors)
a) resource-directing dimensions e.g., +/- few elements +/- here-and-now +/- no reasoning demands	**a) participation variables** e.g., open/closed one-way/two-way convergent/divergent	**a) affective variables** e.g., motivation anxiety confidence
b) resource-dispersing dimensions e.g., +/- planning +/- single task +/- prior knowledge	**b) participant variables** e.g., gender familiarity power/solidarity	**b) ability variables** e.g., aptitude working memory intelligence

TASK DEMAND ⟷ PERFORMATIVE CONTEXT ⟷ LEARNER PERCEPTIONS

↑ INTERACTIONS

Figure 10.1 A componential framework for mapping task, context, and learner interactions (adapted from Robinson, 2001b)

Task-based learning and task design

Other recent research into the effectiveness of classroom instruction has examined the effects of design features of L2 tasks on production and learning. Studying the effects of cognitive design features of classroom learning tasks (which affect the extent of attentional, reasoning, and memory demands the task makes on the learner) can be done while also varying other details of how practice on the tasks is implemented. These include the nature of task participation (such as whether the task requires simple information transmission or two-way information exchange) and of the task participants (such as familiarity or gender). One can then look for effects of these different kinds of factors on L2 learning and performance outcomes (see Figure 10.1).

This research has begun to show that some features of L2 task design, such as the complexity of cognitive demands, do have effects on L2 performance. Performance on more complex tasks has sometimes been shown to lead to greater accuracy (Iwashita, Elder, & MacNamara, 2001; Kuiken, Mos, & Vedder, 2005; Rahimpour, 1999; Robinson, 1995a) and more extensive self-repair (Gilabert, 2004). More complex tasks also lead to more negotiation and interaction and more extensive uptake and incorporation of premodified input (Hardy & Moore, 2004; Robinson, 2001a, 2003b, 2005b). In contrast, simpler tasks have been shown to promote fluency and consolidation of previously learned language

(Gilabert, 2004; Rahimpour, 1999; Robinson, 1995a, 2001a). Task repetition (Bygate, 2001) and the provision of planning time (Skehan & Foster, 2001) have also been shown, in a number of cases, to systematically affect the fluency of L2 production. These initial findings may have potentially important pedagogic consequences for decisions about which design features of tasks to manipulate in order to maximize the effects of task practice on accuracy of production, the amount of interaction that tasks stimulate, and the extent to which tasks can facilitate automatized access to already learned aspects of the L2.

This said, a number of studies have also reported null effects of task design on learner production. As with the FonF research, however, task research has not yet substantially addressed the role of IDs and aptitudes for learning and performance on specific tasks during task-based L2 learning. It is possible, therefore, that learners with strengths in patterns of task-related abilities may be more suited to learning from or production practice on one task versus another. Consequently, IDs in abilities may also interact with L2 task characteristics to systematically affect speech production, uptake, and learning. One learner may be systematically more fluent on one type of task than another, or systematically more accurate, or notice and use more new information provided in the task input. These are important issues for the development of theoretically motivated and researched L2 task-aptitude interaction profiles that can be used to maximize on-task practice and learning opportunities.

Niwa (2000) has done the only empirical research to date that casts light on this issue. She showed that as L2 tasks increase in complexity, IDs in cognitive abilities increasingly differentiate performance. This is consistent with the predictions of the Cognition Hypothesis of task-based L2 development (Robinson, 2001b, 2003b, 2005b, in press). It claims that increasing the cognitive demands of tasks will have L2 performance and learning effects (i.e., that performing complex tasks leads to more noticing, uptake, and incorporation of input and interlocutor feedback, greater accuracy and complexity of production, but less fluency on complex tasks relative to simpler versions) but that these effects will be more differentiated in the population than the fluency effects induced by performing a series of simpler versions (e.g., greater speech rate, less pausing and hesitation, fast lexical access). This relatively greater sensitivity of complex task performance and learning to IDs in relevant abilities has been well documented in other domains and has been shown in many previous studies of aptitude treatment interactions (see e.g., Ackerman & Ciancolo, 2002; Fleishman & Quiantance, 1984; Snow, Kyllonen, & Marshalek, 1984). In her study, Niwa (2000) assessed the influence of IDs in WM, aptitude, and intelligence on speech production during narrative tasks performed at four different levels of reasoning complexity.

TABLE 10.5 EFFECTS OF INDIVIDUAL DIFFERENCES IN APTITUDE, WORKING MEMORY, AND INTELLIGENCE ON L2 NARRATIVE PRODUCTION AT FOUR LEVELS OF REASONING COMPLEXITY IN NIWA (2000)

		Narrative production						
	Accuracy	Fluency						Complexity
Reasoning complexity	EFT	TIME	WPS	SBP	WPP	WPT	SPT	TTR
Narrative 1 (simple)	ns.	Apt* −.48	ns.	ns.	ns.	ns.	ns.	ns.
Narrative 2	ns.	Apt* −.5	ns.	ns.	ns.	Apt* −.59	ns.	Apt** .61
Narrative 3	ns.	Apt* −.42	ns.	ns.	ns.	ns.	ns.	ns.
Narrative 4 (complex)	Int* −.45	Apt* −.44	ns.	Apt/* WM* −.45/ −.55	WM* −.47	ns.	ns.	ns.

Key: *= $p < .050$; ** = $p < .01$; EFT = % error free T-units; TIME = time on narrative; WPS = words per second; SBP = seconds between pauses; WPP = words per pause; WPT = words per T-unit; SPT = S nodes per T-unit; TTR = type token ratio; Apt = aptitude (LABJ); WM = working memory; Int = Intelligence (WAIS-R)

As can be seen in Table 10.5, the strongest pattern of significant correlations was found for IDs in intelligence (measured by a short form of the Wechsler Adult Intelligence Scale), L2 learning aptitude (measured using Sasaki's LABJ), and WM (using a measure of reading span) on the accuracy and particularly the fluency of speaker production on the most complex version of the narratives. This suggests that IDs in cognitive abilities do lead to increasingly differentiated L2 speech production by learners on complex versions of tasks high in their reasoning demands.

In a further study of the effects of increasing reasoning demands of L2 narrative tasks, Robinson (2003b, 2005b) found that as tasks increased in complexity, learners increasingly incorporated premodified L2 input available in the task materials into their own production. However, it is possible that the greater uptake and learning from premodified input on complex tasks found in this study is also related to IDs in the abilities contributing to aptitudes for task-based learning and L2 practice. If so, the ID variables that predict this may well differ according to the dimension along which the task is made complex: for example, IDs in reasoning ability in the case of the reasoning demands dimension versus attention control in the case of the single-to-dual task dimension.

In summary, the frameworks for research, accumulating findings, and research agendas at the three levels of instructional context are important since they can help to base pedagogic decision making about optimum L2 learning conditions, task types, and FonF interventions on an empirical footing. What is additionally needed is research into the interaction of instructed L2 learning – under different conditions of exposure, via different FonF techniques, and via practice on different types of tasks at different levels of complexity – with IDs in the cluster of abilities contributing to aptitudes for those specific L2 learning conditions, techniques, and tasks.

Contemporary approaches to aptitude(s)

The issue then is how best to describe the ID factors and their combinations in such a way as to define sets of aptitudes or optimally conducive sets of abilities for learning (becoming aware of the input and subsequently elaborating and processing it at higher levels than those of initial registration) during exposure and practice under one condition, or on one task, or accompanied by one FonF technique versus another. Conventional measures such as MLAT are not well suited to this and were not intended to be (Cook, 1996, p. 101). They were developed to be parsimonious, optimally predictive tests of global learning over schooled courses of instruction following years of exposure in audiolingual language programs during the 1960s – not learning in contemporary L2 classrooms during practice on cycles of pedagogic tasks or during content-based instruction.

As Skehan argues (2002), and as some of the studies reviewed above show, no doubt the subtests of MLAT and similar aptitude batteries, such as Pimsleur's PLAB or Sasaki's LABJ, do capture some of the abilities that contribute to learning in contemporary communicative and immersion classrooms. A number of longer-term studies show this (e.g., Ehrman & Oxford, 1995; Harley & Hart, 1997; Ranta, 2002). Studies have also shown that the GS subtest of MLAT is a particularly good measure of metalinguistic ability and that scores on it correlate significantly and positively with L2 learning by post-critical-period learners but not with learning by those with substantial amounts of pre-critical-period exposure to the L2 (see DeKeyser, 2000).

While valuable, such long-term studies clearly lack the temporal and operational granularity of the experimental studies reviewed earlier. It is not clear precisely which instructional options and practice activities experienced in the lengthy communicative and immersion programs were facilitated by learner aptitude (as measured) and which were not. The experimental studies reviewed above do suggest that incidental

TABLE 10.6 PROCESSING STAGES AND POTENTIAL APTITUDE COMPONENTS
(FROM SKEHAN, 2002)

SLA processing stage	Aptitude component
1. noticing	auditory segmentation
	attention management
	working memory
	phonemic coding
2. pattern identification	fast analysis/working memory
	grammatical sensitivity
3. extending	inductive language learning ability
4. complexifying	grammatical sensitivity
	inductive language learning ability
5. integrating	restructuring capacity
6. becoming accurate, avoiding error	automatization
	proceduralization
7. creating a repertoire, achieving salience	retrieval processes
8. automatizing rule-based language, achieving fluency	automatizing, proceduralization
9. lexicalizing, dual-coding	memory, chunking, retrieval processes

learning is not well predicted by the MLAT or LABJ. Additionally, the small number of subtests in traditional aptitude measures limits the ways in which learner differences can be classified. Is memory-oriented versus analysis-oriented a true classification or simply an artifact of the MLAT, since it measures little else? While it may not be wrong, it is almost certainly incomplete (cf. Sternberg, 2002, p. 36). Consequently, there is a need to develop more contextually sensitive measures of aptitude if progress is to be made in linking IDs in cognitive abilities to the daily conditions of classroom learning and practice in a useful way. Two approaches that have explicitly tried to do this are reviewed below.

Skehan's Processing Stage model of aptitude

Skehan (2002) proposes that the components of aptitude for instructed learning must be differentiated according to the SLA processing stage they correspond to (see Table 10.6), and he identifies four broad stages: *noticing* the input, *patterning* the input to facilitate further analysis and generalization, *controlling* the analyzed knowledge in production, and *lexicalizing* or variegating the patterns learned to suit different communicative and situational contexts. This sequential processing stage approach to identifying the components of aptitude is similar in conception to one adopted by MacIntyre and Gardner (1994) for measuring the effects of anxiety on L2 learning and use at the input, central processing, and output stages. Each proposed stage in Figure 10.2 is matched by a hypothetical description of the cognitive abilities and resources a complementary aptitude component would measure. Skehan notes that in the approach he describes, "We are not taking existing aptitude tests and seeing if SLA relevance can be perceived for each of them. Rather we are taking SLA stages, and exploring whether aptitude would be relevant for each of these stages" (2002, pp. 89–90). While some stages do relate quite clearly to the abilities measured by the MLAT and other subtests, in other cases the model "reveals where it would be useful to produce aptitude tests if we are to be able to predict effectively in acquisition-rich contexts" (2002, p. 90).

The first stage concerns noticing and registration of the input. In addition to measures of attentional management and WM, Skehan identifies the phonetic sensitivity subtest of MLAT as a particularly relevant measure of what he calls "phonemic coding" ability. This first stage – as with the subsequent stages Skehan describes – requires an interacting cluster or "complex" of abilities rather than a single subtest to measure the components of processing. Stages 2–5 in Table 10.6 broadly concern pattern analysis. Here the GS and inductive language learning measures of MLAT are proposed to capture some of the abilities contributing to these aspects of language processing, but Skehan notes that Stage 5, "integrating," involves capacity for "restructuring" – an aptitude component not well-matched by any existing tests. Similarly, current aptitude subtests do not capture well the abilities contributing to control of analyzed knowledge in Stages 6–8 and the cumulative proceduralization of knowledge in fluent performance over time. One suggestion is that – as in dynamic tests of other aptitudes that involve an authentic trial learning session – a cumulative measure of ability to profit while engaged in learning would be appropriate here. In such tests (see Sternberg & Grigorenko, 2000), aptitudes for learning are assessed at least in part in terms of pre- and post-test performance on some learning activity. One option that may be suitable, as in Grigorenko et al.'s CANAL-F aptitude test (2000) and Sick and Irie's (2000) Lunic Language Marathon, is to develop an aptitude component which involves actual learning of, and also tutoring in while learning, a miniature artificial language. This would involve two stages. In an initial self-study stage, learners attempt to understand the rules of the artificial language alone and are then tested. Following this, there would be a period of instruction in the language, followed by a further test. Performance on the second part of the test would be assessed by measuring gain from the first test of unaided self-study against results of learning following tutored instruction on the second test. Gain could then be taken as a measure of what Skehan calls "the capacity to proceduralize with linguistic material" (2002, p. 92) while profiting from tutored exposure, as happens in real-time teaching and learning classroom environments.

Finally, the last of Skehan's processing stages, lexicalizing, involves "going beyond rule-based processing" to build a fluent lexical repertoire. Since this involves an aptitude component that measures storage and retrieval memory processes that provide access to interlanguage during language use, current aptitude measures such as MLAT again are not appropriate here, since they measure only paired-associate, rote memorization abilities.

Implications of Skehan's model for matching aptitude to conditions of practice

Skehan's programmatic proposal suggests that some components of existing aptitude tests may be useful for capturing the abilities involved at different stages of L2 processing, but that – as has been stressed throughout this chapter – further development of complementary subtests will be necessary. As with the approach of Robinson described below, aptitude subtests are also seen to operate in differentiated clusters to determine the complexes of L2 processing abilities appropriate to each of the four broad noticing, patterning, controlling, and lexicalizing stages.

The validity of aptitude tests as theoretically motivated measures of fine-grained SLA processes is thus prioritized in this approach to aptitude test design and development in contrast to the traditional concerns of parsimony, i.e., have as few subtests as possible, and pragmatism, i.e., ensure brevity of administration. It should be noted here that while the tension between validity and thoroughness versus parsimony and pragmatism was understandable in the 1960s and 1970s when aptitude tests could only be administered at one sitting in classrooms, in the present day computerized, self-paced delivery and scoring of aptitude subtests has become a very feasible alternative, relaxing the traditional concerns over test administration.

The sequential, processing stage approach taken by Skehan also suggests that aptitudes for learning at each stage may differ, with the consequence that some learners may have poor aptitude for input processing and noticing (Stage 1) but better strengths in aptitudes for patterning the input (Stages 2–5), or for proceduralizing and automatizing analyzed input (Stages 6–8), or for lexicalizing learned rules of narrow domain applicability (Stage 9). This suggests that where weaknesses exist in capacities for L2 processing, such an aptitude measure could be used to diagnose, and subsequently support, learner areas of weakness through supplementary, more structured, and extensive practice activities. For example, activities involving task repetition such as story retellings have been studied by Bygate (2001), and such sequences of repeated task performance, across a variety of L2 genres and discourse domains, may be particularly beneficial to learners who have poor aptitude at Stage 8 in Skehan's model and who need support in proceduralizing and automatizing access to an existing L2 repertoire. Alternatively, it may be possible to develop learner training activities to enhance capacities in the areas that are weakest (see Oxford, 2003). For example, Gass and Mackey (2000) have described techniques for stimulating recall of prior episodes occurring during classroom interaction in which teacher and learner together watch video clips of interactional exchanges. Teachers' directed questions can be used to stimulate learners' recall of thoughts about problems that they may have experienced or cognitive and communicative strategies that they were using during an activity. Such questions can also be used to elicit learner awareness of what they noticed about specific aspects of language used, either in their own or an interlocutor's production, and thus to ascertain whether learners noticed the gap between their own production and a targeted recast (see Mackey et al., 2002) or a more explicit form of negative feedback. Such structured rewatchings may be important practice activities for learners who are weaker in aptitude for Stages 1 and 2 in Skehan's model and may help improve attention management during communicative interaction, leading to greater and more effective noticing and subsequent uptake of negative feedback.

Skehan's model thus has potential diagnostic value, which can be used to identify areas of needed support in processing for L2 learning. But beyond this it is not clear whether such an aptitude test could be used to match learners to more specific options in classroom activity, such as decisions about optimally learner-effective FonF techniques, or about matching learners to optimally effective task types during accuracy, fluency, and interaction practice in communicative classrooms. In fact, this lack of contextual specificity is in one way a strength of Skehan's proposal, as it enables aptitudes for L2 language processing under conditions of practice in naturalistic as well as instructed settings to be compared within the same framework. That is, Skehan takes different stages of global L2 information processing, rather than the specific conditions of instructed L2 exposure, as his operational platform for proposing aptitude components. However, considerations of the relationship of aptitude(s) to the specific conditions of instructed L2 classroom exposure and to options for pedagogic interventions are the major motivation for and the operational platform of the Aptitude Complex / Ability Differentiation framework.

Robinson's Aptitude Complex / Ability Differentiation model of aptitude

Robinson, adopting the interactionist approach of Snow (1987, 1994), identifies a number of "aptitude complexes" or combinations of cognitive abilities that are differentially related to processing under different conditions of instructional exposure to L2 input. Strengths in one or another of these complexes of abilities can be expected to be important to learning from one instructional technique or under one condition versus another. Sternberg has commented on his own attempts to learn three different languages, with very different degrees of success, saying that "my aptitude was not internal to me, but in the interaction between my abilities and the way I was being taught" (2002, p. 13). Robinson's model of L2 aptitude for instructed learning is an attempt to specify the information-processing details of this observation and to relate them to current issues in SLA theory and pedagogy. There are two closely related hypotheses that define Robinson's basic framework, which taken together make predictions about how to optimally match learners to instructional options.

THE APTITUDE COMPLEX HYPOTHESIS

The first Aptitude Complex Hypothesis (see Snow, 1987, 1994) claims that certain sets or combinations of cognitive abilities are drawn on in learning under one condition of instructional L2 exposure versus another.[2] Figure 10.2 describes instructional options and options in types of practice conditions in terms of techniques for intervening during communicative task activity to focus on form. These techniques include *recasting*, providing orally or typographically salient *input floods* to enhance forms and so facilitate incidental learning, and providing *rule explanation*. Not all learners can be expected to have equivalent aptitudes for learning from each of these options. It follows, therefore, that if the effects of communicative practice are to be optimized for learners, focus on form during task performance should be delivered by those techniques to which learners' aptitudes are best matched. The details of how aptitude complexes can be matched to these instructional options are motivated in part by findings from the laboratory and from FonF research reviewed above, as the following discussion illustrates.

Figure 10.2 describes four *aptitude complexes* (see n. 2). Aptitude complex 1, for learning from *recasting*, is a combination of the aptitude for noticing the gap (NTG) between the recast and the learner's prior utterance (see Schmidt & Frota, 1986) and memory for contingent speech (MCS). These two ability factors are argued to be important for holding the interlocutor's recast in memory while comparing it to the learner's own prior utterance (MCS) and also for noticing critical formal

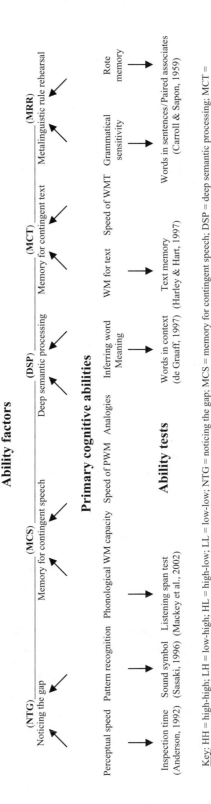

Figure 10.2 *A hierarchical model of aptitude complexes, ability factors, and cognitive abilities*

differences between the two (NTG). Figure 10.2 proposes that the two ability factors (NTG and MCS) contributing to this L2 aptitude complex are themselves combinations of domain-neutral *primary abilities*, i.e., perceptual speed and pattern recognition (in the case of noticing the gap, NTG) and phonological WM capacity and speed (in the case of memory for contingent speech, MCS). Tests of these primary abilities are nominated at the lowest level of Figure 10.2. In the case of NTG, Anderson's (1992) measure of inspection time is proposed as a measure of the ability drawn on in fast responding to perceptual stimuli, and Sasaki's (1996) measure of phonological sensitivity is proposed as a measure of the ability to identify patterns in aurally processed input. Both of the abilities measured by these tests are proposed to contribute jointly to the higher-level factor, NTG, and so strengths in both of these abilities are proposed to enable a learner to notice the gap between his or her own utterance and another person's feedback on it during oral interactive practice. This model is hierarchical in its organization of the structure of abilities, in the tradition of Cattell (1971) and Carroll (1993), while also capturing the insight of Snow (1994) that specific combinations of abilities (aptitude complexes) may be related to specific options in L2 instructional exposure.

It is important to add that the operational tests of abilities nominated in Figure 10.2 are in many cases motivated by findings reported earlier in this chapter. For example, evidence for the strong relationship between performance on the LABJ sound symbol test of phonological sensitivity and L2 classroom learning from recasts was discussed earlier (i.e., findings of Robinson & Yamaguchi, 1999, described in Table 10.4). In the case of memory for contingent speech (MCS), Mackey et al. (2002) used a listening span test of WM, which positively predicted the ability to notice and learn from recasts during L2 interaction.

The second aptitude complex in Figure 10.2, for incidental learning from oral input containing a flood of particular forms, is made up of memory for contingent speech (MCS) described above and deep semantic processing (DSP). DSP contributes the ability to process the semantic content of input containing the flooded item(s) deeply – and may be measured by tests of the primary ability to infer word meaning (as was used in de Graaff's 1997 study, described earlier) or to construct analogical representations of meaning and so to establish greater semantic coherence between aspects of the input (see e.g., discussion by Sternberg, 1985, of analogical reasoning and tests of this). The third aptitude complex, for incidental learning from floods provided in written input, differs only in that memory for contingent text (MCT) rather than speech combines with DSP. Finally, Figure 10.2 illustrates a fourth aptitude complex – aptitude for learning from a brief rule explanation, supplemented by examples written on a classroom board, and then applying the rule (while remembering and rehearsing it) in subsequent comprehension (as in input processing instruction) or production activities. This complex is made up of the ability factors memory for contingent text as well as metalinguistic rule rehearsal (MRR). MRR is proposed to be measured well by two existing subtests of aptitude: the MLAT words in sentences / GS and paired associates / rote memory subtests. Table 10.3, reporting findings for strong significant positive correlations of rule-instructed learning with performance on these subtests in Robinson (1997a), supports this claim. The findings for low, *nonsignificant* correlations of performance on these subtests and *incidental* learning in Table 10.3 also support the separation of MRR from aptitude complexes 2 and 3 for incidental learning and practice in meaning-focused conditions, as shown in Figure 10.2.

THE ABILITY DIFFERENTIATION HYPOTHESIS

The second part of this framework, the Ability Differentiation Hypothesis, is based on findings described by Deary, Egan, Gibson, Austin, Brand, and Kellaghan (1996) as well as work on language-based learning abilities and disabilities by, among others, Ganschow and Sparks (1993) and Grigorenko (2002). Work on language-based learning disabilities and developmental dyslexia has shown that some learners have extensive L1-based impairment to, for example, phonological WM capacity or specific difficulties in mastering morphosyntactic paradigms in their native language. Ganschow and Sparks (1993) further argue that such L1-based disabilities underlie poor aptitude for L2 learning. Deary et al. (1996) have also shown, in the field of general intelligence research, that when comparing adults and children or high IQ with lower IQ groups, performance on the subtests of traditional measures of intelligence (such as the Wechsler Adult Intelligence Scale) is more differentiated (i.e., there are multiple abilities and a weaker general factor or G) for adults and high IQ groups than for children and lower IQ groups. These findings suggest that patterns of strengths in abilities contributing to aptitude complexes in Figure 10.2 may also be very differentiated for some (especially older and/or higher aptitude) L2 learners, such that, for example, the noticing-the-gap ability is high while the memory-for-contingent-speech ability is low. This possibility is captured in the top left HL quadrant in aptitude complex 1 in Figure 10.2. Alternatively, strengths in both NTG and MCS may be high (HH), meaning recasting is a particularly suitable option for focusing on form for these learners. Strengths in both of these factors may also be much lower (LL), suggesting either that alternative FonF techniques are more suitable or that some remediative training in developing the abilities in question may be a necessary option. Further, the research on age-related changes in abilities that Deary et al. (1996) report additionally suggests that aptitude profiles for older learners may well be considerably more differentiated than they are for younger learners (see also Deary, 2000) and, therefore, that older learners in particular will very likely benefit from matching patterns of abilities to conditions of learning and practice, in ways consistent with the framework previously described.

In summary, the Ability Differentiation Hypothesis claims that some L2 learners may have more clearly differentiated abilities – and strengths in corresponding aptitude complexes – than other learners and further that it is particularly important to match these learners to conditions of practice which favor their strengths. This is in contrast with other learners who may have less differentiated abilities and equivalent strengths and aptitudes for learning under a variety of conditions of exposure and classroom practice.

Further comments and conclusions

In line with Snow's view of aptitude described at the beginning of this chapter, Robinson's framework describes aptitudes for learning and practice as variegated but constrained by a theory of the learning situations they operate in. Learning situations were described as implicit, explicit, and incidental, as options in FonF techniques, and as specific options in types of pedagogic tasks. The framework thus draws on the findings reported earlier from laboratory, FonF, and task-design studies to motivate a number of the claims about the primary and secondary abilities contributing to aptitude complexes.

In the cases illustrated by Figure 10.2, instructional contexts in which opportunities for practice occur are proposed as interacting with aptitudes to affect learning from exposure to L2 input. These contexts are described with reference to options in FonF techniques, such as recasting, incidental learning from oral and written input floods, and explicit rule learning. Options in such techniques are not infinite, so matching aptitudes to conditions of practice which deliver focus on form via one or another of these techniques is a manageable research program with foreseeable beneficial results for learners.

At another level, situations can also be described in terms of the specific features of task design described in Figure 10.1, contributing to the cognitive demands they impose on the learner. Most generally, Niwa's study (2000) suggests that IDs are more influential during practice and performance on L2 tasks that are more complex. This general finding is in line with much of the work of Snow and his colleagues on the relationship between abilities and academic tasks in a variety of domains (Ackerman & Ciancolo, 2002; Corno et al., 2002; Snow, Kyllonen, & Marshalek, 1984). It will also be important to chart the interaction of strengths and weaknesses in the abilities contributing to aptitudes, with specific design features of L2 tasks, such as those described in Figure 10.1. With the framework described in Figure 10.1 in mind, it is possible that IDs in the ability to switch attention between task components described by Segalowitz (2003) could be an important component of the aptitude complex for learning and performance during practice on L2 tasks, such as those that increase in complexity within the resource-dispersing single-to-dual task dimension (Robinson, 2001b; Robinson, Ting, & Urwin, 1995). This dimension is operationalized as tasks requiring only one component step (e.g., describing a route already marked on a map) compared with tasks requiring two simultaneous steps (e.g., thinking up the route while also describing it – see Robinson, 2001a, for such a study). In addition a number of measures of reasoning ability (see e.g., Stanovitch, 1999) could be adapted to assess aptitudes for performance and learning during practice on tasks along the resource-directing –/+ reasoning demands dimension of complexity. The essential principles (aptitude complexes and ability differentiation) of Robinson's framework could therefore be applied in developing measures of aptitudes for practice on tasks that increase in complexity along different resource-directing and resource-dispersing dimensions. Such research would do much to illuminate the extent to which learner perceptions of the difficulty of the task inhibit or accentuate task-based language processing and provide a basis for matching learners' patterns of abilities to those types of practice that are most beneficial for L2 learning and performance.

Notes

1. Perruchet and Vintner (2002) argue that all adult learning begins with phenomenal, aware experience and that subsequent unconscious processes operate on the representational content of phenomenal experience, with the result that all knowledge is explicit:

   The only representations people create and manipulate are those which form the momentary phenomenal experience. The main challenge is to explain why the phenomenal experience of adult people consists of perceptions and representations of the world which are generally isomorphic with the world structure, without needing recourse to a powerful cognitive unconscious. Our proposal is that this isomorphism is the end-product of a progressive organization that emerges thanks to elementary associative processes that take the conscious representations themselves as the stuff on which they operate. (p. 297)

   But adult learners differ in the eventual extent of L2 learning, so it follows that IDs in the cognitive abilities learners bring to the task of processing L2 input should be related to the extent of initial noticing, as well as to the extent of higher levels of awareness of the input (Robinson, 1995b, 1996b, 2002b, 2003a). It also follows that different patterns of abilities will likely be relatively more sensitive to or inhibited by the conditions under which input, or feedback, is presented.

2. To help make the organization of Figure 10.2 clear, consider an analogy with aptitude for sporting activities. Figure 10.2 illustrates four proposed aptitude complexes and five ability factors that contribute to these complexes. The cognitive abilities contributing to these factors are described in the third level of Figure 10.2, and the lowest level nominates tests of these abilities. Now consider archery, for example. It requires both good eyesight and a good arm. These are two ability factors that determine aptitude for archery. Eyesight can be assessed by two direct measures of physical abilities such as color discrimination and depth perception. High scores on these two measures mean that a person can be characterized as high in the abilities drawn on by the eyesight factor. A good arm can be assessed by measures of grip strength and steadiness. A person who scores well on all of these four tests of physical abilities, is high in both factors (good eyesight, good arm) and can be classified as HH (high-high) in aptitude for archery. Someone with good eyesight but a poor arm would be classified as HL (high-low), and the aptitude for archery would be average. If a person scored poorly on all of these measures, he or she would have bad eyesight and a poor arm (LL) and no aptitude for archery. But that person could well have the physical abilities needed for success in another sport that is very different, such as surfing! The important point is that, physical abilities, like the cognitive abilities described in Figure 10.2, have their effects in combinations. To learn from recasts presented during practice activities, as illustrated by the first complex, a learner needs to be able to notice the recast (NTG) *and* to remember it for long enough to be able to process it (MCS). If a learner is low in the cognitive abilities NTG and MCS draw on, another condition of exposure and another FonF technique may be better suited.

References

Ackerman, P. (2003). Aptitude complexes and trait complexes. *Educational Psychologist, 38*, 85–93.

Ackerman, P., & Ciancolo, A. (2002). Ability and task constraint determinants of complex task performance. *Journal of Experimental Psychology: Applied, 8*, 194–208.

Anderson, J. R. (1993). *Rules of the mind*. Hillsdale, NJ: Lawrence Erlbaum.

Anderson, M. (1992). *Intelligence and development: A cognitive theory*. Oxford: Blackwell.

Bialystok, E. (1994). Analysis and control in the development of second language proficiency. *Studies in Second Language Acquisition, 16*, 157–68.

Bygate, M. (2001). Effects of task repetition on the structure and control of oral language. In Bygate, M., Skehan, P., & Swain, M. (Eds.), *Researching pedagogic tasks: Second language learning, teaching and testing* (pp. 23–48). Harlow, UK: Longman.

Carroll, J. B. (1993). *Human cognitive abilities: A survey of factor-analytic studies*. New York: Cambridge University Press.

Carroll, J. B., & Sapon, S. M. (1959). *Modern Language Aptitude Test*. Washington, DC: Second Language Testing Inc.

Cattell, R. B. (1971). *Abilities: Their structure, growth and action*. Boston: Houghton Mifflin.

Cook, V. (1996). *Second language learning and language teaching.* London: Arnold.

Corno, L., Cronbach, L. J., Kupermintz, H., Lohman, D. F., Mandinach, E. B., Porteus, A. W., & Talbert, J. E. (2002). *Remaking the concept of aptitude: Extending the legacy of Richard E. Snow.* Mahwah, NJ: Lawrence Erlbaum.

Daneman, M., & Carpenter, P. A. (1980). Individual differences in working memory and reading. *Journal of Verbal Learning and Verbal Behaviour, 19,* 450–66.

Deary, I. (2000). *Looking down on human intelligence: From psychometrics to the brain.* Oxford: Oxford University Press.

Deary, I., Egan, V., Gibson, G., Austin, E., Brand, R., & Kellaghan, T. (1996). Intelligence and the differentiation hypothesis. *Intelligence, 23,* 105–32.

de Graaff, R. (1997). *Differential effects of explicit instruction on second language acquisition.* The Hague: Holland Institute of Generative Linguistics.

DeKeyser, R. M. (1995). Learning second language grammar rules: An experiment with a miniature linguistic system. *Studies in Second Language Acquisition, 17,* 379–410.

DeKeyser, R. M. (1997). Beyond explicit rule learning: Automatizing second language syntax. *Studies in Second Language Acquisition, 19,* 195–221.

DeKeyser, R. M. (2000). The robustness of critical period effects in second language acquisition. *Studies in Second Language Acquisition, 22,* 499–533.

DeKeyser, R. M. (2001). Automaticity and automatization. In P. Robinson (Ed.), *Cognition and second language instruction* (pp. 125–51). Cambridge, UK: Cambridge University Press.

DeKeyser, R. M., Salaberry, R., Robinson, P., & Harrington, M. (2002). What gets processed in processing instruction? A commentary on Bill Van Patten's "Processing instruction: An update." *Language Learning, 52,* 805–23.

Dörnyei, Z. (2002). The motivational basis of language learning tasks. In P. Robinson (Ed.), *Individual differences and instructed language learning* (pp. 137–58). Amsterdam: John Benjamins.

Dörnyei, Z. (2005). *The psychology of the language learner.* Mahwah, NJ: Lawrence Erlbaum.

Doughty, C., & Varela, E. (1998). Communicative focus on form. In C. Doughty & J. Williams (Eds.), *Focus on form in classroom second language acquisition* (pp. 114–38). New York: Cambridge University Press.

Doughty, C., & Williams, J. (1998). Pedagogical choices in focus on form. In C. Doughty & J. Williams (Eds.), *Focus on form in classroom second language acquisition* (pp. 197–262). New York: Cambridge University Press.

Ehrman, M., & Oxford, R. (1995). Cognition plus: Correlates of language learning success. *Modern Language Journal, 79,* 67–89.

Ellis, N. C. (1993). Rules and instances in foreign language learning: Interactions of explicit and implicit knowledge. *European Journal of Cognitive Psychology, 5,* 289–318.

Ellis, R. (Ed.). (2005). *Planning and task performance in a second language.* Amsterdam: John Benjamins.

Fleishman, E. A. & Quaintance, M. K. (1984). *Taxonomies of human performance: The description of human tasks.* New York: Academic Press.

Ganschow, L., & Sparks, R. L. (1993). "Foreign" language learning disabilities: issues, research, and teaching implications. In S. A. Vogel & P. B. Adelman (Eds.), *Success for college students with learning disabilities* (pp. 282–317). New York: Springer-Verlag.

Gass, S. M., & Mackey, A. (2000). *Stimulated recall methodology in second language research.* Mahwah, NJ: Lawrence Erlbaum.

Gilabert, R. (2004). *Task complexity and L2 oral narrative production.* Unpublished doctoral dissertation, Department of Applied Linguistics, University of Barcelona, Spain.

Grigorenko, E. L. (2002). Language-based learning disabilities. In P. Robinson (Ed.), *Individual differences and instructed language learning* (pp. 95–113). Amsterdam: John Benjamins.

Grigorenko, E. L., Sternberg, R. J., & Ehrman, M. (2000). A theory-based approach to the measurement of foreign language aptitude: The CANAL-F theory and test. *Modern Language Journal, 84,* 390–405.

Hardy, I., & Moore, J. (2004). Foreign language students' conversational negotiations in different task environments. *Applied Linguistics, 25,* 340–70.

Harley, B., & Hart, D. (1997). Language aptitude and second language proficiency in classroom learners of different starting ages. *Studies in Second Language Acquisition, 19,* 379–400.

Hulstijn, J. H. (1989). Implicit and incidental language learning: Experiments in the processing of natural and partly artificial input. In H. Dechert & M. Raupach (Eds.), *Interlingual processing* (pp. 49–73). Tubingen: Gunter Narr.

Hulstijn, J. H. & DeKeyser, R. M. (Eds.). (1997). Second language acquisition research in the laboratory: Special issue. *Studies in Second Language Acquisition, 19,* 2.

Iwashita, N., McNamara, T., & Elder, C. (2001). Can we predict task difficulty in an oral proficiency test? Exploring the potential of an information processing approach to task design. *Language Learning, 51,* 401–36.

Krashen, S. D. (1982). *Principles and practice in second language acquisition.* Oxford: Pergamon.

Kuiken, F., Mos, M., & Vedder, I. (2005). Cognitive task complexity and second language writing performance. In S. Foster-Cohen, M. P. Garcia-Mayo and J. Cenoz (Eds.), *Eurosla yearbook. Vol. 5* (pp. 195–222). Amsterdam: John Benjamins.

Kyllonen, P. C., & Lajoie, S. (2003). Reassessing aptitude: Introduction to a special issue on honor of Richard E. Snow. *Educational Psychologist, 38,* 79–83.

Leeman, J., Arteagoitia, I., Fridman, B., & Doughty, C. (1995). Integrating attention to form with meaning: Focus on form in content-based Spanish instruction. In R. Schmidt (Ed.), *Attention and awareness in foreign language learning* (pp. 217–58). Honolulu, HI: University of Hawaii Press.

Logan, G. D. (1988). Toward an instance theory of automatization. *Psychological Review, 95,* 492–527.

Logan, G. D. (2004). Working memory, task switching and executive control in the task span procedure. *Journal of Experimental Psychology: General, 133,* 218–36.

MacIntyre, P. (2002). Motivation, anxiety and emotion in second language acquisition. In P. Robinson (Ed.), *Individual differences and instructed language learning* (pp. 45–64). Amsterdam: John Benjamins.

MacIntyre, P., & Gardner, R. (1994). The subtle effects of language anxiety on cognitive processing in the second language. *Language Learning, 44,* 283–305.

Mackey, A. (1999). Input, interaction, and second language development: An empirical study of question formation in ESL. *Studies in Second Language Acquisition, 21,* 557–87.

Mackey, A., Philp. J., Egi, T., Fujii, A., & Tatsumi, T. (2002). Individual differences in working memory, noticing of interactional feedback and L2 development. In P. Robinson (Ed.), *Individual differences and instructed language learning* (pp. 181–210). Amsterdam: John Benjamins.

MacWhinney, B. (2001). The competition model: The input, the context, and the brain. In P. Robinson (Ed.), *Cognition and second language instruction* (pp. 69–90). Cambridge, UK: Cambridge University Press.

Matthews, G., & Ziedner, M. (2004). Traits, states and a trilogy of mind: An adaptive perspective on intellectual functioning. In D. Y. Dai & R. J. Sternberg (Eds.), *Motivation, emotion and cognition: Integrative perspectives on intellectual functioning and development* (pp. 143–74). Mahwah, NJ: Lawrence Erlbaum.

Niwa, Y. (2000). *Reasoning demands of L2 tasks and L2 narrative production: Effects of individual differences in working memory, intelligence and aptitude.* Unpublished master's dissertation, Department of English, Aoyama Gakuin University, Japan.

Oxford, R. (Ed.). (2003). Special issue: Language learning styles and strategies. *International Review of Applied Linguistics, 41* (4).

Perruchet, P., & Vintner, A. (2002). The self-organizing consciousness. *Behavioral and Brain Sciences, 25,* 297–388.

Pienemann, M. (1998). *Language processing and second language development.* Amsterdam: John Benjamins.

Pimsleur, P. (1966). *Pimsleur language aptitude battery (PLAB).* Washington, DC: Second Language Testing Inc.

Rahimpour, M. (1999). Task complexity and variation in interlanguage. In N. O. Jungheim & P. Robinson (Eds.), *Pragmatics and pedagogy: Proceedings of the 3rd Pacific Second Language Research Forum, Vol. 2* (pp. 115–34). Tokyo: PacSLRF.

Ranta, L. (2002). The role of learners' analytic abilities in the communicative classroom. In P. Robinson (Ed.), *Individual differences and instructed language learning* (pp. 159–80). Amsterdam: John Benjamins.

Reber, A. S. (1993). *Implicit learning and tacit knowledge: An essay on the cognitive unconscious.* Oxford: Clarendon Press.

Robinson, P. (1995a). Task complexity and second language narrative discourse. *Language Learning, 45,* 99–140.

Robinson, P. (1995b). Attention, memory and the "noticing" hypothesis. *Language Learning, 45,* 283–331.

Robinson, P. (1995c). Aptitude, awareness and the fundamental similarity of implicit and explicit second language learning. In R. Schmidt (Ed.), *Attention and awareness in foreign language learning* (pp. 303–58). Honolulu, HI: University of Hawaii Press.

Robinson, P. (1996a). Learning simple and complex second language rules under implicit, incidental, rule-search and instructed conditions. *Studies in Second Language Acquisition, 18*, 27–67.

Robinson, P. (1996b). *Consciousness, rules and instructed second language acquisition*. New York: Lang.

Robinson, P. (Ed.). (1996c). *Task complexity and second language syllabus design: Data-based studies and speculations*. University of Queensland Working Papers in Language and Linguistics (Special issue).

Robinson, P. (1997a). Individual differences and the fundamental similarity of implicit and explicit adult second language learning. *Language Learning, 47*, 45–99.

Robinson, P. (1997b). Generalizability and automaticity of second language learning under implicit, incidental, enhanced and rule-search conditions. *Studies in Second Language Acquisition, 19*, 223–47.

Robinson, P. (1999). Second language classroom research in Japan: Issues, studies, and prospects. In T. Fujimura, Y. Kato, & R. Smith (Eds.), *Proceedings of the 10th IUJ conference on second language research* (pp. 93–116). Tokyo: International University of Japan.

Robinson, P. (2001a). Task complexity, task difficulty, and task production: Exploring interactions in a componential framework. *Applied Linguistics, 22*, 27–57.

Robinson, P. (2001b). Task complexity, cognitive resources, and syllabus design: A triadic framework for investigating task influences on SLA. In P. Robinson (Ed.), *Cognition and second language instruction* (pp. 287–318). Cambridge, UK: Cambridge University Press.

Robinson, P. (2001c). Individual differences, cognitive abilities, aptitude complexes, and learning conditions in SLA. *Second Language Research, 17*, 368–92.

Robinson, P. (Ed.). (2001d). *Cognition and second language instruction*. Cambridge, UK: Cambridge University Press.

Robinson, P. (2002a). Learning conditions, aptitude complexes and SLA: A framework for research and pedagogy. In P. Robinson (Ed.), *Individual differences and instructed language learning* (pp. 113–33). Amsterdam: John Benjamins.

Robinson, P. (2002b). Individual differences in intelligence, aptitude and working memory during adult incidental second language learning: A replication and extension of Reber, Walkenfeld, and Hernstadt (1991). In P. Robinson (Ed.), *Individual differences and instructed language learning* (pp. 211–66). Amsterdam: John Benjamins.

Robinson, P. (Ed.). (2002c). *Individual differences and instructed language learning*. Amsterdam: John Benjamins.

Robinson, P. (2003a). Attention and memory during SLA. In C. J. Doughty & M. H. Long (Eds.), *Handbook of second language acquisition* (pp. 631–78). Oxford: Blackwell.

Robinson, P. (2003b). The Cognition Hypothesis, task design and adult task-based language learning. *Second Language Studies, 21*(2), 45–107.

Robinson, P. (2004). Rules and similarity processes in Artificial Grammar and natural second language learning: What is the "default"? *Behavioral and Brain Sciences, 28*, 33–34.

Robinson, P. (2005a). Aptitude and second language acquisition. *Annual Review of Applied Linguistics, 25*, 46–73.

Robinson, P. (2005b). Cognitive complexity and task sequencing: A review of studies in a Componential Framework for second language task design. *International Review of Applied Linguistics in Language Teaching, 43*, 1–32.

Robinson, P. (2005c). Cognitive abilities, chunk-strength and frequency effects in implicit Artificial Grammar and incidental L2 learning: Replications of Reber, Walkenfeld, and Hernstadt (1991) and Knowlton and Squire (1996) and their relevance for SLA. *Studies in Second Language Acquisition, 27*, 235–68.

Robinson, P. (in press). Criteria for classifying and sequencing pedagogic tasks. In M. P. García-Mayo (Ed.), *Investigating tasks in formal language settings*. Clevedon, UK: Multilingual Matters.

Robinson, P., & Ha, M. (1993). Instance theory and second language rule learning under explicit conditions. *Studies in Second Language Acquisition, 15*, 413–38.

Robinson, P., Ting, S.C-C., & Urwin, J. (1995). Investigating second language task complexity. *RELC Journal, 26*, 62–79.

Robinson, P., & Yamaguchi, Y. (1999). *Aptitude, task feedback and generalizability of focus on form: A classroom study*. Paper presented at the 12th AILA world congress, Waseda University, Tokyo.

Sasaki, M. (1996). *Second language proficiency, foreign language aptitude, and intelligence*. New York: Lang.

Schmidt, R. (1990). The role of consciousness in second language learning. *Applied Linguistics, 11*, 127–58.

Schmidt, R. (2001). Attention. In P. Robinson (Ed.), *Cognition and second language instruction* (pp. 1–32). Cambridge, UK: Cambridge University Press.

Schmidt, R., & Frota, S. (1986). Developing basic conversational ability in a second language: A case study of an adult learner of Portuguese. In R. Day (Ed.), *Talking to learn: Conversation in second language learning* (pp. 237–322). Rowley, MA: Newbury House.

Segalowitz, N. (2003). Automaticity and second language acquisition. In C. J. Doughty & M. H. Long (Eds.), *Handbook of second language acquisition* (pp. 382–408). Oxford: Blackwell.

Shavelson, R. J., & Roeser, R. W. (Eds.). (2002). A multidimensional approach to achievement validation: Special Issue. *Educational Assessment, 8*, 2.

Sick, J., & Irie, K. (2000). The Lunic Language Marathon: A new language aptitude instrument for Japanese foreign language learners. In S. Cornwell & P. Robinson (Eds.), *Individual differences in foreign language learning: Effects of aptitude, intelligence and motivation* (pp. 173–86). Tokyo: Aoyama Gakuin University.

Skehan, P. (1998). *A cognitive approach to language learning*. Oxford: Oxford University Press.

Skehan, P. (2002). Theorizing and updating aptitude. In P. Robinson (Ed.), *Individual differences and instructed language learning* (pp. 69–94). Amsterdam: John Benjamins.

Skehan, P., & Foster, P. (2001). Cognition and tasks. In P. Robinson (Ed.), *Cognition and second language instruction* (pp. 183–205). Cambridge, UK: Cambridge University Press.

Snow, R. E. (1987). Aptitude complexes. In R. E. Snow & M. J. Farr (Eds.), *Aptitude, learning and instruction, Vol. 3: Conative and affective process analysis* (pp. 11–34). Hillsdale, NJ: Lawrence Erlbaum.

Snow, R. E. (1994). Abilities in academic tasks. In R. J. Sternberg & R. K. Wagner (Eds.), *Mind in context: Interactionist perspectives on human intelligence* (pp. 3–37). New York: Cambridge University Press.

Snow, R. E., & Farr, M. J. (Eds.). (1987). *Aptitude, learning and instruction. Vol. 3: Conative and affective process analysis*. Hillsdale, NJ: Lawrence Erlbaum.

Snow, R. E., Kyllonen, P. C., & Marshalek, B. (1984). The topography of ability and learning correlations. In R. J. Sternberg (Ed.), *Advances in the psychology of human intelligence* (pp. 47–103). Hillsdale, NJ: Lawrence Erlbaum.

Stanovitch, K. E. (1999). *Who is rational? Studies of individual differences in reasoning*. Mahwah, NJ: Lawrence Erlbaum.

Sternberg, R. J. (1985). *Beyond IQ: A triarchic theory of human intelligence*. New York: Cambridge University Press.

Sternberg, R. J. (2002). The theory of successful intelligence and its implications for language aptitude testing. In P. Robinson (Ed.), *Individual differences and instructed language learning* (pp. 13–44). Amsterdam: John Benjamins.

Sternberg, R. J., & Grigorenko, E. L. (2000). *Dynamic testing: The nature and measurement of learning potential*. New York: Cambridge University Press.

Sternberg, R. J., & Wagner, R. K. (Eds.). (1994). *Mind in context: Interactionist perspectives on human intelligence*. New York: Cambridge University Press.

Tomlin, R., & Villa, V. (1994). Attention in cognitive science and second language acquisition. *Studies in Second Language Acquisition, 15*, 183–203.

VanPatten, B. (Ed.). (2004). *Processing instruction: Theory, research and commentary*. Mahwah, NJ: Lawrence Erlbaum.

White, J. (1998). Getting the learners' attention: A typographical input enhancement study. In C. Doughty & J. Williams (Eds.), *Focus on form in classroom second language acquisition* (pp. 85–113). Cambridge, UK: Cambridge University Press.

Williams, J. N. (1999). Memory, attention, and inductive learning. *Studies in Second Language Acquisition, 21*, 1–48.

Conclusion: The future of practice

Robert M. DeKeyser

Agreed-on goals in language teaching

The goals of language learning and teaching in general and of practice in particular are manifold. In fact, they are characterized by such a complex array of partially overlapping distinctions that few people ever reflect on this whole array, focusing instead on the distinctions that are most relevant to their own interests or experiences. If practice is to be a set of means to reach a set of goals, however, it is important that we stop and reflect on those goals before continuing.

Even the layperson who has barely set foot in a second language classroom will recognize the distinctions between oral and written language and between the ability to produce and to comprehend. Combining these two distinctions, we get the traditional division among the four skills: listening, speaking, reading, and writing. It is clear for all to see that even in one's native language, and a fortiori in a second language, different people have different levels of need for and proficiency in these four skills. Many people do not aspire to be good writers, even in their L1, and some, even in these days of instant global communication, care more about their ability to understand written text in a second language than about their ability to speak that language because their careers as students or professionals require massive L2 reading but hardly any spoken interaction.

Applied linguists typically make at least three more important distinctions. One is shared with experienced language learners: accuracy, fluency, and complexity can be seriously out of sync in a second language, sometimes simply because they require somewhat different abilities or learning opportunities, but often also because they are not seen as equally important goals. Learners and teachers alike may stress the ability to speak fluently rather than correctly or may experience the need for a large vocabulary rather than the need to retrieve it actively and quickly. A somewhat less obvious distinction concerns rule use versus formulaic language use. One cannot tell easily from listening to an L2 speaker whether what is being uttered is the result of rule application or formula use, and even the speaker may not always know. Certainly, nobody starts learning a language with the goal of being a formulaic speaker or a rule-based speaker. Which of the two goals is realistic for certain aspects of the language at a certain point in the learning process, however, is a relevant question, and the answer to that question will determine what may be the best way to practice the aspects of language in question for that learner at that time.

Two other distinctions are more familiar to psychologists than to applied linguists but are seen more and more commonly in our field: implicit versus explicit and declarative versus procedural (see the introductory chapter to this volume). While explicit knowledge is not the ultimate goal for L2 learners, with the possible exception of future language professionals, it may be an intermediate goal on the road to spontaneous use for at least some learners, depending on one's views on the interface issue (see e.g., Carroll 2001, 2002; DeKeyser, 1998, 2001, 2003; N. Ellis, 2005; Hulstijn, 2002; Muranoi, this volume; Leow, this volume) and on individual differences such as age and aptitude (see e.g., DeKeyser, 2000; Muñoz, this volume; Robinson, this volume). Note, on the other hand, that implicit knowledge in the sense of the absence of awareness of structure can never be a goal in itself. The real goal is fast, accurate, spontaneous, effortless use of knowledge, which is better described as automatic than implicit. While these two concepts tend to go together, there certainly is a difference (see the introductory chapter to this volume). Even at the endpoint of the acquisition process, highly automatized knowledge may remain largely accessible to awareness, while some implicit knowledge may be used only very hesitantly, haltingly, or haphazardly.

In terms of goals to be achieved by L2 practice activities, therefore, the declarative/procedural or the more detailed declarative/proceduralized/automatized distinctions are more useful. It is clear that a high degree of automaticity, however hard it may be to achieve, is the ultimate goal for most learners, both because of its impact on the quality of linguistic output and because of how it frees up resources for processing message content instead of language (cf. Segalowitz, 2003, p. 402). Even more clearly, procedural, not declarative, knowledge is the ultimate goal. A large literature exists, however, showing how skills in many domains, including perceptual, motor, and cognitive skills, can develop from declarative to procedural to automatized knowledge through practice. In contrast, empirical research on this point in applied linguistics is very scant, but from what is available it appears that at least some aspects of language can be learned (best) in this way by at least some learners (see esp. DeKeyser, 1997). Here again, therefore, an important question when selecting practice activities is whether declarative knowledge or incipient proceduralization may be the best intermediate goal for a given structure and a given learner at a given point in time, and what that implies for selecting the most effective form of practice.

Agreed-on means: The praxis of practice

While goals may be relatively easy to agree on, the question of means is far more complicated, for at least three reasons. First, there is the conceptual confusion about what is meant with practice: the narrow sense of repeated, focused exercises to optimize retrieval of what one has learned, the slightly wider sense of any kind of L2 use that will encourage expansion and fine-tuning of existing knowledge, or the widest sense of any kind of contact with the L2 that will improve knowledge of it at some level (see the introductory chapter to this volume). Second, there are the broader theoretical disagreements in the field about whether language learning, in particular in adults, can or should be implicit or explicit (see esp. DeKeyser, 2003; Doughty, 2003; N. Ellis, 2002, 2005), whether interface between explicit and implicit knowledge is possible, to what extent practice should be form-focused (see esp. Doughty & Williams, 1998; Long & Robinson, 1998), and even whether competence should be distinguished from performance in L2 learners (see esp. Carroll, 1999; Truscott & Sharwood Smith, 2004). Third, there is the tendency to overgeneralize from research on the acquisition of certain elements of a certain language by certain kinds of learners without taking into account the big differences in psycholinguistic difficulty that characterize the acquisition of vocabulary versus grammar versus formulas, or of rules versus items versus prototypes. These different learning targets presumably require different learning activities, in interaction with the special challenges posed by children versus adolescents versus adults (see Muñoz, this volume), and by learners with very different aptitude profiles (see Robinson, this volume). This section will deal with relatively well-agreed-upon means for achieving the goals listed in the previous section; the next section will tackle some of the more controversial issues.

Improving declarative knowledge is not often thought of as practice, but various kinds of practice in a broad sense can be seen as doing just that. This applies not only to repeatedly going over a list of vocabulary items to make sure one has memorized them correctly, for instance, but also to the variety of consciousness-raising activities discussed in Leow (this volume). The purpose of the crossword puzzles and other activities discussed by Leow in the attention-focusing strand is clearly to make grammatical patterns salient in order to let students induce a rule representation at some level. These rules, whether full-fledged metalinguistic statements or incipient hunches about the nature of some patterns, are clearly declarative in nature and can be seen as a first stage in the skill acquisition process. Those who do not believe in such an approach to second language learning would simply see them as triggers to jump-start a process of implicit acquisition.

In most cases, of course, learners will want to be able to use rules, not just know them, and not just after leaving school but in their language classes. In other words, they want to learn the behavior that consists of applying certain rules to specific sentences, whether it be in comprehension or in production. Obviously, this is a necessary first step on the way to fluency. In skill acquisition theory it is called the proceduralization stage. What is fortunate about proceduralization is that it does not have to take much time. Being required to use a rule a limited number of times to process a set of sentences is all it takes. The learning curves in DeKeyser (1997), for instance, show that a dozen or so relevant sentences were enough to make learners adopt the right behavior, i.e., applying their new morphological knowledge to understand or produce a sentence correctly (but of course this is still a long way from fully automatizing it). More generally, Anderson, Bothell, Byrne, Douglass, Lebiere, and Qin say, "According to this analysis, during the warm-up trials, which are typically thrown away in an experiment, the participant is converting from a declarative representation and a slow interpretation of the task to a smooth, rapid procedural execution of the task" (2004, p. 1046).

What is unfortunate about proceduralization is that being required to use a rule to process a sentence is not as obvious as it may seem. Just like the experimenter in the lab, the teacher in the classroom cannot check what rules, if any, are going through the learner's mind during what appears to be a rule application. Is it the expected rule, a rule that is much narrower or even only vaguely similar but which happens to yield the same result within the narrow confines of the experimental block or the classroom exercise, or not a rule at all but rather a largely formulaic use that will do for a set of very similar stimuli? This problem is at the very core of the question of what constitutes good classroom practice. If the behavior practiced in the classroom exercise does not consist of using the target language rule or something *very* close to it, then it may be of little use. The problem, however, is that the poor results of exercises that do not stimulate use of the right rule often do not show up till after the student has left the classroom. In a study abroad context, for instance, it is very common to see students misuse or completely fail to use a rule, which they learned *and* practiced intensively in their first year of study, well enough to get perfect scores on the corresponding classroom tests. Such observations are often seen as rather trivial examples of how classroom knowledge does not easily transfer to the real world, but something much more fundamental from the point of view of skill acquisition theory is going on here. What kind of rule knowledge did students ever have, regardless of transfer to the real world? Was it the correct rule at the declarative level or only a prototypical example? Was it the correct rule at the procedural level or only a narrow subcategory of examples processed to practice the rule? In the latter case, it is likely that the procedural rule is too narrow in scope, regardless of how the declarative knowledge may be represented in the same learner's mind, and that, therefore, even in this obvious sense of rule content processed, the classroom exercise did not constitute "transfer-appropriate processing" (see the introductory chapter to this volume), let alone in the sense of the exact information-processing conditions under which it was practiced. While such narrow proceduralization may dramatically speed up the initial learning process (for experimental evidence see Rothkopf & Dashen, 1995), it leads to poor transfer (for evidence on this point, see Allen & Brooks, 1991), and it is one of the many examples of how practice that appears best initially leads to worse results in terms of transfer or delayed testing (see Schmidt & Bjork, 1992, for other examples of this).

A good example of how rules are too narrow in scope can often be observed in English-speaking learners of Spanish trying to express the equivalent of the English verb *like* in their L2. They may know perfectly well that "I like coffee" is "me gusta el café" and maybe even that "she likes sweets" is "le gustan los dulces," which seems to indicate they have learned the different argument structure of the Spanish verb, in the sense that what is the grammatical subject in English is the indirect object in Spanish and what is the direct object in English is the subject in Spanish, but as soon as a slightly more complex proposition needs to be expressed, such as "this is the brand of coffee that I like" or "this is the student who doesn't like sweets," learners are likely to fall back on English case assignment. This shows that they don't really have an abstract representation of the valency structure but rather some sort of a prototype that works well enough for most simple sentences – assuming they *do* all manage to get all of those correct and do not get stuck at an even more narrow rule or prototype, allowing them only to produce a correct equivalent for "I like" but not for "they like," for instance, due to the high frequency of practice sentences in the first person for this verb, both in the classroom and the real world. These are not instances of lack of automatization; the learner simply does not have the production rules to be automatized. Nor is this a matter of lack of declarative knowledge that can simply be resolved with a longer lecture on differences in valency structure between English and Spanish for certain verbs. The core of the problem is lack of opportunity for proceduralization: lack of sufficiently challenging, that is, sufficiently different and complex example sentences to be processed for practice while the supporting rule knowledge is still highly active in declarative memory.

Moreover, while proceduralization may be fast, the resulting knowledge is not going to be very robust if the production rules are hardly ever used after that stage, let alone automatized. Production rule application is always a messy probabilistic business: "The key idea is that at any point in time multiple production rules might apply, but because of the seriality in production rule execution, only one can be selected, and this is the one with the highest utility. Production rule utilities are noisy, continuously varying quantities just like declarative activations and play a similar role in production selection as activations play in chunk selection" (Anderson et al., 2004, p. 1044). A very weak and/or incomplete rule will only make its selection at the right moment even less likely. On this point the classroom fails even more often from the point of view of what students need once they leave the classroom. By the time they go abroad for a semester, typically at the end of their second year of college language study, they have largely forgotten their partially proceduralized rule knowledge from the first year instead of reinforced it, let alone partially automatized it (see DeKeyser, this volume).

The last stage in skill acquisition, automatization, is the most problematic of all in the classroom context, of course. When one compares the thousands of hours of deliberate practice accumulated by highly skilled musicians as documented in Ericsson, Krampe, and Tesch-Römer (1993), or the tens of thousands of hours claimed to be necessary for the slow establishment of form-function mappings in language acquisition by N. Ellis (2002, p. 175) with the amount of accumulated practice second language learners get in school or even in a semester abroad program, then second language practice may look like a rather quixotic enterprise. That is a typical case, however, of seeing the glass as half empty rather than half full. If musicians, chess players, or athletes are not ready to perform in an international competition after taking a couple of courses or going to a summer camp but manage to draw on these early learning experiences as stepping stones towards their ultimate goal, thousands of hours of practice later, then why can't we see L2 practice in the classroom in the same way – as a necessary but far from sufficient condition for the development of second language skills? Proceduralization with minimal automatization is not enough to perform at the highest levels, but it is a necessary step and one that the classroom can facilitate much better than any other environment.

All of this does *not* mean, of course, that different structures should be practiced one by one, from declarative to procedural to automatic, before going on to the next one on the list. Good practice needs to involve real operating conditions as soon as possible, which means comprehending and expressing real thoughts, and this necessarily involves a variety of structures, some of which will be much further along the declarative-procedural-automatic path than others. That means that the teacher and/or learner cannot expect the same level of accuracy and fluency for each of these structures at any point in time, certainly not if complexity is also a goal. While one can argue about exactly how important these three aspects of skill are for certain types of learners – and for certain elements of the language – it is clear that fostering all three to some extent will be the goal for most learners and most structures. As all three are desirable, the question becomes how practice can foster all three, if not at the same time, at least at some point. Research on the effect of tasks and task conditions by a variety of researchers has taught us that different degrees of briefing, planning, time pressure, feedback, repetition, and debriefing have a clear impact on the degree of accuracy, fluency, and complexity that one can expect in the learner's performance and that these task conditions can favor or disfavor one or more of the three dimensions (for reviews, see Muranoi, this volume, Robinson, 2005; Skehan & Foster, 2001). It is important to keep in mind, however, that, while performance on these three dimensions may be correlated negatively across task conditions, it tends to correlate positively across individuals; i.e., those individuals who are more fluent are also more accurate. This area of research has always used short-term performance measures. Taking into account the multiple studies documenting a trade-off between short-term and long-term performance in various domains outside of language learning (see esp. Schmidt & Bjork, 1992), it would be unwise to read too much into these studies about what they imply about eventual performance. The amount of literature is actually rather limited to allow drawing conclusions even about immediate uptake, given the somewhat inconsistent findings, the small numbers of subjects in most studies, and the usual problems of generalizability across structures and learners. We will return to this issue in the next section(s).

The question of how to pursue the complementary goals of fluent rule use versus fluent use of chunks is easier to answer, at least in principle. In both cases, large amounts of practice are required, i.e., many opportunities to use the rule or chunk in question: but of course the nature of the practice will be different. In the case of rule use, what is needed is repeated rule retrieval under increasingly demanding task conditions after initial proceduralization. In the case of chunk use, ample short-term recycling of the same sentences with minimal change is required. Gatbonton and Segalowitz (1988) provide some examples of communicative exercises that naturally lead to such recycling. Beyond these two basic forms of practice, however, the curriculum needs to provide opportunities for learners to change their knowledge representations from lexical to syntactic and vice versa. Given that a combination of both types of knowledge is needed to ensure both fast and creative language use, the learner needs what Skehan (1998) calls a "cyclical syllabus" on this point, with opportunities to turn initial formula knowledge (acquired under conditions of meaning primacy and communicative pressure) into rule knowledge with a wider scope and frequently produced strings of words into chunks that can be retrieved as a whole for faster, more errorless production. As

R. Ellis points out, production practice plays an important role in both processes:

Production, then, may constitute the mechanism that connects the learner's dual systems, enabling movement to occur from the memory-based to the rule-based system and vice-versa. If this interpretation is correct, learners may not be so reliant on input as has been generally assumed in SLA. They may be able to utilize their own internal resources, via using them in production, to both construct and complexify their interlanguages. Such an account affords an explanation of what Swain might have meant when she talked about output helping learners to stretch their interlanguages. (2003, p. 115)

This brings us to the importance of production versus comprehension. Both are obvious goals for almost all learners, but that does not necessarily imply that both need to be practiced. In fact, the profession has seen a shift from almost equating practice with production practice (as in structural drills) to strongly questioning the value of production practice (R. Ellis, 1992, 1994; Krashen, 1982; VanPatten & Cadierno, 1993). In recent years, though, a middle position has clearly emerged. On the one hand, both theoretical psycholinguistic research by MacWhinney and associates (see esp. MacWhinney, 1997) and more applied research on second language learning in the classroom by VanPatten and associates (see esp. VanPatten, 2004a) have convinced researchers and practitioners alike of the importance of practicing form-meaning links in comprehension in order to counteract the tendency to pay selective attention to different morphosyntactic cues depending on one's L1 and universal tendencies rather than on the grammar of L2. On the other hand, both theoretical and empirical arguments from both skill acquisition theory (esp. DeKeyser, 2001; Singley & Anderson, 1989) and second language acquisition research (esp. DeKeyser, 1997; Izumi, 2002; Shehadeh, 1999, 2002; Swain 1985; Swain & Lapkin, 1995) have confirmed the importance of practice in production, if production ability is the goal, but even for stretching IL competence more generally. Muranoi (this volume) summarizes the various benefits of production practice (besides the obvious improvement of fluency, he lists noticing new features, reflecting on structure, formulating hypotheses, and testing hypotheses; cf. Swain, 1985). And VanPatten (2004b) now recognizes at least two benefits: not just increasing fluency in production, but also stimulating noticing.

The question is not so much whether comprehension and production skills both have to be practiced but what constitutes good comprehension practice and good production practice and how there can be cross-fertilization between the two. DeKeyser (1998) and Wong (2004), coming from very different angles – skill acquisition theory for the former and processing instruction for the latter – make quite similar statements on this point; the former about production practice, the latter about comprehension practice.

Drills make sense only if they are defined in terms of *behaviors* to be drilled, but the so-called mechanical drills are defined in terms of *structures*, not behaviors. Declarative knowledge of these structures is useful for the development of procedural knowledge, but only if it is kept in working memory during the actual behaviors to be automatized. . . . The behavior actually engaged in by students in most mechanical drills is not even a psycholinguistic behavior in the sense of linking form with meaning. (DeKeyser, 1998, p. 54)

Creating activities without first identifying a processing strategy is like a doctor passing out medication without knowing what is wrong with the patient. (Wong, 2004, p. 61)

Both agree, in other words, that good practice consists of activities that make students process form-meaning links.

From the perspective of skill acquisition theory, processing these links in comprehension and production are very different things, requiring different kinds of procedural knowledge, i.e., different sets of production rules (note that production here has nothing to do with production in the psycholinguistic sense). This does not mean, however, that practice activities for one skill cannot contribute indirectly to development of the other. Again, skill acquisition theory and the theory of processing instruction have more in common than it may seem at first. Both insist on the importance of explicit/declarative knowledge of structure as the basis for developing procedural knowledge/processing strategies (see esp. DeKeyser, 1998, 2001; VanPatten, 2002a; Wong, 2004), and this declarative knowledge of structure can be reinforced or even transformed in the process of proceduralization/processing instruction, thus improving the declarative basis for the opposite skill (cf. Singley & Anderson, 1989). It is even conceivable that in many cases the advantage of processing instruction over traditional instruction, as documented in a number of studies (for summaries see esp. VanPatten 2002a, 2004b), is largely due to the depth of processing of the form-meaning link at a merely representational (declarative) level fostered by the activities typical of processing instruction. Conversely, production practice can lead to noticing and hence to declarative knowledge, as recognized by Swain, VanPatten, Muranoi, and others. In other words, "the output component represents more than the product of language knowledge; it is an active part of the entire learning process" (Gass, 1997, p. 27).

It is important, furthermore, not to see this development of skills through practice in a vacuum. Practicing production and comprehension of specific form-meaning links does not have to mean language lab drills. Ortega (this volume), for instance, makes it clear that, even in a foreign language teaching context, production practice can be made communicative and interesting, not just meaningful, in a variety of ways while still ensuring that the exercise be competence-expanding by manipulating various parameters, such as planning, rehearsing/recycling, or gradually increasing the stakes, to name just a few. Teachers have ever more technology at their disposal to enhance the possibilities of the classroom on this point, i.e., to integrate true communication with systematic practice rather than to disconnect practice from communication as the old-fashioned language lab used to do. Chatrooms, e-mail, and electronic journals, for instance, are a means to motivate students to interact with native speakers of the L2 (see Ortega, this volume), while providing a good context for proceduralizing second language knowledge. Because the medium is written but there is a certain amount of time pressure, electronic chatting functions as a slowed-down form of speaking rather than as writing, and this is exactly what is needed for proceduralization: performance of the target task at slow speed, allowing the learner to draw on declarative knowledge (for empirical evidence on this point, see Payne & Whitney, 2002). Increasing time pressure from journals to e-mail to chatrooms, or increasing opportunities for monitoring from chatrooms to e-mail to journals can provide the teacher with a natural task sequencing for increasing fluency or increasing accuracy. All of this can be done in a context that, rather than being disconnected from real life, makes L2 knowledge and technology go hand in hand as tools to facilitate the kind of communication that comes naturally to young people in many parts of the globe. From an affective point of view, this use of technology is one aspect of what Van den Branden (this volume) calls providing a safe environment, in the sense that anxiety levels are held down, confidence is boosted, and ample opportunities are available for experimenting with the target language and negotiating meaning.

On the other hand, of course, such open-ended and relatively unsupervised practice opportunities always raise the specter of unacceptable levels of accuracy. Teachers cannot monitor such high volume of communication in detail, and many errors will go uncorrected. While that may be true, the fact that there is real communication going on, and with a native speaker, will provide an incentive for "comprehensible output" (Swain, 1985), i.e., for going beyond the classroom dialect that can become the norm, especially in immersion situations (see Ranta & Lyster, this volume).

This brings us to a more general consideration of the role of feedback in practice. While a respectable amount of literature on feedback has started to accumulate (for reviews see Leeman, 2003, this volume; Nicholas, Lightbown, & Spada, 2001; Russell & Spada, 2006), most of that research looks at feedback in a more or less decontextualized fashion, without taking into account how provision of or kind of feedback interacts with the individual learner's stage of skill acquisition for a specific element of L2. While some researchers have taken a step in this direction by gauging success of feedback as a function of the learner's readiness for specific structures (e.g., Mackey & Philp, 1998), this is still very different from assessing the learner's readiness in terms of stage of skill acquisition. Yet, the importance of the latter is not to be underestimated for error correction. Researchers such as Johnson (1996), Larsen-Freeman (2003), Lyster (2004), and Leeman (this volume) are among the few who do not just conceive of error correction as a way to improve competence but more directly as a way of improving performance. Improved performance is a sign of improved skill, even though not necessarily a sign of improved explicit knowledge/declarative knowledge/linguistic competence. Lyster (2004; see also Ranta & Lyster, this volume) points out, for instance, that prompts can be a very effective feedback technique because they provide students with opportunities to practice and thereby proceduralize rule-based knowledge of emerging target forms. Clearly, the same level of success could not be expected for this technique with students who do not have the relevant declarative knowledge yet or who are already far along in the automatization process. Much remains to be done in this area to determine how teachers can foster optimal interaction between type of structure, stage of acquisition, and type of feedback.

Finally, any answer to the question of what constitutes good practice will also depend on a number of individual differences, such as age, aptitude, and personality. Less research effort has been spent on determining how teaching techniques and practice in particular can be adapted to the age of the learner than to the effect of age on learning. Similarly, while a substantial literature exists that documents the correlation between a variety of cognitive and affective aptitudes on the one hand and L2 learning on the other, the amount of aptitude-treatment interaction research in applied linguistics is still quite limited. In most existing studies in that category, treatment is defined very broadly; for instance, at the level of approach or curriculum design, rather than at the level of techniques for practice. Yet, researchers such as Cameron (2001) and Muñoz (this volume) argue convincingly that practice activities can be adapted to the cognitive and affective characteristics of children, adolescents, and adults, and Robinson (2002, this volume) formulates a wealth of hypotheses and some initial empirical findings about how different aptitudes, and especially combinations of aptitudes at various levels of specificity, predict differential success at various stages of the acquisition process or with various teaching techniques. Just for recasts, for instance, Robinson (1999) found that phonetic sensitivity and rote memory were good predictors for amount of learning with this technique, and Mackey, Philp, Egi, Fujii, and Tatsumi (2002) found a similar advantage for amount of learning from recasts among learners with good phonological working memory.

Outstanding questions

While the means for systematic practice discussed in the previous section are relatively uncontroversial, many difficult questions remain, in part because of seemingly contradictory research results. The debate about processing instruction is a case in point. VanPatten (2002a, 2002b) and DeKeyser et al. (2002) come to very different conclusions after reviewing existing research on the value of input processing practice versus traditional output practice. VanPatten attributes divergent results to a failure by some researchers to replicate the conditions of the original studies (as Wong [2004] explains, that largely means failure to identify and train a processing strategy), while DeKeyser et al. cite a lack of generalizability to different structures. Clearly, this is an empirical question that can be answered only by more research, documenting a variety of structures being learned in a variety of languages by a variety of learners, practiced in input and output format, with and without explicit teaching of structure, and with and without processing strategy training so that the most relevant variables or interaction of variables can be identified.

The issue of generalizability, of course, is not limited to the processing instruction debate:

- How useful are recasts for grammar compared to vocabulary or pronunciation? Mackey, Gass, and McDonough (2000) provide very suggestive evidence that intake after recasts is much more likely for vocabulary and pronunciation than for grammar, but more studies of this kind are needed before one can be certain that the issue is an interaction among these three areas and recasts and not, for instance, among these three areas and error correction in general, or between specific elements of grammar and recasts, or even between specific elements of grammar and error correction.
- How much systematic practice is needed for proceduralization? DeKeyser (1997) provides evidence that suggests a dozen items are more than enough to learn the morphosyntactic rules under investigation, but how much would be required for other, morphologically more complex, or semantically more transparent elements of morphosyntax? And how about proceduralization of phonological rules in pronunciation? Given how stubborn pronunciation errors can be, and how abstract many phonological rules are, the answer is almost certain to be very different there.
- What are the ideal parameters of task design to ensure gradual automatization of structures, avoiding undue bias toward accuracy or fluency? Given the limited number of studies, the limited number of participants in them, the somewhat inconsistent results, and the variety of possible interactions with different structures and previous learning and practice

experiences, we cannot claim to have an authoritative answer to this question at all.

- How can a skill acquisition perspective be integrated with various forms of communicative language teaching, in particular with task-based learning? There certainly is nothing incompatible about the two approaches. On the contrary, a careful sequencing of tasks on the basis of non-linguistic criteria is what is needed for skill acquisition, but of course narrowly focused research on the acquisition of specific elements of grammar from a skill acquisition perspective is not only very scant, but also has been carried out in very rigid, largely noncommunicative contexts. As Segalowitz puts it, "The challenge then is to incorporate activities that promote automaticity into the language learning situation in a manner that respects transfer-appropriate processing and other positive features of communicative practices" (2003, p. 402). For the time being, research cannot give much guidance on this point; teaching, in this respect, is more of an art (or a balancing act?) than a science.

While for some of these questions existing research has received divergent interpretations, in most cases the lack of clear answers reflects lack of directly relevant empirical research more than anything else. Therefore, in the last section, we discuss the need for and promise of certain kinds of research on practice.

Implications for a research agenda

It should be clear from what precedes that progress in research on L2 practice can only be made if the perspectives of cognitive and educational psychology are brought together with those from second language acquisition research. Applied linguistics needs a meeting of the minds between these two worlds. At a very broad level, merely defining what can be expected to be hard in a given L2 for learners of a given L1 may be largely the domain of second language acquisition research, but for a given individual the question of whether something is learnable, how, or in how much time cannot be answered without knowledge of the individual's age and aptitude profile and knowledge of how these factors interact with specific (psycho)linguistic variables.

For a variety of more specific questions, the linguistic focus of SLA research and the learning focus of cognitive psychology should be able to illuminate jointly a number of issues. At the top level of grammar selection, the decision of which form-function relationships should go into the curriculum can be left to linguists with their knowledge about frequency, usefulness, and learnability of the structure, but to what extent it makes sense to practice use of this structure for specific skills and subskills is a question for cognitive psychologists. In the past, linguists have almost totally ignored this question, and psychologists have tended to provide general answers without taking any of the specifics of given elements of the language into account.

At the next level, that of presentation and subsequent practice of specific elements of grammar, linguists may be able to determine the best way of presenting "the rules," taking into account the facts of L1 and L2 and the requirements of a pedagogical grammar, but psychologists may be able to provide more precise plans for how to proceduralize and automatize such knowledge.

At the fine-grained level of feedback during practice, cognitive psychologists may be able to provide hypotheses about how explicit and how frequent negative feedback should be at different stages of skill acquisition, but their hypotheses will need to be tested for different elements of the L2, and even for speakers of different L1s, based on where the second language acquisition literature predicts specific problems.

For other questions, applied linguists may be on their own. How can one best achieve Ortega's (this volume) objective of a "purposefully selective but relatively unobtrusive focus on the language code within a wider context of communication"? How can more activities be designed like the one described in Lynch and Maclean (2001), which provide enough repetition to help with systematic skill acquisition but that, because of their resemblance to real-life situations, are not perceived as repetitious?

It appears then that there are a great many questions, quite a few educated guesses, and here and there a beginning of a body of empirical evidence, but that, all in all, issues of practice in second language learning are vastly under-researched. While there may be many reasons for this state of affairs, the main reasons are probably the lack of research tools available to applied linguists in the 1960s and 1970s – when practice was discussed frequently in the L2 literature – and the theoretical distrust of the concept of practice in the 1980s and 1990s (cf. DeKeyser, 1997). Now that a variety of developments in second language acquisition research and applied linguistics – from a renewed focus on form (see, e.g., Doughty & Williams, 1998) to a renewed reflection on what constitutes good tasks and good sequencing brought about by the discussions about the task-based syllabus – have brought issues of practice back into the spotlight, and now that an increasing array of high-tech tools are at our disposal for the fine-grained tracking of learner's knowledge and behavior in interaction with equally detailed documentation of treatments (see, e.g., Chapelle, 2003; Jenkins, 2004), it is time to meet these questions head-on.

A variety of research approaches are possible, from narrowly focused experiments in the laboratory, to broader quasi-experiments in the classroom, to correlational and observational studies. There are multiple challenges, however. One is to focus squarely on practice while taking the wider environment into account, from the macro-sociolinguistic and institutional context to the individual's aptitude profile and learning history. Issues of grammar practice, for instance, cannot be understood completely without taking into account how much focus on form the students have been used to or how much prestige the (standard variety of) L2 has among the learners. Another challenge is to reconcile two almost incompatible requirements on research on practice: that it be very fine-grained, to allow for tracking of stimuli and responses in milliseconds, certainly at the more advanced stages of learning, while being longitudinal in nature – after all, no experiment lasting only a few weeks is representative of the long-term dynamics of real-world language learning. Perhaps new technology can solve this problem by allowing for massive data collection *and* sophisticated analysis at the fine-grained level *and* longitudinally, from many learners, without losing sight of the importance of individual differences. Potential materials designers or publishers in computer-assisted learning should be motivated to work with second language acquisition researchers on such projects, however, because without such research their materials are a bit of a stab in the dark. Computers offer tremendous promise for massive *and* sophisticated *and* highly individualized practice, but much more language acquisition research as well as research and development in the area of language technology is necessary before that promise can be fulfilled.

References

Allen, S. W., & Brooks, L. R. (1991). Specializing the operation of an explicit rule. *Journal of Experimental Psychology: General, 120*(1), 3–19.

Anderson, J. R., Bothell, D., Byrne, M. D., Douglass, S., Lebiere, C., & Qin, Y. (2004). An integrated theory of the mind. *Psychological Review, 111*(4), 1036–60.

Cameron, L. (2001). Teaching languages to young learners. Cambridge, UK: Cambridge University Press.

Carroll, S. (1999). Putting "input" in its proper place. *Second Language Research, 15,* 337–88.

Carroll, S. E. (2001). *Input and evidence.* Amsterdam: John Benjamins.

Carroll, S. E. (2002). Induction in a modular learner. *Second Language Research, 18*(3), 224–49.

Chapelle, C. A. (2003). *English language learning and technology.* Amsterdam / Philadelphia: John Benjamins.

DeKeyser, R. M. (1997). Beyond explicit rule learning: Automatizing second language morphosyntax. *Studies in Second Language Acquisition, 19*(2), 195–221.

DeKeyser, R. M. (1998). Beyond focus on form: Cognitive perspectives on learning and practicing second language grammar. In C. Doughty & J. Williams (Eds.), *Focus on form in classroom second language acquisition* (pp. 42–63). New York: Cambridge University Press.

DeKeyser, R. M. (2000). The robustness of critical period effects in second language acquisition. *Studies in Second Language Acquisition, 22*(4), 499–533.

DeKeyser, R. M. (2001). Automaticity and automatization. In P. Robinson (Ed.), *Cognition and second language instruction* (pp. 125–51). New York: Cambridge University Press.

DeKeyser, R. M. (2003). Implicit and explicit learning. In C. Doughty & M. Long (Eds.), *Handbook of second language acquisition* (pp. 313–48). Oxford: Blackwell.

DeKeyser, R. M., Salaberry, R., Robinson, P., & Harrington, M. (2002). What gets processed in processing instruction? A commentary on Bill VanPatten's "Processing instruction: An update." *Language Learning, 52*(4), 805–23.

Doughty, C. (2003). Instructed SLA: Constraints, compensation, and enhancement. In C. Doughty & M. H. Long (Eds.), *Handbook of second language acquisition* (pp. 256–310). Oxford: Blackwell.

Doughty, C., & Williams, J. (1998). Pedagogical choices in focus on form. In C. Doughty & J. Williams (Eds.), *Focus on form in classroom second language acquisition* (pp. 197–261). New York: Cambridge University Press.

Ellis, N. (2002). Reflections on frequency effects in language processing. *Studies in Second Language Acquisition, 24*(2), 297–339.

Ellis, N. (2005). At the interface: Dynamic interactions of explicit and implicit language knowledge. *Studies in Second Language Acquisition, 27*(2), 305–52.

Ellis, R. (1992). *Second language acquisition and language pedagogy*. Clevedon, UK: Multilingual Matters.

Ellis, R. (1994). *The study of second language acquisition*. Oxford: Oxford University Press.

Ellis, R. (2003). *Task-based language learning and teaching*. Oxford: Oxford University Press.

Ericsson, K. A., Krampe, R. T., & Tesch-Römer, C. (1993). The role of deliberate practice in the acquisition of expert performance. *Psychological Review, 100*(3), 363–406.

Gass, S. (1997). *Input, interaction, and the second language learner*. Mahwah, NJ: Lawrence Erlbaum.

Gatbonton, E., & Segalowitz, N. (1988). Creative automatization: Principles for promoting fluency within a communicative framework. *TESOL Quarterly, 22*(3), 473–92.

Hulstijn, J. (2002). Towards a unified account of the representation, acquisition, and automatization of second-language knowledge. *Second Language Research, 18*(3), 193–223.

Izumi, S. (2002). Output, input enhancement, and the noticing hypothesis: An experimental study on ESL relativization. *Studies in Second Language Acquisition, 24*(4), 541–77.

Jenkins, J. (2004). Research in teaching pronunciation and intonation. *Annual Review of Applied Linguistics, 24*, 109–25.

Johnson, K. (1996). *Language teaching and skill learning*. Oxford: Blackwell.

Krashen, S. D. (1982). *Principles and practice in second language acquisition*. Englewood Cliffs, NJ: Prentice-Hall.

Larsen-Freeman, D. (2003). *Teaching language: From grammar to grammaring*. Boston: Heinle.

Leeman, J. (2003). Recasts and second language development: Beyond negative evidence. *Studies in Second Language Acquisition, 25*(1), 37–63.

Long, M. H., & Robinson, P. (1998). Focus on form: Theory, research, and practice. In C. Doughty & J. Williams (Eds.), *Focus on form in classroom second language acquisition* (pp. 15–41). New York: Cambridge University Press.

Lynch, T., & Maclean, J. (2001). "A case of exercising": Effects of immediate task repetition on learners' performance. In M. Bygate, P. Skehan, & M. Swain (Eds.), *Researching pedagogic tasks. Second language learning, teaching, and testing* (pp. 141–62). New York: Longman.

Lyster, R. (2004). Differential effects of prompts and recasts in form-focused instruction. *Studies in Second Language Acquisition, 26*(3), 399–432.

Mackey, A., Gass, S., & McDonough, K. (2000). How do learners perceive interactional feedback? *Studies in Second Language Acquisition, 22*(4), 471–99.

Mackey, A., & Philp, J. (1998). Conversational interaction and second language development: Recasts, responses, and red herrings? *Modern Language Journal, 82*(3), 338–56.

Mackey, A., Egi, T., Fujii, A., Philp, J., & Tatsumi, T. (2002). Individual differences in working memory, noticing of interactional feedback and L2 development. In P. Robinson (Ed.), *Individual differences and instructed language learning* (pp. 181–209). Amsterdam / Philadelphia: John Benjamins.

MacWhinney, B. (1997). Second language acquisition and the competition model. In A. M. B. de Groot & J. F. Kroll (Eds.), *Tutorials in bilingualism: Psycholinguistic perspectives* (pp. 113–42). Mahwah, NJ: Lawrence Erlbaum.

Nicholas, H., Lightbown, P. M., & Spada, N. (2001). Recasts as feedback to language learners. *Language Learning, 51*(4), 719–58.

Payne, J. S., & Whitney, P. J. (2002). Developing L2 oral proficiency through synchronous CMC: Output, working memory, and interlanguage development. *CALICO Journal, 20*, 7–32.

Robinson, P. (1999). Second language classroom research in Japan: Issues, studies, and prospects. In T. Fujimura, Y. Kato, & R. Smith (Eds.), *Proceedings of the 10th IUJ conference on second language research* (pp. 93–116). Tokyo: International University of Japan.

Robinson, P. (2002). Learning conditions, aptitude complexes, and SLA. In P. Robinson (Ed.), *Individual differences and instructed language learning* (pp. 113–33). Amsterdam: John Benjamins.

Robinson, P. (2005). Cognitive complexity and task sequencing: Studies in a componential framework for second language task design. *International Review of Applied Linguistics in Language Teaching, 43*(1), 1–32.

Rothkopf, E. Z., & Dashen, M. L. (1995). Particularization: Inductive speeding of rule-governed decisions by narrow application experience. *Journal of Experimental Psychology: Learning, Memory, and Cognition, 21*(2), 469–89.

Russell, J., & Spada, N. (2006). The effectiveness of corrective feedback for the acquisition of L2 grammar: A meta-analysis of the research. In J. M. Norris & L. Ortega (Eds.), *Synthesizing research on language learning and teaching* (pp. 133–64). Philadelphia / Amsterdam: John Benjamins.

Schmidt, R. A., & Bjork, R. A. (1992). New conceptualizations of practice: Common principles in three paradigms suggest new concepts for training. *Psychological Science, 3*(4), 207–17.

Segalowitz, N. (2003). Automaticity and second languages. In C. Doughty & M. Long (Eds.), *Handbook of second language acquisition* (pp. 382–408). Oxford: Blackwell.

Shehadeh, A. (1999). Non-native speakers' production of modified comprehensible output and second language learning. *Language Learning, 49*(4), 627–75.

Shehadeh, A. (2002). Comprehensible output, from occurrence to acquisition: An agenda for acquisitional research. *Language Learning, 52*(3), 597–647.

Singley, M. K., & Anderson, J. R. (1989). *The transfer of cognitive skill.* Cambridge, MA: Harvard University Press.

Skehan, P. (1998). *A cognitive approach to language learning.* Oxford: Oxford University Press.

Skehan, P., & Foster, P. (2001). Cognition and tasks. In P. Robinson (Ed.), *Cognition and second language instruction* (pp. 183–205). Cambridge, UK: Cambridge University Press.

Swain, M. (1985). Communicative competence: Some roles of comprehensible input and comprehensible output in its development. In S. M. Gass & C. G. Madden (Eds.), *Input in second language acquisition* (pp. 235–53). Rowley, MA: Newbury House.

Swain, M., & Lapkin, S. (1995). Problems in output and the cognitive processes they generate: A step towards second language learning. *Applied Linguistics, 16*(3), 371–91.

Truscott, J., & Sharwood Smith, M. (2004). Acquisition by processing: A modular perspective on language development. *Bilingualism: Language and Cognition, 7*(1), 1–20.

VanPatten, B. (2002a). Processing instruction: An update. *Language Learning, 52*(4), 755–803.

VanPatten, B. (2002b). Processing the content of input-processing and processing instruction research: A response to DeKeyser, Salaberry, Robinson, and Harrington. *Language Learning, 52*(4), 825–31.

VanPatten, B. (Ed.). (2004a). *Processing instruction. Theory, research, and commentary.* Mahwah, NJ: Lawrence Erlbaum.

VanPatten, B. (2004b). Input processing in second language acquisition. In B. VanPatten (Ed.), *Processing instruction: Theory, research, and commentary.* Mahwah, NJ: Lawrence Erlbaum.

VanPatten, B., & Cadierno, T. (1993). Input processing and second language acquisition: A role for instruction. *The Modern Language Journal, 77*(1), 45–57.

Wong, W. (2004). The nature of processing instruction. Theory, research, and commentary. In B. VanPatten (Ed.), *Processing instruction. Theory, research, and commentary* (pp. 33–63). Mahwah, NJ: Lawrence Erlbaum.

Glossary

This glossary contains a number of terms that are used in various chapters in this book. It is not meant to be a general glossary of SLA, nor does it provide all possible meanings of the terms below in all areas of SLA research.

ability. The propensity to learn from exposure to a variety of forms of information in a variety of cognitive and behavioral domains. Sometimes used interchangeably with *aptitude*, sometimes to refer to more stable, inherent characteristics of an individual (innate or acquired early in life) as opposed to aptitude, which often refers to readiness to learn at a specific point in time as a result of ability, knowledge, and experience.

ability differentiation hypothesis. The proposal that one of the effects of aging is that adults become increasingly differentiated in their patterns of strengths in cognitive abilities. Some adults, however, show more differentiation than others.

ability factor. A hypothetical construct underlying effective cognitive and behavioral functioning which draws on a number of separately measurable cognitive or physical abilities. For example, "noticing the gap" has been proposed (see the chapter by Robinson, this volume) as a factor contributing to learning from recasts during oral interaction in second language learning contexts.

aptitude. Readiness to learn from exposure to a variety of forms of information in a variety of cognitive and behavioral domains. This can include physical and affective characteristics, as well as previous knowledge, but the term is most often used in the more restricted sense of cognitive aptitude. In the domain of second language acquisition, the most frequently used measure of aptitude has been the Modern Language Aptitude Test (MLAT). On the other hand, sometimes the term is used in a very wide sense, interchangeably with *ability*.

aptitude complex hypothesis. The proposal that aptitudes affect learning through specific combinations, or complexes, during learning and practice. The effects of strengths in one variable (e.g., working memory capacity) are multiplied by (not simply added to) the effects of strengths in other variables (e.g., processing speed) relevant to the processing demands of specific learning and practice contexts.

attention. A selective process that focuses the mind on a subset of the stimuli or information it has access to, necessitated by the fact that human information processing is of limited capacity. Attention is essential for learning and access to consciousness but in its widest sense does not require awareness.

attentional / attention-focusing tasks. Pedagogical tasks designed to promote noticing of targeted forms during instructional exposure to L2 data or while engaging in meaningful interaction; these tasks aim at fostering L2 development by raising learners' awareness of particular grammatical features of the language.

automaticity. The capacity to carry out a task at high speed and with minimal interference from or with other tasks, resulting in a low error rate and little variance in performance depending on task conditions. It is the result of the process of automatization.

automatization. The gradual improvement in terms of speed, error rate, and effort required that characterizes performance of highly practiced tasks. Sometimes used in the narrow sense of mere speedup of the same elementary task components, more often in a wider sense of improvement in task performance that is due at least in part to the restructuring of subcomponents.

aware and unaware learners. Various measures of awareness are assumed to capture the presence or absence of the subjective correlates of experience of second language processing phenomena. These coordinates include explicit memory for, and focal attention to, second language percepts. Awareness can therefore be at a number of different levels, varying from phenomenological awareness of instances of L2 percepts to metalinguistic awareness of those instances and percepts. Learners can be classified at each of these levels, as aware or unaware, using operational measures appropriate to the cognitive processing demands they are assumed to implicate.

cognition. Encompassing term for higher mental processes such as memory, problem solving, reasoning, and strategy use; in other words, any mental process that involves the acquisition, storage, and use of knowledge.

cognition hypothesis. The proposal that as the cognitive demands of second language tasks increase, learners become more attentive to, and process more deeply, the input provided. The cognition hypothesis also proposes that as the conceptual demands of tasks increase, learners attempt to make their language production more accurate and complex.

communication task. A classroom activity that involves learners in solving some sort of problem through using the target language. Learners' primary attention is focused on meaning or communication rather than form. Communication tasks can be used to provide learners with systematic, meaningful, and contextualized practice.

content-based instruction. A form of language teaching in which the primary focus is on content conveyed, such as math or social science, but in which second language learning is an important secondary goal, encouraged mainly by providing learners with extra help with terminology and other aspects of school language.

contingent speech. Utterances adjacent to those of first or second language learners in oral interactive discourse and which may contain negative feedback from a parental, NNS, or NS interlocutor.

declarative knowledge. Knowledge that can be explicitly expressed ("declared"), such as a historical fact, a law of physics, or an explicitly learned grammar rule, as opposed to knowledge that can only be performed (procedural knowledge), such as how to swim, do mental arithmetic, or speak fluently. Sometimes called knowledge THAT as opposed to knowledge HOW.

error correction. Negative "feedback" provided in response to learner error. The term is often avoided in SLA research due to the implication that "feedback" leads to elimination of error; used more often in educational approaches (as opposed to "evidence" in linguistic or "feedback" in psychological approaches), but less frequently there recently in favor of "corrective feedback" or "teacher feedback."

explicit learning. Learning with awareness of what is being learned. In second language acquisition this term is most often used to refer to the learning of phonological, morphological, and syntactic structure, as well as pragmatic function.

explicitness of a task (degree of). The extent to which a task helps learners extract explicit knowledge about a particular L2 structure or form. Often, such knowledge is arrived at by means of conscious strategies such as hypothesis formation and testing.

feedback. Information provided after a given process regarding the success or failure of that process. May include information about accuracy, communicative success, and/or content of learner utterance. May include positive evidence, negative evidence, prompts, and/or metalinguistic information. Used most often in psychological approaches (as opposed to evidence in linguistic or error correction in educational approaches).

fluency. The capacity to produce language at a reasonable speed, i.e., without undue pauses, frequent or slow repairs, or searching for words.

grammatical sensitivity. A proposed ability to grasp grammatical structure. It predicts the acquisition of grammatical knowledge in an L2 (to different extents depending on age and learning context) and is often operationalized as Part IV (Words in Sentences) of the MLAT.

immersion. A form of second language education where the student uses nothing but the second language for most of the school day, at least in early stages of the curriculum. Such programs exist for students of all ages but are most typically designed for grade school or middle school students and often start in first grade.

implicit learning. Learning without awareness of what is being learned. In second language acquisition this is most often used to refer to the learning of phonological, morphological, and syntactic structure, as well as pragmatic function through mere exposure to examples, without any attempt at analysis.

incidental learning. Learning without the intention to learn. In contrast to implicit learners, incidental learners may become aware of the objects of processing at a variety of levels, such as simple noticing of the stimuli, or form hypotheses about word meaning, phonological, morphological, and syntactic structure, and pragmatic function.

input. The linguistic data (typically combinations of form and meaning) that learners receive either in the formal classroom or in a naturalistic setting.

input flooding. Providing the learner with oral or written input that is highly saturated with a specific type of target structure.

input processing. What learners do with input during comprehension, including intake influenced by previous instruction.

intake. The part of the input that has been attended to by second language learners while processing. Intake represents stored linguistic data that may be used for immediate recognition and does not necessarily imply language acquisition.

interaction. Verbal exchanges of communicative value during which language learners engage in a variety of processes (e.g., negotiation, modified output, comprehensible input, feedback) that are argued to contain critical linguistic information and shown empirically to benefit L2 learning; considered necessary but not sufficient for SLA.

metacognitive knowledge. Self-awareness or knowledge of one's own cognitive processes (e.g., ability to self-monitor and self-evaluate).

metalinguistic awareness. Awareness of a variety of properties of (a) language, from the level of sound to that of meaning. Often, but not necessarily, leads to the ability to talk about these properties.

Modern Language Aptitude Test (MLAT). A test of abilities supposed to contribute to successful instructed second language acquisition. These include grammatical sensitivity, rote memory for lexical paired-associates, phonetic coding ability, and inductive learning. These abilities, and optimal tests of them, were established through statistical factor analysis and do not correspond completely to different sections of the test.

negative evidence. Information that certain utterances or types of utterances are impossible in the language being learned.

negative feedback. Responses that provide information that a process was unsuccessful.

negotiation. An interactional process during which interlocutors modify their interaction, for example, by providing feedback, requesting clarification, checking comprehension, and making adjustments to linguistic form, conversational structure, and/or the content of their utterances in order to achieve mutual comprehension.

noticing. The registration of the occurrence of a stimulus event in conscious awareness and subsequent storage in long-term memory.

noticing the gap. A higher level of cognitive processing than mere noticing. Experience of one perceived L2 stimulus is compared to another in working memory, and some difference between the two, i.e., the gap, is registered in short-term memory. This short-term memory may subsequently be (though it is often not) consolidated as a long-term memory, and so contributes to L2 learning. Noticing the gap involves, therefore, not simply awareness and noticing of an L2 stimulus but recall of a prior, related stimulus to which it is compared.

output. A learner's production of the target language. Depending on the situation, this may include anything from mechanical drills to spontaneous conversation with native speakers.

output hypothesis. The hypothesis that output plays an important role in second language learning, more specifically through noticing, hypothesis formulation, and testing, as well as metalinguistic awareness and a shift from merely semantic to syntactic processing.

output practice. Any activity designed to provide L2 learners with opportunities to produce output with the goal of facilitating cognitive processes involved in L2 learning.

positive evidence. Information that certain utterances are possible in the target language; frequently used to refer to exemplars of possible utterances.

positive feedback. Responses which provide information that a process was successful.

power law of practice. Law invoked to describe the specific way reaction time and error rate decline as a function of practice during the acquisition of a wide variety of skills. The word *power* refers to the fact that the mathematical equation describing how reaction time and error rate are related to practice expresses the rate of learning as an exponent. The most common form of the equation is $T = a + bN^{-c}$ where T is the time needed to perform the task, a is the shortest possible time, b is the total amount of speedup possible, N is the number or practice trials, and the exponent c is the rate of learning.

practice. Activities engaged in repeatedly with the goal of becoming better at them. Often called deliberate practice to emphasize this goal orientation as opposed to the incidental nature of practice that comes with activities engaged in frequently for work or personal routines.

proceduralization. The process of creating procedural knowledge by merging declarative knowledge with more encompassing procedural rules. This takes place when learners repeatedly engage in a task that calls on the same broad procedural rules and declarative knowledge.

procedural knowledge. Knowledge that can only be performed, such as how to swim, do mental arithmetic, or speak fluently. Sometimes called knowledge HOW as opposed to knowledge THAT (declarative knowledge).

procedural rules. The algorithms of the mind, i.e., the concrete form taken by procedural knowledge. Often referred to as if-then rules: if in a given (combination of) situation(s) X is present, then carry out an (or a set of) action(s) Y.

processing speed. A cognitive ability variable that measures the speed of responding to physical stimuli and which does not implicate higher-order, conceptual processing, e.g., quickly deciding if one line on a visual display is longer than another line presented simultaneously.

prompt. Teacher feedback move (such as elicitation, metalinguistic clues, and clarification requests) that withholds correct reformulations and instead pushes learners to self-repair.

pushed output. Language produced in communicative contexts by a learner who is under pressure to make sure it is as correct as he or she can make it; the pressure comes from the need to be understood perfectly and/or to be valued socially.

recast. A response to a non-targetlike utterance in which the interlocutor reformulates the utterance, eliminating the error (whether grammatical, lexical, or phonological) but maintaining the original meaning.

repair. In second language acquisition research, the correct reformulation of an error as uttered by a learner in a single turn. Studies using conversation analysis, however, refer to repair as the entire sequence of turns resulting in the correct reformulation.

restructuring. In skill acquisition theory, a qualitative change over time in the way a task is executed typically through reorganizing its subcomponents in terms of the division between them and their sequential (or possibly parallel) ordering. This psychological mechanism may or may not lead to a behavioral change in the sense of different structures being used to express the same thing.

scaffolding. The support that a teacher or an adult provides the learner to use his or her language and cognitive skills in a way that he or she could not do without such support (e.g., by means of focused questions or supportive encouragement).

skill. The capacity to carry out a specific kind of task, whether cognitive or psychomotor.

skill acquisition theory. An attempt at describing and explaining the development of all skills by positing a common set of learning mechanisms and stages of development.

Speech Production Model. A psycholinguistic model developed by Willem Levelt which describes and explains processes involved in language production. Three major processes are posited: conceptualizing, formulating, and articulating.

task-based learning. An approach to instruction in which the goal is the accomplishment of target tasks that are not primarily linguistic in nature. These tasks are often selected according to the results of a needs analysis and usually sequenced according to nonlinguistic considerations of difficulty.

transfer-appropriate processing. Executing a (learning) task in such a way that transfer to a new task is likely because cognitive operations involved in the new context, task, or test are highly congruent with those engaged in during initial learning.

ultimate attainment. The highest level of proficiency a person reaches in a second language, marked by the cessation of progress at that level.

uptake. A learner's utterance that immediately follows feedback and that constitutes a reaction in some way to the hearer's intention to draw attention to the learner's ill-formed utterance. (Uptake is also sometimes defined as what learner's claim to have learned from a particular lesson.)

working memory (WM). The mechanisms involved in the active and temporary maintenance, control, processing, and manipulation of information (e.g., numbers and their relationship or elements of language and their relationship) in the service of complex cognitive activities (e.g., arithmetic or listening/speaking). Often held to be a strong predictor of L2 learning.

Index

Page numbers in *italics* refer to figures and tables.

power law of practice, 3–4, 64–65, 77n5
PPP (presentation, practice, and production) model, 11, 51, 149–50
practice
applications of, 289–97
institutional contexts, 139–40
reaction to concept of, 1
usefulness of, 12
See also definition of practice; input practice; meaningful practice; output practice
practice activities
age-specific activities, *232, 234, 236, 239,* 244–48, *245, 246*
cognitive development and, 230–31, *232*
demands and support balance, 229–30, 248n1
drills (*see* drills)
goals for, 287–88, 289
good practice, 294–97
L1 use during, 190–91
learning methods and, 227
multiple repetition, 11–12
study abroad programs, 212–15
to support aptitude deficiencies, 272–73, 297
teaching methodologies and, 9
technology-based strategies, 195–98, 296
practice effect
benefits of deliberate practice, 5
on competence, 7
complexity of tasks and, 4
on performance, 7
on skill acquisition, 169–71, 259–60, 292–93
skill-specificity issue, 8–9
transfer between tasks, 3–4
presentation, practice, and production (PPP) model, 11, 51, 149–50
problem-solving abilities, 230–31
procedural knowledge / proceduralization
automatization, 3–4, 33–34
declarative knowledge, transfer of skills, and, 6, 7, 9, 116, 117, 149, 215–16

feedback and, 117
immersion program instruction, 151–52
processing stage model, *270*
research recommendations, 298
skill acquisition and, 3, 33–34, 288, 290–92
study abroad programs, 213–14, 215–16, 290–91
processing instruction
awareness, role of, 39–40
benefits of, 29, 63–64, 216
characteristics of, 28
complexity of tasks and, 41–42
contradictory research on, 298
definition of, 20
feedback and, 118–19
goal of, 27–28
L1 use during, 190
research on, 27–31, 34–35, *36*
role of attention in, 28
role of practice in, 295
theoretical foundation of, 27
processing stage model (Skehan), *270,* 270–73
production practice
age of learners and, 238
benefits of, 294
comprehension practice vs., 33–34, 294–95
good practice, 294–96
output practice and, 63–65
receptive practice vs., 34–35, 166
role in learning, 293–94
production rules, 3, 149, 291–92
proficiency. *See* fluency and proficiency
pronunciation, 241–42, 244
pyramid model, 171

readiness, 257
reading activities, *246, 247*
reading skills, 211, 287
recasts
definition of, 92
effectiveness of, 115, 167, 219, 264–65, *265*
focused recasts, 126
in immersion programs, 152, 153